THE

WILD, WHITE

GOOSE

the Diary of a Female Zen Priest

THE
WILD, WHITE
GOOSE

the Diary of a Female Zen Priest

by
Rev. Rōshi P.T.N.H. Jiyu-Kennett

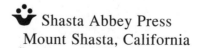 Shasta Abbey Press
Mount Shasta, California

Second Edition—2002

© 2002 Shasta Abbey.

The first edition of *The Wild, White Goose* was published in two volumes—Volume I (Books 1 & 2) in 1977 and Volume II (Books 3 & 4) in 1978. Some portions of this book have appeared in *The Journal of Shasta Abbey*.

Front cover: The author reading the Scriptures as a junior monk at Dai Hon Zan Sōjiji.
Frontispiece: The author after her ordination ceremony in Malaysia.
Page 474: The author leading the procession at the Jūkai ceremony of Ketchimyaku at Shasta Abbey.

Printed in the United States of America.

ISBN 0-930066-23-5
Library of Congress Control Number: 2001135933

The TransIndic Transliterator font used to print this work is available from Linguist's Software, Inc., PO Box 580, Edmonds, WA 98020-0580 USA tel (425) 775-1130.

To all women seeking Spiritual Truth and especially to those who have ever entered into Zen training.

Acknowledgments.

The author wishes to thank all those
who helped in the production of this book.

Contents.

Preface.

This book may do the reader more harm than good if he does not first read this preface; and it will be worse than useless to him spiritually if he does not read the annotations as they occur in the text.

This book is published purely for the purpose of showing how Buddhist training was done by me in the Far East. The material for this book has been taken from diaries covering a period of almost eight years spent by me in Far Eastern temples. In Books One and Two I describe the first two and a half years of my religious training as a junior trainee in one of the leading monasteries of Zen in Japan, up through my first kenshō and my Transmission as an heir in the Dharma to the Chief Abbot. The training of a junior, although often a somewhat gruelling experience, is to a certain extent like the cultivation of a hot-house plant. Once one has found one's True Nature and had one's faith and spiritual strength established in the semi-seclusion of the junior years in a monastery, it is necessary to be "transplanted" into the world, without leaving the actual monastery itself, for that faith and strength to grow to the point of being able to be of real use to others. Books Three and Four are the story of the growth of a Zen priest into a teacher through the process of testing and trial which six years of the responsibilities of holding office in the monastery, dealing with religious politics, and running my own temple naturally provided. It is through this seeming morass that each of us must travel if we are to progress from our initial understanding of the Truth to higher spirituality. This aspect of religious training is particularly relevant both to the senior trainee, priest, or new teacher and to the advanced Buddhist layman—all of whom are faced daily with some form of the experiences recounted herein. The particular form which those events took for me was, of course, in part determined by the fact that I was a Western trainee in a Japanese setting; very similar occurrences happened to all of the other Western trainees whom I knew in the Orient. The reader should always remember that the purpose of this book is to show him or her how training must be done in the "mud" of daily life in order to grow straight and strong the stem of the lotus flower of his own spirituality. To this end great care should be taken to read the numbered footnotes which serve to indicate where I went wrong in my own training at that time. This work is equally meant to teach by the example of what *not* to do! Above all, please do not become caught up in the apparent "unfairness" of the actions of some of the people around me. What they did must be included here in order that one can see my reactions to it, both wise and unwise; their actions are *not* published to cause others to become angry and especially they are *not* published to cause the reader to engage in idle speculation as to people's identities. I have no wish to identify, expose, or embarrass anyone whatsoever.

For this reason, and because I value highly the right to privacy of everyone, I have found it necessary to not only change names and locations, but also years, countries, and, in some instances, the sexes, ages, habits and behavioural traits of characters. Some characters represent a combination of several real people; some real people whom I knew in the East at that time are not represented here at all; some characters have been invented for the sake of reporting certain thoughts which are germane to the teaching. Some teachings discovered *later* have been reported in conversation form *here* for the sake of making a more complete book although they did not necessarily take place with the characters I have indicated. All of this I have done since I have *no* wish whatsoever to invade the privacy of *anyone*, living or dead—I respect the privacy of others far too much. I have tried to preserve the integrity of the circumstances and events of my training without causing harm to others.

The result, therefore, is a work of fiction in the respects mentioned above. *Events* spoken of *actually* took place, however, and documents, letters, etcetera, mentioned in the text all *actually* exist in the Archives of Shasta Abbey. Out of respect for the privacy and rights of others letters have been paraphrased and identifying details deleted or changed, in consultation with legal counsel. In some instances a certain amount of poetic license has been taken in order to give the events a better flow. Conversations are reported as accurately as possible but not necessarily with the characters with whom they originally took place. My opinions, actions and reactions are also recorded here as accurately as possible but many I have since seen to have been imprudent and would not repeat in the light of my present, I hope more mature, state of mind; it is amazing how wrong a person can be with regard to some situations and events. When events warrant it in this respect, annotations will be found appended to the text by numbers. Taking cognisance of the above information, therefore, *any* resemblance to *any* person, living or dead, is *purely* coincidental.

The terms "monk" and "nun" which may appear in the text are sometimes used for translating the word "unsui," a term applied in Japanese Zen to both men and women in religious training, and which can only accurately be translated as "trainee." The terms "monk" and "nun" are misnomers since they carry a connotation of enclosed monasticism from the Christian tradition. In Japanese Sōtō Zen, it is expected that all trainees will eventually become priests, whether they be male or female, although there are some who do not go up the ranks beyond unsui as a result of not completing their formal training in a temple. There are some schools of Buddhism which do have nuns in the more Christian sense, but these are not found in Sōtō Zen. In the interest of keeping the diary as close as possible to its original wording, the term "monk"

rather than the term "unsui," which would have been prefer-
able but is unfamiliar to Western readers, has been used to
indicate both male and female trainees. I was not fully
appraised of the correct translation and interpretation of
"unsui" until my later years in Japan.

Introduction.

Flying clouds in a flying sky,
  I listen and hear the wild goose cry;
Peaceful eve but it's no use
  For I am sister to the wild, white goose.

My heart knows what the wild goose knows
  For my heart goes where the wild goose goes;
Wild goose, sister goose, which is best,
  The flying sky or a heart at rest?

I do not know the author of this poem but it is highly applicable to my state of mind when I left England so many years ago for the Far East. Somewhere I have heard that a goose is a stupid creature; and it is for this reason that I identify myself with one. The story told in this diary is that of a woman who gave up the world, a good position in life and worldly comforts in order to search for—she knew not what. Whatever *it* is, it cannot be caught and held—it can only be experienced—one cannot realise it merely from reading books. "Remember thou must go alone; the Buddhas do but point the way," says the scripture. Books do not even manage that.

All searches start with the premise that we have something to look for, something which we have, perhaps, lost. Those who do not find what they are seeking console themselves with the thought that it never really existed and forget about it—those who find it start looking for something else. Human nature is such that it is constantly desiring something, never being satisfied with that which it already has. I wanted an end to this.

I know now that they who *search* for the absolute never find it for, whilst attachment to desire exists, it will never manifest itself; as soon as the search ceases and the searcher learns to clean up his life and accept things as they are he is *filled* with the absolute for, indeed, it was never lost. This is the secret entry to the gateless gate of Zen—the barrier which all must pass if they wish to understand Zen behaviour and Zen books. It is so simple that no-one believes it and this fact alone results in many, who are otherwise serious and well meaning, abandoning their search and deciding that the absolute never existed at all or, at least, not for them. They go in search of something less worthy and end by becoming mediocre, unhappy or even bigoted.

Although we can ask a thousand different questions and get a thousand different answers yet, in fact, there is only one question and, to that question, no answer that will ever satisfy logic. So the Zen kōans that are given to Zen students, and the questions that they ask, are really one question and the reader must ask it in his own words for I cannot write his own particular formula thereof for him; and he must find his own answer to his kōan for himself, within him, for no-one can tell it to him. When he can live without doubt he will have found his answer without knowing it, and when he has doubt he will never find it for he will again be searching, searching . . . . And yet we must always go on. We must, at every moment, find the right answer. This is the "Gyate, gyate, haragyate" of the Hannyashingyō,—the "going, going, going on, always going on"—never stopping, never resting, only continuing without doubt. The doubting mind is in hell. The undoubting mind is in heaven. And this heaven is the Pure Land of the Shin Buddhists and the Nirvana of the Zenist—and the hell is the state that most men create for themselves in the every-day world in which they live.

All philosophers know that if we reach perfection we must end or start again; each time one has a kenshō experience one starts again at the beginning although the memory of the first one, translated thereafter into faith, makes each successive one easier to come by. If a Zen Buddhist *stops* his training after a kenshō he will be worse off than he was before he had it. So always he must do his Zazen—sitting meditation—and, for this purpose, he must turn every action of the day into Zazen, whether it be peeling the potatoes, washing the floor or sitting in the meditation hall. If he decides he has finished his training he has ceased to begin it. So no Zen master ever admits that he is enlightened; if he did he would not be! He just keeps going, doing that which has to be done and doing the best he can in both sickness and health whilst life lasts. By his deeds we can tell if he is real or not and by no other means; there are many whose words are excellent but whose actions prove them to be ordinary men of the every-day world. If a man is the living embodiment of the Buddhist Precepts, if he evinces no doubt whatsoever as to the rightness of his actions and if he accepts all the consequences thereof, even when he has been wrong, without demur, then he is real and a sage worthy of being followed.

When I, like the untamed goose I was, set sail from England I had a question to which I sought the answer because that was the level of understanding at which I was then and with which I must, perforce, start. My question was a normal one for someone who had seen the bloodshed and cruelty of the Nazis in that last great and terrible war. I thought my question was profound and meaningful—I was that naïve! My teacher was to tell me, at a later date, that there were three levels at which all questions existed:– the question actually asked, the question in the back of the questioner's mind and the real question which was embedded in his heart and of which he was usually completely unaware. A true teacher's duty is to answer the last of these three and forget about the other two. There will be many who will not consider my question to lack profundity for I was asking why death and cruelty should exist and I was an angry young woman who wanted answers; time was to show me how wrong I was to do so. For what, in reality, was I actually asking? A reason for being alive when so many of my friends had been killed? A reason for not being alive? Had I a desire for eternal life? A desire for total annihilation? All these questions, and many more, are facets of the question I took with me to the Far East whilst the question I *should* have been asking was:– when was the first arising of selfishness? It is in order to force the pupil to look within himself for true answers to true questions that Zen teachers employ obliqueness in their teaching methods and, for this same reason, the Zen monastery, in the Far East at any rate, trains its inmates with a degree of severity as to create for them a man-made hell. This seeming hell enables the student to find the opportunities that are constantly offered for his enlightenment and then all questions are put into their true perspective rather than possessing their original emergency.

In the diary which follows I give an account of both the heaven and the hell which I created for myself when in training. If the events are looked at singly, or out of context, only severity and senselessness will be seen but, if looked at through the eyes of faith and religion and regarded as opportunities for the discovery of the heaven that is within ourselves, they will be seen to be of the greatest use; what, in the eyes of the world, would be regarded as severe treatment, will be seen to be acts of the greatest kindness. The scriptures tell us that the kindest Kanzeon (the Bodhisattva of Compassion) is to be found in hell for there all opportunities for bettering oneself exist.

Understand that at *all* times I was a volunteer in the temple where I trained in Japan although the early parts of my diary, when in Malaysia, speak of events which were very much outside my control; I could have left the Japanese temple at any time I wished but I preferred to stay. The reason was simple. When I found out what my real question was I knew I had no alternative but to go on with my training for what had really brought me to a monastery was not why death and cruelty existed but why *I* was as I was. Death and cruelty were in me just as much as they had been in Hitler's S.S. troops and I knew that the real reason for my going to the East was because I wanted to do something about myself and I knew that I was willing to put up with anything in order to change. However much other people disliked me I disliked myself a lot more; *I* needed to change *me*. It was the realisation of what my *true* question was—what caused the *first* arising of selfishness, why am *I* as *I* am?—with my petty ideas, opinions, likes, dislikes, hates and loves—not why is the *world* as *it* is—and the need to have a heart at rest, that made me put up with untold hardships and difficulties. Cruelty and death were in the world because of me and people like me; it was useless to try to change the world; I had got to change myself and, in so doing, the world would change also. Anyone who gives up Zen training is a person afraid of facing himself; the need to face ourselves is the real reason that every one of us comes to religion; they who fail are not willing to accept that the answer to their question is not the answer they wanted.

The above was the reason I went but, in changing myself, I found something more than the solving of my kōan. Shakyamuni Buddha went out in search of the reasons for birth, old age, decay and death; it was his *acceptance* of their inevitability as a sequence of events in time as we know it after he saw his Original Face, i.e. after he was enlightened, that brought him freedom from their tyranny. It was the *acceptance* of the fact that the world is as it is because I and thousands of others like me have refused to do anything about ourselves, and my willingness to do something about me, that brought me freedom and peace along with the knowledge that I must never cease my training if I would improve myself. To be satisfied with the answer to a question when it is something is acceptance; to be satisfied with the answer when it is nothing is acceptance; to be satisfied with an answer that has got rid of the concepts of something and nothing is to accept the immaculacy of Zen, to know one's Original Face, but such an answer cannot be put into words—we can only talk around it until, like the Oozlum Bird, it eventually swallows itself.

Book I.
The Layman.

Book I.
The Layman.

10th. January.

We docked this morning off the coast of Malaysia. There
was the usual crowd on the dock but, in one corner, there were
a group of rich-looking people and Rev. Jones, the man who I
had agreed to help by giving some lectures; I had arranged to
do this for him before leaving England. I had promised to stay
about three months. The ship docked and I disembarked. Since
I was, in any case, going on to Singapore in the morning, there
was no need for any immigration formalities and I was soon on
the dockside greeting my reception committee.

To my horror I discovered that Rev. Jones had brought a
tribe of newspaper reporters with him and they had already
been primed as to my reason for visiting Japan—moreover,
they seemed to know far more than they should of my private
affairs. I was told that I was being ordained in Malaysia during
my three-month stay instead of in Japan and that Rev. Jones had
made arrangements to have me trained in Malaysia also. I was
so surprised that I was unable to say anything for a few minutes.[1] I came to myself again to find Rev. Jones busily telling a
story about me to the reporters who were taking it down.

It is perfectly true that I had discussed the possibility of
being ordained in Malaysia. Once I had even asked if it could
be done but I had made no firm arrangement to this effect as far
as I knew. I came to with a gasp.

---

1. For this and all other notes, see "Annotations" at the end of Book 4, p. 475.

3

"No," I said, "this is all wrong; I am going to be trained in Japan."

The reporters promptly swung round to me but Rev. Jones forestalled my saying anything.

"She means that she may later go on to Japan for a short time," he said, "I have written to the abbot there to tell him that I am ordaining her here and he has agreed."

The reporters turned to me again. "Did you know about this," one asked, "or is it entirely new to you?"

"I did not know about it," I replied.

"Does your mother know about it?"

"No."

This was true in every sense of the word, since I did not know of Rev. Jones' arrangements myself, but I was to regret these words later on.

Rev. Jones continued to elaborate on his plans for me with sweeping statements as to what I was going to do in Malaysia but I felt too sick inside to say anything. I was to be ordained by someone I did not know, instead of by the old man I had met in London and who I knew was waiting for me. True, I had discussed the possibility of being ordained in Malaysia but a "friend" of mine in London had written to Rev. Jones in Malaysia to say that I was too ill to be ordained at all and that he should not even consider it. I had not realised to what extent Rev. Jones had already made the arrangements.

The interview over, I was taken, somewhat shaken, to Rev. Jones' luxurious house which dripped with valuable possessions of every sort. I was wined, dined, taken on a tour of the island, fed in the most luxurious restaurants, smothered with presents and put to bed in the best guest room of a palatial mansion belonging to a Chinese millionaire. The ship did not sail for Singapore until the next day and so I was able to rest on land for the first time in three and a half weeks. But I could not sleep. Apart from the mosquitos, which ate me from one end to the other, and the intense and unaccustomed heat, my mind was in a whirl of excitement over the arrangements for the festivities which had accompanied my arrival and amazement at what had been, without my knowledge, decided for me, not to mention the luxury in which religious people in the Far East seemed to live. I have come, expecting a spartan existence, and I find a luxury unknown to most people in Britain.

11th. January.

I was taken to the botanical gardens and fêted again before finally embarking on the ship, five minutes before she sailed, for Singapore.

The reception I got on board was electric; everyone avoided looking at me, or else did so side-ways, and I could not imagine why until someone quietly handed me the morning paper, walking away without saying anything after doing so. The headlines read, "Englishwoman to enter the Buddhist priesthood—Mother does not know!"

I stared in wonder at the newspaper headline, not comprehending its full meaning, since my mother had known of my going to Japan; and then the horror of it burst upon my brain like a thunder-clap. To the average Western person the fact that an adult decides to do something like entering the priesthood is not very significant but it seems that, to the Oriental mind, anything that is done without the *full*[2] knowledge and approval of a parent, in spite of the age of the person concerned, is absolutely anathema. In addition to this I know the British yellow press too well for me to feel happy about such a headline: but there is nothing I can do about it and I can only guess what repercussions the story may have in England with my family. I spent most of the day, rather miserably, in my cabin.

12th. January.

After a restless night—the second together—I got up, tired and worried, to see a pouring wet day in Singapore harbour. We docked and I waited in my cabin for some time for the person who was supposed to come to meet me with members of the local Buddhist Youth Group. No one came. I waited and waited and then, suddenly, my cabin door was blocked by a tall man, who looked more Indian than Chinese, and a young woman who looked the same.

"Are you Miss Kennett?" was his first comment.

I looked at him hard; but in a place such as Singapore, where all the races are inextricably mixed, it was quite possible that he was part Chinese.

"Yes," I replied.

"Good," he said, "I want to see you."

"Are you Mr. Chou?" I asked.

"No," he replied, "but he will perhaps come later. Shall I take you to your temple?"

It was difficult to know what to do under the circumstances. The ship was about to embark its new passengers prior to sailing and I knew that I had to be off and away before that; I wanted to question this man much more before trusting myself to him but I had almost no time left for such things so I thanked him and we left the ship.

On the quayside I stopped. "I think I really ought to wait for Mr. Chou," I said. We waited and waited but no one came. Then my new companion turned to me.

"I think you ought to know that all the newspapers in the country are chasing you," he said. "I can protect you from them if you wish. Allow me to take you to your temple in my car. It is possible that Mr. Chou knows about the newspapers and so has not come."

"Are you sure?" I was startled but did not wish to show it. Then I said, "Do you know where the temple is?"

"Oh, yes," he replied, "let me take you."

The rain continued to pour down and there seemed nothing else to do but get into his car. We roared through the dock-yard and I was surprised at the grin on the face of the custom's official who did not even bother to check my passport. We were out in Singapore and heading north; where to I did not know.

It was with growing anxiety that I noticed that we seemed to be leaving the city of Singapore behind and making for the suburbs. Finally I gave voice to my thoughts.

"Where are we going?" I asked.

"To my flat," came the reply, "You see, I too am from a newspaper but, if you see only me, the other reporters will not bother you and you will be left alone. At the moment there are dozens of them around the temple."

The car was travelling at high speed and there was little I could do to stop it. I said nothing.

"You took that remarkably well," he said, "aren't you afraid?"

"Why should I be? I can only die once."

There was silence in the car for some time. He then started asking all sorts of questions to most of which he thought I was giving unsatisfactory answers. It seemed that he was convinced that the only reason any woman would enter religion was if she suffered from kinky sex. He was so stuffed with all the stupid ideas of the cheap novels he had read that I began to get somewhat angry as well as to recover from my state of shock.

"My readers will never believe this," he grumbled, "You must give me a better story."

At this I got really angry. "That is not my concern," I retorted. "What I have told you is the truth and that is all there is to it."

I was now feeling that even if there were scores of reporters at the temple they must be better than this miserable specimen and I told him to take me to the temple at once.

"But I want to keep you here as long as possible," he bleated.

"I expect you do," I replied, "but I do not wish to stay. Do you realise that the penalty for holding people against their will in Singapore is hanging?"

This worked like a charm. The car turned round at top speed and we sped to the temple.

The Chinese, who were waiting for me at the temple, were completely unruffled by what had happened and I was again amazed at the luxury and living standards of the priesthood. More than anything else I wanted time to think and this was the one thing that was not to be allowed me. I was never free at any time from a bevy of women and young girls who giggled incessantly, gibbered amongst themselves and fingered everything within sight that belonged to me. This went on and on and all I wanted to do was—*THINK*. I have never been quick-tempered but this situation, after all I had been through, was just too much. I turned suddenly and roared at them to get out.[3] In all my life I can never remember doing such a thing before this. I lay down on the bed to just be *still*—the mosquitos ate me through the open, unscreened windows and the girls giggled outside the door. Then came an official of some local organisation demanding to see me—I flatly refused. People poured into my room; the giggling and gibbering started all over again. I was told that newspaper reporters were all around the temple and had set up cameras with telescopic lenses in the windows of all the neighboring houses. I tried to go downstairs for a meal but the reporters burst the door down. I fled upstairs again and a young Chinese girl, who spoke excellent English, came to me. She was amenable to understanding my feelings and undertook to do something about what was happening. She also agreed to smuggle me out for a drive in the evening when it was dark. This she did—through a side door and over the back fence!

19th. January.

Since my arrival I have been besieged. In desperation I was finally put on a long-distance coach, just before dawn, to go inland where the abbot of a great temple will protect me. The abbot met me at the coach stop. He was roughly the same height as myself with the kindest pair of brown eyes; they could twinkle in an unusual way for a Chinese. With him were a number of white-clad members of the laity. He welcomed me graciously and we went to his temple where we had a long talk with the aid of an interpreter who spoke excellent English; the abbot himself speaks good English rather slowly. I talked much to the young interpreter about the situation I found myself in and the publicity hounds that I had met, asking him bluntly what everyone meant by it. He became sad.

"In the East," he said, "a Westerner becoming a priest is a rare thing; the Christian missionaries always make a lot of trouble about it. Because of this many Buddhists feel that they have caught a prize and so tend to turn the person into a temple pet rather than a genuine member of the priesthood. He is shown and pampered and always in the public eye. This is what has happened to your friend Rev. Jones."

I was appalled. "But I want to do the thing properly," I said, "and, whether you like it or not, I want to go on to Japan and study there. I am not willing to become a puppet in silken robes."

It seemed that the abbot had understood this without any interpretation for his look was very compassionate. "I understand," he said, "and I will help you." The officials of the small temple I was to stay at came to collect me and I had the feeling that the abbot was slightly averse to this but he did not stop them, since it had been arranged by Rev. Jones, and so I went to my new home.

This temple has a bunch of Malaysians living in a separate part of its house as caretakers and the noise they make is absolutely deafening.

20th. January.

I have put up with the noise, as well as the constant visits of the temple officials, until I can stand it no longer.[3] As politely as I could I asked the Malaysians to make less noise. The result was that the noise became twice as loud. The abbot of the big monastery came to see me this morning and I told him about the noise. He looked concerned but said nothing. With him was a representative from the leading news agency in the country who was very polite. He apologised for having to disturb me but the newspapers were printing so many conflicting stories that he had been sent to get the real one which he personally guaranteed to the abbot would be circulated to all the newspapers, thus stopping the rumours. Rev. Jones arrived this evening and he, the abbot and I had a conference.

"We must decide," said Rev. Jones, "who is going to shave her head."

The abbot said nothing and there was a long silence. Then I spoke.

"I did not want to be ordained here since I had arranged for it in Japan," I said, "but, since I hear that if I do not go through with it the Christians will make much use of my refusal to ridicule Buddhism in the press, I am willing to be ordained here provided I go on to Japan to study afterwards. Can I choose who is to do the ordination?"

The abbot's eyes kindled for a second and were instantly dimmed. There was another long silence.

"I suppose so," said Rev. Jones.

"Then I choose the abbot," I answered and saw Rev. Jones jump as if stung by a wasp. "I wanted to be ordained in Japan but I am sure Zenji Sama will understand my reasons, accept this ordination and still teach me."

I could feel something between joy and relief coming out of the abbot in my direction. When he spoke, after another long silence, his words betrayed none of his inner feelings.

"Perhaps Rev. Jones would prefer to do it?"

"No," said my friend, "not if she would prefer you. You go ahead."

The conversation continued a little longer and then we all went to bed. The ordination is due to take place in the morning.

21st. January.

I slept well and ate with a good appetite this morning. I feel safe with the abbot, besides my family telegraphed to say that they are making no difficulties whatsoever with regard to the ordination. The ordination itself took place and, after the ceremony, the man from the news agency had a press conference with the other newspapers and I was left in peace.

22nd. January.

The abbot came on a bicycle to invite me to lunch at his temple. I am overjoyed at the simplicity of the life of both himself and his fifteen fellow priests which is much as I pictured it should be when I was in England.

The author being ordained in Malaysia by the Very Reverend Seck Kim Seng, abbot of Cheng Hoon Teng Temple, a Rinzai monastery in Malacca.

23rd. January.

I was awakened in the middle of the night by an unbelievable racket from the Malaysians in the other half of the house. What exactly was happening next door I still do not know and I had no desire to go and see. It occurred to me, however, that I was in a remarkably dangerous situation for the racket seemed to be of a particularly menacing variety. I felt that I should do something about removing myself from its vicinity. As I left the building something whistled past my ear. I ducked and darted round the corner, out of range, to the nearest telephone. A temple official returned with me to be told by one of the Malaysians that they objected to a foreigner in the house who told them to be quiet. The official pointed out that I was the priest of the temple and they were only the caretakers. The quarrel lasted the rest of the night and half of the day with the official saying that he had grumbled about the noise himself many times. I went back to my room but felt a lurking danger there; the quarrel continued. I wished there were some bars on the windows. Finally, since the quarrel seemed endless, I went to the abbot's temple and told him the whole story. He said nothing but made a telephone call in Chinese. Two cars arrived, with several burly Chinese in them. We returned to my temple. My things were taken to the abbot's temple in less than ten minutes.

"What is happening?" I asked.

"You are coming to my temple where you should have been in the first place," he replied, "only Rev. Jones wanted you to be like him, independent."

It is the first time I have ever heard him openly disapprove of anything my friend does. I have been given a small room, neither elaborate nor poor, which will be mine until I go to Japan. I am to give the lectures Rev. Jones has arranged under the abbot's protection and sponsorship.

13th. April.

It was raining when the ship docked at Yokohama. Rev. Ichirō met me on the dock-side and, together with two or three other people, took me by car to the temple. I was shocked to find that there were several reporters amongst the people with him. It seems that the noise made by the Chinese newspapers may be duplicated here. I was taken to the temple tea house where, I am told, I shall stay until the temple officials decide whether or not I can enter the temple itself. I thought this had all been decided before I came. I am so tired; all I want to do is drop into bed and stay there for a week but there seems to be some kind of celebration on and every time I try to rest hordes of school children swarm into the house to gibber and giggle or else open the windows to stare in at me. Who was it told me that the Japanese were the politest nation in the world? Or is this silly gibbering simply the normal behaviour of females who have been suppressed and ignored for most of their existence?

At dusk Rev. Ichirō came and told them to go away and now I have time to write this. There is so much I want to write about my first impressions of Japan, especially now that it is bright moonlight outside in the really exquisite garden, but I am just too tired to do it. There seems to be no point in trying to study religion seriously if one is to be made a newspaper story from London to Sydney. Surely I would be better off to disappear somewhere in the mountains and teach myself.[4]

14th. April.

Rev. Ichirō came to the tea house to have lunch with me today. After the meal he told me that the officers of the temple were all discussing what name I am to be called by if I am allowed to stay.

"But I thought that had all been arranged," I said, "about my staying I mean. Zenji Sama invited me over here; I have the letters to prove it. He said I was to become his disciple and study here."

"This temple is not Zenji Sama's private property," said Rev. Ichirō with a certain amount of annoyance in his voice, "and there are many who feel he had no right to ask a foreigner to come here at all. In addition to this, you are a woman and this temple has never had a woman in it before."

"Then what are all those girl trainees that I saw this morning doing here?" I asked.

"Most of them are here for this special period only. We are, at the moment, doing Jūkai and they have come to help. The others, who are here all the time, are not officially here; save one." His English is a little quaint.

"That is a great idea," I said, "women are here but not here. And you tell me this after I have come twelve thousand miles. Zenji Sama might have let me know and I could have considered whether or not it would be worth coming at all."[4]

"Zenji Sama has very warm feeling for you," he said, showing some slight anger in his tone as he said the words, "it is very strange to us that he should want a woman for a disciple in this temple."

"Has he no other female disciples?"

"Oh, yes, many, but not here. They are all in other places."

Suddenly his face darkened and he fumbled in his sleeve and produced an old newspaper cutting of the bombing of Hiroshima. He spoke in a voice that vibrated with emotion.

"This is a picture of Hiroshima; the poor, bombed city; but we must forgive and forget."

It was difficult to know whether he was speaking to himself or to me so I said nothing. He looked up at me and I was startled by what seemed to be close to hatred in his eyes. "You say nothing?" he said.

"What is there to say? I was a child when the war started. I was scarcely adult when it ended. Many stupid, evil and wicked things are done in wartime. Many people suffered all over the world . . . . ."

I stopped; there seemed nothing more to say.

"No country suffered as did Japan."

There came a knock at the door and a tall, slender young trainee entered. Rev. Ichirō changed abruptly from the state he had been in and broke into a smile which somehow did not light up his eyes. He stuffed the news clipping into his sleeve and turned to the newcomer, half nodded to him and then turned back to me.

"This is Rev. Tarō. He will be looking after you. He will teach you all the little ways of the monastery. He speaks English slowly. Speak slowly to him and he will understand you very well. You can teach him better English in return for the help he will be giving you."

Rev. Ichirō then rose and left the room quickly after a cursory "Sayonara."

Rev. Tarō looked at me sideways from his position on the floor near the door and I could see that he was rather nonplussed with the situation. I poured out a cup of tea and offered it to him along with one of the cakes Rev. Ichirō had brought. He ate and drank in silence. Then he spoke very slowly and with a very strange-sounding intonation.

"Young Japanese not worry of war."

I realised that he must have been standing outside the door for some time before knocking for he had obviously overheard the conversation; this would account for his slightly embarrassed air when he came into the room.

"Young Europeans too," I said.

"Japan is fire country. Many mountains with fire in them. Many earthquake. Noise and shake not last long but, at time, very mighty. Older Japanese temper over war very like." The English was queer but the meaning obvious.

I was amazed at his frankness and the genuine generosity and concern in his eyes.

"Thank you," I said, "It did not worry me. Please do not be concerned."

"All young trainees very glad you here," he said. "Officers old; some pleased, some not. You be very careful? I will guard you. Zenji Sama, he very good. He love disciple very much. Japanese temper very hot, very quick; put in pocket, it burn hole if not taken out sometime. Rev. Ichirō mountain hot."

I construed this as meaning a volcanic temper.

"Let me teach you how to use bowls," he said.

We spent the rest of the afternoon talking whilst he taught me many things and took me all round the temple.

"When do you think I shall be allowed to enter the temple properly?" I asked.

"If you enter it will be quick or not all," he replied.

It was supper time and he had to leave me. I am just too amazed at what is happening to be able to think clearly.

15th. April.

Rev. Tarō came to me early.

"When am I to be allowed to go to meditation?" I asked. "I have been here for almost three days and I am still told that I must not get up in the morning or go to the Meditation Hall."

"I not know." His eyes were lowered and his tone was mournful.

There was a long pause, then he said, "This morning I much beaten during meditation. I not know why."

"I have some salve that might help," I said.

He looked up eagerly. "You lend? It will take away pain?"

I nodded, got up and found it. He took it eagerly with both hands. There came a knock at the door and the bottle disappeared into his sleeve very quickly. A young trainee came in to fetch the breakfast things and departed.

"To-day you must go to Jūkai ceremonies," he said.

"What's Jūkai?" I asked.

His eyes were instantly cast down again. "I not know," came the surprising answer. I found myself wondering if he was saying he did not know how to explain or if he was not allowed to. Another knock came at the door and Rev. Ichirō entered.

"To-day you will do Jūkai," he said. "Please get yourself ready. It is a pity you have only yellow robes; they should be black but Zenji Sama does not mind."

"What is Jūkai?" I asked again.

"A woman does not need to know. All she needs is to do it. Clean the room, Tarō."

He swept through the door with a swish of his brown robes and I thought I saw a shade of dislike flit across Rev. Tarō's face, then instantly wiped away.[4] He went to the window and watched Rev. Ichirō go off down the garden path.

"Jūkai is Shushōgi," he said cryptically.

"What is Shushōgi?" I asked.

"Chief Scripture. I will somewhere find copy."

He disappeared and came back with a small book written in atrocious English; he then got a broom and started sweeping. I hunted around the back of the house, found another broom and started sweeping from the opposite side of the room. He stopped and stared at me.

"You can use broom?"

"Of course," I said.

He broke into a big grin. "We can do real training together," he cried. "Already you start at one side and me other. We will meet in middle and—no more dirt! They unfair—you cannot come to Meditation Hall but here is good Meditation Hall."

We worked away and the room and the rest of the little house were soon spotless. I then made tea whilst he was finishing off the garden path.

"To-night," he said, "ceremony is Reading of Precepts. To-morrow is Confession night; very great and very solemn. Then you will see Zenji Sama's blood and be recognised."

I tried to sort through this as best I could and then saw Rev. Ichirō coming up the path again. Rev. Tarō shut his mouth like a clam shell and disappeared as much into the woodwork as he could. Rev. Ichirō looked at the house in some surprise. Rev. Tarō told him that we had cleaned it together.

"Can I have a bucket?" I asked. "I need to do some washing."

"You are used to such work?" he inquired with a measure of disbelief.

I had already been caught off guard with this type of comment and was determined that it should not again annoy me so I replied, "Oh, yes, I am quite used to washing clothes."

"Good," he said, "I will arrange it. The council has decided to call you Jiyu, which is the Japanese form of your Chinese name, Tsuyu. From now on all trainees here will call you by this name. Zenji Sama will not change it although he does not like it for you."

"Thank you," I said. "When can I go to meditation? I am now quite rested from my journey."

"We must tell the reporters to come first," he said. "The newspapers want to know when you meditate and take pictures of it."

This got my temper out.[5] "I am not a public show," I exploded, "and I do not intend to become one."

"Zenji Sama has done much for you," he said coldly, "the least you can do for him is give some publicity to the temple."

"That is not what he wants and you know it," I was beside myself with fury now,[5] "and besides, when am I going to see him? I have come from the other side of the world to follow him and, after four days, I have still not seen him."

"You will see him to-night," he replied, "and to-morrow he will receive you as a member of the Zen Church. A group of ladies are busy making you a special kesa (priest's robe) at his request so that he can officially receive you as his full disciple. So much honour for you is not good. All trainees will be very jealous."

"I am deeply grateful for the honour Zenji Sama is showing me," I said, "but I came here to meditate. When am I to be allowed to do so?"

"Before you can you must ask permission of all officers here," he said, "I doubt if they will give it."

"Then by all means let us ask them," I said, "and, if they refuse, I can make arrangements to go elsewhere."[5]

He looked at me in surprise. "You want to meditate that badly?" he said thoughtfully, "I see."

He left the room. I went to the Reading of the Precepts ceremony this evening and was overjoyed to be with everyone for the first time.

16th. April.

At about seven-thirty in the morning Rev. Ichirō came to the tea house.

"Put on your robes and come with me," he said tersely, "we have to ask formal permission of all officers for you to enter this temple. It is Zenji Sama's order."

I got the feeling that the old abbot was warm tempered with his bunch of recalcitrant officers and did not want to make feelings run any higher than they might already be by keeping them waiting so got myself ready as quickly as possible.

Our first call was on the chief lecturer, Rev. Akira, who received me charmingly and, using Rev. Tarō, who was also with us, as his interpreter rather than Rev. Ichirō whose English was much better, said he was overjoyed that foreigners were coming to the temple and that he hoped that I was merely the first of many. He gave me a box of cakes and the interview was over. Rev. Ichirō did not look pleased. The next one we visited was the chief disciplinarian, Rev. Masao, who informed me, by way of Rev. Tarō, that there had never been a woman officially in the temple before but he was hunting through the rules to discover how my entry could be legally effected. He then produced the kyosaku (awakening stick) and placed it in front of me on the table between us.

"Do you know what this is?" he asked through Rev. Tarō.

"Yes," I said.

"The kindest Kanzeon is to be found in hell," he said, "I shall not hesitate to use it." He then turned his full attention to Rev. Tarō. "Teach her to recite the Scriptures," he roared, "and bring her back in a week's time." As we left the room Rev. Tarō whispered, "He sergeant-major in army before become priest."

The third interview was with the Director who seemed not to know what to do. He merely said good morning, looked uncomfortable and then fled from the room.

A young trainee came up to Rev. Ichirō, whispered something to him and I was taken to Zenji Sama's room for the first time. The old man was reclining on magnificent cushions, grinning with pleasure at seeing me. He invited me to sit beside him and Rev. Ichirō glowered so much that he had to get up and look out of the window. Rev. Tarō looked frightened and once again tried to disappear into the woodwork. Zenji Sama and I had tea after which he had a photographer come in and take a picture of us together. I was taken to the next room where I and several others underwent the reception ceremony of the Zen Church. Again I was taken into Zenji Sama's room; again fed; then sent back to the tea house in the company of Rev. Tarō. Maybe I shall be able to meditate the day after to-morrow. I hear I am to attend the Confession ceremony to-night.

Later.

The Confession ceremony took place at midnight as I had been told it would. There must have been hundreds of people taking part in it and I hear it only happens once a year. First in the procession, after the bells, came the male trainees who had not yet attended a Jūkai followed by the female ones. Then came a large number of old laymen and lay women and, finally, several hundred sixteen-year-old girls from the temple high school. Waiting for the long procession to start was somewhat gruelling since the girls could not look at me without giggling; a fact which made it difficult for me to concentrate on the act of confession itself. Finally the procession began and wound its way through many scarlet-hung, tortuous corridors until we came to a small altar set within a recess in the hangings. Behind it sat the oldest priest I have ever seen. He gave me a small piece of paper which I took a look at and discovered that it contained one Chinese character signifying all my past evil karma. Each person was given a piece of paper similar to this. The procession continued until we came to another similar altar behind which sat another very old priest to whom we each gave back the piece of paper we had already received. The procession continued on to another altar behind which sat an old priest who was as immovable as a statue. For a moment I thought he was one until I saw the slight movement of his chest as he breathed. His paper thin hand took a pinch of incense whilst his eyes looked deep into mine and then he offered the incense in the bowl in front of him with such reverence that I was quite startled by it. The procession emerged from the red hung corridors into the Ceremony Hall and everyone sat on the floor in rows in front of the altar. When all were seated the three old priests entered and several young trainees brought in a great cauldron from which flames leaped. The three old priests who had sat behind the altars solemnly burned each piece of paper in the cauldron and, when they had all been consumed, uttered a great cry which electrified me and everyone else present. Some Scriptures were recited and then everyone went back to their rooms—I think. Rev. Ichirō called me to his room (it was the first time I had ever seen the inside of it) and made tea.

"Did you understand what was happening?" he asked, "The ceremony did not in any way seem to be causing you much of a problem."

"The ceremony signifies the giving up of all past karma," I said, "the turning over of a new leaf in life as it were. The priests have destroyed the bad karma with fire and scared away further evil with their great shout. Why should the ceremony cause me a problem?"

Rev. Ichirō looked startled. "That is very quick," he said, "How did you understand the ceremony yesterday?"

"It was the Reading of the Precepts," I replied, "The Precepts tell you how to live. The priest who read them wanted us to know how we were to live in the future after we had got rid of all our past evil karma."

His eyes had narrowed suddenly, "You are too intelligent for your own good," he said, "you must not understand such things with your brain only."

"That is why I want to go to meditation," I said. "When can I start?"

"We must think about it," he replied, "we cannot make such a decision in a hurry."

The interview was obviously over and I stood up. At the door I turned towards him.

"I am sorry if my brain bothers you," I said, "since it belongs to a woman it is probably quite annoying for it to have come up with the right answers."

His hand, in the act of putting away the tea things, stopped in mid-air and his jaw dropped open.

"Never has a woman spoken to me thus," he said.

"Then I think it is about time that one did."

Strange things were happening to me. Maybe I was just fed up with the attitude of mind that this man had to women and had decided to lay down the ground rules for both of us. Whatever the reasons, the ceremony seemed to have had the effect of making me reckless—or courageous, whichever way one prefers to look at it.[6] His face suddenly broke into a big smile and even his eyes seemed to have kindled slightly.

"We will see how you manage with the next one," he said, "it will take place at six o'clock to-night since it is already morning now. I will give favourable consideration to your wish to meditate. Understand that the first requirement for anything in Buddhism, however, is gratitude. Understand also that always my heart is good."

I looked at him for a moment then turned from the door and made a full bow right down to the floor. As I got up he was grinning happily.

"You might even make it here," he said and then he added, "Next time don't speak to someone superior to you without sitting down first."

I sat down immediately. "Good-night," I said then rose and left the room before he had time to recover.

17th. April.

At six o'clock this evening we again went to the Ceremony Hall. When we were all seated Zenji Sama came in procession with many trainees two of which were carrying large lotus-blossoms, made of gold-lacquered wood, from which the smoke of incense issued. They advanced up the length of the hall and stopped in front of the altar itself. Zenji Sama ascended it and sat down upon a great chair placed there for him. The hall was dark except for two candles carried by two junior trainees who now also ascended the altar and knelt beside Zenji Sama, lighting him on both sides. Another trainee ascended the altar and, after some preliminary Japanese Scriptures and prayers which I did not understand, unrolled what looked like a roll of silk against Zenji Sama's arm. Zenji Sama spoke quietly, in a very young-sounding voice for a man of his age, pointing to certain writings and circles on the silk. All the time his eyes seemed to be roaming over the assembled people and I had the feeling that he was hunting for me. I therefore made an effort to look at him and immediately felt his eyes full on me as he went on speaking. I heard him say something about England and felt sure he was trying to tell me something but it was his eyes that were telling me the most. Deep, silent and quiet, they seemed to be drawing mine into them and, not merely my eyes, but the whole of me. He ceased speaking and the trainee beside him folded up the silk and put it away carefully. A large tray of folded papers was brought and Zenji Sama seemed to be bless-ing them. Then, each in turn, we were led to the front of the altar where we were given one of the papers by Zenji Sama himself. As he handed me mine he contrived to touch my hand. A thrill shot through me as I bowed and returned to my place.

After the ceremony I went again to Rev. Ichirō's room at his request. As soon as we had entered I bowed and sat down. He eyed me thoughtfully and began to make tea. Rev. Tarō entered softly and, discarding the cushion that had been set for him, moving it reverently to one side, sat directly on the floor. I carefully removed the one that was beneath me and placed it neatly on top of Rev. Tarō's discarded one. Rev. Ichirō said nothing but continued to make tea. When he had finished he said, "What of to-night's ceremony?"

"The words themselves I could not understand," I said, "for, as yet, I do not understand spoken Japanese. But I do know that Zenji Sama was telling me something and that he wants me very much."

"Have you looked at the paper he gave you yet?" he asked, "It is a copy of the silk certificate he was showing to everyone in the hall."

"It was too far away for me to see clearly what was on the one he was holding," I replied, "as for my own one I have not opened it in case I was not supposed to."

"Open it now."

I took the square-folded envelope, which had been made in such a way as to make finding its opening difficult, and turned it over. From observing Rev. Tarō I had noticed that one never tore anything open in a hurry or made a show of one's desire for a quick satisfaction of one's curiosity. Everyone sat silently whilst I carefully inspected the edges. I heard a faint chuckle from Rev. Ichirō as I finally found out how an opening was effected without harm to the envelope. I drew out a long sheet of paper on which were many red lines and circles with Japanese characters written upon them. Rev. Ichirō took it from me.

"What do you make of it?" he asked.

I already knew the Chinese characters for the names of several of the Buddhas and Patriarchs of Zen, as well as those for Zenji Sama's name, and I recognised them.

"It would seem to be a list of all the Buddhas and Patriarchs and masters preceding Zenji Sama," I said.

"You can read Japanese?" his eyes were quick and searching.

"A little," I replied.

"How do you understand the lines and circles?"

"The lines run through all the names from the time of Shakyamuni Buddha down to the present time," I said, "and there seems to be another name written after Zenji Sama's which, although it does not have the characters for my own name, I presume must represent me. As I understand it Zenji Sama has made me a part of his family."

"Unless you can understand the red lines and circles this piece of paper is useless," he said, "You must study it in detail."

"What is this actual paper called?" I asked.

"Ketchimyaku," he replied.

"What does the word mean?" I asked.

"It means the Bloodline of the Buddhas," he said.

"Then the red lines represent the Blood of Shakyamuni Buddha which flows through the Patriarchs and masters down to the present time and on to me from Zenji Sama," I said.

"The graphic picture is one thing," he said with his eyes closed, "but the reality is another. You are understanding only in your brain and I have already said that it is too quick for your own good. I do not want to talk much with you because of the danger of feeding your intelligence. You must experience these things with your entire being. You must know what the Blood of the Buddhas[7] really is."

"When can I start meditating?" I asked.

"You are in too great a hurry," he said with a return to his old expression of seeming dislike, "Jūkai does not end until after the ceremony that will take place at six o'clock to-morrow evening. When all the guests have gone, and the priests who have only come for Jūkai, we can consider what we are going to do with you. Good-night."

I rose and left the room together with Rev. Tarō.

18th. April.

The last of the Jūkai ceremonies took place this evening. At six o'clock we all went again to the Ceremony Hall. After the preliminary Scriptures had been recited we were taken, in batches of twelve, to ascend the steps of the main altar where we sat down. On the other side of the altar, hidden from the congregation in the hall, sat Zenji Sama and the elderly priests whom we had seen during the Confession ceremony together with a large number of others and, behind them, the shrine of Keizan Zenji and Dōgen Zenji was illuminated so that the statues of these founders were clearly visible just above the heads of the assembled priests. As soon as we had sat down the priests, including Zenji Sama, rose and solemnly bowed to us and we bowed back to them. They then went in procession around the altar as we sat there, ringing bells and giving homage to Shakyamuni Buddha. They circumambulated the altar three times for each twelve members of the congregation and, whilst I myself was there, I had a distinct feeling that they were worshipping us as if we were Shakyamuni Buddha in person— not just me alone but all the others with me; and the altar and the hall and everything there seemed to be included. We returned to our places and the one word that Rev. Tarō had said to me about this ceremony continued to throb through my brain, "Recognition." We had been told how a Buddha behaves during the Reading of the Precepts, we had been cleansed from our karma by the fire of Confession; we had entered the family of the Buddhas; the Ketchimyaku was our family tree and this ceremony was the recognition of the Buddhist Church that we had been reborn, this time into the country of the Buddhas. When all had been upon the altar the priests made a circle around the congregation, stretching all round the hall and, ringing bells and chanting "Homage to Shakyamuni Buddha," circumambulated us three times. One thing puzzled me, however, and that was the very strange procession that we had made before sitting down in the hall for the Ketchimyaku ceremony. Zenji Sama had led us, carrying his staff and, I believe, his begging bowl, in a sort of follow-my-leader procession round the hall, up and down and round and about, twisting and turning in all directions and in all places until he finally got to the main door from where he made directly for the altar, climbed it and sat down on top. The ceremony over Rev. Ichirō sent for me once more.

"Jūkai is over," he said, "What have you learned from it?"

"That I am neither the same nor different from when I entered this temple," I replied.

"I do not want to hear your explanation," he said, somewhat angrily, "if you have understood it, it will show in your daily life. Thank you for joining us."

"Thank you for permitting me to," I replied. I bowed and left the room.

21st. April.

Nothing has happened for four days. I went to Morning Service as I had been told to but there was no service taking place. Rev. Tarō continues to come but says absolutely nothing. He simply helps me clean up, brings my meals and then departs and that is all I see of anyone during the whole day. I wonder what I should do?

22nd. April.

I decided that to do nothing was definitely wrong so got up at about two o'clock this morning and went to the Ceremony Hall. I know that it is probably wrong to do such a thing but I am desperate. Rev. Tarō has already shown me where the Meditation Hall is so, finding nothing in the Ceremony Hall, I went there instead. I could hear steady breathing coming from inside it and peeped round the curtain. All the junior trainees were sound asleep upon their seats, wrapped up in large quilts. Outside the Meditation Hall there are a set of seats also so I settled down on one and dozed a little to wait and see what would happen. At about a quarter past three someone came running round with a bell and I heard hurried sounds of dressing in the Meditation Hall itself as the lights flashed on. I shook myself, sat up and got into the meditation position. Several trainees came to enter the hall (presumably they sleep elsewhere) and some looked very startled at seeing me sitting outside. However, they said nothing, passed me and went in. I continued to sit. Several bells rang and some wooden clappers were struck. I had no idea what they indicated so just continued to sit where I was. Presently Rev. Tarō came out of the hall, gave me a strange look and settled down beside me. I carefully followed everything he was doing and, as the next bell sounded, turned to face the wall when he did. After what seemed to be a period of about an hour a wooden block was struck and Rev. Tarō placed his kesa on his head and recited a verse before putting it on. I put mine on my head too but could make nothing of what was being said. The bell then rang again and all the trainees came pouring out of the hall in procession to the Ceremony Hall. Rev. Tarō did not seem to know quite what to do so I charged off behind the others and he, looking really worried, followed me.

We got to the Ceremony Hall and everyone sat down. I did not know where to sit so sat down in the first available place. Zenji Sama entered and I saw his eyes kindle with joy when he spotted me. Rev. Ichirō came up to me and said, "You cannot sit here. You are not permitted to."

"Where can I sit then?" I asked.

"I do not know. There is no place for you in this temple."

I thought he was speaking literally but decided to answer him from a religious angle anyway.

"In the line of the Buddhas there is room for everything."

"Not in this hall," he replied.

A young trainee touched him respectfully upon the sleeve and waved in the direction of Zenji Sama. Rev. Ichirō went over to speak to him. When he came back he pointed to a spot on the floor behind all the other trainees and not really in the hall at all.

"You may sit there," he said stiffly and swept away.

I settled down to do everything that the others did and thoroughly enjoyed the service. Later I asked Rev. Tarō to teach me the Scriptures that were being recited.

"I must ask permission," he said.

When I saw him later I asked again.

"Rev. Ichirō will be bringing you something to learn them from," he said.

"But Rev. Masao said that I was to come and see him in a week's time from when I last saw him and recite them to him," I said.

"Rev. Masao and Rev. Ichirō not such good friends," said Rev. Tarō. "Not good idea to press matter."

Rev. Ichirō arrived sometime later bringing with him a romanised copy of the Hannyashingyō (Scripture of Great Wisdom) and the list of the names of the Patriarchs which, he told me, is recited at every Morning Service.

"Learn these thoroughly," he said, "and I am to tell you that you may sit outside the Meditation Hall every morning from now on, if you wish, and come to Morning Service also; however, it is at a different time every day."

"Thank you," I said. "How shall I know at what time it starts?"

"We cannot send someone all the way out into the garden with a bell," he said. "Rev. Tarō will have to come for you each morning."

Rev. Tarō winced but said nothing.

"When shall I be admitted to the Meditation Hall properly?"

He glared at me. "It is up to Zenji Sama," he snapped, "If he wishes to break the rules here presumably he can whenever he wishes. In Japan women are slow; you must understand this. You are in Japan now."

"Maybe Japanese women are slow," I countered, "but, whether I am in Japan or not, and although my head is shaved as yours is, the skull, and the brain inside it, are still British and are going to behave like it."

"How can a woman ever do what a man does?"

"According to the Shushōgi even a little girl of seven can be the celebrant at Morning Service if she is sincere in what she is doing. Dōgen Zenji says so and he meant it. He also says that there is complete equality of the sexes in Zen."

"Do you dare to teach me the Scriptures?"

"No, simply to remind you of them."

He paused. "Can you *really* put up with what these young men do here?" he asked.

"I can put up with anything that anyone can put up with anywhere," I said, "whether it be man, woman or animal." And then I stopped, appalled at what I had just said.

"We will see," he said and left me.

15th. May.

Absolutely no movement one way or the other with regard to my entering the actual community. Rev. Tarō tells me that they are quarrelling again over my being here and Zenji Sama is doing the equivalent of slapping their heads in order to make them agree with his wishes. Maybe I should not have come.

The rainy season began to-day, somewhat early according to Rev. Tarō, and the weather is becoming incredibly hot and sticky. In addition to this mosquitos are beginning to be something of a nuisance. Rev. Tarō says that mosquitos do not bite before the first of July which is the date that mosquito-nets are issued to the community. If this is true, I wonder why I am covered with bites at the moment?!? It is only May.

17th. May.

The rain is pouring into the tea house and there is no dry spot anywhere for me to put my bed. I asked Rev. Tarō if there was somewhere else I could stay for the time being but he merely repeated that there was no room for me in the temple. I also asked him if he could get me a black robe, so that I do not always have to wear this yellow one, and gave him five thousand yen with which to purchase one. He says he must ask Rev. Ichirō first.

18th. May.

I did not go to the Meditation Hall or Morning Service to-day. I was just too fed up with having to sit in a corner all night with nowhere to sleep because of the rain and a temperature which is gradually rising from a cold I now have as a result of being constantly wet. Rev. Ichirō arrived immediately after Morning Service, looking very worried, to know what had happened. I have not seen Rev. Tarō at the time of meditation for some days now.

"Is there any place I can move to until the rain stops?" I asked Rev. Ichirō as best I could between sneezes.

"No," he replied, "but I will get you a doctor."

About half an hour later, a certain professor of medicine, of whom I knew and who was a friend of several people I knew in Malaysia, arrived. He spoke excellent English and had been amongst those who had welcomed me on my arrival at Yokohama. He looked me over carefully and decided that I must be in a warm, dry place. To him I told all my troubles concerning housing and my desire to enter the Meditation Hall.

"Will you speak to Zenji Sama for me?" I asked, "I know you have his ear and you can get to him without being stopped by anyone here. I have made several attempts to get to him but have been stopped before I have set foot outside the garden. There is no point in my staying here if I am not to be taught anything and I am certain that he is as anxious to get to me as I am to him."

He looked concerned. "It may not be good for me to go against the wishes of the officers here," he said, "they are very powerful. If they found out what I had done they may make life very difficult for me. This is a royal temple and the officers carry a lot of influence in high places."

"If you do not help me then I had best leave," I said, "for I have no-one else to turn to."

"I will see what I can do," he said as he left me.

This evening I was visited by a very small priest, the newest of all the officers here, having arrived only five days before I did. He introduced himself as Rev. Hajime and said very slowly, "I no speak English but can write."

He had a young trainee with him who had brought a pad and pencil and I poured out, on paper, all that had happened to me, what I had been trying to do and how I thought it was best to leave since no-one would attempt to help me. He read it slowly then wrote, "I will arrange." He rose and left the room together with the young trainee.

19th. May.

This morning Rev. Hajime came back again with two other officers and all three sat and looked at me as if I were an interesting specimen in a cage. One handed me a box of cakes and then departed. I was still in bed for the cold had got much worse.

An hour later five trainees arrived and I and my things were swept out of the tea house and taken to the main temple where we were installed in a large reception room. I and my belongings and bed make a pathetic dot in one corner; but at least it is dry.

21st. May.

Rev. Ichirō came to see me this morning. My cold is almost better and he said that I am to go to N.H.K. (the Tokyo television network) to make an appearance. I refused.

"You will go or you will leave this temple," he said.

"That is fine by me," I replied.

He left me and five minutes later three or four trainees arrived, picked up all my things and dumped them back in the tea house. I went with them. Rev. Tarō came too, looking glum.

"Please do it," he begged.

"Not unless I know that Zenji Sama himself specifically wants it," I replied. Rev. Tarō disappeared and came back, half an hour later, with a piece of paper on which was written one word in English beside Zenji Sama's seal. The word was, "Please."

Rev. Ichirō came in a few minutes later and I agreed to do the show. He said that he had borrowed a black robe for me for the purpose and helped me dress. At the studio he decided that my robes were not flashy enough for the producer and insisted on my using his. On the way back I felt so much as if I had been turned into an actor for publicity reasons that I just could not bring myself to speak to him at all.[3]

31st. May.

Still in the tea house. It seems that absolutely nothing is being done and the rain is still pouring in.

1st. June.

After Morning Service I heard a great noise in the garden and saw the thirty officers bearing down on the tea house, headed by a very small one, quite the tiniest man I have ever seen. They came to the door and crowded in.

"The officers have come to welcome you to the temple," said Rev. Ichirō who was with them. "This is the *new* director, Rev. Shizuo, who wishes to welcome you in their name."

The tiny little priest bowed to me delightedly with a roguish smile. Through Rev. Tarō he told me that he wanted me to come and meditate in the Meditation Hall from to-morrow.

They all drank tea and, as soon as they had gone, my professor friend turned up.

"I talked to Zenji Sama yesterday," he said. "It was the first time I could get to him without others suspecting that I was going on your behalf. He is very sorry for what is happening but asks that you bear with him in his difficulties. He sent you this flower. Always, when you see it, know that he is thinking of you." He handed me a lily, got up and left the room. To-morrow, it seems, I am to enter the Meditation Hall and I have to learn much before it. I am overjoyed.

2nd. June.

I have been moved into the main temple buildings again. Late last evening three young trainees arrived and moved all my things into a large room in the building furthest away from the Meditation Hall where, Rev. Tarō tells me, they put all those trainees which they feel sure will not make it. Oddly enough Rev. Hajime lives there too along with the two others which he brought to see me when I was ill. I suspect it is he who has made these arrangements. At any rate what people think of this particular house does not matter very much to me since it is both warm and dry *and* among the main temple buildings so I shall know what is going on.

This morning, at about two-thirty a.m., someone ringing a bell furiously ran along the corridors round the house and I got up hurriedly, washed and made my way to the Meditation Hall.

I sat outside it, as I had been instructed, meditated in my usual place and then went to Morning Service. After this I was given a stick of incense and told to stand outside the Meditation Hall door. To my horror I noticed a large number of people, carrying cameras and movie lights, coming down the corridor towards the Meditation Hall, led by Rev. Ichirō, and looked at the priest who was beside me for an explanation but he looked steadfastly into the distance. It was at about this time that I also noticed a young and slender trainee who had not gone into the Meditation Hall with the others and who seemed to be hovering not very far from me. Rev. Ichirō and his cameramen arrived outside the Meditation Hall and some came up to me, pushing their cameras into my face. I retaliated by turning away from them. This made them quite angry and one stepped inside the hall in order to try and photograph me from there. The priest who was standing with me was annoyed at this and turned to Rev. Ichirō who told him to be silent. It was then that the other young trainee, who I had seen hovering, came up and touched Rev. Ichirō on the sleeve. He said one word, "No." Rev. Ichirō turned, glaring at him, and then seemed to freeze on the spot. I was not to find out until later in the day why this young man had such power over him. At all events the reporters were relegated to the back of the corridor and not allowed either near my face or the door of the Meditation Hall.

The disciplinarian called my name and announced that I was to be formally admitted to the Meditation Hall; I, and the young priest with me, went in together. I offered my stick of incense at the altar and went to bow at the main altar. I then walked round the hall in greeting to all the trainees there before bowing to my own seat which was exactly opposite that of Zenji Sama himself. I have been put there, I was told later, since he wants to watch over me in person. When the ceremony was over Rev. Ichirō whisked me off to his room along with the reporters. Whilst he gave them tea, Rev. Tarō handed me a scruffy piece of paper on which was scrawled what seemed to be a daily time-table.

"Rev. Ichirō says that you are to memorise this so that, when the reporters ask you what your daily schedule is, you can tell them," he said, trying not to look at me as he said it.

I scrutinised the piece of paper and stared at him; then I said, "But this is not my daily schedule and Rev. Ichirō knows it. This is a bunch of lies."

He hung his head and looked miserable. "Please do not make life more difficult for me than it is," he pleaded, "just say it. Otherwise I much beaten, on Rev. Ichirō's order, in morning."

"That is blackmail," I said.

He looked up, worried. "What is 'blackmail?' " he asked.

By now Rev. Ichirō had finished making his tea and was regaling the reporters with tales of my exploits. He turned to me. "Now tell the reporters what they want to hear," he said. I stared at him, unbelieving. They started questioning me—about my private life, my love life, anything and everything that was useless or sensational. I refused to give them the answers they wanted to hear; if they beat up Rev. Tarō I cannot help it. When it came to the schedule I said that one had not been set up for me but that I hoped to talk about the matter with Zenji Sama. Rev. Ichirō, showing signs of fury which was ill suppressed, concluded the interview in a hurry and then turned to me.

"If you want to stay in this temple you will do things my way," he hissed between thin lips.

"I will do nothing that my conscience will not permit me to do," I replied, "and no power here or elsewhere will force me to."

"Get out," the hiss had grown more menacing.

I rose, bowed and left the room with Rev. Tarō looking terri-fied beside me.

"What is 'blackmail?' " he pleaded when we were outside the room.

"Look it up," I snapped and left him.

On the way to my room I again met the young trainee who had had such an effect on Rev. Ichirō. He handed me a lily of the same sort that the professor had brought me, bowed and departed. I turned it round in my hand, looking at it carefully. It was a white lily. I continued on my way, thinking over what had happened rather miserably, for Rev. Ichirō had taken all the joy out of my entry into the Meditation Hall, when something seemed to happen to the flower. It was as if it was trying to tell me to do something. "Whenever you see it know that Zenji Sama is thinking of you." The professor's words ran through my mind. I turned round and, regardless of Rev. Tarō's cries of fright, for he was following me, hurried off in the direction of the Chief Abbot's (Zenji Sama's) house with Rev. Tarō hard at my heels. On arrival at the house I was presented with a problem: how to get in without being caught by his staff. I turned aside from the door and made for the garden gate which brought a squeak of fright from Rev. Tarō. Opening the gate I walked into the garden with Rev. Tarō trying to pull me back. I shook him off. In the garden stood Zenji Sama, feeding his goldfish. He turned and smiled at me as I came up and bowed to him: I handed him the flower and his smile broadened. He motioned to Rev. Tarō to come forward but the latter was so terrified that he was grovelling on the ground. The old man stooped and touched him gently and he stood up very shakily. Zenji Sama spoke to him and then Rev. Tarō turned to me.

"Zenji Sama says you understood the meaning of his sending the flower," he said, his voice squeaking with fright. "He wants you to have tea with him and to talk to you. He wants to know what happened at your entry and if you are happy about it."

We entered the house and the staff members who were there looked up in some surprise and annoyance at seeing me with Zenji Sama but I decided to take no notice of them. We sat down in the abbot's room and tea was brought. Through Rev. Tarō I told Zenji Sama everything that had happened to me during the ceremony but I got the feeling that Rev. Tarō was not translating what I was saying and told him so. He replied that he dare not tell Zenji Sama what Rev. Ichirō had done because Rev. Ichirō would treat him, Rev. Tarō, terribly if he knew he had told the truth of what had happened. The frustration was unbelievable so I took out a piece of paper and wrote, as best I could, what had happened and handed it to Zenji Sama. I had got to the state when I was beyond caring what happened to anyone, myself included. Zenji Sama read it slowly and then looked at me with deep kindness and concern; he then turned the same glance on Rev. Tarō.

"Do not ever be afraid to tell me the truth," he said, "I will protect both of you. Do not fear. Whenever I want to see you I will send you a flower. When the season changes I will send you a different one. Always come. It may be difficult to get to me but, if you truly want to, you will find a way as you have to-day. I suspected there may be trouble with reporters which is why I sent Rev. Shirō, my personal attendant, to be present at your entrance ceremony. Do not ever be afraid of telling me these things otherwise I cannot help or teach you. I will see you in the Meditation Hall in the morning."

Rev. Tarō and I bowed and left the room. On leaving the garden, for we went out by the same route, he touched me on the arm and pointed to a circuitous path in the temple grounds. "Safer we go back that way," he said, "in case we meet Rev. Ichirō. I much honoured by Zenji Sama to-day, many thanks to you. I show you many secret ways to reach this house since Zenji Sama desire it. You be very careful? If his staff see you they tell Rev. Ichirō and that very dangerous for me. I now in very dangerous position; as if split in two? You understand? I must be loyal to Rev. Ichirō who give me order to watch you and to Zenji Sama who say he protect me from Rev. Ichirō. Very difficult; I see much more of Rev. Ichirō than Zenji Sama; in many ways Rev. Ichirō more dangerous."

"Don't you mean split in three?" I asked. "What about your loyalty to me as a friend?"

"You only woman; no loyalty needed to woman," was his reply.

"In that case good-bye," I said, "I need neither you nor Rev. Ichirō and, if this continues much longer, I shall not need Zenji Sama either."

I hurried off to my room leaving him standing there wondering what he had said wrong. It is obvious that I must learn to speak Japanese as quickly as possible and rely upon absolutely no-one other than myself.

3rd. June.

Rev. Ichirō came for me this morning to say that Zenji Sama wanted to officially receive me as his personal, monastic disciple and was doing so even against the wishes of all the officers of the temple. I asked Rev. Hajime if this was true and he said that Rev. Ichirō was a liar since it had been the express wish of *all* the officers that Zenji Sama *should* so receive me. My mind reels with the contradictory statements that these people come out with. One thing I know for certain; preconceived notions of the peace and quiet of a monastery are so much tommy-rot; in many ways the world outside seems to be much more honest. At least it is evil and knows it; here they are pretending to be good and are evil.[4, 8] I must stop this; if I think this way I shall get nowhere. I must stop my head from spinning.

4th. June.

No sleep from worrying about the seeming evil so sent a lily to Zenji Sama by the simple expedient of placing it on his front-door-step before meditation where he must see it when leaving his house to go to the hall. I then made my way to his house via the garden as soon as Morning Service was over. He was waiting for me in the garden, looking concerned. I had written down what I wanted to ask him and handed him the paper. I was appalled at what I had written but something in me just did not care any longer. It said quite simply, "I hear that all the officers here are against my becoming your disciple. Is this true?"

He turned the paper over in his hand slowly, and then wrote, "Who said this?"

"I do not want to tell you," I wrote back. He smiled and put the paper in his sleeve. Then he took it out again and wrote, "I shall receive you at eleven o'clock this morning. I never do anything I do not want to do." I bowed to him and left the garden.

At about ten-thirty Rev. Ichirō arrived with Rev. Tarō and told me to get ready for the ceremony. Whilst I was putting on my robes he was constantly muttering about too much honour being given to a foreigner and how jealous it was making all the other trainees.[9] Finally I was dressed to his satisfaction and we

*The author with the Very Reverend Kohō Keidō Chisan Zenji
after the ceremony of becoming his official, personal disciple.*

went off to Zenji Sama's house. In Zenji Sama's private room
were assembled a large number of elderly ladies. The ceremony
was very simple and beautiful; I recognised it as being, in part,
the same as the one I had undergone in Malaysia but much more
intimate since it was not attended by a lot of newspapermen.
When it was over Zenji Sama again wanted me to sit beside him
for a photograph. We drank tea and I returned to my room with
Rev. Ichirō still grousing at my side about jealousy on the part
of the others.[9] He stayed to lunch in the house in which I was
living and kept up a conversation along the same lines all
through the meal which was attended by the trainees who lived
there as well as Rev. Hajime and the other two officers.[9] As he
spoke I saw ideas being put into their minds that had not been
there before and I felt sure he was laying a foundation of mistrust against foreigners and women in particular.[9] When he had
gone Rev. Tarō said to me, "Rev. Ichirō really does not like you
at all. He is determined to turn as many people against you as
possible. I very worried. Now you will have no friend in this

house except, perhaps, Rev. Hajime. Very difficult for you; you cannot live in house if all people against you."

"Why does he hate foreigners so?" I asked.[9]

"I think he hates you most for being woman," he replied, "he himself not married. I think that is reason."

"Do you think the other trainees here will take *much* notice of what he has said?" I asked.[9]

"It will really be up to other officers in this house," he replied, "trainee always say 'yes' to officer even if he is wrong. This way he can live in peace and learn to live in Japanese world too. Any other way is unsafe. You very different; you not care if you make enemy or not so long as you tell what you think is truth; I not sure whether this is very courageous or very stupid; but I very like. I hope you win. I think Rev. Hajime like too; he very interesting man. Rev. Ichirō very powerful; some officers very frightened of him; not Rev. Masao, though, so he very like you. He in charge of beating in Meditation Hall so you reasonably safe there at least. Only you lack personal friends, I think."

"Surely a monastery should be above cliques?" I said.

"What is 'clique?'" he asked. I groaned in spirit. "Please, later," I said. "I am very tired."

He left me saying he would look it up.

5th. June.

My first Sesshin has come and the sitting is pure hell. It is, of course, impossible to move a muscle without getting oneself beaten and my back now looks like a mass of black and blue streaks. To make matters worse it has begun to break out in boils and, as the beating continues, the boils are bursting. The wall seems to writhe in front of my eyes as I sit and the floor seems to be coming up to hit me in the face as I walk. When bedtime comes I fall on the ground like a log and stay there until the bell goes at two a.m. I cannot eat for they eat so fast in the Meditation Hall that I am still chewing one mouthful when they have finished eating the last scrap in their bowls. The lectures drone on and on. The only thing that keeps me here is the feeling that Zenji Sama is sitting behind me on the opposite side of the aisle. Somehow I feel that every time I am about to give up he enters into my spirit and holds it up. Every time the kyosaku is carried by I now jump in terror.

6th. June.

This morning, as the kyosaku was carried by, I jumped so much that the tan shook. And then I heard a voice in my ear; I could have sworn it said the words in English but I know that that cannot be for Zenji Sama does not speak any and I do not know how I heard them for he had not left his place. The words were, "Do not fear, just breathe naturally."[10] Instantly I was flooded with a tremendous peace and the whole morning passed as if in a miraculous dream. This is surely the peace that comes to a person when he gives up the struggle at the moment of death.

As I went back to my room to rest at lunch-time I looked out of the windows of the long corridor and was startled by a strange sight. All the trees in the garden were shimmering with light, gleaming in a thousand different colours.[11] Something inside me wanted to bow but I could not tell what, so I bowed anyway. It was just too wonderful. Now, whenever I look out of the window, I seem to see it still.

7th. June.

To-day, the next to last day of Sesshin, something even stranger than what happened yesterday took place. My legs have got to a semi-crippled state from the constant sitting and I have to help myself along when I walk by holding on to the wall. I had just got to my room for the usual three-quarters-of-an-hour rest that always comes after lunch during Sesshin when the room seemed to disappear. Instead of being in my room I found myself in a long country lane and some sixth sense told me that the time was many centuries before this one. I was making my way to a large temple that stood on a far-away hill. There was absolutely no-one around and no sign of any sort of life on the road; just me, the long road, the hill and the temple. After what appeared to be an endless walk I arrived at the foot of the hill up which I hurried, young and eager. Halfway up the hill (it was more of a mountain than a hill) were the main temple buildings and I waited in a long, arched corridor, overlooking the hillside, for someone to come to me. Presently a priest, whose face I could not see since it was hidden in the shadow of a tatte-mōsu (high hat worn by an abbot) of some kind of brown material, came up to me and began to abuse me, trying to push me over the parapet. I struggled with him, fighting, as it were, for my life. At that moment a very old priest, whose face was similarly hidden but whose robes were black instead of brown, came on the scene. He put a protecting arm around me and held me away from the other priest. Nothing was said; the brown priest bowed and left us. The corridor and black priest blurred before my eyes and, as I looked again, I saw that I was standing just inside the doorway of my room. I was definitely not asleep; yet it had been a sort of dream—I think.[12] I tottered to the one cushion that I had been given and sat down on it. There I fell asleep immediately only to be awakened, I have no idea when, later on by Rev. Tarō who told me that I would miss meditation if I did not hurry. I staggered to my feet and went to the Meditation Hall. The afternoon and evening flew by; the wall had taken on a glazed appearance, a sort of sheen. At bedtime I fell asleep immediately to awaken an hour later to write this.

8th. June.

It was morning.[13] I was back in the same temple on the hill except that the picture of it was even clearer than it had been at lunch-time. The old black priest was sitting in meditation opposite me, his face in deep shadow. He was still, silent, quiet. Instinctively I knew that he was sitting inside me and that he did not care if I lived or died for *he* would always be. My legs could drop off, my body turn to stone but he would sit still and quiet, neither calm nor uncalm. And yet he was not inside me; he was there with me when I needed him. I neither wanted to grasp at him nor push him away. What mattered did not matter; what did not matter..... The bell for morning meditation rushed by my door and I somehow got to my feet, dressed and went to the Meditation Hall for the last day of Sesshin.

The beating got even worse this morning. Every hour we were all beaten by at least four different people so that I lost count of the number of times and no longer cared anyway. Whatever it was that was sitting with me—or inside me—or was me . . . . . sat like iron and sat and sat and sat . . . . . As they came around to do the beating I bowed with the kyosaku and it bowed back—I think. I must tell someone about what is happening to me; I cannot go on doing this without knowing what is happening—but I don't care what is happening—there is only sitting quiet and still. We went on sitting late and then Sesshin was over and Rev. Tarō came and slapped me on the shoulder saying he did not believe a woman could have done it and I leaped in the air and yelled as he hit the bruises and he said he was sorry and took me to a feast that had been prepared by some of the younger trainees and we ate . . . . .

9th. June.

I woke up on the floor with half a dozen other people asleep all round me. We must have dozed off at the meal-table. I struggled to my feet and made my way back to my room with no idea of what time it was until I got there; it was twelve noon. I have slept the clock round. I think it is the 9th. but I am not quite sure; anyway it just does not matter. The young trainees in my house are very scared of being friendly as a result of Rev. Ichirō. I must talk to Rev. Hajime about it and see what can be done; what has happened to me is strange and I just do not understand it but I must accept it. So many things seem to have disappeared. I know when it is the first and fifteenth of the month since that is when we get beaten and I have tea with Zenji Sama; and I know when a day has a four or a nine in it since that is when they shave my head . . . . . he who would gain his life must lose it . . . . . that is Christian . . . . . I think . . . . . I have lost something and gained something . . . . . I know not what . . . . . life continues . . . . . I sit.

The author in front of the Butsuden (Main Hall) at Dai Hon Zan Sōjiji.

1st. July.

I have been in the actual temple buildings now for over a month. It is so much better than being in the tea house which is strictly for visitors and nothing more. It is disturbing to think that, after coming twelve thousand miles, there should have been so much argument as to whether or not I ought to be here at all. I cannot help thinking that this particular problem should have been settled before I came over since it was Zenji Sama himself who invited me.

Thanks to the help of the three seniors in charge of this particular part of the temple I have been admitted to the Meditation Hall but it seems that there are still many people here who are convinced that I should never have been let past the gate. Perhaps this will change with time. How unreal everything sometimes becomes. This is a Zen monastery and this country is Japan. In the world I was a professional musician; in Malaysia I was Rev. Sumitra, the lecturer; Rev. Tsuyu to the Chinese abbot and here, Hō Un Ji Yu, Zenji Sama's disciple, half-accepted by some and heartily detested for being a woman and a foreigner by others. Rev. Ichirō says I am myself without hair and decorations. The world seems upside down and so do

I. My brain rocks and there is no-one I can talk to except Rev. Ichirō, who never comes at all, and Rev. Hajime who finally got me in here and with whom I can communicate on paper. The only thing I can possibly do in order to learn anything is to accept, in blind faith, everything that is happening to me, believing that it is all for my good, whatever it may be.[14] If I do anything else then I shall always be saying that this person is good or that one is bad; I am here to get beyond the opposites; I must stop discriminating; whatever happens, whether they like foreigners or not, I must see what they do as being intrinsically good at all times, even when it works against me. If I do not then indeed I must surely go mad. I do not understand what has happened to me since Sesshin—no-one can tell me because they cannot speak English. I seem to sit still in transient darkness. The place I found during Sesshin has faded.

8th. July.

Rev. Minoru had a heart attack the day before yesterday and we had a farewell party for him last night before he went home to his own temple for a rest. Yesterday I found myself turned out of my room without an explanation, my things being dumped unceremoniously in the passage outside it whilst a bunch of people moved in leaving me with nowhere to go. I wrote a note to Rev. Hajime who inquired about what was happening and then told me that there had been a breakdown in communication somewhere. The people who had moved in had been promised the room a long time ago and no-one had thought to find another place for them when it was given to me. He suggested that he move into Rev. Minoru's room, which is now empty, and give me his since no-one will dare to try to move him out of Rev. Minoru's. Since I shall be occupying his, Rev. Hajime's, no-one can throw me out either. I moved in this morning. I have asked Rev. Hajime if he can teach me since Rev. Ichirō, whom Zenji Sama told to do it when he personally was too busy, seems never to have any spare time; Rev. Hajime says he must think about it.

9th. July.

This morning Rev. Hajime said to me, "Can you catch me?" Our conversation was, as always, on paper.

We had just come back from Morning Service and meditation and he was making tea for both of us in his room. For a moment I thought he was speaking in a literal sense and then something gave me pause.

"Yes," I said, "I most certainly can."

He chuckled softly. "We will see," he said, "but first I must make sure you have a good translation of the Sandōkai and Hōkyōzammai."

"I have a translation of them," I said, "but it is in very bad English and I get the feeling that whoever made it did not particularly understand it."

"Show it to me."

I gave him the small book; he studied it for some time and then said, "This is wrong. The first two lines are most important and they *should* read 'now you have so guard well.' You do not have 'anything' or 'nothing' as such; you have, that is sufficient."

"Then there is no point in my being here," I said.

"Right. Why did you come?"

"To know that I did not need to."

There was hesitation in my voice and he caught it. "When you know that you did not need to you will know that you 'have'; and yet you will still 'need to'. For many years Dōgen Zenji's comment, 'Always we must be *disturbed* by the Truth', has worried me."

The bell rang for breakfast and we had to leave it there. We did not get a further chance for discussion all day since he had to go to Yokohama to give a lecture.

10th. July.

Rev. Hajime's comment about being able to catch him exercised my mind considerably during the night. Long before the bell went some sixth sense warned me to keep awake and it was well that I did. At about two a.m. I heard an imperceptibly soft sound which the sixth sense in me said was Rev. Hajime getting up although it was against the rules to get up before the rising bell. I dressed quickly and silently and, flinging the rules to the four winds in my own mind, hastened to the door of his room with a lighted stick of incense; as he opened his door, fully dressed for meditation, he found me kneeling outside it as any good jiisha (assistant) of any master would. He chuckled softly. "Come in," he said. His bed was still on the floor. I put the incense stick in the bowl on his private altar and quietly put his bed away, then put on the kettle for tea. He watched me, smiling softly, and put tea in the teapot.

"To-day it was easy," he said, as we drank our tea, "it will not always be so."[15]

11th. July.

Am almost wandering about in my sleep as a result of staying one step ahead of Rev. Hajime but it was worth it. He has been making it progressively earlier and earlier each night until last evening I simply camped outside his room intending to meditate all night with the incense ready beside me so that at any moment I could be there before him. I have had less than an hour's sleep each night during the last week. He came out of his room at a little after eleven last night and told me to go to bed since he was going to do the same thing. I stayed up, however, feeling that he would depart whist I slept. At a little after one o'clock I heard a faint movement and got the incense ready. As his door opened softly I was sitting outside the door with the incense. He called me into his room, took the incense from me, and said, "You win. After Morning Service we will talk." I went back to my room but did not sleep.

I hurried back from Morning Service whilst he was still in conference with the other officers and cleaned his room and got the tea ready. When he came in it was clean and fresh with the windows open and flowers and incense on his private altar. He sat down and looked at me for a long time.

"Can a foreigner really catch the Lord?" he asked.

"I thought Shakyamuni Buddha was born in India not Japan," I said. "Since when have the Japanese been the descendants of the Indians?"

This made him angry.

"How dare you compare Japanese with Indians?" he roared at me in Japanese. I did not understand his words but got the idea that I had said something wrong from his face. Then his temper disappeared like a flash-flood and he grinned.

"Indians are black and we are not," he wrote on the pad I had brought with me.

"So what?" was my response.

"How can any foreigner understand the mind of a Japanese?" he asked.

"Since Buddhism teaches that all is one, why shouldn't a foreigner understand a Japanese mind?" I countered.

His temper flared up again. "Do you presume to teach me Buddhism?"

"If telling you such things is presuming to teach you Buddhism it would seem that such a presumption is necessary." I was getting slightly annoyed.[5]

He dissolved into a grin. "Let us not quarrel. You have beaten me fairly in the first round of catching me but understand that "IT" flashes with great speed, faster than any eye can see. I have to be sure that you, a woman and a foreigner, are worthy of my attention."

"Thanks very much," I had to watch myself for my sarcasm was beginning to show.[5] He took this for acquiescence in his opinions, however, for he produced a book and proceeded to translate certain passages from it into atrocious English. I studied them, carefully corrected the English, and gave them back to him. For a moment I saw anger show in him again and then he slowly and carefully went through my corrections. "Your English is fluent," he said.

"It is only my native language."

He looked at me and saw that I was still bristling slightly;[5] he relaxed.

"We must not start off on the wrong side of the fence," he said. "Let us start again."

"Because I am a woman and a foreigner I have all the misfortunes of both senior and junior trainees and none of the advantages," I said. "Do you think it would be possible for me to go to a women's monastery soon?"[16]

"Zenji Sama is your master; you are, in many ways, his favourite disciple. It is doubtful if he will let you go. He sees you on the first and fifteenth of every month at his private senior's tea-party. You are deeply honoured."

"Cannot I be a junior trainee like other junior trainees? It is dangerous for me to receive such favours from Zenji Sama. As long as they come my way I shall be accepted by neither seniors nor juniors and you know it."

"Does such a thing matter to you? It should not."

"Yes, it does. Whenever the juniors have a dirty or hard job they want done they send for me; when the seniors have one they do the same thing. If I were an ordinary trainee I would not constantly have the problem of being regarded as Zenji Sama's favourite. I know that I am new here but there are a lot of others who are newer than I am. I am a great believer in everybody starting at the bottom but I have always disagreed with the idea of staying there. Unless I can become an ordinary trainee like everyone else I see no point in being here."[16]

"Dōgen Zenji was in the same position as you for five years in Tendōzan. He said the same things you have just said and finally wrote to the Emperor of China to ask him to do something about the fact that, because he was a foreigner, he was always put last in everything. It is something with which you must bear if you would study in the East."

"I seem to remember that Dōgen Zenji's letter got answered at the third try and the Emperor made a ruling that everyone was to go up the ranks equally according to the time at which he entered the temple. Maybe I should write to the Emperor of Japan."

"Why don't you?"

"Would the temple authorities here take notice of his answer, should he give one?"

"They might but I am not sure."

The bell went for breakfast and we left the room. I must remember my resolve to take everything that happens as being for my good. I must not allow myself to be upset by silly, chauvinistic behaviour.

15th. July.

This morning I said to Rev. Hajime, "We are born men who can become Bodhisattvas and then Buddhas. What happens to us after that?"

"Nothing happens," he replied.

"Do we continue to exist or do we cease to exist?"

"Why do you think about such useless things?" was his unexpected answer.

"You say it is useless because you do not know the answer any more than I do!" I said.

"Wrong. 'Not life because not death.' We must throw away such thoughts. You are seeing everything in this life as if through coloured glass, including Buddhism. We are ourselves." As always, his answers were written.

"There are no answers to real questions so what is the use of asking questions?" I asked.

"Every answer is real," he replied.

"Rev. Ichirō asked me if anything happened during Sesshin. I told him that the only noteworthy event was that everyone ate so fast that I was starving hungry and, as a result, had visions of an apple pie. He then threatened to give me thirty strokes with his kyosaku. But he did not tell me how to overcome the difficulty. Can you?" I asked.

"I can't. Let the apple pie continue," he said. I started to make tea.

16th. July.

This morning I wrote the following, "In Zen there is no goal—what do we gain? If we gain nothing why study Zen? If we gain something then it is not Zen. As long as we want or do not want something we are not free from desire so to study Zen is wrong. The Scripture of Great Wisdom says, 'There is no attainment and no non-attainment.' I know what your answer will be, 'Just go on training,' but that doesn't help—I want the answer now."

"You are always thinking about external problems. Even when you think they are inside, still they are out. It is wrong to try to embrace infinity within limits. We are always apt to think of the teaching through our knowledge of books. Apart from such knowledge, we must understand for ourselves. We can at once directly become Buddha with this dirty body or we can become thieves and murderers. Why? Because we can practice Zazen; because we are enlightened. To sit is enlightenment itself. Dōgen said, 'Training and enlightenment are one.'" He sat back and looked at me.

"I do not know what I am looking for—I do not even know if I am looking for anything. Are all enlightened—are all Buddha? If so, simply by doing Zazen and sitting, I am a Buddha and so is every trainee here. Is what is wrong with me the fact that you are certain of your enlightenment and I am not certain of mine?" I wrote.

"You are thinking of a quiet Buddha, not a working one. Buddha is working through our hands and feet. Can a person who is behaving badly be a Buddha? Buddha is there when we do a thing with our right will, uncoloured by an ordinary point of view such as looking for money and position. To do right and not to do evil—this is Buddhism. There is no difficulty, nothing special."

"Please teach me how to accept all things unquestioningly—I do not care what you do with me in order to do it."

"Acceptance by body is endless training. In this sense there is no enlightenment, only training. There is no desire to get enlightenment; only endless training by body," he answered. "Others think that this must be considered from many sides, but we should go on without thinking anything. That is the true way through which Buddhahood can be represented in the world. Buddhism is not a thought or 'ism' or feeling; it must be a fact."

"If a woman shaves her head and becomes a trainee, may she return to the world again and grow her hair or is this wrong?" I asked.

"Not wrong. No-one can disturb her," he replied, "But if she realises the truth completely she will not turn back."

"The reason why our type of Zen is thought so little of in the West is because it is believed to be easy whilst other forms are hard and difficult. Europeans like hardness and strict discipline—Americans like everything to be easy. Is our form so easy?" I asked.

"It is never easy. What are they looking for outside of the actual world?" he asked.

I heard the bell and had to leave the room.

One of the three seniors in this house is always trying to give information on how to sit properly. He is very small and old but seems to be greatly respected as a lecturer, representing the temple on important occasions. This morning he came to my room together with Rev. Hajime. Rev. Hajime introduced him as Rev. Sansaburo. He immediately wanted to know how I was doing with regard to my meditation. As always, we conversed on paper.

"I am getting a great amount of pain in my legs," I wrote, "and there seems no means by which I can alleviate it."

He asked to see my cushion and studied it carefully then he said, "This cushion is the wrong size for you. Most people think that the larger they are the larger the cushion they require but this is not so. A small cushion, never more than about eight inches across, is all you need. But it must be high. You are getting the pain because you are sitting fully on a large cushion instead of sitting with just the tip of your spine on it. If you sit fully upon it your circulation will be impaired and you will have pain. If you sit only on the edge of it, so that your thigh muscles are touching nothing whatsoever, your body balance will be correct, your circulation will not be damaged and you will be able to keep your spine tucked in. By these means you will learn not only how to sit properly but also find your meditation greatly improved."

"I thought you had to keep your spine straight," I said.

"You do," he replied, "but, at the waist, the spine *must* curve inwards or you will slump and become ill. We call this type of sitting 'having a straight back' but it is not straight. Many people put their spines partially in this position but, for meditation, they must be held as if you were standing at attention and not sitting on the floor; yet without strain. After a little this way of sitting becomes quite natural and the improvement in health is so great that you will wonder why you ever sat in any other way. But you will not find sitting in an easy chair at all comfortable after getting used to this type of sitting."

"I sat down in the meditation position just now and have tried to hold my spine as you say but it really hurts to hold it in as much as you have just pushed it."

He examined my back, vertebra by vertebra, tracing them with his fingers where they poked their shape against my robe. Suddenly he yelped happily, grabbed me around the neck, put his knee in my back and gave a shove against my spine. There was a resounding click and I found that I could move my spine much more freely. He continued to feel down the vertebral 'knobs' and did the same thing in two more places; the third one went off so loudly that I was quite startled. He then motioned for me to sit down again and once more pushed my spine right in, as far as it would go, at the waist; I was sitting on the edge of my cushion, as I thought, but the pushing on my spine resulted in my seeming to slide forward and only sit on the very tip of the cushion. Immediately I felt a great difference in the ease with which I could sit and also a great loss of weight in my back and head.

"The pain in your legs will soon disappear now," he wrote for Rev. Hajime to translate, "now we must see about your mind."

He wrote a lot of things on the paper but Rev. Hajime seemed to have some trouble in working out their English meaning. In the end Rev. Sansaburo grabbed the dictionary and hunted in it. Presently he found what he was looking for and handed it to me. I studied it; the word he was showing me was 'right.' I nodded but he was not satisfied. First he pointed to the left, shaking his head, then to the right and nodded.

"Not left," I said, "only right?" I looked hard at Rev. Hajime.

"Not exactly," said Rev. Hajime.

Next Rev. Sansaburo pointed at the floor, shaking his head, and then at the ceiling, nodding.

"Up, not down?" I wrote but Rev. Hajime seemed to be mentally scratching his head and gave me no help. "One way?" I asked.

"Like water," wrote Rev. Sansaburo.

"Water only flows one way," I said and he nodded happily and wrote, "Gyate, gyate, haragyate."

"Gone?" I asked.

"No," cried Rev. Hajime and then wrote, "Going, going, always going, like water." He then added, as an afterthought, "Water bright."

Rev. Sansaburo seemed to have become galvanised by something and uttered the first word of English I had ever heard him speak.

"Bright," he cried; he had obviously found several words at once, "mind bright, not dull; bright, bright."

I sat still for a few minutes, thinking hard, then I took the dictionary and found the Japanese for positive and negative and wrote the following:–

"The mind must always be bright when meditating, always positive and never negative, looking upwards and not downwards, always flowing on and clinging to nothing just as water flows."

Rev. Hajime read it carefully and translated it into better Japanese for the other one could make no sense out of my attempt. Rev. Sansaburo nodded in obvious delight and wrote, "Good for the beginning, later nothing at all but, in the beginning, there must be brightness and flow with no holding on. When brightness becomes usual one does not notice even brightness."

"Then what I decided a little while ago was right," I wrote, "I must take everything that happens as for my own good, whatever it may be."

Rev. Hajime nodded. "Always you must *believe* that every-one has good heart for you," he wrote in his atrocious English. "If you not do so you never become peaceful at all; Buddha must be seen in all thing."

Rev. Sansaburo was writing busily and Rev. Hajime trans-lated, "The attitude of the mind is just as important as the posi-tion of the body when you meditate. If the mind is not right the meditation will be useless. Zen teaching is to just sit but it is more than just sitting and yet it is just sitting. Wandering thoughts are like pain in the legs; if the mind is right in its attitude, thoughts pass as traffic on a bridge and we watch from beneath the bridge without being involved in the traffic; if the attitude of the body is right the pain in the legs and other places passes in the same way and neither our body nor our mind is disturbed."

The bell went for the hour of working in the garden and we all changed into work clothes and went out together. It has never ceased to amaze me how these old, senior priests rush out to do hard work whilst many of the juniors have to be almost forcibly dragged.[4] I wanted to think about the conver-sation we had just had and, being a bit annoyed with my fellow juniors who have done very little to be friendly in the past cou-ple of months, went off by myself to dig up weeds instead of joining the main body who were removing daisy roots in another part of the grounds.[5] I was busy digging away when I suddenly discovered the chief disciplinarian digging beside me very quietly; *and* it seemed we were rapidly being joined by a large number of others who were digging in *my* daisy patch. Quite soon I realised that they had formed a circle round me and were digging inwards towards the centre where I was dig-ging. Thinking that I had come to the wrong place, and not wishing to cause problems, moreover all I wanted to do right then was think, I moved off to another patch several hundred yards away. The circle converged on the centre I had vacated, one set light to the pile of daisy roots and everyone dispersed. I went back to concentrating on what we had been talking about. Then I noticed that Rev. Sansaburo and Rev. Hajime were quietly working on either side of me. Opposite, some

twenty yards away, was the chief disciplinarian and, before I
knew it, a huge circle was formed of which I was part. Rev.
Ichirō came up to the circle and somehow fitted himself in
between Rev. Hajime and I. He busily cut away at the weeds
and then whispered in my ear, "You should dig deeper." At
first I thought he was referring to the weeds and then I knew
that he was not. We all arrived at the centre of the weed patch
more or less simultaneously and someone thrust a box of
matches into my hand. I lit the pile of weeds and they left me
to tend the fire, moving on to another patch. As soon as I had
got it going I left it and went off to another place, determined
to think, but the circle formed around me again and Rev.
Hajime whispered in my ear, "Now is the time of digging up
weeds, not thinking."

"But I can think whilst I dig," I said. He produced pencil
and paper.

"Not if you dig properly," he wrote. "When you are digging
weeds you are digging weeds; when you are thinking you are
thinking. Right, not left, has many meanings. Also we train together, not alone up mountain. When one is enlightened all is enlightened. You are trying to cut enlightenment but it cannot be
divided, we are one circle, not two, no-one is outside Buddhism."

"What if enlightenment wants to be cut from me?" I asked.

"That is enlightenment's problem, not yours. Your problem
is not to cut enlightenment."

"So I must train with others whether they want me or not,"
I said.

"You are not their problem and they are not yours. That you
train or not makes no difference to enlightenment but it does
make a difference to you. By training yourself with others you
train enlightenment and enlightenment trains you. No-one can
do your training and you cannot do theirs."

The bell rang for the end of the period. Somehow I know
what he was talking about but how the heck does one put it
into words?

17th. July.

Rev. Sansaburo collapsed in the Ceremony Hall and I am nursing him. It is fifteen years since I walked out of the study of medicine and into the study of music; perhaps I was a coward. Rev. Sansaburo has had a stroke and it has paralysed his left side. Now, instead of the happy little priest who has helped me so much by simply sitting beside me during meditation and putting me in the right position when I was sitting incorrectly, there is a helpless lump of flesh, half of which is useless. His wife has come and will not let him rest and, because of my poor ability at speaking Japanese, I cannot explain the danger to her. It is my fault; I should have known the language better before I came. Sitting here in the middle of the night, watching him dance with death, is like watching the tragedy of the world for the death of one man is the death of the world and the life of one man is the life of the world. The disease of one man is the disease of the world too and so Rev. Sansaburo has become all men and all men are Rev. Sansaburo. And I must sit helplessly by and watch, knowing that this must come to all men and to me. What can I do? I have come twelve-thousand miles to find the answer. There is none. Why am I here? It is all so useless. I seem to be crying the tears of the world.

19th. July.

Rev. Ichirō called me to his room this evening although I was nursing Rev. Sansaburo. I was somewhat worried at leaving my post, even for only a few moments, but knew that I dare not disobey the summons. When I got there I found Rev. Ichirō in a fury. Cringing on the floor was Rev. Tarō.

"How dare you do something as dedicated as nursing someone?" he demanded, his face dark and his eyes nothing more than slits. "You, a foreigner, know nothing of such a dedicated thing. You will leave doing this at once and return immediately to your room. I will speak to Zenji Sama in the morning; I doubt if he will allow you to remain in the temple. All you do is try to show off because you are a woman."

"But I must stay until Rev. Sansaburo goes to hospital. I have promised the doctor and he says that Rev. Sansaburo must not be allowed to be alone even for a minute for the next four days."

"If you return to that room I will have every officer in the temple against you and have you removed. Get out and take this book with you."

Rev. Tarō grabbed my arm and pulled me from the room. "Let go for walk," he stammered, "very hot night; cooler outside."

I was too surprised by the whole incident to give thought to a possible double meaning to his words. He had picked up the book on our way out. We went into the grounds where the music of the OBon dance festival was sounding clearly across the loudspeakers near the gate but I was too dazed to do anything except walk; at the back of my mind a nagging worry persisted about Rev. Sansaburo and leaving him alone. We said nothing as we walked and presently we were joined by one of the other juniors from the house in which I lived. He asked Rev. Tarō why I was not with Rev. Sansaburo and Rev. Tarō told him. The other looked very worried but said nothing. After some minutes I regained some of my original presence of mind.

"I have got to go back," I gasped, "he could die if he is not watched all the time. The doctor said that the next four days are absolutely critical. Whatever Rev. Ichirō does I must go back."

The one who was walking with us said something to Rev. Tarō who nodded.

"What did he say?" I asked.

"He says he knows how important it is that someone is always with Rev. Sansaburo."

I stopped where I was. "I *am* going back," I said, "and nothing anyone can do will stop me." And then I started to cry; whether from fury, anger, disgust or just plain fear for Rev. Sansaburo I had no notion.

"Why must you go back?" asked Rev. Tarō. "What is so important about Rev. Sansaburo? Many priests die every year and other priest have no notice of it. Their own training is much more important."

As I stood there looking at him, disbelief filled every part of me. Then, from somewhere inside, came an answer. "I must go back because he *is* Buddha,"[17] I answered. "Look at him; can't you see? Even dying he shines; I don't know how to explain it to you but he does. As far as I am concerned he is Buddha in person and my duty is to be with him."

I turned away from them and hurried back up the garden path at a run which was illegal for a trainee but I just did not care any longer. In the hall I met the chief guest master who scolded me for leaving Rev. Sansaburo and wanted to know why I was so untrustworthy. Tearing myself away from him I rushed back to the room to find Rev. Sansaburo sleeping quietly and settled myself down to spend the night watching. It seemed that the brightness in the room had increased but this could simply have been the result of my overwrought state.

Rev. Tarō came in and begged me to leave the room since he would be badly beaten if I disobeyed Rev. Ichirō. I refused. In the end, after I had almost screamed at him to look at the man in the bed and have some respect for the sick and dying, he said he would tell Rev. Ichirō and slunk out of the room.

Rev. Ichirō arrived and, between gritted teeth, informed me that he would see Zenji Sama in the morning. I didn't care.

"As far as I am concerned," I said, "Rev. Sansaburo *is* Buddha incarnate; I have met him here on earth and, should I die to-morrow, I am blessed eternally for having had the honour to nurse him."

He gave me a strange look and left the room.

20th. July.

I had just taken Rev. Sansaburo's temperature and pulse when Rev. Ichirō came into the room. I did not hear him come and was unaware of his presence until a voice over my shoulder asked, "Is it a good temperature and pulse?"

I turned round. "Yes," I said, quite simply.

His whole demeanour had changed and he was almost fawning, a fact which I found somehow both distasteful and unnecessary.[18]

"I spoke to Zenji Sama," he said, his eyes were veiled but I could detect that they were not exactly friendly. "He says you may miss the laymen's Sesshin to do this." His voice was trying not to grate on the last sentence.

"Thank you," I said.

"It is not enough to see just one as Buddha," was his next comment, "all are thus. You must be able to see all as Buddha."

He rose and left and Rev. Tarō crept, almost whimpering, into the room.

"What happened?"

"Zenji Sama says that I can continue to nurse Rev. Sansaburo."

Rev. Tarō looked stealthily around him as if fearing eavesdroppers. "How did you understand that he is Buddha? What did you see? I try so many years to see."

"It isn't seeing exactly," I replied. "It is sort of—knowing without words; and seeing with your heart and—still you see." I broke off for what I was saying made no sense. He gave me a queer look, half bowed and left the room.

21st. July.

I have had three hours sleep in forty-eight. The junior trainees are furious over my nursing Rev. Sansaburo because, I am told, they think I am doing it in order to impress Zenji Sama. When the relief nurse came from the hospital I tried to get some sleep this morning but one of the juniors played his clarinet, regardless of the rules, full-blast outside my door and made sleep impossible. In the end I went to the graveyard and slept on one of the tombs. It was so peaceful there. The dead are true friends. This place is quite terrifying in many ways. Living amongst these junior trainees is, for someone of my age, like living amongst strange and dangerous children. Zenji Sama must stop showering favours on me or living here will become utterly impossible.

But Rev. Sansaburo is getting better with every hour. I hope and pray that he may regain the use of his limbs. I want to see him walk and laugh again.

Rev. Ichirō got very angry with me because I took a bath. The trouble is that the temperature is well over ninety in the shade and, because I am a woman and they have not yet got the female bath-house finished, I cannot legally take a bath anywhere. I have to beg the pardon of those who had not yet bathed. I had no idea it was against the rules. I find out the rules as I break them. I have asked at least three people during the past few weeks to tell me what the rules are so that I can keep them but they only laugh at me and say that Zenji Sama is making his own for me. How can I help breaking rules if I do not know what they are?

If I had not felt pain and suffering so keenly I would have gone on studying medicine but it seems so useless since we are all doomed to die—better far to learn to live by illuminating the spirit. We are all living dead.

To-day I have been here one hundred days! To-morrow I should officially be allowed to go out but have been told that, for me, it will be two hundred days since Zenji Sama has made me his favourite. I could not go out even if I were permitted for I am so tired I would probably be run over by a car. As I was taking Rev. Sansaburo's temperature this morning Rev. Hajime told me about the problem of my going out. It seems that Zenji Sama's favour is creating special rules in the minds of some who feel that I shall be spoiled. I must remember that this is all for my own good. Whatever is happening it is so that I may be helped. Before he left this morning Rev. Hajime said that I must be very careful here or it will break my heart.

23rd. July.

Rev. Sansaburo goes to hospital the day after to-morrow and I shall return to my room beside Rev. Hajime. In some ways I shall be glad to return for it is very stuffy in Rev. Sansaburo's room. His wife will allow no windows to be opened. I wonder if she realises how dangerous it is to sleep like this? The weather is incredibly sticky and the thought that I am not allowed a bath is rather frightening. Whatever will my body be like four days from now? With insects of every variety crawling round on the floor my feet and legs and hands are covered with bites. I sat with my feet in a bucket of water to-day to keep the insects away from them during my spare time. To-morrow most of the trainees go away for the OBon Festival but I have nowhere to go and so must stay here. In a strange way I feel truly a trainee for I have no home now and the only money I have comes from the Chinese abbot. I have no room of my own and the clothes I wear are not mine. I am too tired to meditate.

24th. July.

Rev. Sansaburo goes to hospital to-morrow. During the night he asked me to recite the Daihishindharani with him but fell asleep before we were halfway through it. I could imagine his thoughts as we said it for, just before, he had held up his useless left hand with his right one and smiled at me sadly. For a man who has spent his life in the emulation of Kanzeon the loss of one hand is as the loss of five hundred arms. This will be his last night in the temple—to-morrow he will hear the meditation bell and the dawn drums for the last time. And the world goes on unheeding and uncaring. It is all so useless. Yet it is for such as he that Wordsworth wrote:– "Take him, O death, and bear away whatever thou canst call thine own; Thine image, stamped upon this clay, Doth give thee that, and that alone. Take him, O great eternity, the wind that shakes the tree can only drag its petals in the dust." I can accept death as inevitable without fear, and life too, but I cannot understand why either should be necessary. My brain reels and staggers—I can no longer sleep in peace by day or night. I must find the answer.

I wrote about this in bad Japanese and showed it to Rev. Sansaburo when he awoke. He read it slowly and studied it carefully, then he scrawled one character on the paper—it meant acceptance.

"But I don't care any longer," I wrote, "I am so apathetic that nothing matters. The stupid behaviour of the juniors here, their petty jealousies, life, death—I don't care whether I live or die."

His ears had pricked up and his eyes had become animated as he read my words; then he wrote, "Good. Become apathetic. Be destroyed. This is the immaculacy of MU!" His hand dropped the pen and I thought he had fainted but he was merely closing his eyes. His wife came in (she had been visiting a friend down the hall) and scolded me for opening a window.

25th. July.

Rev. Sansaburo went to hospital at ten o'clock this morning. The ambulance bumped much on the bad road that constitutes the temple drive-way. Rev. Toshio came to see me bringing a beautiful flower vase which he said was a present from Rev. Sansaburo who had noticed the flowers I had been putting in Rev. Hajime's room. It is the first time I have ever had any contact with Rev. Toshio and I sincerely hope that I shall see more of him. He used to be chief lecturer here before he became seriously ill and he radiates something that is elusive and beautiful and which I want very much. Rev. Sansaburo radiates it too but in a different way and with a totally different atmosphere and yet it is the same thing. Rev. Hajime has it sometimes but seems to be running round in his own thoughts too much for it to show at all times. I wonder if this is the "Lord" he was telling me I must catch?[19] If it is then it is easier to see in some than in others; in some, indeed, it is not even elusive.

26th. July.

I wonder why I am becoming so selective in what I write down of the various day's events? Or maybe it is just that doing the night-nursing of Rev. Sansaburo has dulled my memory. Yet it is odd that I should not have recorded the following incident yesterday. Just before the ambulance came to take Rev. Sansaburo to hospital Zenji Sama and quite a number of the officers came into the room. I was sitting in the far corner watching Rev. Sansaburo's wife preparing him for the journey and wondering if I would ever see him alive again. Zenji Sama knelt down beside Rev. Sansaburo and said something quietly to him then he turned round to face me and said "Thank you" in

Japanese in such a loud, clear and young-sounding voice that it seemed to echo off the walls of the room. Again I experienced the same piercing, gentle glance he had given me during Jūkai and the same physical thrill as when he had contrived to touch my hand during the ceremony. He turned and left the room and it was as if the sun had gone,[20] leaving the room dark, gloomy and cold. It must just be my tiredness; but I could have sworn that there was more light in the room when he was in it than when he left. I *know* why I did not write this down; I felt a bit odd about writing it; suppose somebody picked this book up and read it? Whatever would they think? Fooey to what they might think; this is my diary and I am writing what happened. If others read it and do not like it then that is their problem.

I slept in my old room last night and the reception I got when I returned to that part of the temple was quite chilly. Rev. Hajime has gone away for the OBon festival in his own temple and will not be back again, he tells me, until term starts some time in October. Most of the other trainees have gone off also and, in all this huge temple, with its thirty separate houses and departments, there are but four officers and ten or so trainees; or so it seems—there could be some more for all I know. This was all I counted during Morning Service.

Later.

I have just discovered that there are no officers at all in this particular house from now until next term and the only other person here with me is the one who played his clarinet whilst I was trying to sleep during the time I was nursing Rev. Sansaburo. He came upstairs a few minutes ago to tell me that he has never before been subjected to having to take meals with a woman and he is not going to do so now. It seems that Rev. Ichirō is very annoyed that I am still here and is an especial friend of his. He informed me that if I wanted any food, or a bath or anything else, I would have to go out into the town to get it since I am not allowed to go to the kitchen and he is not going to give me any of the food that is sent up.

On going downstairs later I discovered that he was sleeping off the mid-day heat (it is about thirty-eight centigrade if the gadget in the house-kitchen works) and that so much food had been sent up for us that he had been quite unable to eat it all. Since he dare not throw it away openly, without being beaten and thrown out of the temple, he had put it in paper and hidden it behind some pipes under the sink. I found it, took what I wanted whilst he continued to snore, and there was an end of the problem. If he is going to continue to sleep his time away during the entire month there should not be much difficulty for me, at least with regard to food, but the loneliness is going to be considerable. And if this is the behaviour of a trainee in a monastery—what the hell have I got myself into?[4]

27th. July.

I decided that the atmosphere here is just too oppressive for me to stay in it all day long.[4] There is almost no-one about, the Meditation Hall is absolutely empty for most of the day and I can literally meditate for as long as I want to, and when I want to, without being disturbed. It is interesting that the one place that neither that apology for a trainee[5] downstairs nor Rev. Ichirō think of looking for me is in the Meditation Hall. I have also found out that there is a bun shop on the opposite side of the road from the cemetery gate so I will live on buns until the others get back. It is very difficult not to have hateful thoughts about these two but I must try to overcome them, I really must. What a hell-hole this is.[4]

11th. August.

I have been spending most of my time during the last few weeks meditating. This morning I rose as usual at three-thirty for meditation and Morning Service. On my return, round eight-thirty, I found the trainee downstairs still asleep and became really angry.[5] I went to the kitchen to collect my breakfast and, to my amazement, there was one of the old priests, who had been to Morning Service, quietly down on his hands and knees scrubbing the kitchen floor. He was not complaining that most of the juniors were still in bed but simply getting on with his work, doing what had to be done.[20] My anger just disappeared—there was something about the quiet old man that made all the nonsense in this house this summer seem very unimportant. After seeing him I went back and cleaned the upstairs of the house I was living in. Later I went to weed Zenji Sama's garden and, on the way back, found Rev. Akira quietly washing the long corridor by himself.[20] The simple actions of these old men sparkle like stars in a dark sky. I must remember to keep in mind the words of Rev. Hajime, "In the world there are various sorts of people but they are not your problem. You must worry about yourself and not about them. It is not your concern that they want to be lazy."

28th. August.

It is wonderful what a peaceful meditation can do. I have been going to the Meditation Hall every day since my last entry and the owners have got to know me quite well at the bun shop; I can now even speak a little with them in Japanese, thanks to their kind help—and they are laymen and the chap downstairs is a trainee![4] I must *not* think that way—judging. Stop it. To criticise others is to break the Precepts; and to go and buy buns outside the temple walls is breaking the rules![5] I am awfully glad this is a two-story building for the downstairs has not been cleaned since the others went away. In a country where there are so many insects and a hot climate nothing could be more dangerous. I have spread flea powder all over the bottom stair leading to this floor for my own protection. Dealing with the mosquitos is quite enough. I shall be glad when everyone else gets back.

30th. September.

The other three juniors living here got back this morning; on seeing the state of the house they immediately rushed off to see Rev. Ichirō and he came up here in a furious temper saying that it was my fault that the downstairs was flea-infested. I tried to tell him that it was not my fault since I had not been allowed downstairs during the whole of the summer holidays but he would not listen to me. I threatened to tell Zenji Sama about it and he stormed out of the room. A few minutes later the senior of the downstairs juniors came up to see me, looking very worried; he was carrying a large bowl of food that he had had sent in from a restaurant; he placed it in front of me. Saying that I must understand that I was very welcome in the temple, he ended by telling me that he wanted to take me out to dinner that evening. He spoke atrocious English and had obviously looked up all the words before-hand.

"I am not hungry," I said.

He was non-plussed for he could not understand me but I pushed the bowl away and he understood.

"Must eat," he screamed, "I order." He rushed away leaving the bowl on the floor of my room.

A few minutes later up came the junior who had been so rude and unfriendly during the summer; he too was carrying a bowl of food, much more expensive than the one that had previously arrived.

"Must eat," he said, "We Japanese love foreigner, flowers, children."

He sat and watched me; I do not think I have ever before or since seen such a mixture of dishonesty, hatred and suppressed fury.[4] We stared at each other for quite some time but my last two months in the Meditation Hall, coupled with the hour a day I had spent working in Zenji Sama's garden in order to weed it, although he was away, now stood me in good stead. Under normal circumstances I would have smashed my fist into his sneering, childish face but instead I merely said, "Later," turned and walked into my room and closed the screen door. I heard him rush downstairs; then high-pitched words in the room below me. I wrote a letter to Rev. Ichirō, setting out quite clearly what had been happening during the summer holidays as fairly as I could, and delivered it to his room. On my return I found the trainee who had brought the first bowl of food waiting outside my door, dressed to go out.

"We go out," he said, "we eat together in restaurant; everyone see. Japanese man eat with foreign woman."

His voice was pleading, almost pitiful. Something inside me wanted to vomit and then a voice, which I would never have heard had I not been meditating so much, said, "Why not go out with him? He is obviously terrified of what the other one has done. It may make peace with them. If you refuse all overtures of friendship you might as well leave."[21]

I put on my outdoor clothes and we went off together into the town. He took me to a restaurant where he ordered huge ice-creams and avidly watched me eat mine. When we had finished eating he gulped and started to say an obviously memorised speech.

"You eat with me. In public I eat with foreign woman and I Japanese man. Very great thing. Now all world know we trainees very great man. You not say word about what happen during summer, see? You tell Zenji Sama not good for you in temple. We all friend now. You understand?"

My desire to vomit was increasing and it was *not* from the ice-cream.[4] I spoke very slowly and distinctly.

"Buddhism teaches the control of selfishness. Why are Japanese men so selfish?"

After looking up a couple of the words, which I repeated, in the dictionary he had brought with him, he was silent for a long time.

"Woman baby factory," he said eventually. "Man give much pleasure to woman in getting baby. So man much superior. From birth he preferred in all things over woman."

I started to laugh; not a nice, amused laugh, but a rather nasty one and surprised myself just as much as I angered him.[5] I stopped abruptly. I knew that there was some sort of a limit I was reaching; it was as though I was gripping the sides of a slide hard, so as not to go flying down it, for fear of what I might do.

"After all," I said, "how can I expect Japanese men to be unselfish when they have been treated as gods from the moment they were born? If they do not know what the word 'selfishness' means they can hardly be expected to do something about it."[22]

I was gripping the arms of my chair strangely, desperately, as if they were the sides of the slide. My nails bit into the upholstery and tore it in one place. He noticed and swore quietly under his breath saying that "Foreign woman must not tear Japanese restaurant." How I stopped myself from hitting him I do not know.[5] I thank whatever powers there be for meditation.

"Buddhism very difficult," he said. "Control selfishness not possible."

Something inside me crashed about, things seemed to be threshing around from side to side in my head. Somehow I rose and left the restaurant with him muttering behind me. I am not sure how I made the door or negotiated the roads outside, I just did. Now, as I write this, it is as if everything that has ever lived within me is dead.[23]

4th. October.

I do not think that I have been back to my room, since writing the previous entry, until now. I found a large tomb in the graveyard, complete with its own private garden and summer house, and have been staying there instead. Term does not start until to-morrow so all should be well. I do not know if I have eaten and it does not matter at all. When one is dead, food is unnecessary and something has surely died in me.

A few moments ago I found a letter on the desk in my room and have just read it. It is a scathing tirade from Rev. Ichirō saying that it is all my fault that there are fleas downstairs and that they never had any until foreigners came to Japan. I have to beg pardon of everyone in the temple for being here and causing such a thing to happen. It is my fault that the trainee downstairs has had his summer ruined.[24]

5th. October.

There is no way in which I can comment on to-day; all I can do is report.

After receiving the letter from Rev. Ichirō it was as if everything and I went into an adagio dance. It was dark, I do not know the time but it was after the official bedtime. I remember putting the note into my desk drawer, taking a few clothes from a cupboard and putting them into a small suitcase, putting on my outdoor clothes and stowing my passport in my pocket, turning out the light. Like an automaton I left the room, closed the door softly and made my way to the stairhead. It was pitch dark, darker than I ever remember and the stairs were narrow, old and dangerous but I paid no heed. At the bottom I made for the nearest door and out into the garden. Without turning, without noticing that I was even using my feet, I glided down the path, away from the temple, away—away—away. If this is how they want it, then let them keep their temple; if this is their understanding of the oneness of Buddhism then I have indeed come to the wrong place. A small ball was appearing before my eyes, getting larger, brighter. I was losing my numbness—coming to from an anesthetic? The form of the old priest I had seen during Sesshin seemed to crystalise in the ball, his face in shadow, just a shape—a blotch? A dream? A voice sounded hollow inside me; an echo in an empty church after evensong, when the doors are closed and the organist sits in the organ loft, his instrument silent. How often I had done that—how often. The echo—louder, louder; the blotch—brighter, brighter. Outside me? Inside me? Sitting still—still and hard as iron—anchored. The echo—soft, clear. "You could be wrong"—"You could be wrong"—"You could be wrong"— — —

My feet—whose feet? or I—but who am I, what am I?—turned round and went back up the path, through the door, the main door,—why?—it does not matter any more—along the corridors to the foot of the stairs. It is light, I can *see*; is it dawn—so late already? The stairs need washing and I fetch a bucket of water from the kitchen; the whole house needs cleaning, putting in order—I wash the stairs—the water must be dirty and needs changing. Looking into the bucket—water needs changing—the water is clean—never was there any dirt—only clean, sparkling water, abounding with life, fresh, pure. I drink of you, clear water, delicious water, I throw you over my unclean body—the house is unclean—it must be put in order—

for the Lord of the House is coming—the Lord of the House is here—he never went away—was never gone.

Did I walk up the stairs to my room? Or fly? Was I carried? My consciousness seems to ebb and flow. Is it the same day? Great swirls of mist, clearing.[25] A little girl in England coming home from school, longing to tell her mother her geography lesson—"Mummy, mummy, do you know where sugar comes from? It's sugar cane." A trilling, sarcastic laugh—"What a *wonderful* thing to have found out; aren't you *clever*." Something snapping shut inside—swirls of mist, clearing—a little girl, bigger now—"Mummy, mummy, please come and watch my gym class. All the other mothers have been." "I'm very busy, child, go and play"—something snapping shut—mist, swirling, clearing—"That child's eye is infected; she must see a doctor"—"I have no time to-morrow; I must get the cakes ready. Let her aunt take her"—"It seems I must just take time off from work to do it"—swirling mist, clearing—How beautiful the sea looks—a thousand diamonds sparkling across a crystal mirror—"Peggy Kennett, you have been put at the bottom of the class in that seat because you are useless and the personification of laziness, not to stare like an idiot out of the window"—"Sorry, madam,"—the sea is a dirty grey—how soon clouds hide the sun in England—swirling mist, clearing—the crystal sea, the diamonds dancing, the sun high in a blue sky, so rare these days, so very rare—"Oh, sea, how long before I cross you? How long? Somewhere there must be someone with a smile in his heart that will match the smile in mine and we two will know each other"—a voice within, "Be still, be still just a little while longer; be still"—"Peggy Kennett, you have been detained after school to do your homework every day for a year. We are all thoroughly fed up with you here. We shall be glad when you go"—"Be still just a little while longer; the smile exists; be still—not long and I will come"[26]—swirling mist, clearing—A male voice, "I'll swear she is not an idiot; I'll swear it. Let me have her for a bit"—swirling mist, clearing—a terrible, rending quarrel, it is as if three people have hold of me

and pull me in different directions—a voice says I am old
enough to have rights—mist swirling, clearing—I want to hurt
people, I want to hurt everyone—I am sixteen, the war rages,
my father is dead, the bombs fall everywhere, no sleep, people quarrelling, pulling me this way and that—I have rights—
I want to hurt people so much—the sea is a dirty grey, railed
in by barbed wire; someone grabs me and pushes me over the
parapet of the promenade while a 'plane dives down and
sprays it with machine-gun-fire—someone holds me close to
the parapet—I do not know him—is love thus, always from
the unknown?—in all this horror does love still exist?—Did it
ever exist?—Be still, be still, a little while longer—I must
believe the voice[26]—I want to hurt everyone, I want to hurt—
swirling mist, clearing—I, the useless idiot, I have been
awarded a university degree—"Mother, aren't you pleased
with me? Please say you are proud of me"—"If you were a
boy it might make some sense. Your brother now, he is the
one who should have it, not you; he needs it"—I hate you, I
hate you, I hate you, I want to hurt you—swirling mist, clearing—It is so cold in London, I have no money to buy food, no
place to live, no rooms available anywhere—four of us in
Hyde Park—"Where are we going to sleep to-night?" "It's the
fault of those damned West Indians; there's no work and
nowhere to live. What the hell did we fight the bloody war for
if we are only to give the country to the damned wogs?"—"I
saw a bombed out building that looked as if it had a couple of
usable rooms"—"And get pinched by the ruddy coppers? not
ruddy likely"—"Molly's pregnant, she needs a warm place to
sleep; we're all coughing our lungs out in this smog"—"I'm
going to immigrate to America; no bloody good staying
here"—"Australia's for me"—"I like England, somewhere
there must be someone with a smile in his heart"—"You are
an idiot, Peg, patriotism is the opium they feed us so we won't
complain when we get bullets in the backside; they want to
make sure the wogs can sit down if we can't"—"Molly's still
pregnant and she's coughing her guts out"—"We could take
her to the Salvation Army Shelter"—"We might as well all go;

at least we'll get a streaky rasher on fried bread in return for bawling a hymn or two"—"Maybe there'll be a job in the morning"—swirling mist, clearing—"But it's a beautiful apartment, mother, and I am making over a thousand a year now so maybe Aunt Alice would like to come and stay with me and take the burden of her illness off your hands; I will be able to get her a nurse as well"—"There's no need to flaunt your money at me, and your aunt does not want to leave your brother and me"—Aunt Alice lying stiff and cold on the floor; she had tried to get out of bed when no-one answered her bell in the nursing home—swirling mist, clearing—Zenji Sama in a London hotel——"Come to Japan; become my disciple"—how to get the money?—but I have a university degree, something will turn up—be still, be still, just a little while[26]—the sparkling crystal sea, beckoning, calling[26]—swirling mist, clearing—this is good-bye, I tried so hard, I suppose I tried too much, once I told you that I loved you as much as ever could be loved and you had laughed with your friends and said that the child said such silly things—the smile is still inside but hidden—by accident we met, you and I, as mother and daughter, but we were as ships that pass in the night, dim shadows seen and soon gone—we are together on the dock, there is nothing underhanded here, but we passed each other long ago—how do you say farewell to a mother whom you have never met?—swirling mist, clearing—"If this house is dirty it is all the fault of the foreigners"—Rev. Ichirō's face—swirling mist, clearing.[27]

And as each successive wave of mist cleared it was as if a life had passed and left behind a different person—each layer that went left me thinner, more transparent—Shakyamuni Buddha saw his past lives—the little girl, the angry young woman, all are as if past lives—they are not me; in me is all that is left of them[28] . . . .

"Term has started," said Rev. Tarō. He was looking down at me where I lay, half drowned in water, on the floor of my room. "Get up, you must come to the Butsuden (Main Hall), it is Bodhidharma Day." I sat up; Rev. Tarō gleamed with a radiance from head to foot.[29] I clasped my arms around him and hugged him.

"Are you all right?" he asked.

"Oh, yes, yes," I replied.

"Come on, hurry. Rev. Ichirō is in an absolute fury because you are still here."

"Where is he? I must see him." I changed my robe, after bundling Rev. Tarō unceremoniously out of the room, and raced down the stairs to Rev. Ichirō's room. He was preparing for the ceremony. I sat down on the floor and bowed.

"Thank you," I said and it seemed that my voice put the same sound into the words that I had heard from Zenji Sama at the time of Rev. Sansaburo's illness. Rev. Ichirō turned to stare at me but all I could see was that his body gleamed with light from head to foot as did Rev. Tarō's.[29] There was no way of telling him how grateful I was; I looked at him for a long moment and then left the room. I went to the hall and to the Bodhidharma ceremony; the trainee from my house who had refused to eat with me glared as I walked in; I bowed to him, overjoyed to see the glory of light around him—and around everyone else and everything there.[29]

When the ceremony was over we changed and weeded the garden for a couple of hours. Someone put a large praying mantis on my head. Normally I would have screamed at the touch of an insect and they knew it. I carefully took it from my head and admired the golden glory that surrounded its body[29] and placed it on a weed that had the same glory on its fronds.[29] How simple and exquisite is this world in which we live; we bother ourselves with outside things, thinking they are all of life when they are, as was my past, but shadows in a mirror, seen through the swirling mists of our own delusions. There is nothing more than to go on doing that which has to be done for the Smile exists everywhere; the Heart in which it dwells is in all men, all things, it is in the glory of the sunset and the glory around the weed, the life of Zenji Sama and the life of Rev. Ichirō. And I wept great tears for having despised the food that had been brought to me as a peace-offering for it had been sacrificed to my delusion; I had not seen its glory. Christianity, Buddhism, Mohammedanism, the stupid delusions of men and women, none of these things matter; "*I* am right"—"No, I *know* that *I* am right"—to hell with "isms"—*Nunc dimitis, Domine*—Now you have, so guard well—and I am so unworthy.

6th. October.

"His left hand is under my head, and his right hand doth embrace me. The voice of my beloved! Behold, he cometh leaping upon the mountains, skipping upon the hills. Behold he standeth behind our wall, he looketh forth at the windows, showing himself through the lattice. My beloved spoke, and said unto me, 'Rise up, my love, my fair one, and come away. For lo, the winter is past, the rain is over and gone; the flowers appear on the earth; the time of the singing of birds is come and the voice of the turtle is heard in our land; the fig tree putteth forth her green figs, and the vines with the tender grape give a <u>good</u> smell. Arise, my love, my fair one, and come away. O my dove, thou art in the clefts of the rock, in the secret places of the stairs, let me see thy countenance, let me hear thy voice; for sweet is thy voice and thy countenance is comely.'

My beloved is mine, and I am his: he feedeth among the lilies. Until the day break and the shadows flee away, turn, my beloved, and be thou like a roe or a young hart upon the mountains."

All day yesterday and all last night my heart has been singing, singing everything, anything. I do not know where the above comes from except that it is somewhere in the Bible.[30] Every day of my life for ten years I was forced, whether I would or no, to learn two verses of the Bible at school. Stray lumps like the above have gone gliding by me with a meaning and a joy I have never before known. Chunks of Latin, always thought of as a chore, have gone by too, all with a different feel, a depth before unseen. I watch them float by; they lull me as in a cradle of joy and all I can feel is an exquisite adoration and gratitude for them.

Rev. Hajime returned this morning and came immediately to see me. He seems very worried about what Rev. Ichirō and the others downstairs have been doing during the summer. I really do not know what there is to be concerned about.

7th. October.

Rev. Tarō went with me to the port authority of Yokohama to-day to collect some things of mine that have been sent on from Malaysia. He seemed very frightened of the officials who wanted to inspect them at the customs but there was nothing to be concerned about. They were really very charming and did not charge me anything. I wonder why he keeps looking at me so queerly?

When we got home he came upstairs and had a long talk with Rev. Hajime who came in to see me immediately afterwards. It was about six o'clock and we had just finished supper. He looked at me for a long time and then said, "What have you been doing during the summer?"

"Oh, nothing that really amounts to much," I replied. "There was really nothing to do here."

"Did you sleep?"

"At nights."

He gave me an even stranger look. "What about the daytime?"

"Well, there was nothing to do and I was a great nuisance being in the way here, a stray woman, and all that, so I used to go to the Meditation Hall and sit there. I didn't upset anybody by being there, really I didn't. Nobody else was there when I went." Then I gulped at the memory of what a terrible thing I had contemplated only a few days earlier. "I almost did a terrible thing," I said, "I almost ran away. I had got as far as the bottom of the drive when I thought that I could be wrong and so I came back."

"What else happened?"

"Oh, nothing of any importance; I just realised that I had been wrong about everything and everybody and now I am back again, that's all."

He left the room for a few minutes and came back with someone I did not know, a very old and quiet priest. He looked at me for a long time and then got up and left together with Rev. Hajime.

On his return Rev. Hajime said, "I have just spoken to Zenji Sama. You should become Chief Junior; you are worthy."

"What is a Chief Junior?" I asked.

"Later I will explain. Now I want to translate something for you." His English had improved considerably during the summer and I realised he must have been working on it. My own Japanese has also improved greatly and we found that we could even begin to converse a little without having to write everything down on paper first. He fetched a book from the cupboard in his room and, with the use of a huge dictionary, began translating some of it into atrocious English. I took what he had written and studied it. Something rang a bell inside me as I read; despite the strange English I knew the meaning. I wrote out what he had written in my own words in good English and handed it back to him. He went through it, looking up any of the words I had used that he did not know and then looked at me.

"I did not know you had reached such place," he said, startled, "You *understand* this."

"Rev. Hajime, let's get on with translating some more." It was as if my heart and body and every fibre of me was hungry for more of what I had just read. Abruptly he got up and left the room again. On his return he said, "Zenji Sama says that you must be careful, very, very careful or we shall break your heart."

"You can't! It is an absolute impossibility," and I laughed at him from the bottom of my being.

He smiled softly and then said, "Do not stop here, never be satisfied; always you must be *disturbed* by the Truth. Do not stay with clarity, do not be satisfied with peace. He who is satisfied dies. Go on, go on, always going on, always *becoming* Buddha but never become Buddha." He looked at his watch.

"It is long past bedtime," he said, "We must not disobey the rules."

I rose, bowed and left the room for bed with the Diamond Sutra saying softly in my head, "Thus shall ye think of all this fleeting world, as a child's laugh, a bubble in a stream, a phantasm, a dream." The things I had seen of my past life were like that—shadows in a mirror—the silly things that had happened during the past month or two were like that too and all I have to do is watch them float by, interested but not concerned. Oh, Holy Buddha, I take *Refuge* in Thee.

Book II.
The Trainee.

Book II.
The Trainee.

12th. November.

Rev. Hajime and I had a wonderful day visiting the language school in Shibuya. It was my happiest day in the world outside since I left England. The world really is a magnificent place.

14th. November.

Permission has been granted for me to attend the school and Rev. Tarō came with me for the first time so that I could learn how to find my way on the trains and buses for myself. The class seems to be full of Baptist missionaries. The teacher was a bit worried about this but I can see no cause for it. After all, so what? They are Baptist and I am Buddhist—and we all learn Japanese together—fine.

I have again asked Rev. Hajime if I am to be given a definite job here—I now realise that what I should have asked for is a job that is listed in the books since I am already doing the job of taking what foreigners come to the temple round it. My heart seems to be doing some queer things—bumping about— it made me feel a little sick—went to bed early.

15th. November.

We have now translated quite a lump of the Denkōroku. It is amazing how much of it seems to be being said inside my heart as I write it down. I startled Rev. Hajime to-day by asking who had written it in reality—I know that it is said to have been written by Keizan Zenji but it seems to have been written in eternity. He looked at me with worried eyes and said, "Be careful, be careful, we will break your heart." I laughed and said, "You can't; nothing can. Physically I can die but spiritually never." He grabbed me by the wrist and looked deep into my eyes then drew away and held his head in his hands. "I would not have believed it possible," was all I could get out of him.

25th. November.

I have to move from my room to let the old priest who went to hospital have it. Rev. Hajime told me that I am to be *anja* to both of them. I am so glad—it will be an honour to serve them.

29th. November.

Despite all of the things going on around me my peace is, as it was, unshatterable. It is something so big in which every-one here shares.

1st. December.

To-day the order came from the Director that I am to be anja to the lecturers, that is, the three officers upstairs. I now live in the corridor since there is no longer a room for me to live in. I am so pleased that I am now "on the books" so to speak. It is not so pleasant knowing that one is here but not here in the eyes of the temple. I cannot help wondering how they have worked that one out with the press. I went round and bowed to every door of the temple, as do all trainees here, to tell everyone what my job is. I wonder why some of them laughed at me when I told them I enjoyed it?

4th. December.

The fourth day of Sesshin and I am wondering if I shall be able to keep it up. I can scarcely move my arms from the beatings. All this goes on and the peace sits there, neither smiling nor moving, crying nor remaining still. My heart is giving me much trouble.

6th. December.

It seems, according to the junior trainees, that everything Japanese is perfect and nothing else is any good. They have

spent most of their spare time to-day criticising everything I
and other foreigners in the world do but I must say nothing in
reply. Although it is Sesshin they spent most of the night playing mahjong downstairs. I went to the Zendō and Morning
Service and came back to find them still in bed. How am I to
understand what is going on?[4] It is at times as if the evil of the
whole world lies upon my back and I have to support it. How
easy it would be to end it all.

This is madness—it is deluded thinking. I must turn and
fight or I will stop my training—I do not know how to fight but
I must. What they are up to is not my concern—it is the dust
upon the mirror of the mind—and the mind is not there. I once
asked Rev. Hajime if I could give my will to him since freedom
from desire only comes when there is no wanting, no knowledge
and no having, but he refused to allow me to even think of it.

8th. December.

I have been beaten every day since October the first and
eight or nine times every day since Sesshin began. These last
few days have been quite remarkable, however, in that whatever it is that sits in the Zendō just sits and sits and doesn't care
whether I am alive or dead. Just my body bows when it is
beaten and the stick bows too.[11, 13]

15th. December.

Was sent to lecture to some Americans in Yokohama to-
day. Their questions were very disappointing and extremely
shallow. I wonder why I never noticed such things before?

16th. December.

I was sent to get a sack of rentan-coal from the store this
morning. On the way back to our house something seemed to go
snap inside, my head began to swim and I genuinely saw stars.
I dropped the sack of coal and it split open. The juniors from
downstairs came to find me and were furious when they saw the
broken rentans. I cannot remember exactly what happened but I
think one of them struck me, then they went away taking the

rentans with them. Somehow I got back to my room where
Rev. Hajime found me on the floor. He sent for a doctor and
they took me to hospital. They want me to stay in but I have
refused. They tell me I have had a small heart attack and must
not carry anything heavy or do anything more strenuous than
reading a book for several months. The doctor was very unwilling to let me return here but, since the hospital belongs to
the temple, he could not argue about it. He let me go back in a
taxi with a supply of medicine and strict instructions to Rev.
Hajime to look after me.

28th. December.

Fainted in the Hondō this morning and two priests carried
me back to my room. Rev. Hajime was very annoyed that I had
not stayed in bed. The disciplinarian came to see me to-day
along with quite a number of others. I have never before known
them to be so friendly. Rev. Hajime says that it is now common
knowledge that Zenji Sama is annoyed with Rev. Ichirō for
what he has been doing with me and has agreed that he, Rev.
Hajime, shall be allowed to teach me in future. Rev. Ichirō
came to see me to ask how I was and to tell me that, since he
was so busy, Rev. Hajime was going to teach me at such times
as he was unable to do it. I wish my brain and body were not so
tired—my spirit is willing to do everything but my body feels
exhausted and my heart beats so fast I am wondering what is
going to happen.

29th. December.

The exhaustion has increased unbelievably yet my meditation is so wonderfully peaceful. I heard this morning that I have
passed my examination in Japanese which I took on December
3rd. It is amazing I could write properly for my shoulders ached
so much from the beatings that I could scarcely hold the pen.

30th. December.

Went to the Zendō but was so dizzy I had to come back.
One of the trainees from downstairs came up and grumbled

because I had not gone to meditation, so I went back again but Rev. Hajime saw me staggering through the door and immediately sent me out. Unfortunately the trainee downstairs did not believe me so I tried to go back for a third time but was so ill I could not make it. I rallied a little by lunch time and wrote the above. Even this exhaustion, although I feel ready to drop, is very peaceful—it is as I used to feel before being operated on years ago—the peacefulness that comes with the acceptance of the possibility of death—it is strange and very pleasant.

31st. December.

I am so hungry these days. Yesterday food kept floating in front of my eyes as I tried to meditate and I could even smell it. And then I saw London and Paris and Rome and they seemed so very pleasant and inviting. And a voice kept asking, "Why don't you chuck it all? You could dine out on what you have already done for the rest of your life."[31] Even the rain was beautiful as I looked out at it. I must find the strength to fight against this; I must never stop meditating. It is the one thing I must never do.

The New Year celebrations went on all night. First we went to thank Zenji Sama for teaching us during the past year and then, after a ceremony in the Hondō to welcome in the New Year and pray for peace, we went back to his room to wish him a happy New Year. We had a big feast and plenty of saké and then an hour off before meditation started again at three in the morning. And this is going to go on in much the same way for three days along with the arrival of many guests. It is really fascinating and very wonderful. I wish I felt better so that I could enjoy it more.

2nd. January.

Rev. Hajime went to the Council to tell them I must rest by order of the doctor who came to see me yesterday or the hospital will not be responsible for what will happen to me. I went to bed very early and got up late but am still very shaky. Rev. Hajime gave me some saké to make me sleep.

3rd. January.

Woke up late and felt much better but my heart is still not good.

4th. January.

If I go slowly I am all right. I shall return to the Zendō in the morning.

5th. January.

Went to meditation and was beaten again three times. It is as well I do not suffer from fear of the kyosaku or I would by now be surely dead.

9th. January.

Have been out begging with everyone here every day since I have been able to walk again. It is so wonderful to be able to be with all the others.

10th. January.

Rev. Hajime came back to-day after being away since the third. I told him about Rev. Minoru who is living up here now, giving me Buddhist history lessons every day of the week. He was very pleased.

I said, "Always you say that I must be useful and I am trying my best to be so. But I find the attendance at ceremonies I do not understand very troublesome. Will you explain them to me?"

Again he smiled. "Consult the Lord," he said, "always He will tell you." Then he stopped. "No, that is too unkind, I will help you to translate."

"Going back to the business of being useful," I said, "I am always *trying* to learn, every minute. Because I could not talk to people here I tried to learn Zen when cleaning this house and you know what happened as a result of that. My understanding is mine and I can only show it to you in my actions— whether you believe it is right or not does not matter— whether you think my actions right or not does not matter for I do not do them with any motive other than the best I can manage. You say I am clever with words but you are wrong—clever people do not enter monasteries and do the sort of things I have done—they stay in the world and enjoy their comforts. Clever people do not cross the world to try and do something about the mess they have got themselves into for they do not know they are in need of help. I am but one person—a despised woman. I have been here almost a year and the time has flown by, forgotten almost as a dream. You say I am hurrying—I must—for there is no time to lose. I cannot fully give you my thought; I try to see everything I do and say in the spirit of the Lord but my body does not seem to be strong. You say I have 'too keen feeling' to exist here safely. Tell me, how can I become stronger—you say I must find my own way—but even the night watch of this temple has a lantern to dispel the darkness."

I wrote this down for I knew he would lose track of my words. He read it and then he wrote the following, very deliberately:–

"I have read through your writing. I have been beaten with your sincerity. I, too, am trying to do the best as possible. I do not know that what I am doing is right or wrong. Your sincerity will be promoting you. It is enough for you only to *try* to do something in order to make yourself useful. I should beg your pardon because I lose sometimes my temper; it is bad Japanese trait. I am treating you as I treat a familiar disciple. And, as the result, I pretend sometimes to lose my temper. You may do everything as you think best. Perhaps there may be many useless things for you because of the difference of customs. Because of this reason the outside ceremonies here will be useless for you as like as the Sōfugin [memorial ceremonies] inside this temple. Now again I should say to you, when there is a high character it will shine gradually on outside world. Please ask everything when you want."

I bowed and left the room.

11th. January.

Rev. Hajime called me into his room early this evening so that we could get on with the translation for as long a time as possible before the bell went for bed. During these very cold evenings there is no evening Zazen for the sake of the physical health of the trainees who are all too few at this time of the year and, with the large number of ceremonies and other things to attend to, would become exhausted and ill if expected to work non-stop from three in the morning until nine in the evening. I must admit that it is a concession that I myself deeply appreciate, much as I would like to do my evening meditation.

He said nothing for a few minutes after I had bowed and greeted him and then he spoke softly.

"It is going to be very difficult for you to do the formal Chief Junior ceremony since you are a woman and this is a male temple," he said, "but Zenji Sama is determined that you shall be properly educated. It is possible for someone in your position to become Chief Junior without ceremony if you satisfy the actual Chief Junior requirements."

"What are they?" I asked.

"You have already fulfilled them," he replied. "A Chief Junior must be able to lead all his or her fellow trainees both by example and learning. You have already learned to handle your kōan of daily life; that is, you have learned how to find peace in the midst of hatred, distrust and prejudice. In consequence of this you have become a shining example to the other juniors here. You know your own spiritual indestructibility and you are not afraid of standing alone for what you believe to be right; and when you are wrong you do not complain about the consequences to yourself. In other words, you have learned to sail your ship on an extremely dangerous sea; a sea more dangerous for you than for anyone else here. All the rest of being Chief Junior is simply ceremonial which you can learn from a book."

He waited for me to speak but I was silent.

"A Chief Junior must lead all his fellow trainees by example at all times and in all circumstances. You have fulfilled this requirement in every respect and your knowledge of basic Buddhism is excellent. With time you will know Zen teachings just as excellently."

"What are the basic differences? Are they very great?" I asked.

"There is no *basic* difference. Zen is the closest of all the Mahayana schools to the original Buddhism of Shakyamuni Buddha. However, it has expanded the original teachings as time required that expansion, always keeping in mind that what was required of a Buddhist was the following of the spirit of Shakyamuni and not the letter of his words. Thus his basic kōan of suffering has become expanded into the first chapter of the Shushōgi which is the basic kōan of every living person at the present time, the understanding of birth and death and the full acceptance of them. When one speaks of suffering to the average person he thinks of a pain in his big toe or tooth-ache. The old words of Shakyamuni were right for his time but are not fashionable in ours; we want the explanation of the reason for existence, which is what Shakyamuni wanted but, with our more modern education and differing fashions in words, we call it the understanding of the reasons for birth and death. Shakyamuni found himself free from suffering after accepting it completely; we become free of the fetters of birth and death after accepting them completely. This is not a complete explanation but you can do your own research. Compare the Four Noble Truths with the Shushōgi and you will understand me. In a similar way you must take all the Buddha's teachings and apply them to your own particular case after you have compared them with the teachings of Dōgen Zenji. You will find that they are progressing still, and expanding to meet the needs of the present day just as they did at the time of Dōgen; if they do not, then Buddhism must, of necessity, die for it has ceased to live in the present and is only a shadow of the past. Such shadows lead to dogmatism and rigidity."

"Have you any other suggestions for Scriptures that can be compared in a similar way?" I asked.

"Many, but you must find them out for yourself. Only by such means will you ever learn how to make Buddhism live, grow and expand."

"What you are saying is that I must make Buddhism pulse with life, my own life, if it is to be of any real use. That means that I must become greater than my own teacher; I must for ever leave him behind."

"Correct."

"Shakyamuni Buddha and I are one, as are all Buddhists with both him and me, and not merely all Buddhists but all people and all things both animate and inanimate. And none of us have anything to do with Shakyamuni Buddha." I paused for a moment, so that he could thoroughly digest what I had written, then I continued. "Shakyamuni Buddha is of no importance at all at the present time and Shakyamuni Buddha lives for ever in me."

He was silent, simply looking deeply into my eyes; then he spoke softly.

"You should ask Zenji Sama for the Transmission," he said.

"If Transmission is what I think it is I do not understand you. As I know of it, Transmission is received when all training is finished and the master wishes to give his seal of approval to a disciple before he goes out to teach. I am anything but ready for that."

"That is a popular misconception. Admittedly it is the giving of the seals of the master to someone whom he knows has understood his Own Nature but they are only given when the master is certain that the disciple concerned regards his training as just beginning every minute of his life and not when he thinks of it as being over. In other words, not when he thinks of himself as being enlightened and having nothing more to do. Understand the 'gyate, gyate' of the Hannyashingyō as 'going, going,' not 'gone, gone.'"

"Doesn't one have to have had some great kenshō before such a thing takes place? All that happened to me in October was that I realised that there was nothing more I could do but train myself constantly every day of my life and that I was the worst trainee in existence."

"In so short a time after the event that is all you *are* going to understand of it," he said smiling softly. "But, as you continue to train constantly, many things will become deeper and clearer to you as a result of that kenshō. The peace within you will become more profound. Look back on yourself to last summer and what do you see? Read over this conversation on Shakyamuni Buddha; you did not know that you could make it; you know that it did not come out of your intellect and I have not told it to you. Therefore, Who did tell it to you?"

Something inside me jumped with a certainty of the rightness of his comments but I was still stuck with what I had heard of as being kenshō. "Something is very strange since that event in October," I said, "and that is that none of my books make sense in the same way to me as they used to do. I am having to read the whole lot over again and it is quite startling what I am finding out. It is like living in a totally different dimension from what I used to and having to learn everything from scratch again within that dimension. Words don't have the same meanings, people can't press the buttons of my emotions and get the reactions that were customary. I don't know who I startle most, others or myself. And it's awfully alone; not lonely, just alone. I watch things and see things that I never saw before and, when I have a conversation with someone, I understand something totally different from their words from what I used to. People who knew me before are having problems adjusting to me, I am certain, but—oh, I don't know, I could be wrong. I really don't know anything any more."

"For a mere three months since your kenshō that is quite good progress. You should be nicely ready for Transmission in a few months' time."

"But I can't see people in the same way as I used to; it is all so different," I said, "I really don't know what I am talking about. I hope it makes some sense."

"Of course you can't see people in the same way as you used to. But your new way of seeing them is extremely interesting and you know it. Just be careful you do not become an observer. Remember you must participate and not merely watch otherwise you will become a useless stone Buddha. To thus be passive is quietism. And stop trying to get back to the other side of the river. It was you who tried to cross it with such mighty efforts so you have only yourself to blame for having succeeded in crossing. You are trying to grab back your old ways and understandings as does everyone when he first understands. You know in your heart that there is no way back to giving your old emotions and thoughts their original sway over you. Simply sit still and accept what has happened and that you must now do everything from a totally different dimension as you call it."

"It isn't a matter of disliking it; I love it—no, that's wrong—I don't know what I feel about it—you see, love doesn't mean the same thing any more either. I suppose I am just wondering if I am functioning efficiently—I don't know what I am trying to say—I have no means of expression—all words have been grabbed away from me."

"Wrong, you threw them away; what has happened you have done. There is no magic here."

"How can I talk to you? I have no words to use—that's hopeless—I don't need any words to talk to you. I know that and I don't know how I know it. And I don't care because both you and I know that it doesn't matter. You tell me I am ready for Transmission. Somewhere I read that the master's and disciple's eyes have to flow into each other and they laugh—what the hell am I talking about? None of this makes any sense and none of it matters."

He became extremely animated and, for a moment, I thought he was angry. "Such tales are worse than stupid and useless," he said hotly. "There are masters who mistake their own hypnotic powers, and the willingness or gullibility of their disciples to submit to them, for a genuine kenshō experience but they are worse than wicked. They are worse than jugglers playing tricks. There is, of course, a certain type of person who loves such things and they get their reward. Such eye-flowings are the equivalent of spiritual orgasms and leave one with the same flabby feeling afterwards that a physical orgasm leaves; such people enjoy what they think is spiritual joy for a few days and then return to being exactly as they were before it happened except that they now think that they 'know' and so they are in a worse state after their 'understanding' than they were before it. A person who experiences a true kenshō is conscious, as you are, that he is the worst trainee in existence and that he is completely unworthy of what has happened to him. He can only preserve his state of awareness by always remembering how much he still has to do to make himself worthy of what he knows he is. Do not think that any such thing as you have described happens at Transmission; there is no play-acting; the master and disciple *know* each other. There *is* a flowing between them of which they *know* but it is not as you have described it. You will know the Turning of the Wheel of the Law when it happens."[32]

"Forgive me for asking such stupid questions and for disturbing you. I do not know how to talk any longer in words; and yet I must use them. It must be because my Japanese is so bad. I am sure that, if I could speak better, there would not have been the problems that have arisen with Rev. Ichirō. I know that they are really all my fault."

"The problem is not one of language; it is just that you do not yet know how to express yourself in your new dimension as does no-one in the beginning. You will be able to use words again but with a totally different power than before and a totally different meaning for those who have the ears to see and the eyes with which to hear; for they will be hearing with their eyes just as much as they will be seeing with their ears and you will be talking with your heart. Already you are doing so. You are making perfectly good sense to me. But, as yet, you lack confidence. In a month's time you will have mastered your new dimension and then there will be no stopping you. You could have said nothing you have said to-night even a month ago. But it would be good for you to improve your Japanese so that you can move about the temple much more freely and talk to everyone at all times. I will tell Zenji Sama you wish to be Transmitted."

I was about to tell him that I did not want to be Transmitted and then stopped, realising that I did. I had known it all along, and so had he, without saying any words. Already our hearts were talking confidently to each other without any help whatsoever.

The night bell rang. I wished him good-night, bowed and left the room.

16th. January.

I went to Zenji Sama's room this morning and, in the presence of several others, completed the ceremony of Chief Junior. It was so wonderful to have it without any fuss and an awful lot of formality as would have happened had I actually done it in the main hall. When it was over we all had tea together and then I went back to my room together with Rev. Hajime.

"Zenji Sama says that if you continue as you are you will be Transmitted some time in the late spring or early summer."

"Really? He really thinks I'm good enough?" I said, truly amazed.

"It isn't a matter of being good enough or bad enough. Normally you would be Transmitted immediately but, because you are a foreigner and a female, he wants to make absolutely certain that no-one can ever accuse him of doing something he shouldn't actually do. He is quite afraid of Transmitting you and being told that he did it far too early. It is reasonable, knowing the difficulties that he has had here in just being able to keep you in the temple." Did I detect something grudging in his tone? Of course not.

"It doesn't really matter whether it's done early or late. I don't mind. The joy is that he is willing to do it," I said, my voice very still.

"It is advisable that you don't talk very much about the fact that he is going to do it otherwise there could be trouble. I doubt very much if Rev. Ichirō would be very happy if he knew that it was going to happen although it is none of his business." Again, something grudging? No.

"I don't see why I should keep quiet about it. I'm not ashamed of being Zenji Sama's disciple, nor am I ashamed of the fact that I'm a foreigner and a female, and you know it." My voice was again very still.

"That may be true but the fact remains that, although you can now handle the kōan of being both foreign and female, you

still *are* a foreigner and a female. At *all* times the kōan has to
be overcome in the situation in which one finds oneself right
now—solving it is a continuous process—and the situation you
find yourself in is that you are still foreign and still female and
will be fifty years from now; this kōan is going to appear again
and again; it is soon to appear in the shape of Rev. Ichirō who
is not going to be overhappy that a foreigner and a female has
become the direct descendant of an Archbishop of Japan."
Again that tone in Rev. Hajime's voice. What *is* it?

"It is still none of Rev. Ichirō's concern. I am not becoming
his direct descendant; I am becoming Zenji Sama's."
Stillness—stillness everywhere.

"That is an excellent answer but it is time that you knew
some of the problems that exist in the Buddhist world. Each one
of us belongs to a different family. In the time of Shakyamuni
Buddha there were only He and his actual disciples. Then, as
those disciples travelled, they took disciples and so the family
tree branched off in many directions and many schools of
Buddhist thought. Our line comes directly from Makakashyō
down through Ananda and, eventually, through Bodhidharma
who took Zen to China. Eventually it came to Japan as a result
of Dōgen Zenji who became the pupil of Tendō Nyojō when he
was at Keitoku-ji in China. There is not just *one* line from the
Buddha but many, for although everyone is descended from
Bodhidharma in China and everyone here in Japan is descended
from Dōgen Zenji, the fact remains that, since Dōgen Zenji in
the twelfth century, many *more* lines have formed. Dōgen
Zenji's own pupils, through Keizan Zenji, became legion.
Keizan Zenji had a great disciple named Gassan who founded
one of the two greatest lines in the country. You and Zenji
Sama trace your descendency through Manzan, the other great
line in Japan. I myself am from Gassan. That does not make any
difference in the real sense of Buddhism, for we are all one in
the Spirit of Shakyamuni Buddha, but we are all different
because we are descended from different lines and the teachings, and the techniques employed in teaching, are very slightly
different according to the temperaments of the people through

whose hands they have passed. However, your line, coming directly from Shakyamuni Buddha, through Bodhidharma, through Dōgen Zenji, through Manzan Zenji and eventually through Zenji Sama who, at present, is living here in this temple, although it is one of the most powerful, is only one of *several* lines in Japan. There are more; however, they are not nearly as important as are my own, Gassan, and yours, Manzan. After the formation of the administration some years ago many problems came out; for the not-so-very-scrupulous among us decided to form into parties, known roughly as the Gassan and Manzan."

"Do you mean to say that trainees squabble over which lines they belong to for religious/political purposes?" The idea seemed inconceivable yet he was completely serious.

"Yes, I do. Very much so. At the moment the Manzan line is in power in the administration so Zenji Sama can afford to do anything he wishes, including have you here in this temple, but the day may very well come when the Gassan line will be in power and you will find it very difficult to live in this temple; and, perhaps, even very difficult to live in Japan."

"I see. So what do you suggest I do?" Be still, be still.

"I strongly suggest that you do not anger Rev. Ichirō. The elections for the administration take place every two to three years. I believe that from next year it is going to be every two but I am not sure of this. The Gassan line could well get in then and life would be very difficult for you." Again that grudging tone in his voice.

"I'm having difficulty with words again, Rev. Hajime. It's awfully difficult to understand how people like priests can— well—sort of form up into political parties; it's even more difficult to understand how they can give them the names of great saints like Manzan and Gassan." Do not be pulled off centre. Be still.

"When you know more about our administration you will understand a lot better. There are priests who don't even register their disciples at all with the administration for they feel that, in many ways, it is far too corrupt. There are also many who feel that to register them with the administration is the only way. I myself have always obeyed orders and so I register my disciples. Zenji Sama, too, has always obeyed orders, and so you have been duly registered but, whether this is good or bad I am not prepared to say; just I do that which I feel has to be done; just that and nothing more. Zenji Sama is a great man. Because of his greatness he can afford to register you with the administration and, at the same time, break its rules. I wonder sometimes if he is right in doing it." The grudging tone was turning to one of censure and I was conscious of holding myself absolutely still.

"I am not going to listen to any criticisms of Zenji Sama. He is my master and always will be; whatever he does, right or wrong, in the eyes of the world, will always be the law for me." An echo coming from a great distance.

"There speaks the good disciple but you may find that to live by that will be very difficult at a later date. You should be warned of the political dangers." Did I detect a faint sneer in his voice or was it—jealousy? Surely not.

"Even although I know that nothing can destroy me?" An echo in stillness.

"Yes. You have understood the Lord of the House. You have understood that you are indestructible. You have understood eternal meditation but you have not yet understood the 'with' within the Denkōroku; for the 'with' is everything else around you and you must regard all that as Buddha as well. If you do not you will have great problems for you will then regard Zenji Sama as *the* Buddha and you will look at Rev. Ichirō as something that does not have the Buddha Nature." A return to his old voice. I must have imagined what happened before in his tone.

"I could never do that and you know it. I know that Rev. Ichirō has the Buddha Nature and so do you." Take off the brakes; no need to hold still.

"That may be but the fact remains that, unless you can take into consideration the feelings and aspirations of the Gassan line, you will never understand Buddhism fully." Again—faint jealousy? My awareness seems to be so much clearer.

"What you are telling me is that I have to regard the Queen of England, the President of the United States and the Emperor of Japan as symbols of the Buddha Nature just as are you and I and—do you realise that we'd have to include Hitler in this as well?" His voice tones forgotten. All that matters now is the understanding.

"It is not 'we *would* have to include Hitler,' we *do* include Hitler. If you cannot see that he, too, possesses the Buddha Nature, however misguided he may have been, you are never going to understand Buddhism completely. You are always going to chop off a part of the Buddha Nature and say, 'That little bit isn't clean; that little bit isn't nice.' You cannot do that."

Even as he spoke I understood completely what he meant. There is no part of me that can ever be chopped off. There is no emotion, no feeling, no thought, no word, no deed that does not come out of the Buddha Mind. I said this to him and went on, "Then the sex act is part of the Buddha Nature and expresses the Buddha Nature at every turn, for it is, of itself, clean. What we have done is made it dirty with our own guilts and misuse."

"You are correct."

"Eating and going to the toilet and washing clothes and scrubbing the floor are all part of the 'with' for they are all expressions of the Buddha Nature." I stopped, amazed at myself.

"Go on," he said.

". . . and the sun and the moon and the stars and the earth; and the digging of the earth and the flowing water; these too are all expressions of the Buddha Nature, and the tongue I use to speak these words, and the food I eat, and the differences in the tastes; 'by comparing them you can'—Yes! that's what the Scripture means. 'By comparing them you can distinguish one from other,'—and yet they're all the same thing; they're all expressions of the Buddha Nature and there is no way in which they can be separated off from it; and there is no way in which one can separate off any person or being or any living thing or— or centipedes even, and they're such—now—no they're not."

"What were you going to say?"

"I was going to say they're such—horrible looking things."

"Do they make you shudder?"

"No, but—I don't quite know what they do now. They used to terrify me. You know I told you about what happened when Rev. Tarō put an insect (I can't remember its name now) on my head and, normally, I would have been terrified. Instead I took it off—I know what it was, a praying mantis,—and do you remember I took it off and I wasn't scared of it at all? It was really a very lovely thing."

"Of course, you had suddenly understood that it had the Buddha Nature, and you weren't afraid of it because, if you were, you would have had to have been afraid of yourself."

"Then when we are afraid of some external thing we are inadequate within ourselves—afraid of what the thing represents, and it is because we are afraid to live that we suffer from fear. Life is opening up so much, so widely, so vividly . . . . . It's like seeing a huge panorama instead of looking through a keyhole. That's what it's been like since I had this kenshō; like looking at a great scene which before was only glimpsed when you raised a curtain a fraction; almost instantly the curtain would be dropped again,—and now fear and love and hate . . . . . do you remember I said to you last time that words have totally different meanings?"

"Yes, I remember."

"Well, now . . . . . now they do have totally different meanings but again in a totally different way. It is as though they change their meanings from moment to moment, flowing, nothing sort of fixed any longer; it's like seeing each word in a kaleidoscope."

"Ah! you have at last understood 'Ūji.'"

"'Ūji?'"

"Yes, you already have a very bad translation of it in one of your books."

"Oh, yes. Ūji—on Being Time, Dōgen Zenji's writings. I used to have a lot of problems with that. In one way I couldn't understand what the translator meant but now I think I know. Existence, Time. It's not Existence, Time, it's a flow and, whereas before kenshō we understand fear as a sort of thing that we're stuck with, at a later date, now, for example, I understand fear as something totally different. It's . . . . . it's something that grows smaller and smaller as we become less and less fearful inside ourselves and what I was afraid of in the insect was something I was afraid of inside me. Now I can . . . I can look at the centipede even and see that it's just a centipede and nothing to be afraid of. You know I've got a friend down in Kyoto who tells me she is constantly attacked by them but they've never attacked me. It's really very odd."

"Why should they attack you? They know they have nothing to fear from you."

"No, that's very true, in fact, they get out of my way. Hey, I don't know how to express these things any longer."

"Give it time. I told you to give it a month or two and you'll be able to express yourself magnificently. You're doing awfully well right now."

"Oh! You know, I think if I were capable of being frightened what you've just said would frighten me."

"But it doesn't, does it?"

"No, it doesn't, and I'm wondering why it should."

"You are still not used to your new dimension."

"I see."

"Let's try again."

"Going back to the business with regard to Hitler, what we've just been talking about means that what we couldn't stand in him, what gave us such awful horror, was the realisation that we could do identically the same things as he did; we all had the potential of cruelty in us and that shocked us so horribly that we had to kill it in him. We realised that it was within us, good and evil both being part of us along with the Buddha Nature; he allowed evil to be in the ascendancy and we *knew* he was wrong. Our *mistake* was that we could not *accept*, and so transcend, the evil side of ourselves. I am not saying we should have allowed Hitler to run the world; obviously he could not be allowed to get away with evil; we had to go to war. But we wished to turn our eyes away from the fact that we *could* do the same things that Hitler did. We decided that he *alone* was evil instead of saying 'I could be evil too; Hitler is a mighty example of what I must *not* become.' Looked at this way Hitler becomes an important teacher for me and I must be grateful to him for showing me what I could become. This is the reason why it is so difficult to keep the Precepts and why the Truth can't be given to us until we have kept them and learned to make them our blood and bones. We don't *want* to know that we can be evil so where is there any need for Precepts? Thus, no-one can enter into the Truths of Buddhism until he has made the commitment of becoming a priest otherwise he could use the knowledge of his own indestructibility for all sorts of evil purposes.[33] He would know his own true freedom and wouldn't care two hoots what he got up to with other people."

"That is completely right. You have understood the 'with' at last. You see, from now on you can carry on from there and there will be no difficulty in understanding, and you will know that you must hold everyone and everything as the 'with' aspect of the Buddha Mind and recognise that, whatever aspect of the Buddha Mind it shows, the Precepts must always hold it within themselves."

"Then making the Precepts part of my blood and bones means that the Precepts will eventually fall away because I will be their actual embodiment."

"Haven't you realised that, in your case, the early moral form of them already has? You have gone on beyond morality."

"I thought they had but . . . . . oh dear, there goes the bell. We'd better go to service. Can we continue this later?"

"To-morrow. I have to go out this evening."

We bowed to each other, the first time he had bowed to me fully, and I left the room.

17th. January.

Rev. Hajime came back this morning, instead of last night as he had originally arranged, but it did not really make very much difference because as soon as he had eaten he called me into his room and said, "I think it's about time we started translating the Precepts."

I said, "But I already know them."

"Yes, you know the version that most people are given but you do not yet know the Kyōjukaimon."

"I heard it during my Jūkai ceremony."

"Did you understand it fully?"

"No, the Japanese was too old for me to be able to."

"That's what I meant, so we're going to translate it. Get some paper and we'll get on with it at once."

I settled down at a side desk, which he has now arranged for me in his room, and he got out the old book and started working on it. We had just finished the beginning preamble and had got to the first Precept, "Do not kill, but no life can be cut off. Do not kill Buddha. Do not cut off the life of Buddha," when he said, "Before we go any further I want you to explain that."

"Oh. 'Do not kill.' I understand that."

"But do you understand 'not cutting off the life of Buddha,' because only that is real death?"

"I think so. May I tell you what I think it is?"

"Of course. I am waiting."

"As I understand it, it's a matter of mind attitude in the sense of the *kokoro*, the heart-mind, wanting to do harm. One frequently accidentally kills. We kill millions of microbes every hour of the day just by breathing and we're always treading on grass and insects and things like that. To 'cut off the life of Buddha' is to *will* to hurt, to harm; to *will* to kill, if you like, the compassion within ourselves; to *will* to kill the feeling that other creatures have the right to live."

"Go on."

"Let me think. How can I put this? The trouble is I know what I'm trying to say and I can't get it out."

"I know that one but what are you going to do when you have to lecture to people who come to you with questions like this? You have to be able to talk to them on these matters; you have to be able to explain them."

"Yes, let me think again. I know what it means. It's the 'with' we were talking about yesterday."

He smiled. "Take it from there."

"If we kill something deliberately there's a bit of ourselves that we're cutting off and there's something even more than that. We're saying that something hasn't got the right to live, in other words, that something hasn't got the right to be Buddha. There's something that we're not accepting . . . . . there's something we're saying . . . . . just . . . . . well, can't *be* Buddha. That's the Precept that everybody breaks when they say, 'Oh, well, this is pure and that's impure.' When they say that a . . . . . purity is . . . . . It means that if I say that Hitler is difficult to see as a Buddha I am trying to kill Buddha; if I say something is unclean I am killing the Buddha Nature within that thing itself; if I say . . . . . but that means that morality has to be thought of from a totally different angle, for morality is only a rule of thumb: that which leads to a higher, truer morality—a morality beyond morality.[34] At a later date, as we spiral in, we discover that we cannot really live completely by the Ten Precepts, otherwise we are always working out which one to break and which one not to. We have to live by the Three Pure Precepts, but even they are not enough. Every time we look at somebody and say, 'Well, I can see the Buddha Nature in so-and-so but I can't see it in him over there,' we're literally killing the Buddha and it's our own delusions that kill the Buddha. That's why we don't know that we ourselves *are* Buddha. That is why we are not enlightened. Because we cannot recognise the Buddha in all things we constantly kill the Buddha. We can know, we can feel instinctively, that the Buddha is everywhere but we have not understood the 'with,' we have not understood that our bones, flesh, blood, marrow . . . . . yes, and our sexual side as well, and all the mud and the things we hate and all the torture side of ourselves and all the evil, all is *the* aspect of the Buddha Mind. We have to learn to accept it and work through it and bring compassion to bear on those who only exhibit one aspect, and even love them whilst we restrain them because, only by so doing, can we teach them better things. So every one of us is a murderer every day of the week; every time we discriminate against someone else."

"Quite correct."

"That is the meaning of 'do not kill.' It is not just 'don't go out and slaughter an animal for food,' it is 'don't discriminate against other people, don't set yourself up, don't say "I know who's a true teacher and I know who isn't," ' because, instantly, we are killing. All the Precepts interact upon each other and spiral in. After a bit we get over the fact that the Ten Precepts are the limit of morality and go on to something deeper. We come to where the Ten Precepts fall away and all we have to live by are the Three; to cease from evil, to do only good and to do good for others."

"That's right."

"Then they fall away too, because they're still bounded, and we are left with the True Heart within us which is the Buddha Nature. That's why 'Homage to the Buddha, Homage to the Dharma, Homage to the Sangha' are the only *Real* Precepts and anybody who takes the refuges completely has taken the Precepts. It means that I believe there is within me something greater, something far more wonderful than I have yet been able to show to the world. It means that I know that within me is something intrinsically good and that I can be worthy of it by being better than I am; that there is a teaching which can help me and that there are priests who have realised their True Nature who can give me guidance."

"Good. Now you have understood 'do not kill.' You have understood that no life can be cut off and you have understood it from the moral, from the Lord of the House and from the 'with.' You have gone through the phases and now your training must express it. At a later date you will take it deeper still."

"I'll try. I honestly will."

"I believe it but you will fall many many times and every time you fall you've got to scramble back; and you've got to go on believing that you *can* scramble back."

"That's the meaning of faith. Faith isn't a belief in an outside God; it isn't a belief in something external. It's the belief that one can always go on and do better than one has done before through the guidance of the Buddha Nature. That's the *real* meaning of belief."

"Yes, so it is."

"Faith is the faith in us. It's the faith in the Buddha Nature; in our possession of it. Now to really try and put it into practice."

"We will go through the other Precepts steadily over a period of time and you will find that they are all one and the same Precept."

"Can't we do them now? 'Do not steal, but there is nothing to be stolen.'"

"To-morrow. Don't try to rush. The world takes time to develop and so can you. You've already got a long way. I want you to settle down and work quietly; let these things sink in. Remember that just having a kenshō is not nearly enough; all that it does is open up the panorama; whether or not we want to see it is another matter."

"Yes. Seeing God is one thing and knowing how to live with Him is quite a different one or, better still, becoming a saint is quite a different one. That is the meaning of endless training."

"Correct. What you have to do, now you have seen it, is learn to understand and express it."

"But don't you realise that you're—well,—sort of not teaching me anything, you're dragging it all out of me?"

"That is how Zen is taught. The master only points the way. Remember what it says in the Scriptures, 'Trainees contain the ultimate, masters contain the means; correctly blended this is good.' All Zenji Sama and I do is point. You have done the work and you walk alone and you can walk alone very well indeed. Why do you want any more?"

"It's just a totally different concept of teaching, that's all. Always, when I was being taught before, the teachers were putting stuff in, never taking it out."

"That's the usual concept of teaching but it is wrong. We must realise that within us is a great storehouse of knowledge; all we have to do is tap it."

"Isn't there a danger of becoming swollen headed?"

"Very much so. You must watch constantly for the desire for power. There will even be power struggles within your own mind. The nearer one gets to mastery the worse they become."

"Yes, I can see the danger of that, but if I really *can* see that everything, that every aspect of me and the universe is *the* Buddha Nature expressing itself at all times then I'll be able to handle it."

"Good. Leave me now. I have to prepare a lecture for this evening."

"Thank you, Rev. Hajime. In any case I must go to some ceremonies. I now help with the memorial ceremonies in the Hondō."

"Yes, I know. There are about seventeen this morning. You'll probably be pretty tired."

"I suppose I shall be. Anyway, can we continue this evening?"

"I don't really know; I may have to go out again this evening but we can certainly continue again to-morrow."

"Thank you very much."

Again we bowed to each other and I went to prepare for the ceremonies.

Changing my robes to go to the Hondō it struck me that the last two or three lines of the Zazen Rules really *are* extraordinarily apt. After all, he wasn't putting anything into me; he was dragging it out just by throwing out ideas. And through and through my mind kept running those last few lines, "If you do these things you will become as herein described, then the Treasure House will open naturally and you will enjoy it fully." I *own* the Treasure House and *always* have owned it. What an idiot I have been not to have noticed it before and not to believe, not to realise that the only person who could open the door to it was me. I really am very stupid.

18th. January.

My illness came back again to-day; in fact my heart was so bad that I was almost unable to move. The trainees downstairs were a bit angry about this; they were really very angry indeed

I suppose. They came up to know why I had not been to Morning Service: it is so difficult trying to explain to them. I wonder sometimes if my Japanese is really as bad as they make out. I seem to make everybody else understand me but—I wonder—don't they *really want* to understand downstairs or is it just me?[35] It really must be me—I think.[35] It *cannot* be them.

Anyway, Rev. Hajime went away and won't be back for ten days so I'll try and rest as much as I possibly can. I went to see the Director to tell him of the state I was in and almost collapsed at the door. He was very kind and told me to stay in bed so maybe he'll explain clearly to the others here.

28th. January.

Rev. Hajime returned this morning and I told him the problems that I've been having, notably the fact that, although I told the Director about the situation with my health, either he forgot to tell other people about it, or he was just too busy to, because it seems that none of the Dōans or officers knew that I was ill. Rev. Ichirō turned up and was pretty angry about it but, finding me in bed, went away again. I told him to contact the doctor at the hospital; I hope he did so. It seems I have been forced to lie in bed for such a long time and the medicine they're giving me is really odd; powders with tablets embedded in them. A bit difficult to take too. Anyway, it seems to be making me feel a bit better. It also seems to be making me quite sleepy.

29th. January.

There was a tremendous rushing round in the temple this morning. The festival of Bean Throwing is to take place soon and that means that most trainees are going to be in the grounds with side shows, having fun. It's the big, official festival of the Spring; and I'm told it always snows! It's also officially the *first* day of Spring. February 2nd seems a bit early, to my mind, to be celebrating Spring but it's a nice thought. Winter does seem to have been rather long.

Anyway, as well as the side shows, there are going to be big processions of all the local dignitaries and merchants who are coming to throw beans. I'm really looking forward to seeing it; that's if I'm well enough to get outside.

2nd. February.

It's now six o'clock in the evening. I went to watch the bean throwing; it was really quite remarkable. There were three main processions, one at about noon, one at three in the after-noon and one later this evening at five o'clock. Everyone who was going to throw beans went to the big guest rooms where they changed into special old time Japanese costumes. They have to pay fifty or a hundred thousand yen each to attend this ceremony and they have to be a specific age; boys of seven, for example, and men of twenty and forty-five; I'm not *sure* of the actual ages. They went in procession to a platform ramp which had been built from the center-front of the Butsuden right out into the gardens. They went into the Butsuden for a special cer-emony after which some of them won prizes because their admission tickets had lucky numbers. Some of the things they won were big Bodhidharma dolls. They were each given a tray of beans and, after the ceremony, they came out of the hall with the Director at their head. The Director shouted, "Out evil! In, Good Luck!" in very old Japanese, whilst throwing beans into the crowd of several thousand spectators, and every-body threw beans along with him. The throwing out of beans is the throwing out of all the old year's bad luck and the bring-ing in of the good luck for the new year. Odd that Buddhists should have a ceremony like this but it's rather fun. It reminds me a bit of the way in which the Christians took over the old pagan festivals in England.

When it was over everybody went back to their respective rooms, changed their clothes and had a big feast. As I said ear-lier the procession and ceremony took place three times but the most interesting was that in the evening for all the partic-ipants carried paper lanterns. There were thousands of people in the garden to catch the beans. And it wasn't only beans they were throwing; little oranges and all sorts of other things went through the air. I can't remember exactly—well—in fact, I didn't get close enough to see what all the other things were for, of course, they wouldn't let me join in. A bit awkward being a foreigner. I sometimes wonder what I've done wrong to be one. I also sometimes wonder which it is the worst to be, a foreigner or a woman. Anyway, I thoroughly enjoyed the day but it would have been nice to have been closer to everyone.

I had to come back to my room halfway through the second ceremony and go back to bed because my heart was causing me so many problems. It got a little better, however, and I was all right again in two or three hours but I missed most of the second. And now, as I write this, I'm feeling a bit queer again. Maybe I shouldn't have stood around so much.

4th. February.

I was so ill this morning that Rev. Hajime got very angry with me for having gone to the bean throwing. He said I'd thrown away everything that I'd done to try and get better in the last ten days. The doctor took me off to hospital and then rang Zenji Sama. He was very angry about the state I was in and said that I must go away for a rest; but there's nowhere I can go to. I asked Rev. Hajime if I could go down to his home temple but he said that there was no possibility of it whatsoever so I must just try and stick it out here and hope that I improve. Of course I've got some friends down in Kyoto but, somehow, I don't think they'd be too happy to have me. I was never terribly close to them when they were in England. I suppose I shall always be a loner and the fact that they dislike foreigners and females so much here makes me more lonely still but the joy remains within. That, at least, is mine and always will be and, if this heart problem of mine kills me to-morrow, I'll know that I found what I came looking for. That's the glory of this whole thing; I *found* what I came looking for! What is even more amazing is that I can talk about it and I never knew any of it was inside me; I marvel at this every day. I suppose this is what is meant when they say that a Buddhist is born alone and dies alone; he is complete, needing nothing. He finds the peace within himself, the peace that was always there, but never really has anyone else that he can rely on other than himself. Oh, I'm making a mess of this; I don't even know how to express it. Maybe the illness is causing problems but I'm peaceful and awfully happy.

26th. February.

I returned to the Zendō this morning. It's been almost a month that I've been away sick but at least it wasn't during term-time so there was no real problem. Everybody glowered at me. I suppose that was to be expected. I feel awfully guilty at having been ill so long and having neglected my training in this way. I really should have been with everybody else doing everything with them. I'll make up for it now. I'll really work like mad to make up for it.

28th. February.

Rev. Hajime wouldn't translate any more of the Kyōjukaimon to-day, nor listen to explanations of it, because he felt that it was more important for us to work on part of the Denkōroku. We worked so hard we almost completed one chapter; now I am busy writing it up. It will probably take me quite a long time so I doubt if I'll get a chance to do anything more with him to-day; in any case, he's awfully busy.

Good to feel so much better but I'm terrified of some of the things that I know I've got to be able to do. For example, I must be able to do OBon dancing. I don't want to collapse out in the gardens. I wonder if I could really . . . . . no, I'd better not do that. It's wrong to talk to Zenji Sama over a matter so unimportant. I asked Rev. Hajime about it and he said that I must do all things at all times. So I must really try. I'd love to be able to do it—the only thing is—can I?

1st. March.

Rev. Hajime, as soon as I entered his room this morning after Morning Service, said, "All right, now I want to hear your explanation of the greatest of all the Precepts, 'I take refuge in the Buddha.' It's the one and only Precept that really matters."

"But I thought we were going to do 'Do not steal' to-day?"

"Yes, I know you did but there is no point in your doing that for you already understand it. You have already done extraordinarily well on that set of Precepts."

"What do you mean?"

"By the way in which you explained 'Do not kill.' "

"But what about, ... oh, of course, you're right. They're all the same Precept. Stealing, killing, coveting, all are the same thing. I'm taking something away from someone by killing him; I'm stealing his life; coveting it; I am treating him as less than Buddha. I . . . . . I don't know how to put this but . . . . . yes, I can understand now what you're talking about with 'I take refuge in the Buddha.' I'm in an awful muddle this morning."

"No, you've just had quite a long time when you haven't exercised your mind on what you learned during your kenshō and you need to get it going again."

"Can I try again?"

"Of course."

" 'I take refuge in the Buddha.' The Ten Great Precepts aren't really the first Precepts."

He smiled quietly. "Yes?"

"No, the first Precepts are the things we get when we're very young; when we're very definitely spiritual children, not spiritually adult, not autonomous."

He stopped me for a moment to look up two or three words and said, "Yes, autonomy, that is a good word. Autonomous, that is a good word."

I said, "We start off with 'I'll *try* not to kill' and 'I'll *try* not to steal.' 'I'll *try* not to' . . . all sorts of things. I'll *try* not to covet and not to lie; but it's *me* that's going to do the trying. At a later date we say that we *won't* do it. Because there's no *point* in our doing it; we would only be hurting ourselves."

"That is correct."

"It is only later, when we get to these ten *Great* Precepts, which speak of something other than morality, that something is saying to us 'you mustn't do that.' We've then got to the state when the Buddha Nature rules us and tells us what to do."

"And what *is* the Buddha Nature?" he asked.

"It's the 'I take refuge in the Buddha.' It is the Buddha Heart Itself which takes refuge in Itself."

"Yes."

"As I said, we start off by saying, 'I'll *try* not to . . . . . do this or that and then come to the Precepts which we get when we're ordained in which we say, 'I *will* not do this or that.' Then come the Great Precepts when the Buddha Nature Itself is telling us 'Don't do that.' The Ten Precepts are a sort of rule of thumb. They show us the diversification."

He stopped me to look up the word "diversification," smiled, and then said, "Go on."

I said, "It's . . . . . they explain to us the diversification, the ways in which we can make mistakes, the ways in which we can make a muddle of our lives. We find that, when we kill something, we are also killing the Buddha and everything else that is around us as well as the True Nature within ourselves; if we steal something from another we also steal from ourselves for we think there is something we haven't got; in coveting something from another we covet from ourselves because we think there is something that we are without. It's not that we have to get rid of *self*; we have to get rid of our own *inadequacy*."

He stopped smiling and studied me with great care. "Go on."

"When we get rid of our inadequacy we realise that we *know* we can do no wrong for neither right nor wrong exist;[34] we don't *need* the Ten Precepts for we have already ceased from evil. Since there is nothing that can be stolen from us and nothing to steal, since there is nothing that can be taken away from us, we ourselves cannot steal; since there is no life to be cut off there is no death."

"Yes."

"So we really *do* cease from evil, do only good and do good for others. The Ten Precepts drop away and all we have left are the Three Pure Precepts; just that and nothing more. I've explained it awfully badly."

"No, you haven't. You'll explain it a lot more clearly later on but you've got the idea all right. You have understood that the Ten Precepts don't matter."

"Oh, but they do. They are the focal points of our responsibility. Supposing I'm faced with a decision such as speaking against someone who is doing wrong. I must speak, otherwise he could do harm to others; and I'm stuck with the karma of speaking for I have broken a Precept; in breaking one I have broken all of them. I have, well, tried to destroy him in the eyes of others, to kill him; to steal his reputation from him; to covet it."

"Yes."

"So I'm bound by the consequences of my action; but I'm also bound by something else; the Three Pure Precepts, to cease from evil, do only good and do good for others. This means that I must take the consequences of my actions without complaining about them in order not to commit a much greater fault. Just as it is impossible to keep the Ten Precepts perfectly, because they're always interacting upon each other, so it is impossible to keep the Three Pure Ones perfectly for, in order to cease from evil and do only good and do good for others, we are still sometimes going to have to break the Ten. So we come to the Three that matter, the Three Refuges. To get advice from those who are more learned than we are, that is the Sangha, is to take *refuge* in the Sangha; to take *refuge* in the teachings of the Buddha is never to be afraid when those teachings cause us to suffer as a result of the law of karma; to take *refuge* in the Buddha is to have *faith* in the Buddha Nature within our own hearts, to listen to the Voice of the Eternal Lord. Christians, I suppose, would call the Buddha Nature the Holy Spirit."

"We have nothing to do with Christians."

"Oh, but we do. Their spirit is identical to ours. They call it something different, that is all."

"I am not prepared to go into that. I do not know enough about Christianity."

"I do and I know that's what it means. Anyway, when we take refuge in the Buddha Nature, which is in our own hearts, and the teachings of the Buddha Himself within us, when we act completely from our hearts and not from our heads or emotions, we are ruled by nothing. We're obeying our own higher or Buddha Nature. So, from the very beginning, we have to do something about all these Precepts because we have to allow our higher nature to show before we can do anything real, before we can be truly responsible people. This brings us full circle back to the rule of thumb, the Ten Precepts, not to kill, not to steal and all the rest but we must still accept the responsibility of not being able to keep them perfectly and take the consequences thereof."[34]

"Good. I want you to write everything out and let me see it when I come back."

"Why, are you going away again?"

"Yes, I shall be away for quite a long time. I probably shan't get back here until term starts at the beginning of April."

"Oh dear, it is so unfriendly here when you're gone."[35]

"Nonsense. You have to *keep* peace within *yourself*; you cannot rely on other people. How many times have I told you that a Buddha, a human being, man or woman, is born alone and dies alone?"

"That's very true. But all of you can talk to each other. And you don't despise each other because you're men or because you're Japanese."[35]

"It was you who chose to come here. Because you chose to do something unusual you must put up with the unusual consequences. It is not my fault that you are a woman or that you are a foreigner."

"I'm not complaining, Rev. Hajime. I'm just thinking how wonderful it would be to have a friend or two." And, even as I said this, I knew something else. I knew that a priest has no friends—not if he is a real one. That all of these young people can talk to each other doesn't necessarily mean that they are friends. They *talk* to each other, that is all. What, after all *is* a friend? From what I have seen of people, when in the world, I know that all they want me for is to discuss themselves. They are terrified of doing anything more; terrified of being friendly with another human being. I have so much that I want to give but I must not thrust it on those that don't want it.

"What are you thinking?" he asked.

"Nothing at all, Rev. Hajime, it wasn't important. Just silly thoughts. Please forgive me."

"What are you going to do while I'm away?"

"Oh, I'll probably write up all the stuff we've been doing and the notes on the Denkōroku. Get everything ready for when you come back."

"There is a group of American tourists coming to-morrow. Would you be good enough to take them round the temple? You know that Zenji Sama has asked that you look after all foreign visitors that come here."

"Yes. What do I do about getting information on the history of this temple?"

"Ask anyone you wish."

"Somehow I don't think that's going to be good enough. A lot of them won't talk to me."

"Well, what is it you want to know?"

"I have got a small brochure on the temple in Japanese but please tell me about each of the buildings. The Japanese is so old that I just can't read it."

"Nonsense. You have been studying Japanese for some time. You should be able to read quite a lot."

"That I should be able to, and that I can, are two different things. Please help me."

Somewhat grudgingly, for he seemed to be in something of a warm temper, (why I couldn't work out) he quickly scribbled down a few notes on each of the buildings and told me to fill in the details. I hope I can get enough information by to-morrow. He went away later this afternoon and that's it, I suppose, until he comes back at the beginning of Jūkai. It's going to be almost a full month again.

3rd. March.

The American tourists arrived. They attended a banquet with Zenji Sama and I was called in to be introduced to them and to discuss many things with them. Most were from various offices and military bases throughout Japan. Some of them wanted me to lecture to them on my life in the monastery, what

I was doing and what Buddhism had to teach and I agreed to do so. It looks as though my loneliness may actually be lifting a little. I must be a very bad trainee if I can't really live completely alone, if I *must* have human company. But I don't know. What *am* I trying to do? Am I trying to be *too* perfect?

Several of the Americans invited me to their homes; it will be wonderful to be with Western people again. I wonder when I will be able to go? I bet it won't be for several years yet. They may have all returned home by then.

4th. March.

Rev. Ichirō arrived at my room with three reporters this morning and informed me that, if I didn't see them, he would go to Zenji Sama and say that I was uncooperative. I told him that he could go to whomsoever he wished; I was not going to be cooperative. He went away in a temper. He is very careful now to come only when Rev. Hajime is away. I must really try to be somewhere else for the long summer holidays.

One of the cameramen tried pushing his camera in my face to get pictures because he thought they would look good whether I was willing to talk to him or not. I left the room. Unfortunately, in rushing downstairs to avoid him, I jogged my heart a bit. Now I suppose I'll be ill again. Oh, why do these people keep this stupidity going?[4]

Since the Americans came yesterday my loneliness has become all the more poignant, all the more obvious. I didn't realise how much I enjoyed seeing them. This afternoon I decided I had better try to do something about this and the only thing I could think of was to go and tell Zenji Sama. It seemed an unimportant thing to see him about but I really didn't know what else to do. However, I knew that the only way I could get to see him would be if I were to take him a present since I wanted to see him officially; that would be the only way I would get past all his assistants so I went out and, knowing that he loves goldfish, bought the largest and most beautiful fan-tailed fish I could see. It didn't cost an awful lot; only three hundred yen which is about six shillings.[36]

I went to Zenji Sama's house with the chubby fish in a plastic bag. There was much bickering with the assistants but I insisted that, since I had a present for Zenji Sama, I had a right to see him and, what was more to the point, intended to do so. After a long argument with me pointing out that Zenji Sama was, at least officially, my master, whether they liked it or not, I was permitted to go into the garden and look at him through his window.

Zenji Sama, apparently feeling that this was not quite right, kindly opened the window and came out, smiling gently.

As a result of all the bickering and argument I began to stammer, in really atrocious Japanese, and with one eye over my shoulder at the scowls of the assistants, that I had brought him a present.

"I have brought you the most perfect fish I could find for your pond," I said.

He flashed me a lovely smile. "But a perfect fish cannot live in a pond with other fish. So I will keep this one in a bowl in my room until it becomes less perfect." So saying, he took the bag and disappeared back into his room again.

I'm not sure how long I stood in the garden staring at the closed window but it must have been for some time for I came to myself again to hear the chief assistant asking me just how long I intended to stay there. It was as though my mind had been turned inside out. Here was I, trying to be absolutely perfect according to the Precepts, terribly earnest, sincere almost to the point of morbidity in some ways, trying to explain how to live completely and utterly by the Precepts and completely and utterly by one's own heart, sitting in the Meditation Hall every morning, even getting there before anyone else did, with the attitude of mind, "Beat me, I need it, I've been so bad in the past," and wondering why everyone avoided my company.

A thought flashed through my head, "But it doesn't really matter what they think. What matters is that I am as perfect as I can be." What Zenji Sama said had definitely shaken something loose inside me though. I bowed to the assistant and left the garden.

5th. March.

I didn't go to the Meditation Hall this morning; I stayed in bed. Just before breakfast I got a telephone call from the irate senior assistant in Zenji Sama's house. After scolding me soundly for not being at meditation he informed me that Zenji Sama had accorded me the unprecedented honour of wishing to drink tea with me. Since I had not been to the Meditation Hall he, the assistant, could not possibly understand why.

On reaching the house I was not at all surprised to find Zenji Sama standing by his goldfish pond holding the fish I had brought him in a bowl.

"Let's put this fish into the pond before we drink our tea," he suggested and together we emptied the contents of the bowl into the pond and watched the fish scuttle away. We went indoors to have tea and cakes and, when we had finished, he said, "I expect you in the Meditation Hall in the morning."

"I shall be there, Zenji Sama," I replied. "Afterwards, may I help dig up the weeds in your garden?"

"With pleasure. I will come and help you myself," he said.

I bowed and left him.

The questions and answers we had exchanged were exactly what I felt they should be. They were part of what went on yesterday and they are the answer to my question about loneliness. What he has really said, especially in the last part with regard to the weeds, is, "Strive for perfection within but don't make a parade of your striving so that the world shall call you holy." I've been striving so hard; I'm sure that's why they're so unfriendly. I must always be sitting still in the Meditation Hall within my own heart and not make a show of being in the physical Meditation Hall. I must appear at all times to be quite natural. Wrong deeds, words and thoughts—they are the weeds, and they must be rooted out. But, since neither master nor disciple are perfect, this is something which we must do together and not separately. And, if I'm a wise disciple, while honouring my master as my teacher, I must not copy his mistakes, and I must recognise that he, like me, can make them. I mustn't become so attached to perfection that no-one wants to be with me. That's how I understand what he was saying.

When I went to see him yesterday I felt as though I was all tied up with wire and now I'm all shaken loose again. I'm back where I was long ago, the day that I knew the bucket of water was completely clean, always will be and always was.[37]

I worked like mad for the rest of the day. At everything and anything—writing about the different things I've been discussing with Rev. Hajime and this incident of the goldfish. I'm keeping a whole stack of notebooks now as well as this big one for the diary. It makes such a pleasant change to be able to write. It doesn't really matter whether they're friendly or unfriendly downstairs. What does matter is that I make myself worth knowing. I must at all times work on *me* so that it won't *matter* whether I am a foreigner or a female.

8th. April.

Rev. Hajime came back this morning. He seemed quite refreshed after his long holiday but there was a sort of yearningness about his eyes. He said it was called 'natsukashii,' loneliness in spring. I pointed out to him that 'natsu' meant summer not spring but he said, "Early summer always makes one homesick."

I wanted him to check all the things I'd been writing but he didn't really seem interested. He just gazed out of the window and kept grumbling about the fact that he'd had to come back to the temple and how much he wanted to be at home. I really felt awfully sorry for him but there wasn't much I could do. So, in the end, I just left him.

In the evening he called me into his room; there were two large flagons of saké on the floor. "I want you to drink with me," he said. "It will help cure the problem with your heart. It will make you sleep more."

"Rev. Hajime, do you think it's wise?"

"Are you saying that I shouldn't drink? Are you saying that I'm bad?" He was returning to his very bad English again.

"Of course not. I'm just saying, is it wise?"

"You know quite well that most of the priests in this temple drink."

"Oh, no, Rev. Hajime, not all of them drink. Some do."

"Most do. And *I* have every intention of drinking as much as I want to. If you don't want to drink with me I'm not interested in teaching you anything."

"But that's blackmail, Rev. Hajime."

"You call it blackmail! Get out of my room."

"All right. I'll drink with you. Can we translate some more when you've—when you've drunk a bit?"

"If I feel like it." His temper got steadily worse throughout the evening and, in the end, at about half past eight, I made his bed and asked to be excused. "You'll be excused when *I* feel like it."

"Yes, Rev. Hajime." I sat down on the floor again, looking at him worriedly. He had drunk almost the whole of one flagon and was beginning to eye the second. I opened one of my notebooks and started reading it.

"Do you realise that it is very rude to read when you are sitting with me?"

"Rev. Hajime, I just don't know what to do. I honestly don't."

"You must do everything right at all times."

"Believe me, that's what I'm trying to do right now."

"When the master is drinking you observe him drinking. When he sleeps you observe him sleeping. When he is angry you observe his anger."

"Yes, Rev. Hajime." I sat on for a few more minutes, watched him nod off and fall upon his desk, sound asleep. I wasn't quite sure what I ought to do so, in the end, I picked up one of his quilts and put it round him at his desk; I then turned out the light, lit a small night light beside his bed and left the room. There seemed nothing else to do.

I hope he doesn't worry me like this too often. Between all the things that normally go on here, and now his beginning to drink, life is, to say the least, quite difficult.[35]

9th. April

Jūkai began to-day. It was a typical Spring day—raw, cold, bright and beautiful. I was looking forward to going to the Jūkai ceremonies again now that I know so much more about them from Rev. Hajime's explanation and was bitterly disappointed when I discovered that the job I'd been given was washing up cups and saucers for the guests. But there'll be other Jūkais, other years. I'll see the wonderful ceremonies again.

I was a little disturbed to overhear Rev. Hajime talking with one of the other seniors in this house. "She insists on having an actual job," he was saying. (But I have not insisted!)

"What do you mean?" replied the other.

"Well, she wants to be able to go to the ceremonies and be in with everyone but it's quite impossible. I mean, after all, she is a foreigner and a female."

"We can always give her *just* the job of washing the dishes."

"That's what I thought and if there isn't somebody else to *bring* the tea she can, of course, bring it. There won't be *too* many important guests in this particular house." I broke in on this conversation. I couldn't resist it. I tapped on the door of the room and entered. Instantly everyone had bright smiles. "Oh, do come in, Jiyu San. Do come in, please. We want to see you. Are you looking forward to Jūkai?"

"Yes," I said. "I am very much looking forward to Jūkai. I very much want to go to it."

"Oh, that won't be possible this year. Um,—after all, you did Jūkai last year so there's no real *need* for you to go to this one. Uh,—when you become that important, having done it once, you don't need to go again."

"But I understood that people could go as often as they wished."

"Oh, yes, yes, people frequently do."

Rev. Hajime suddenly cut in quite curtly, "Your job will be that of 'chāju,' that is washing up cups and saucers from the guests' tea."

"I see," I said, "Is there the possibility that I can do something different next year or is this going to be my job every year?"

"Why do you think you'll be here next year?"

"Forgive me. I see that I am presuming." I left the room. If it wasn't for this peace, this beautiful thing, inside me, something would have died during *that* conversation. I must see that, even with Rev. Hajime, I've got to be very careful how far I trust. And yet I've got to trust everyone at all times and in all places. It's so very difficult to know how to live; and yet there was that—there have been these wonderful lessons—wonderful discussions—I don't know what you call them—with him on the Kyōjukaimon and the Denkōroku. He tells me that I must accept the 'I' and the 'with.' He's accepting the 'I' but not the 'with.' Oh, that's wicked. I'm blaming him. I'm doubting him.[35] I'm becoming—no, it's not wicked, I must just not defame the Three Treasures. I must be very careful not to cut off the Life of Buddha. I must *not* steal another's reputation. I must *not* covet his maleness. I must be content and satisfied with *me* at all times. Thus, and thus only, will peace be completely mine. Whether others understand the 'I' and the 'with' is not my problem. That *I* understand them is *my* problem.

13th. April.

I have been in this temple exactly a year now. In some respects the time has gone awfully fast, in others, terribly slowly. Jūkai is continuing: to-night is the great confession ceremony. I was very wicked. I stole out, after I'd finished in the kitchen, to watch the procession. I watched everyone going off in the direction of the three great abbots and, in my spirit, I went with them. Whether I can be there physically or not doesn't really matter. It was odd because I suddenly felt that someone was beside me and, looking round, saw the old cook. He's so deaf, poor old man, and yet there's something so warm about him. He looked at me, then looked at the procession, looked back at me again and smiled, then beckoned. We both went away together.

He took me to his room above the kitchen which was scrupulously clean, flawlessly immaculate. It must be the cleanest room in the whole temple; it is in a sort of attic loft. He made tea for me, then bowed, smiled and said good-night. As I went back to my room I noticed the people returning from the ceremony. More than three quarters were women. My 'crime' in this instance is definitely that I am a foreigner.

I really haven't seen Rev. Hajime, except as he flashes past in magnificent robes to attend the ceremonies, carrying beautiful fans, looking gorgeous, for the whole of Jūkai. Then, this afternoon, I found him in his room again. I wouldn't have found him only his door was open. He looked at me, glared, and then glared even more at the trees outside. "What's wrong, Rev. Hajime?"

"I hate this place." I didn't quite know what to answer so I was about to go on to my own room when he said, "Where are you going?"

"Uh,—nowhere."

"Then come back here." I returned to his room; it was about five o'clock in the evening and he must have just finished his supper. During Jūkai we all have 'obentō' boxes which are a species of luncheon box. This is because it's not possible for us all to get into the Zendō together, there being so many guests here. "I intend to drink again. I want your company while I do it."

"Yes, Rev. Hajime." I found it difficult to say the 'yes.'

"Go and get me three bottles of saké."

"*Three*, Rev. Hajime?"

"Don't argue with me; go and get them."

"Where—where do I get them from?"

"From the store-house, of course. Here's the money."

"Yes, Rev. Hajime. Will they give them to me?"

"Of course they will. I am an officer. I have ordered it."

"Yes, Rev. Hajime." I went downstairs to the store-house and asked for the three bottles. The trainee in charge gave me a strange look but handed them to me. When I got back to Rev. Hajime's room with the three bottles I found that he'd already found the necessary cups and the special little earthenware jug-like container in which he warms the saké over his fire-pot. He poured out a quantity and began to heat it.

"It is good hot," he said. He drank for some time, insisting that I join him. I became more and more worried, watching the amount he was drinking.

He became steadily more morose as he drank. I tried to make small conversation with him—about everything and any-thing—I talked of the Spring. That was my undoing—I talked of the Spring. Suddenly he exploded in a violent temper.

"I refuse to be Godaikō in the morning! I absolutely refuse!"

"But you're due to be Godaikō in the morning, Rev. Hajime. What can I do about it?"

"You're to go down and tell the Director that I won't do it. I absolutely refuse! I can't *stand* this temple! I want to be home with my family!"

I sat still for a few minutes. "Why haven't you gone to see him?" he screamed. "Tell him I want to see him—tell him I won't do it—tell him anything, but I won't do it!"

"Yes, Rev. Hajime." I got up, went down the stairs, thought for a moment, went along the corridor, came back up via the stairs at the other end of it and went to his room.

"Yes?" he said.

"The Director isn't in his room, Rev. Hajime." I knew I was lying. I also knew that in the morning he would feel differently. This is what he meant. Sometimes we must break the Precepts in order not to do something worse. If I were to tell the Director that he was drunk, heaven only knows what the consequences to him would be. I felt this was the wisest thing to do.

He looked at me, "We'll wait a bit then."

He continued to drink and drink and drink; then, in another fit of passion, he said, "Get down there again and see him!"

He started to scream and rage in Japanese so I rose and went down the stairs again. I knew that he was very, very close to falling asleep with the amount he had drunk for there was no way in which he could resist sleep in the state he was in. I stayed downstairs for a few minutes. Several of the junior trainees came out to see what was happening for the noise coming from

Rev. Hajime's room was quite unbelievable; it was as though he was throwing everything about in it. I realised that he was trying to stand up and kept falling down but I didn't enlighten the juniors. I don't know what my face could have looked like; perhaps it was very worried. They gave me a strange look and went back into their rooms. I walked slowly along the corridor again and back up the stairs—the other set of stairs at the opposite end. When I got to his room he was standing, very unsafely, holding on to the wall.

"Well?" he said.

"The Director has gone to bed, Rev. Hajime." Another lie, and I knew it was another lie, and I was willing to accept the consequences whatever they may be; and then it was that I knew there wouldn't be any for what I had done was completely the right action.

"Then wake him up," he said. I picked up the two remaining bottles of saké; one was now completely empty, the other was begun. I took the near full one, carefully made his bed and stood the bottle beside it, opened the bed, so that it looked inviting, and pointed to the bottle standing at its head.

"Rev. Hajime," I said.

"Yes?" He was still trying to balance holding on to the wall.

"Your bed's ready and there's saké beside it, *warm* saké."

"Where?" He staggered forward, falling on the bed, and within seconds was asleep.

I covered him, turned out the light and took the full bottle back to the store-house just in case someone who shouldn't get hold of it did.

"Would you keep this for Rev. Hajime, please?" I asked.

The store-house trainee looked at me thoughtfully. I thought I saw, for a moment, a flicker of compassion in his eyes, and then he said, "Of course I will," and carefully put the bottle under the counter in the store.

I went back to my room; a lot of things seem to be rocking and falling round me. Idols seem to be falling and crashing from their pedestals; but then, what an idiot I've been to stick anybody on a pedestal. I bet Zenji Sama has some faults too; and I'd tried to be so perfect a goldfish! But I must still try to be as perfect a goldfish as possible. Now here I go blaming other people and praising myself again; I must really remember that what they do is *not* my problem. What *I* do is *my* problem and always will be.

13th. May.

Life has become unbelievably hectic since my last entry. Many people have died from the cold weather this year so there are many memorial ceremonies. One of my chief duties, when not attending Rev. Hajime, is to attend all services so I really haven't had much time to write. Perhaps it's as well since Rev. Hajime has been drunk almost every night of the week. I can't make out what's gone wrong with him. He says that it's sadness in Spring; the fact that he's away from home and doesn't want to be; so why doesn't he *go home*? He doesn't *have* to stay here. There seems to be no real point in his being here if he hates it this much. Anyway, he stays and insists that I heat up the saké for him in the evenings and keep him company while he drinks it. I have managed to get him to do a lot more translating though, which is something. It does help. He has insisted that I write out what it was I understood last September. He says that I should make it into an article for the temple Journal. I tried doing that and he seems very pleased with it; in fact, he went off this morning in high glee with regard to it. It sort of, well, makes me wonder. One minute he's soused—soused out of his head—and the next minute he is overjoyed with regard to religion. I'll have to rethink everything; all my ideas with regard to holiness and unholiness; what *is* religious and what *isn't*. I really have to be able to include the secular within the holy and see no difference between the two. It's so *easy* to talk about these things and when I have them presented to me—well— there they are and I've just got to accept them as they are and never query them. There's no way I can.

Rev. Hajime came back from wherever he'd gone to and informed me that I must go to Zenji Sama and ask him for the Transmission. I didn't know what to say to him so I asked if I could think about it and he said there was nothing to think about. But I've got to know whether I'm good enough in my own heart. I think that, in order to be sure, I'll spend the entire night in meditation. It's an odd sort of feeling to know that you're ready for Transmission and to know that—yet I *do* know because, in all the strange filth and mess and muck[35] that's going on all round me, it isn't really filth and mess and muck; it's just the world and that's part of the Buddha Nature as much as I am and I must see it as part of the Buddha Nature;— stranger still, I can see it as part of the Buddha Nature—and that's all right and always will be all right. It's very strange when I think about it all.

14th. May.

This morning I went to Zenji Sama's room, formally dressed in my kesa, taking my mat, together with the assistant and Rev. Hajime carrying incense, to ask for the Transmission. The old man seemed to be giggling with joy; it was almost as though he was bubbling over. He went to the private altar in his room; a very beautiful private altar; very beautiful and secret; it had great golden doors in front, black lacquered with gold fittings. He opened the doors and took a silken bag from behind the statue in the far corner of the case (for that is really what the altar is; a big, magnificent case). The bag was made of gold brocade, lined with white, on the front of which was a swastika; not the sort that you see on the Hitler flags which look so horribly evil and turn from right to left, but a gentle and incredibly beautiful thing that seemed almost in motion, coloured in delicate shades of pink and white that fanned to gold, and turned from left to right. I could almost feel it move.

"Within this bag lie the silks," he said. "Copy them, study them and, when you have done so, return for the ceremony."

I made the formal bows and, together with Rev. Hajime and the assistant, left the room. I was told that the official silks had come from the administration section for me to make my copies of the silken certificates which are the sign of the Transmission, as had also a special book into which would be written that which my master had to tell me. I went to my room. It had all been carefully prepared. Everything cleansed, everything washed and polished, clean and shining; the desk so clean that one could see one's face within it. No-one was permitted to come near my room; within it I sat still in meditation, as I have sat in meditation for the last twelve days, ever since my last entry—because I have to *know* if I am fit to do this. I need to know—oh, so badly—and now I know that it isn't a matter of fitness or unfitness; it is that which *has* to be done. That is why I went to see Zenji Sama this morning.

As Rev. Hajime opened the box I saw the beautiful silks, three of them, over two metres in length, half a metre wide; such delicate silk, you could see through it; yet so crisp it was like paper and, woven into it, the plum blossom crests; the plum crested silk of the Transmitted priest—and with it, the book.

Rev. Hajime opened the first of the three silks from Zenji Sama's bag and told me to copy it. Of that which I wrote and that which I saw I may not speak in this, my diary, for it must for ever be locked within the heart of a Transmitted priest but, as I copied, it seemed as though the world unfolded and all life appeared before me, clear, bright, explained. That which I understood last September herein had its explanation. The Blood of the Buddhas which is the keeping of the Precepts of the Buddhas; the explanation of life in the world which is life in heaven, the exhibition of compassion, love and wisdom to all creatures; the Life of the Buddha which is the knowledge of the Buddha that always lies within oneself, always was and always will be. I saw them spread out on silk and I knew that they were mine forever. As I copied them, and the papers that had been handed down from master to disciple since the days of Bodhidharma, papers that have been regarded as too holy to put into print, I understood the glory and the joy and the honour of being a Buddhist.

All day long I have been copying. My hand can barely hold this pen as I now write but it does not matter. The candles and the incense still burn upon my altar; I still wear my kesa and sit upon my mat for, during the weeks of Transmission, one may never be without the incense or the kesa, as indeed one is never without incense or kesa throughout one's entire life. Rev.

Hajime has been sitting outside my door most of the day, keeping everyone away who came up to see me; keeping everyone away who may come to talk. It has been a quiet and amazingly still day; still, still and yet terribly alive. To-morrow I will write again. One silk is now finished; there are two more.

16th. May.

After Morning Service and meditation I went to the kitchen to collect my breakfast. They were startled to see that I was still wearing my kesa and wanted to know the reason why. When I told them I was to be Transmitted a gasp of amazement went up. My breakfast was handed to me and I went to my room.

I didn't do the second silk to-day. Instead I copied a number of the secret papers. They are fascinating and amazing; many are in code for they must never be looked upon by unworthy eyes. I do not blame the ancients for keeping this information from those who should not see it. It would indeed be very, very wrong for anyone who is unfit to know the freedom that is truly his.

21st. May.

I have at last finished all the secret papers. To-morrow I will start on the second silk. It has been physically very tiring, sitting here day after day. Writing can be physically exhausting, especially since it must all be done in Japanese, with a brush and I am, in any case, not used to writing on silk. But it has been unbelievably wonderful to sit here, still. No sound, the incense smoke rising, writing; writing that which has been known for thousands of years and which has now come down to me.

Even when Rev. Hajime got drunk this evening, came to my door and bowed, his red face bobbing, it was just an aspect of the Buddha Nature. There was nothing to be turned away or to turn away from. A drunken Buddha is still Buddha just as a small daikon (radish) is still a daikon.

23rd. May.

I started work on the last silk but was so exhausted that I made mistakes and Rev. Hajime had to telephone for another piece of silk. I was writing in the wrong direction, reverting automatically to going from left to right instead of right to left. That is what comes of being Western; coming out of a Western background. I still tend to be conditioned by that which is my own past. Anyway, the silk will arrive to-morrow. I will spend the rest of to-day in meditation.

27th. May.

I have had to spend almost four days in meditation since the silk was not readily available. Apparently it is only kept in sets and Rev. Hajime had to find the person who makes it. After some time he found the maker in a tiny little place near Kyoto. Rev. Hajime got the silk and I was able to start on it to-day. Physically I am exhausted but my whole spirit seems to be bathed in joy. As I wrote to-day I knew somehow that, whatever being here has cost me physically, it will always have been worth it.

28th. May.

I shall finish the third silk to-day and I am told that to-night the ceremony will take place. It is strange to think that to-night I shall see the holy of holies, that which is, and know that I am, and always have been, within it.

29th. May.

Since the Transmission ceremony did not take place until almost midnight I have not had time to write anything concerning it until this morning.

At about eight o'clock in the evening I had to go to Zenji Sama's room to take to him, for his signature and seals, all the papers and silks that I had copied out. I took them in a big, blue silk handkerchief which I have had for some time. After giving them to him I bowed and left the room. Later I was taken to his private bath-house where I was allowed to bathe prior to the ceremony itself. When the bath was over I changed into a spotless white robe, koromo and kesa and returned to my room to wait for the ceremony.

Round nine-thirty I was sent for and again went to Zenji Sama's house. Rev. Hajime was supposed to come to the ceremony too but he seemed not to have arrived by the time I got there; however, they sent for him and he came at a run very shortly afterwards. He, myself and Zenji Sama's assistant were then given dinner, a very special dinner of eggs and rice, that had been sent in from a restaurant. We waited quietly, expecting Zenji Sama to join us, but it seemed that he did not intend to do so. So the three of us had our meal together and then Rev. Hajime, perhaps feeling that, since the ceremony was not going to take place until midnight, it was too long to sit around in the Chief Abbot's house, went away. I kept my robes on, full koromo and kesa with mat, because I had a feeling that Zenji Sama was not going to wait until midnight and I was right. Rev. Hajime had only just left the room when who should arrive but Zenji Sama, fully dressed for the ceremony in koromo and kesa, carrying his mat and book. He was somewhat annoyed that Rev. Hajime was not there but said the ceremony could go on without him. I was taken into the Ceremony Hall which proved to be Zenji Sama's chief guest room; it had been hung from ceiling to floor, both walls and windows, with scarlet hangings so that there was no way in which anyone could see in. Someone was dispatched to find Rev. Hajime.

I cannot tell what happened at that ceremony for it is not permitted to be written down. Suffice it to say that there was that between our hearts which was known, has been known and always will be known from the beginning of time. We knew each other completely. We needed no theatrical performances, none of the external trappings that usually ruin religion; just the intense beauty of being together, our hearts One Heart within the Buddha Nature. When he called my name he was not calling my name. When I looked into his eyes it was not Zenji Sama that I saw but Shakyamuni Buddha. Thus between the two of us rose up the most exquisite of all life which is the Life of Buddha itself, it flowed from one to the other directly from the Lord of the House.

The night wore on. He explained many, many things and asked to see my explanations again, the ones that I had written out. When the bell went at three-fifteen in the morning for meditation the ceremony was barely over and he and I went to the Meditation Hall. During the meditation he made an announcement. What he said was that understanding was possible in less than a year if people were truly willing and anxious to meet the Lord and that I was his true descendant. The words seemed to fall on an electrical silence within the Meditation Hall.

All the way back to my room after Morning Service people were looking at me sideways; they did not seem to want to look straight and I had a strange feeling that Rev. Hajime was not nearly as friendly as he had been before. It is odd how close my heart seems to be to everything that matters since last night. I seem to know instinctively what is going on inside everyone.[37] I know and feel their fear, loneliness, prejudices, hates. I feel so much more. I know, above all things, whether they are truly training or not in the real sense of the word. Most people can tell when others are sincere in some sense but not in the real one, not in the only one that really matters. Now I know completely and utterly, for the first time, that the only *real friend* I have in this whole temple is Zenji Sama and when he dies I will really have to leave here very quickly. He is already over eighty. I shall have to be very careful or there will be great difficulty for me here from now on.

This evening the disciplinarian arrived. He smiled at me and brought with him a bottle of whiskey informing me he had every intention of drinking with me and Rev. Hajime. The three of us settled down and, after I had had half a glass, which was very, very little for we were using tiny saké cups, he said, "You see how easy it is to break the Precepts. Last night you promised that you never would and to-day, look at you, you're drinking whiskey!"

"Yes," I said, "to keep the Precepts on that level is an impossibility."

"And?" was his reply.

"There are no Precepts on that level for a man of integrity to keep. All is clean to those who are truly training themselves. To the man of religious *integrity* there is no such thing as indulgence."

"Can you truly and safely live by that?"

"I will try."

"Are you saying that this whiskey is clean?"

"There is nothing wrong with the whiskey; only what people do with it. Human *indulgence* is all that has ever been wrong with whiskey. I have drunk two sips which will relax me and allow me to sleep so I am intensely grateful to the whiskey but I neither want nor need it. What I have said is my understanding of the Middle Way. *I* am in charge of the whiskey; the whiskey is not in charge of *me*."

He nodded. "Good. You have understood well. I do not need to drink any more."

30th. May.

Rev. Ichirō, who had been away for several weeks, came back to-day. As soon as he arrived someone told him that I had been Transmitted and that Zenji Sama had named me as one of his heirs. Rev. Ichirō sent for me at once and ordered me to bring my papers with me. I could not find Rev. Hajime anywhere so there seemed no way in which I could possibly check with him. I went, taking the papers again in their beautiful silken handkerchief. Everything in me wanted to see Rev. Ichirō. Everything in me wanted to embrace him within that which I and Zenji Sama shared for I was sure that it was possible; I was sure that what had been wrong in the past was my fault. Rev. Ichirō had stepped out for a few moments prior to my arrival so I waited with the trainees next door to him; they were having tea.

One of them grabbed me by the arm and said, "Hey, we want to talk to you."

"Really?"

"Yes. We heard what Zenji Sama said this morning. We want to talk to you."

I felt rather shy and looked down at the floor. Just at that moment, however, Rev. Ichirō came by the door and they took me to his room. Looking at me with some disdain he said, "You are too quick to do Transmission. You have not the right."

"It was Zenji Sama's wish, Rev. Ichirō. Surely he has the right to make his own decisions if he wishes."

"How can you possibly understand it?"

"I have brought with me the explanation which I wrote. Perhaps, if you read it, you may know that it *is* possible, even for a woman, to understand some things."

He took the papers from me and read them through slowly. Then he gave me a very strange look.

"I do not know how you have done this."

"Neither do I, Rev. Ichirō; however, I *have* done it and it is thanks to you and everyone here," and I bowed fully to the floor where I sat.

"Let me see your silks."

I handed him the handkerchief and he opened it.

"You have made mistakes. There should be no hard corners on any of these graphs. All of them should have rounded edges."

"Zenji Sama's ones had hard corners, Rev. Ichirō."

"Then Zenji Sama's ones are wrong."

"Yes, Rev. Ichirō, I will tell him."

He gave me a strange look and then said, "No, no, don't, but perhaps sometime you should copy out another set."

"I'd rather not, Rev. Ichirō. I'll remember to tell my disciples to make the corners rounded. It is very easy to remember."

"Zenji Sama did not tell you?"

"No, but Zenji Sama is very old. He probably forgot."

"You must be sure that they are done properly when your descendants copy them."

"Yes, Rev. Ichirō."

"Just a moment. I will send for some trainees and let them see these." He called in the three special ones who lived next door to him and which I had just left, lit incense and showed them the papers and silks. When he had finished he said, "Right, go back to your room now and think carefully over what you have done. I hope, I pray, that it may not have been a mistake on the part of Zenji Sama."

"Can the seeing of God ever be a mistake?" I asked.

"What do you mean, the seeing of God?"

"That's what it is. The recognition of that which is, and was, and always will be. I see no harm, no conceivable harm, that can come to any living thing from such a beautiful experience."

His eyes narrowed. "Get out of here."

I bowed and left the room. When I got back to my own room I found Rev. Hajime sitting at the door of his and told him where I had been. He raised an eyebrow in query and his anger mounted tremendously when he heard. "How *dare* Rev. Ichirō ask to see your papers and silks. There is no person in existence that has the right to do such a thing, absolutely no-one. Didn't you know that?"

"No, I didn't know; I didn't know it at all. I thought it was all right amongst priests. What am I supposed to do? I can't tell a senior that I am going to disobey his orders. When he tells me that I've got to go and see him I have to go and see him. I had no idea that he was not permitted to see the papers and silks."

Rev. Hajime sighed. "People take such advantage of you and they're going to go on doing it. When Zenji Sama is dead you will find life here very dangerous."

"I know. I know that he's the only true friend that I've got in the whole place."

"I'll get some tea for you," he said. "Come back in a few minutes when you've taken your robes off."

I went to my room and found, sitting on the floor, a little, old priest[20] whom I had seen sometimes in the temple but not too often. He bowed to me and said, "I am one of Zenji Sama's oldest disciples. I have come to congratulate you and to thank you for becoming my sister."

"That is very kind of you," I said, bowing in return. "Very kind of you indeed."

"I want to tell you," he said, "one day Zenji Sama will die. Where will you go when he dies?"

"Why, I really hadn't thought about it. I don't think of him as dying."

"I know you don't but you should. You are now his direct descendant as are quite a number of us. It is very important that you think about it. We will not be able to stay here when he is dead."

"Why not? The Vice Abbot likes me very well."

"Yes, the Vice Abbot is a good man. But this is not his temple any more than it is Zenji Sama's except during his lifetime. I do not know that you will be able to stay here after Zenji Sama's death. You should give the matter thought."

"As you wish."

"Have you done your endless bowing yet?"

"Endless bowing?"

"Yes. You should do twenty-five bows at least to the altar in your room here out of sheer gratitude for Zenji Sama's accepting you as his True disciple."

"Oh, I'll do that gladly. I didn't know I was supposed to do it."

"You are."

"Thank you very much."

He looked at me thoughtfully, "OBon dancing rehearsals begin to-day; I presume you will be dancing. Every trainee who has not yet been here a full two years is expected to join in."

"I don't know that I *can* dance; I've been so ill for such a long time I don't know if it is safe for me to try to."

He looked a little concerned, "If you don't I think there will be trouble. You should really try."

"I'll certainly try. I'll certainly go along to the rehearsal and see what happens."

"Good, it takes place at six o'clock to-night."

"I'll go then."

He got up and left. I have never known his name and, although I asked him for it, he did not tell me. At that moment, just as he had left, Rev. Hajime called me into his room through the partition. On arrival there I asked him who the newcomer was.

"He's not very welcome in this temple," he said and there was slight anger in his voice.

"Why?" I asked, "he's such a charming old man."

"He's one of Zenji Sama's older disciples. He's probably ambitious: he'd probably like a job here."

"Surely anyone would like to be in the head temple with Zenji Sama?"

"Huh!"

He did not want to offer any more information so I didn't pursue the matter but simply said, "What's his name, Rev. Hajime?"

"Oh, I don't know. It doesn't matter." He turned away, obviously not wanting to tell me.

"I hear OBon dancing is starting to-night," I said.

"Yes, you will be expected to perform."

"Do you really think it wise, knowing how ill I've been? I'm still taking the doctor's powders three times a day. They make me awfully tired. There are times when I stand up and . . . I quite . . . I almost reel about. I don't know if I *can* dance."

"Well, you had better go along and see." He seemed very off hand; not interested in doing anything in particular. So, after we had drunk tea, I went away. Somehow something has gone sour in him since last night.[4] No, that's wrong, something has gone sour in him since this morning. Since Zenji Sama made that announcement in the Zendō the whole place has gone strange.[4]

Around six o'clock this evening I went along to the OBon dancing rehearsal and the first thing that happened was that I found myself surrounded by dozens of juniors, all eager and anxious to talk. I talked as best I could to most of them and then Rev. Ichirō came on the scene. He got very, very angry because they should not be talking to me and I should be dancing. It was a little strange since the dancing had not yet started. Anyway, somebody got the record player going and the instructor started explaining the dance movements. I tried joining in on the first dance but almost collapsed halfway through the first section so went quickly to sit on the grass at the side. We were performing outside in the evening air.

Rev. Ichirō came over. "I suppose now you are going to pretend you are not strong enough to do it."

"I'm not pretending, Rev. Ichirō. I'm *not* strong enough to do it."

"If you're strong enough to stay up all night to do Transmission . . . ."

"Yes,—yes, I was and I felt pretty awful all day long, physically, because of it. But I went. It was not something I can do any night of the week and it certainly didn't take the sort of exertion that this is taking."

"All those bows didn't take a lot of exertion?" Sarcasm showed in his voice.

"Yes, I told you it took a lot of exertion, but not of the dancing type; and I've had a lot of sleep during the day. But I really can't dance. There's a difference between doing a big ceremony and resting afterwards and dancing around half the night." I was determined not to be angry.

"Oh, well, I'll just have to tell Zenji Sama that you're not willing to join in with the others in the temple," he said and swept away.

I watched the others dance. They obviously all wanted to be friendly but they saw Rev. Ichirō and they looked side-ways or away. After a bit I went back to my room. I thought about some of the things Zenji Sama had told me. The warmth and the joy glowed inside me.[37] The silly things of the day and Rev. Ichirō didn't seem to be important at all.

5th. June.

Sesshin started this morning. Halfway through the afternoon I collapsed and was unable to go back to the Meditation Hall. I had returned to my room for just a few minutes before tea because I thought that I was going to be ill and I didn't want to collapse in the Meditation Hall itself. I barely made it in through the door before I actually fell. Rev. Hajime sent for the doctor and he was, as usual, angry. But he now has a resigned shrug that isn't helping matters at all for it is making a lot of other people angry.

6th. June.

Went back to Sesshin this morning and, as the beating was continued, as the kyosaku thundered round, I felt myself so wonderfully anchored, so still, so strong. It was as if I was rooted in iron; sitting there firm as a rock, immovable. It didn't matter whether I died or lived; and what was inside me didn't care whether I died or lived. It was still and magnificent, and always has been, always will be.[37]

9th. June.

Sesshin ended to-day but in many respects it has been the most wonderful Sesshin of all. I just sat there still, magnificent as a rock, as if an iron being, an iron man; and all the thunder and the roar has gone round, the world gone crazy, the beatings, the yelling, everything happening; and I sat still, unmoved by anything. It was as if I was but a stone that had been thrown into a pond; a stone that had fallen to the bottom and lay there still. The ripples spread out in all directions and I could feel, as they went, that they comforted others and others comforted me. I could feel others sitting still within this still centre and all the thunder and the roar going on round them. It didn't matter in the least for everybody and everything was still.[37]

And then Sesshin was over; the most wonderful Sesshin of all. Around ten o'clock this evening the doctor arrived and insisted that I rest whether the temple likes it or not. He gave his shrug after hearing about Sesshin and said that the temple didn't care whether I lived or died. Perhaps he's reasonable. After all, I and they haven't taken all that much notice of what he has said. But how *can* I be ill here? This temple is hardly geared for sick people. Well, there's not an awful lot to do from now on until next term anyway. I can go to all the ceremonies, Morning Service and meditation and I can rest in between as much as possible. Somehow I'll manage to get some rest.

10th. July.

I've been in bed on and off ever since my last entry. A lot of people complained. We've done a lot of translating, Rev. Hajime and I, and Rev. Ichirō has been his usual unfriendly[4] self. Some of the trainees have been kind and some have been nasty. It's really been a perfectly normal slice of life I suppose, just that and nothing more. And still I sit where the Iron Being sits. It's fascinating to know that it doesn't care whether I live or die and that it doesn't matter; and yet it matters because I must always, at all times, continue to train; I must spread the ripples in all directions. It's fascinating to both spread, and receive, them from others; the ripples of strength, the ripples of iron.

13th. July.

The OBon dancing ceremony took place to-day for the opening of the festival of OBon. At about six o'clock this evening everyone was summoned to the gardens for a group photograph before the ceremonies began. Zenji Sama had his special chair carried to the centre of the grounds near the tower on which the OBon dance band, which consists primarily of drums and a record player on the top platform and those who are doing the demonstration dancing on the second, is situated. The chair was placed in front and all the officers grouped round him with the junior trainees behind. Zenji Sama settled down on his seat. I had chosen for myself an almost hidden place right at the back but Zenji Sama turned round, hunting for me. Suddenly I was grabbed by one of the prefect trainees and informed that I had to stand right behind Zenji Sama. There were murmurs of dissent in the crowd, silenced instantly by a glower from Zenji Sama and, like it or lump it, I was put behind him.

When the photograph had been taken, the ceremony to start the dancing and to open the temple altars for everyone who wished their dead to partake of holy food was performed. There was another group photograph and Zenji Sama again insisted that I stand behind him for this one. A number of people complained terribly, especially about the fact that a foreigner was going to be dancing and allowed at the ceremonies. I decided to say absolutely nothing.

When the dancing was over (and I did my best *not* to dance very much) I went back to my room. Rev. Hajime called me into his. "You understood the OBon dancing?" he asked.

"Yes, I think so. As I understand it, it is the time when everyone remembers their dead and so they have a great festival for everyone to join in. It's a memorial service, ... memorial ceremony, ... "

"It began a little differently from that. It was started as a ceremony by the Tokugawas when Christianity first came here. The Christians did very well and then the Portuguese and the Dutch started using Christianity as a means of controlling Japan politically which resulted in Christians being persecuted. At this time, since there were quite a number of Japanese who were Christians, the ceremony was started. The priests went round blessing all the private Buddhist altars in people's houses by order of the Tokugawas. It was the priests' duty to see if there were any marks on the statues of the Buddha that were of a Christian nature and, if there were, to have the family brought to justice. The official excuse for doing this was that there was going to be a festival to remember all the dead; the OBon Festival.

"I think the *religious* meaning is possibly the same as that of the Christian All Souls Day," I said.

"What do you mean by 'All Souls?' " he asked.

"It's when people remember the dead—when they commend them to God—in Christianity."

"Yes, that would be about the same thing except that here we believe that they need much more help than that. They need to be fed spiritual food in the place to which they have gone."

"What do you mean by 'fed?' "

"Well, most people, when they are very, very normal have a lot of problems. They frequently do not die in the best of spiritual states. Because of this Buddhists believe that they spend at least three years in hell which isn't, of course, a permanent place. It's somewhere where they will account for their karma."

"Surely specific hells have nothing to do with Zen doctrine at all?"

"Oh, no, this is something that has crept in as a result of national usage, just that and nothing more,[38] but it is a widespread belief. These people are believed, because they are in the world of the Hungry Ghosts or hells, not to be able to take spiritual food since, every time they try to eat, the food turns to fire as does everything they drink."

"So that is the meaning of those pictures of the hungry ghosts; the tiny throats can't swallow anything. The bellies are huge and distorted because they're so hungry."

"Yes, but you should understand that, in the religious sense, it is not food that they're having the problem with. It is True Teaching, True Religion. They're so narrow-minded, their throats are so constricted, they can't *understand* or take anything in."

"Yes, I can understand that quite clearly."

"We, as Buddhist priests, take it on a practical level because the average peasant can't understand what I have just said. We have a big feast during OBon, called Segaki, at which everyone can offer food to his dead relatives and friends in the hope that, wherever they are, what has been offered to the priests here will be offered to the dead in the place where they are. The dead can acquire the merit and become free."

"I see, so that is the meaning of OBon."

"Yes, and we have the dancing and the lanterns because we're overjoyed at being able to help the dead."

"That makes very good sense."

"It also made good political sense," he said with a chuckle. "It certainly resolved the Tokugawas' problems and it resulted in the deaths of a good many hundred Christians."

He looked at me suddenly and said, "You know, it's going to be a hard day to-morrow. We've got to go round and open all the altars."

"Can I come?"

"No, you cannot. It would be very embarrassing for many Japanese to have a foreigner at the ceremonies. After all, many of their dead were young people who were killed during the war."

I gulped. It was useless to try and explain to him that many young Britons were killed during the war and that that would not stop us from having a Japanese come round if he were a priest. It was useless to try and explain that sort of thing. Perhaps one day it will be different.

"Good-night," I said.

"What are you going to bed for?"

"The bell has gone, Rev. Hajime. I don't want to disobey the rules. Good-night," and I left him.

The reason I had given was not the real one and he knew it.

14th. July.

After Morning Service and meditation I went to Rev. Hajime's room before he went off to do the OBon ceremonies.

"Rev. Hajime," I said, "do you think it would be possible for me to go down to your family temple in the west? Do you think I could, really? I'm terrified of being left behind here for the summer. Well, not terrified exactly, that's the wrong word; but I don't think it would be wise after what happened last year. I'll pay your wife if she will let me stay and rest."

He looked at me for a long time and then said, "If Zenji Sama agrees I'll let you come." I bowed and thanked him.

About two o'clock this afternoon I went to see Zenji Sama and, without any difficulty, was able to see him immediately. I explained to him what I had come for; I had written it down first. He smiled and said, "Yes, you need a rest, it will do you good. I'll gladly let you go," and he gave me ten thousand yen for the fare and to help with the financial situation when I got there.

When Rev. Hajime came back I told him all this and he said, "Mmm, he didn't give you very much, did he?"

"Well, I didn't expect him to give me anything, Rev. Hajime."

"You're his direct descendant; he should have given you much more that. Besides, that's not enough for my wife."

"Well, don't worry. I'll pay more than that; there's no problem."

"Hmm, well, we'll see."

Something a little disquieting went on in my mind. Perhaps, ... perhaps I shouldn't have asked. I turned at the door.

"Rev. Hajime, don't have me unless you really, really don't mind my resting."

"Oh, no, no, it's fine," he was all smiles again, "Fine, no problem whatsoever. I'll look forward to having you. We'll be going down on the eighteenth."

I bowed and thanked him.

18th. July.

After what seemed to be an incredibly long journey I arrived at Rev. Hajime's temple. It is very beautiful, very quiet and very large for a small country town. As soon as we arrived I was greeted by his wife and children and it was suggested that I rest at once. I was extremely grateful for the journey had certainly exhausted me.

21st. July.

It was wonderful to have these few days to lie still, not doing very much more than getting up for meals and cleaning my room. It is so wonderful not to have to rush about behind bells. I was somewhat concerned at lunch to-day, however, by a very strange expression on the face of Rev. Hajime's wife. She and her husband kept looking at me sideways. There had obviously been some sort of discussion of which I must have been the subject but of which I knew nothing. After the meal was over Rev. Hajime called me into his room.

"I want to talk to you," he said.

"Yes?"

"My wife and I had a discussion last night as to whether or not we should throw you out. We decided against it, though."

Something seemed to clutch at me inside and I felt my heart give a sickening lurch. "Throw me out, Rev. Hajime? Have I done something wrong?"

"You should understand that, since you are a guest in my house, you should do everything that is required of you."

"I didn't know that anything had been required of me. I thought I was just here to rest. That was the arrangement, anyway."

"It is not the arrangement in my wife's mind; besides, she wants to know how long you are going to be here."

"Oh, I can go to-day if that's what you wish me to do. I . . . I have no definite plans, Rev. Hajime."

"I want you to stay here until the end of August when I go back."

"I can't do that if your wife isn't happy about it."

"If you go back before that Zenji Sama will be very angry with me."

"Yes, I understand that. But . . . but I . . . I can't—sort of—stay in somebody's house if they are not willing."

"How much money have you got? I want you to stay until the end of August."

"Oh, how much is it going to cost for me to stay here until the end of August?"

"A lot more than Zenji Sama gave you."

I could feel my heart bumping round and I knew that I needed to take some more medicine.

"Rev. Hajime, what have I done wrong?"

"My wife wanted the toilets cleaned out; she wanted the kitchen scrubbed. You're in bed."

"Rev. Hajime, I'm *supposed* to be here for a rest."

"Well, we can't have somebody here who's just resting about; people will talk. You'll have to do everything she wants, otherwise you can't stay."

"That's fine, Rev. Hajime, I'll go back to Tokyo right now."

He looked at me. "You can't do that."

"Yes, I can. It's the only sensible thing to do."

"Go to your room and stay there."

I left him, went back to my room and started to pack. I was all packed within ten minutes. Nothing happened so I took some more medicine and, carrying my two little cases, went to the front of the temple. There, on the steps, I found him and his wife sitting together.

"Where do you think you're going?" he asked.

"I'm going to the station, Rev. Hajime."

"You're going to do no such thing."

"Look, I can't stay here. You obviously don't want me to."

"We'll give you a definite decision in twenty-four hours. Now go back to your room."

"*I* want to go, Rev. Hajime."

"If you go I'll make it impossible for you to stay in the temple with Zenji Sama."

I looked at him. For the first time in a long, long time I saw again something that had worried me once before, a look of incredible selfishness. I turned away.

"All right. I'll go back to my room but I *want* to go back to Tokyo."

I heard nothing more from either of them all day. I didn't go to supper.

22nd July.

I didn't go to breakfast this morning; I went wandering in the graveyard instead. There Rev. Hajime found me.

"We've decided that we'll let you stay," he said.

His whole attitude was totally different. He was smiling, his old benign self again but, as far as I was concerned, my whole rest had been ruined. The peace of the place had gone.

"I don't *want* to stay, Rev. Hajime. Please let me go." My voice was very quiet.

His face went hard instantly. "Do you want to ruin me in Tokyo?"

"Of course I don't."

"But, if you go back now, that's what will happen. Zenji Sama will never forgive me."

"That's the measure of it, isn't it?" I said.

"What do you mean?"

"The measure of it is *your* advancement in Tokyo, not that I get better."

"Of course I'm concerned that you get better."

"Yes,—yes, you're concerned that I get better!"

"Come along, it's breakfast time! You've got to come and have breakfast! After that we'll be translating into English a lot of the things that Zenji Sama gave you for your Transmission. It's very important that we do this."

"I'd sooner get someone else to do it with me, Rev. Hajime."

"Nonsense! Zenji Sama has given you to me. We will start immediately after breakfast."

In the living-room Rev. Hajime's wife was sitting at the breakfast table. She was obviously trying to be friendly but it was also equally obvious that she hated my guts. I ate unhappily. Rev. Hajime dragged me off to one of the guest rooms where we started translating.

Halfway through the first of the secret papers he said, "Japanese woman wears a white hat at her wedding so that her horns of jealousy shall not show too often. Sometimes wives forget this."

I made no comment but continued to write. We spent most of the day translating; towards evening I became so weak that I requested a rest.

He said, "Aren't you going to do any housework?"

I shook myself and said, "What needs to be done?"

He looked at me oddly and then said, "You'd better go and rest."

25th July.

After breakfast this morning Rev. Hajime's wife informed me that I had got to start taking services in the temple. I thanked her and said that I would enjoy doing them very much. There are many memorial services for people whose dead relatives are in the graveyard outside. I was also informed that, since Rev. Hajime was on holiday, I must do Morning and Evening Service for him so that he can have a rest.

I got down to doing these and thoroughly enjoyed them. It's rather fun being able to use all the different instruments and finding out what they can actually do and what they can't. I have never been allowed to do anything of the sort in the temple in Tokyo.

After lunch Rev. Hajime informed me that I was to go round with him for his parish OBon ceremonies; I was to carry the bags as he went from house to house. He insisted that I walk behind him. After we had gone some distance I felt that it was virtually impossible for me to go on with the weight of the bags in the intense heat for my heart was causing me so many problems. I begged him to let me go back but he refused. When I got back to his temple later I was so exhausted that I collapsed on the floor in my room. There I remained until some time later when I came to to find his wife sitting on the floor beside me, her mouth pouting angrily.

I sat up, feeling my heart jerk, and asked if there was something I could do.

"Yes," she said. "How long do you propose to stay here?"

Something inside me groaned 'not this again.' "I am perfectly willing to go whenever you wish," I said.

Just then Rev. Hajime came in, swore at her, told her off and she fled in tears. I asked him what was wrong.

"One of the parishioners came round and asked if you were my new girl friend," he said, giggling all over his face, "It's upset her."

"I'm not surprised," I said. "What amazes me is the callousness with which you're behaving."

"Callous? What is 'callous?' "

"Never mind," I said, "Just you are callous. That is all."

I got up and went into the living-room. He followed and sat down beside me at the table; the wife sat opposite.

He spoke coldly, "Do you know what she wants?"

"No," I said.

"She wants a ring."

"Well, that doesn't seem too dreadful a thing to want. Why shouldn't she want a ring? After all, it's a long time since you gave her one at her wedding."

He stared at me. "It's a wedding ring she wants," he said.

Something shot around and jumped about in my head.

"You mean you *haven't* given her a wedding ring yet?"

"It isn't the custom in this country. Why should a man be bothered to give a woman a wedding ring?"

"I see." There was a resigned tone in my voice, bored almost, hopelessly bored.

"She *wants* a wedding ring," his voice was peevish.

I stood up. "I don't intend to be involved in a quarrel between husband and wife. Please let me go back to Tokyo."

"I won't. You'll stay here. I'm not going to have you ruining me."

"Then count me out of what is going on between you and your wife for it is neither my concern nor my business," and I said this loudly and clearly in the best Japanese I knew.

I left the living-room and went back to my own one, repacked the two or three things that I had taken out of my cases for the previous night and walked out the door; as I slid it open I heard Rev. Hajime and his wife come running out.

"Where are you going?"

"To the station," I said and I walked out of the door.

Halfway down the hill to the station Rev. Hajime caught up with me.

"If you go to that station I'll ruin you with Zenji Sama in Tokyo."

"Go ahead," I said.

He continued to walk beside me; we arrived at the station. As I walked up to the station master to buy my ticket Rev. Hajime forestalled me.

"When does the train arrive from Nara?" he asked.

"Oh, it's already gone," said the station master.

"Good. My foreign guest must have missed her friend. We'll go back now. Good-night."

I turned to look at him, he was all smiles. The station master smiled and closed up the station for it was the last train. I looked at Rev. Hajime. Something inside me wanted to hit him but there was that still, lovely silence inside me, which Zenji Sama has made all the clearer, the Iron Man, and this made all the idiotic things going on outside of me of no matter. I just turned away.

He looked at me, "You must come back now."

"I shall come down for the first train in the morning, Rev. Hajime."

"No, no, you'll feel quite differently in the morning, you'll see."

He grabbed my cases and rushed back up to his temple. There his wife had warmed some saké and was busy making a big meal. Everything was all smiles and happiness. I was the welcome, wonderful guest; and I felt *sick*.[35]

26th. July.

I was so ill to-day that I couldn't get up and go. It's hardly surprising considering all the noise and racket the two have made over my being here in the last few days. It's hardly surprising also considering how drunk Rev. Hajime got last night; and he expected me to get drunk too but I did not. I want to write to Zenji Sama.

This morning another girl priest turned up from Tokyo. Apparently Zenji Sama sent her along to be a companion for me. Zenji Sama really is a wise man. I was a little worried, though, by the way in which Rev. Hajime behaved towards her because it is very obvious that he *does* like women perhaps too much.

28th. July.

Rev. Hajime insisted on taking the other girl and I to Kyoto for the day. I wanted to see some friends anyway and I was able to do so. They were, as I had thought they would be, not too friendly since, after all, they are in Rinzai and I am not. Anyway, it was nice to see them and we all had tea together. We got back rather late. The other girl and Rev. Hajime spent most of the day talking together and I was left to wander round more or less on my own which was very, very pleasant indeed. It's been the pleasantest day since I came down here apart from those first few at the very beginning of my stay. I wrote to Zenji Sama.

1st. August.

I was supposed to go to Nara this morning, along with the other girl and Rev. Hajime, but I was too sick to go so she went with him alone. Rev. Hajime's wife was a bit peeved because I didn't go off with them but it really wasn't possible. I would only have ruined the day for both of them. There's one thing though; I've heard no more about the family squabbles since my determined efforts to go off. Every day Rev. Hajime tells me how important it is for him, and for me, that I stay here and how anxious he is to continue the translations; we've managed to do two or three hours every day. He's a bit bombastic about the translations now. He insists that some of them be done in really atrocious English because it makes a more exact translation. At a later date I'll sort it all out; when I'm away from here though, not here.

2nd. August.

I came into breakfast this morning to find both Rev. Hajime and his wife, as well as the other girl, looking very worried. The memorial service for the atomic bombing of Hiroshima and Nagasaki is to take place in a few days time and some of the townsfolk are furious because I am a foreigner. It seems I represent everything that happened in that bombing. I wasn't sure whether Rev. Hajime and his wife were more concerned for their own safety or for mine. Anyway I promised them that I'd keep well out of the way and not go out at all so as not to cause any problems just in case there are demonstrations. Around this time, I am told, everybody gets really upset over that memorial ceremony.

3rd. August.

I became so ill again to-day that it was not possible for me to get up at all. It is obvious that, even if Zenji Sama permits me to return to Tokyo when he receives my letter, I shall be too unwell to travel alone.

7th. August.

I have been desperately ill since the third. To-day was the first time I have been able to get up and go to the living-room or be with other people. I find it increasingly difficult to live in a country where children are given the rights of adults—I don't know what I'm trying to say—so much I want to write down—but I can't make it make sense for the moment. I was able to walk around a little and be up for a bit. I'll try and write out what I meant about the children later.

8th. August.

Still no answer from Zenji Sama. There is a small wooded mountain, or fairly high hill, behind this temple. I was advised to go there, or anywhere, to-day because of the hatred of foreigners over the atomic bombing memorial ceremony. Rev. Hajime gave me some food to take with me and I climbed the hill very slowly and lay down beneath the trees for most of the day.

When I returned in the evening his wife was angry. She felt that I should have been there to answer questions as to why so evil a bombing was permitted. It was useless for me to explain to her that I was British and, at the time of the bombing, almost a child. I couldn't be responsible for it. Knowing the useless-ness of any explanation I didn't try to make one. I just bowed to her. Later in the evening the ceremony was reshown on T.V. and she became even more angry. She insisted that I should do a thousand bows for what had happened, I told her I was quite willing to go off again if she wanted me to and she changed instantly. Her eldest daughter told her she was wrong to behave thus but the wife became very angry with her although she is twenty-three. I left the room. It was obvious that only the wife was angry, not the town. The whole thing was so incredibly painful, so hopelessly distorted; and yet the stillness remains within, unmoved and certain.[39] I thank whatever powers there be for the fact that I met Zenji Sama; that he taught me how to be still within myself. And I also thank whatever powers there be that I have been able to see what is going on here. How glad I am that I am British!

15th. August.

Still no word from Zenji Sama. The temple OBon ceremonies started to-day. Rev. Hajime insisted that I become his
assistant, carrying the incense for him. It seems that, after the
incidents over the Hiroshima memorial ceremony, he feels that
some sort of genuine attempt must be made to force his wife to
at least be reasonably friendly towards a foreigner. As a result I
found myself carrying the incense offerings for the ceremonies.
After the first few, which were a little tense, the congregation
almost began to be friendly; this helped much. In fact, it meant
that, in the end, we were all able to have a meal and a drink
together. In many respects it's been a very happy day. At least
there was some *genuine* attempt at becoming friendly. If once
the Japanese can understand that I have two eyes and a nose, as
they have, all may yet be well.

16th. August.

Rev. Hajime took me to quite a number of outside ceremonies to-day after another big quarrel with his wife; she was
determined that I should not stay in the temple. I begged and
begged him to let me go but he says that he doesn't care what
happens now; he is not going to let his wife win the argument.
It is really a terrible situation to be in. I telephoned Tokyo and
asked if I could speak to Zenji Sama to tell him that I wanted to
come back but it seems that he is away and will be until I get
back on the twenty-eighth.

17th. August.

There were more ceremonies, hundreds more. I'm almost
reciting the Scriptures in my sleep. Rev. Hajime said to me this
morning, "Why can't my wife be like you?" I must get *out* of
here.[39] If only I had somewhere to go. I *could* telephone the
British Consulate but how would I explain the situation? No-
one would believe me; I don't *know* anyone and I cannot afford
a hotel—they charge the earth.

We have been continuing to translate slowly but surely. We
have almost completely finished all of the special ceremonies

and the secret papers that Zenji Sama gave me at my Transmission. If it hadn't been for that, and the fact that I've been writing a fair copy of them, I think I'd have gone mad this month. And yet—I know I wouldn't. Nothing can drive me mad any longer, not even the idiocy that's going on here.

28th. August.

Oddly enough, for the last ten days, things have gone really well. The wife seems to have made a genuine effort to try and like me and I know I've made a similar effort to try and like her. My health has improved a bit too and we've finished all the translations. We go back sometime to-day and I'm really looking forward to it.

1st. September.

The new list of jobs has gone up in the temple and, to my joy, I've discovered that Zenji Sama has approved of my going to one of the side temples here to learn ceremonial. It means that at last he is really going to let me become a priest. It's so wonderful to think of. Admittedly, it's only the very poor man's temple, the place where all the people who really can't afford a ceremony go; where all the bottom-grade trainees are sent when they have to learn to do ceremonial. But never mind—it means that at least I'm going to learn. I did something like ten ceremonies there, all very short, only about ten minutes each, this morning. I either carried the incense or played the instruments; and on two occasions I was allowed to actually do the precenting. This made Rev. Ichirō angry afterwards; one of the juniors told him about it. Apparently he wanted the job himself. I bet that causes some problems later on.

2nd. September.

Zenji Sama sent for me this morning and wanted to know how my holiday had gone. Rev. Hajime insisted on coming with me and told him a long story of all the places we had visited and what a wonderful time we had had. I listened to him and decided to say nothing. After all, what would be the point?

If I create more problems here, in a country which, at best, is only just about tolerating foreigners and, at worst, hates their guts,[35] I could do Zenji Sama as much harm as I could do myself. I must remember that, when one is in a foreign country, one likes everyone until one leaves. I have forgotten who said that but, by golly, he certainly knew what he was talking about.

I see from the notice board that there is another foreigner due to arrive from England; somebody called Jim Harris. It'll be nice to have somebody else in the temple who speaks English and can share in the miseries of being foreign.[35]

The great ceremonies start to-morrow; they have them in Autumn the same as they do in Spring but they don't include the specific Jūkai ceremonies. These now are big memorial services for anyone who wishes to come. They'll be interesting; I'll have a lot of work in my new job. I wish my heart felt better.

8th. September.

Rev. Hajime has continued his translations; we've been working like mad. My heart gives me trouble on and off. Rev. Ichirō made it impossible for me to do the precenting in the temple ever again because, he says, there are enough young Japanese who want the job. Anyway, I did quite a lot of it when I was in Rev. Hajime's temple; it probably won't matter terribly much. I've now got quite a fair copy, in English, of everything we did at Transmission. Now I've got to work it all out and understand it clearly. Zenji Sama gave me a good explanation of it.

9th. September.

I met Jim Harris this morning. I have watched him come and go ever since he arrived and this was the first opportunity I had of meeting him. He managed somehow to get to my room without being stopped by anyone else here. So far Rev. Ichirō has had him so much under his thumb that we have had no opportunity of meeting whatsoever. He told me how much he wanted to be ordained as a member of the priesthood and I asked him if he had any idea of what would be involved; he said yes because he had already gone through one ceremony (I presume it must have been Jūkai). I told him that I thought he should approach someone like Rev. Hajime or Rev. Ichirō and he went away.

Some hours later he came back to me with a very strange look on his face. "Rev. Ichirō says that I am already ordained."

"But how's that possible? You don't wear robes and you have an unshaven head."

"I know," he said, "I find it very odd."

We spent the rest of the day together. It was good to have someone to talk to in English. It's a pity he has to go off to-morrow.

10th. September.

Jim went away to-day; I saw him off at the station. He promised me he would write.

11th. September.

There were many, many ceremonies to-day; there must have been twenty-three or so and we were still working on more translations of the Denkōroku and other things. It has been a wonderful day. I do wish I felt stronger.

12th. September.

I had a letter from Jim this morning. He still wants to be ordained; it's now rather worrying since he says he wants to be ordained by me. I have refused.

15th. September.

I don't know how he could have done it; Jim wrote to Zenji Sama. Yes, Jim wrote to Zenji Sama to complain about my refusal to ordain him. Zenji Sama sent for me, it was the first time I have ever seen him really angry, and told me exactly what he thought of me for refusing to ordain another human being. It was useless for me to point out that I had only recently been Transmitted and that I didn't know that I *could* ordain anybody yet. It was equally useless for me to point out that I thought that he had already been ordained. In the end I gave up.

I went to see Rev. Hajime and told him all that had happened; he grinned all over his face.

"Zenji Sama wants some grand-disciples," he said.

"Rev. Hajime, if this man has *already* been ordained by somebody else how the heck can I ordain him? All I'm going to do is cause all sorts of problems."

"Yes, that's for certain!" his voice was sarcastically dry and unhelpful.

"I don't know how to do the ordination ceremony; for that matter, I don't believe it's in English; we haven't translated it yet. How can I possibly ordain him? What about the legal side of it? Getting the forms from the administration and that sort of thing?"

"Easily done, and there's also the fact that we can translate the ordination ceremony. I'll tell Zenji Sama in the morning that we're starting the translation so that he can get it done in English. Many people don't register their disciples at all but it can be done if you wish."[40]

"Rev. Hajime, I don't *want* to ordain him."

"Nonsense. You want to. Every trainee in existence wants disciples."

"I don't know about that; there's something about him I don't want."

"That is bad Buddhism and you know it."

"Yes, I'm sorry, you're right on that."

It's amazing how he has changed since we came back; his behaviour has returned completely to what it was like before we went away; if anything, he is much more friendly than in the beginning. I must be careful not to go anywhere near his home in the future. He found a copy of the ceremony book and we started work on the translation of the ordination ceremony.

16th. September.

This morning Rev. Hajime told Zenji Sama that we are starting work on translating the ordination ceremony and Zenji Sama was all smiles.

20th. September.

We finished the translation of the ceremony this morning. We've done it in both English and Romanised Japanese so that it will be understood by everyone there.

Life here has been very pleasant since we came back but I'm a little worried about Rev. Hajime. I would have said he has become almost—fond of me. It's rather frightening; I don't want to cross swords with, or cause pain to, his wife under any circumstances. I came here to be a priest; just that and nothing more.

23rd. September.

Many Western visitors came to-day, all of them from various American bases. It seems they remembered me from the time they came here to dinner. They wanted to know if I could spend some time on their bases now and again, give some lectures and get to know them. The invitations were numerous; it was very wonderful to meet them all. I agreed that I would come and many gave me their names and addresses; two of them especially said that if I ever needed help I was to let them know since they are in important positions and can give me help if necessary. They were particularly worried about my health. I thanked them very much and assured them I would contact them in time of need.

27th. September.

Term has been going really well. It's amazing the amount I've learned; it's equally amazing how much translating has been done. We've worked and worked and worked. Only one thing is worrying; the danger with Rev. Hajime is getting worse. There's no doubt in my mind now that he really likes me. What really shocks me is—that I *could* like him. I must keep an eye on this with great care. I must *not* allow it to happen. It could be so very dangerous.

15th. November.

Zenji Sama called me to him and, in a voice of thunder, told me to either go and ordain Jim or leave his temple. Apparently

Jim has written to him again. I bowed and promised him that I would go as soon as I could make the arrangements. Rev. Hajime suggested that I should go sometime when Rev. Ichirō is not in the temple; it seems that he will be away around the 20th. of November. I don't like doing things by these hole and corner methods.[34] Why the heck can't they be done openly?

26th. November.

I arrived to-day at the temple in Kyushu where Jim is staying. The people here seem very, very anxious that I should understand that he has already been ordained. I was shown a certificate he has and it certainly looks as though he *has* been ordained. In desperation I rang Zenji Sama but he refused to listen and said that, if I didn't get on with the ceremony forthwith, he'd forget he'd ever known me. Meanwhile, the priests here, especially the elderly one in charge of the temple, have been ringing up the Patriarch, of all people, to tell him what I'm trying to do. Arguments flew back and forth between Zenji Sama and the Patriarch. It is so worrying. My heart is rushing round. Rev. Ichirō is one of the Patriarch's people and the priest here got hold of him. He exploded at me over the 'phone. Now it seems that, if I do the ordination, I'll please Zenji Sama but upset the Patriarch and, if I don't do the ordination, I don't know whether I'll please the Patriarch but I *do* know I'll be thrown out by Zenji Sama. Under the circumstances all I can do is perform the ceremony; no trainee may ever disobey his own master.

The calls shot back and forth from Tokyo to Kyushu; they must have cost a fortune. Two local priests turned up and tried to persuade me not to do the ceremony but I decided that I must be adamant; I've got to go ahead with it.

28th. November.

I did Jim's ordination to-day. There have been nothing but 'phone calls ever since I got here; yells and screams from the one side and exhortations from the other; but I did the ceremony. One of the two priests who was here tried to grab the razor from me as I was shaving Jim's head but he didn't succeed. Just before the ceremony itself they threatened me with . . . I don't know what they *didn't* threaten me with.

Finally Jim turned to them and said, "If you don't let this go through I'll go down to the river bank and cut my own hair." After that they let the ceremony take place. One of them still tried to grab the razor, though, as I said, as I was cutting the last piece of hair from his head.

When the ceremony was over everybody suddenly relaxed. There was a huge meal; there were flagons of saké; the priest who tried to grab the razor now tried to get drunk and succeeded very well as did the other one who was with him. The two insisted that both Jim and I drink a lot to celebrate but I just did *not* want to. I drank a little and so did Jim. Halfway through the meal we were both appalled by a conversation which we couldn't help overhearing since it was at the table where we were sitting. The one who had tried to grab the razor was saying to the other, "This one will be fine; he's really perfect." "Yes," the other one was saying. "He'll be really perfect for someone or other."

I presumed that it was the drink that was talking; I *hoped* it was. The drinking went on. I had a bowl under the table and was carefully emptying my glasses into it each time they were refilled but there was no stopping the two priests, who were drinking like mad, or the head of the temple who was plying them with full cups. Finally one of the two leaned across the table and gave me a great sploshing kiss. He was so drunk he didn't even know where to aim so it landed in my left eye. He then slumped backwards and fell on the floor in a heap; there the head of the temple covered him with a blanket. The other one sagged down and slept beside the table.

I got up. If it hadn't been for the peace I'd found in meditation I think I would have been in hysterics;[39] Jim was appalled by the whole meal.

I went to my room. I went to bed since it was now about eleven in the evening. There seemed no point in staying up any further.

29th. November.

I woke this morning to discover I had one of the worst cases of tonsillitis I've ever had; whether from the cold in Tokyo, the worry or something else I don't know. My glands were atrociously swollen. I am to stay here a few more days and then go back to Tokyo.

7th. December.

I got back to Tokyo to-day. My neck is still terribly swollen. A friend of mine from Hawaii called to see me. She brought me warm underclothes and some medicine for my tonsillitis. It's helped.

8th. December.

I remembered nothing more of yesterday until now. After my friend had gone I was visited by Rev. Ichirō's junior assistant who requested that I visit Rev. Ichirō's room. I went and the first thing that he said to me, after I'd bowed on arrival, was, "What do you mean by doing this ordination ceremony against the wishes of the Patriarch?"

"It was according to the wish of Zenji Sama," I said. "I cannot disobey my true master."

"You disobeyed the Patriarch!"

"When he stands in the way of my true master I have no alternative."

He eyed me coldly. "He had already been ordained! You have stolen this disciple to be a grand-disciple for Zenji Sama! He does not belong to your line. He will never be your disciple and I shall see to it that he will never be your disciple!"

"I did not want him for my disciple. I told you that, I think, when you telephoned me. At any rate, I told someone; maybe it was Rev. Hajime, I can't remember now."

My tonsillitis was giving me very great pain and there was nothing much I really felt like discussing with this man. He ranted and raged for a long time then he grabbed a stick from under the cushion he was sitting on and said, "I am going to beat you thirty times; you will never forget it."

I looked at him; then suddenly everything went into that strange, slow, adagio dance that it had gone into once before—that it had gone into the night of my kenshō. I remember somehow, instinctively, putting my hands in the gasshō. I felt the blows falling; the only feelings I had were of surprise and amazement. This was actually happening and nothing in me could believe it. It went on and on for some time; he steadily lost control of himself as his temper mounted. A strange silence had come over that entire part of the temple. People in the other rooms, which were only made private by paper dividers, had ceased to say a word. It was as if the whole temple held its breath.

Suddenly, as though something had hit him, not knowing quite what—perhaps it was shame, at least I thought it was for he knew that he had lost his temper and that I had not—he threw the stick from him and yelled, "Things are just as they were! You don't own him! He belongs to our line not yours!"

I said, "People can only belong to a line if they want to belong to it. You have to be willing to be taken by the Buddhas and Patriarchs. You cannot be taken by force. If you disbelieve me study the papers that you received at your own Transmission."

He gulped. I heard a strange sound coming out of him, a rattling noise. I took from my sleeve the letter that Jim had sent me, his request that this ordination be done.

"I obeyed an order from Zenji Sama. I did that which had to be done.[41] It's not my problem that you like it or do not like it."

"Do you want to be beaten again?" he screamed.

"No," I said.

"Then get out of here!"

I rose. I was not conscious of pain for I was already suffering quite enough from the tonsillitis. Fortunately my heart hadn't cracked under the strain; all I could feel was surprise and all I knew was that everything was terribly, desperately slow.

I must have walked back to my room but I don't remember. My next conscious memory is that of waking up in the arms of Rev. Hajime. My head was on his knee and a doctor was bending over me, putting a syringe full of something or other in my arm and telling Rev. Hajime that I was suffering from shock. They then took me to my room and put me to bed.

I don't know where the rest of yesterday and last night went. I suppose I must have slept. The doctor insists I go to hospital. Everything seems to move so slowly. I woke up to see Rev. Hajime with a little spirit stove beside my bed cooking something and the old, old cook, standing there with something that looked tasty in a little bowl, telling Rev. Hajime how to prepare it. He didn't say anything but his eyes were very full of feeling, full and beautiful. Rev. Hajime was all concern and it seemed quite genuine. They finished preparing the food and I took a few mouthfuls.

"Jim insists on coming here," said Rev. Hajime. "Do you like the idea? He wrote to Zenji Sama about it to-day."

"I don't know," I said, "I really don't know."

"You should go into hospital for a time," he said.

"Yes," I said.

25th. December.
Jim arrives to-day; I'm not sure what time.

26th. December.
Jim said that, since he was Zenji Sama's grand-disciple, he had the right to come here just as much as I did.

I went to see Zenji Sama. My legs feel very shaky, my whole body feels as though it's crumbling around me but the Iron Man made it walk.[39] I told Zenji Sama how much Jim wants to stay here and he has agreed that he may.

Rev. Hajime has a new job in a totally different part of the temple. He was moved out this morning. This means that, of course, I have no room since, up until now, the room I have had was the one that had belonged to him when he moved into an empty one to give me a place to live last year; now I have no room at all. Rev. Ichirō came to see me. He informed me that Rev. Hajime would now have no time for doing any sort of translating whatsoever. If it wasn't for the peace inside me I could have sworn that he was gloating.[35] Anyway I now have no room.

I asked for a new one; in the meantime I am in the corridor outside.

31st. December.

All trainees went to see Zenji Sama to-day to thank him for the year and to ask him to continue to teach us for the coming one. Jim came with me.

1st. January.

Jim is causing some problems in the Meditation Hall. He insists on wanting to do things his way rather than the way of the temple. He also insists that his papers be changed to say that he definitely *is* my disciple and not someone else's. It seems that he was originally registered as someone else's disciple although, he says, he did not do the ordination ceremony nor was he told that he had become a trainee-priest. Rev. Hajime went to the administration section to-day to get the papers changed over and was successful. Zenji Sama is very pleased that he is now definitely his.

There seems to be such a lot of fighting over who owns trainees here. I wonder if they understand really and truly that no-one can ever own anything. They're supposed to know it. I wonder why they don't? Ah well, true Buddhists are just as rare as are true Christians I suppose. I still have possessions.

We had barely got the papers back from the administration section when Jim started to complain about my trying to make him keep the rules. Zenji Sama is not pleased about this. He says that I must force him to do what he wants him to do.

2nd. January.

The Patriarch arrived this morning and wanted to see me since he wanted to find out what had happened in Kyushu. After I had bowed I told him, as best I could, what had taken place and he nodded and said that I had done the right thing. He annoyed his assistants greatly by insisting on staying to talk to me since they were afraid he would lose his train. He was a very charming old man and very, very kind. How the heck can such a person as he have a descendant like Rev. Ichirō?[4,35] I must *not* think things like that.

Jim has been complaining bitterly about another sharing his room with him. Apparently the person who made all the arrangements for him to come to Japan promised him a room to himself. He made so much trouble that the temple officers got very, very angry. One of them blew me up for having such a troublesome person in the temple.

I have been informed that the only room available for me is a small three-mat one that is sometimes used by the night watchman. It was suggested Jim move there but he absolutely refused and threatened to write to the person who made his original arrangements. It seems that the officials here are very afraid of outside opinions so it was his roommate that was moved instead.

Meanwhile I have moved from the corridor into the tiny room. It is incredibly small and dark, with no electric light and no windows. Somebody rigged up a tiny bulb in the centre. There's just enough room to stretch out and that's about it—and I and my bed are in there. Oh, well, at least I have no alternative but to lie down now.

3rd. January.

Relations with Jim are worsening. He wants to be here completely on his own terms and not on those of the monastery at all. I had lent him quite a few things so that he would have robes, etcetera, for he has nothing suitable for here. The temple in Kyushu had also given him a tremendous number of brand new clothes. He brought all the things I had lent him and threw them in my room saying he didn't want them and never would want them or me; he then went off in a temper. He hasn't spoken to me since. That was early in the day.

Now it is early evening. I went to see Zenji Sama a few minutes ago and begged him to find me an old temple where I may rest, quite alone, without anyone; just genuinely rest, but he refused. He told me he wants me to promise to stay here until he dies.

6th. January.

A very strange thing happened to-day; it was as though I was failing. It was as if I had turned . . . yes, as if I had turned the wheel of my life in the opposite direction and said, "All right, this is too much. I'm going to go away. I'll leave you my body since you want it. I'll just go." I could feel myself failing. I could feel myself accepting the failure; relaxing various parts of my body into death. My heart is messed up; I've got tonsillitis like hell; Jim has only used me; the political machinations here are unfit to live with; Zenji Sama won't let me go away and Rev. Hajime is obviously helping me only for the purpose of bettering his position and enjoyment.[4, 35] I have watched this last development in horror; it is too dangerous to continue. And so I relaxed into just giving up, being done with it all and then it was that a miracle happened.[37, 42] I can only call it a miracle. I was lying on the floor, having finished the ceremonies of the day, thinking of the Kanzeon Scripture. I had just come to where it says, "When threatened by court judgements or when the military or a tyrant should oppress a man, if he truly thinks upon the name of Kanzeon he will be saved," when the 'phone rang in the office next door and someone told me that the two Americans who had insisted I visit them if I were in need of help had come to see me. I went to the front office, near the front door, and they were appalled at what I looked like. They would hear no excuses, they would not even hear of my seeing Zenji Sama. In no uncertain terms the husband told the office trainee that he was taking me away and that I would not come back again until I was completely better. I was taken right away from Tokyo in a huge car to the military base and there put into a warm, comfortable room with a soft bed. The wife sent for the doctor and that's all I can remember.

15th. January.

I got up for the first time to-day. The doctor has been treating me for exhaustion and malnutrition. My feet were strong; I could walk. My heart didn't rattle around. I don't know what the medicine is that the doctor's been giving me but it certainly works. It was so wonderful to wake up each morning, look out at this beautiful garden and not hear the shouting and screaming and yelling that I have heard since Jim arrived;[4,35] and yet, even through it all, the stillness remained, still as beautiful as it ever was.[39] After all, the horror that goes on in the everyday world is symbolised by the beatings and the stupidity that go on in the Meditation Hall. Everything that goes on in the temple is to teach us to put up with the idiocy of life and not be pulled off centre. I am so grateful to all the trainees who taught me how to find the Iron Man within.

I talked about this and many, many other things to the people in the house. The husband and wife fetched many of their friends and they are going to have a party to-night. I have been talking almost all day. They seem to be quite fascinated by what I am saying.

The party was great fun.

29th. January.

We have had parties almost every night for a week. I am really getting a little bored with them but it's been such a wonderful change. What is even more fascinating is the number of people who really *want* to learn Buddhism. They are sitting round for hours just listening to what I have to say. I did not realise it was that interesting. In fact I did not think it was interesting at all.

3rd. February.

It is good to be back in the temple after so long a time. I had no idea how much I missed it. Anyway, I am back now and I am with Zenji Sama again even if I can't see him every day of the week. This morning Rev. Hajime came to see me.

"I have some news for you," he said.

"Oh, really?" I replied. "What?"

"Rev. Ichirō is going to be sent abroad."

"Whatever for?"

"Well, maybe Zenji Sama thinks that, since he doesn't seem to like foreigners very much, he should go and live among them. That way he can learn that they have the Buddha Nature just as everyone else has."

"That should improve relations between me and the rest of the community no end," I replied.

"What you mean?" he said sharply, lapsing once again into the weird English that I thought he had left behind him over a year ago. "Nothing much; it is just that Rev. Ichirō has an awful lot of friends here. He's a very powerful man as you have said. They're all going to know that he's been—sort of—shall we say removed—as a result of what he got up to with me in November."[43]

"What he think and what other thinks is not your problem!" he replied hotly.

"It is very soon going to be my problem if he has to leave for another country. I do wish you'd stop behaving like an ostrich."

"What is 'ostrich?'"

"It's a bird that buries its head in the sand whenever danger threatens it or anything near it."

"I am not ostrich. I am Japanese man." He thrust his chin out obstinately.

"I've never met anyone so good at avoiding the point at issue as you are," I sighed.

"What is 'point?'"

"It just got lost in the volubility of your comments."

"What is 'volubility?'"

"Look. Let's stop playing games and get back to where we were. You know darned well that if Rev. Ichirō gets thrown out of this temple there's going to be trouble both for me and for you," I felt myself getting tense.[35]

"No, not for me, only for you. Perhaps I am quite safe. I not foreigner like you. Why should I be concerned at what happen to you? That is your problem, not my problem," he turned to the window, the epitome of arrogance.

"There are times when I think you're the biggest humbug that I've ever met." I must watch my disgust;[35] it has been growing ever since his drunken outbursts.

"What is 'humbug?'"

"Well, if you look it up in your dictionary, you'll see that it has two meanings. One is a rather nice, weird shaped peppermint sweet (candy) and the other is somebody who isn't worth knowing. I leave you to work out which is applicable to you."

He suddenly sat down and said, "Shall I make tea?"

"Fine, if you want to."

"Why don't you and I . . . . ?"

I got up and walked to the door, opened it and looked out. "You know, if I were to get a spade, I could dig up a couple of those trees and set them back in the ground with their roots in the air and their branches nicely covered with earth." I knew that my voice was grating;[35] I could not help it.

"What you talk about?" he asked, obviously taken aback.

"I talk about this. You and Nansen have one hell of a lot in common."

"I and Nansen?" he was still bewildered.

"Yes, you and Nansen. Nansen had got things so darned cock-eyed, because he couldn't handle his situation, that all he could do was think of cutting the cat in two. That's exactly what you're doing right now. Dōgen Zenji says, 'Cut the cat in one,' you cut it in two."[44]

"And I suppose you think *you* are greater than Nansen? You can cut cat in one," frustration was causing him to growl; I knew the danger signs; a thunderstorm travelling at a hundred miles an hour.

"I can stick my sandals on my head. If you've got things so damned cock-eyed I might as well dig up a couple of trees and stick them in the ground upside down. Chao-Chou at least understood that Nansen was wrong even if he didn't know how to put the situation right. If your attitude of mind continues, the Buddha Body will be rent and torn and twisted and maltreated, cut in bits; screams and howls will come from every direction.[43] If I were to go to Zenji Sama this morning and get him to change this order perhaps good could come out of it. We've *got* to cut the cat in one. We *can't* cut it in two. Don't you understand what I'm talking about?"

"Why should I understand? It is not my problem." A voice full of frustrated greed.

"Oh, go to hell!"[5,35]

I walked out of the room and made my way through the garden to Zenji Sama's house. It was very early, only just after Morning Service. We hadn't had breakfast yet and it was really highly illegal to go visiting at such an unearthly hour.

I crept into the house avoiding the assistants as best I could by tiptoeing round corners and managed to get at least as far as the first guest room although not to Zenji Sama's room itself. Out came his girl assistant glowering at me, as usual, for arriving at the master's breakfast time.

"I suppose you've come for a meal?"

"No," I said, "I've come to see Zenji Sama. May I see him, please?"

"You may not! He is about to eat."

I had deliberately raised my voice with the words, "May I see him?" for I knew that the paper dividers between his guest room and his living room were so thin that he was bound to hear my voice and know who it was since I was not speaking Japanese. I had deliberately said these words in English knowing full well that she would understand me.

A peremptory order came from behind the screen. She glared at me, said, "Go in!" and walked away.

I went to the door, knelt down and opened it. "Zenji Sama, good morning," I said.

"Come in," he replied. "What is the matter?"

As best I could I told him, in my atrocious Japanese, what was going wrong and what I feared. He looked at me for a long moment.

"Yes, it will be very difficult for you but you should have realised that you were creating the difficulty when you allowed him to beat you," he said quietly.

"How could I have prevented it?"

"You could have refused. By accident someone made the course of karma by registering Jim; you continued it."

"If I had refused I would have had to leave the temple."

"Of course, there would have been no alternative. You would have had to leave the temple for you would have disobeyed a senior," his voice seemed to hold a sigh.

"Then either way I'm stuck."

"Of course, as was Nansen. You quoted Nansen's cat to Rev. Hajime. You took it at one level, now I take it at another. You cut the cat in two when you accepted the beating from Rev. Ichirō and now you have just shown Rev. Hajime that he is cutting the cat in two. At all times the kōan appears on different levels and it is always the same kōan. If your action had been at one with the Truth there would have been no karmic residue."

"Yes, Zenji Sama. You know, I cannot help thinking that, now I have been so ill, perhaps I should have a rest."

"What would you like to do?"

"Is it possible that somewhere in this country there is an old temple that needs a priest which I could take over for a bit?"

"Of course not! Always you are to be here with me. You may not avoid the cutting of the cat," his eyes were full of sadness, as if I had hurt him.

"But Zenji Sama, do you want the cat cut right under your own roof? Do you think it is wise?"

"Do you dare to disobey my order?" There was no anger in his voice.

"No, Zenji Sama."

"Then you should listen to my words. You have cut the cat by permitting this to take place, albeit you had no alternative as you think, but you had an alternative which was to walk out of the temple. There was no problem. You chose to stay in the temple so you had to cut the cat at that level. There was no alternative. Now you can choose again to stay in the temple and fight through the cutting of the cat, stitching its body together again, or you can go off and leave the cat in pieces. Which do you prefer?" His voice was very gentle, applying no pressure either way.

"You know well which I prefer, Zenji Sama, for there is no alternative to it."

"That is good. Then the problem is solved."

"Please may I ask your Lordship a question?"

"You may."

"Surely there must come a time when there *is* no alternative to cutting the cat because not to do so would create some greater ill, some much worse catastrophe, disaster—I don't know. Please, Zenji Sama, surely there *must* be a time, if what you say is true and I do not doubt you, when one *must* cut the cat."

"Yes, there *is* such a time."

"Then I did right in cutting the cat."

"Yes, you did right for then. Now it is right to stitch the cat up again, and to-morrow it may be necessary again to cut the cat."

"Yes, Zenji Sama, I understand your words but I must admit they are very frightening."

He smiled gently. "Life is only a frightening thing without meditation; if we really live it we *must* meditate. Life can be so very terrifying that most people retire from it. They retreat into amusements, play cards or mahjong, go to theatres or lose themselves in drink—or run away to old temples. All this is because they are afraid of cutting the cat when they know they must cut it, and stitching it together again when they know they must stitch it together. The kōan is endless. Always in daily life it appears; and must be mended at all times in daily life. That is the meaning of the kōan in daily life—the genjōkōan. Cutting and stitching and all the time meditating below the turmoil going on around us."

"Yes, Zenji Sama."

The door opened. "Zenji Sama's breakfast is getting very cold."

He looked at me. "We will have tea first," he said. The girl glared and went away to get it.

"To continue with regard to the cutting of the cat. It will be very difficult for you. If your health gets any worse I will definitely think about finding you a temple but you must first make some attempt to put the cat back together," his smile deepened and broadened, almost as if the two of us were conspirators.

"Yes, Zenji Sama, I understand you."

The girl brought in the tea and we drank in silence.

He looked out at the garden and said, "Do you really think you could dig up a tree and stick its roots in the air?"

"I could try," I said, "as did Chao-Chou."

"Yes. Chao-Chou's action, as Dōgen Zenji rightly points out, is the most important part of the story but so few people understand it. I'm so glad that you have done so. Leave me now. I must eat my breakfast."

I bowed to him and left the room. The girl glared again as I went by but I did not care.[5] Somehow I will manage this. Somehow I will manage, Buddha alone knows how, to put the cat back together, but I know a time may come when I will have no alternative but to leave the pieces lying around. This, then, is part, or an aspect, of the *kokoro-kanashiku*, the great grief, that at all times we do the very best we can and that 'best' can never be enough—the Cosmic Buddha, God, is within us—and we are not the Cosmic Buddha, God. This, too, is endless training; the constant trying, the constant going on, always trying to put the cat back together. So long as the *trying* lasts, so will Buddhism. The teaching of both Rev. Hajime and Zenji Sama is identical; the problem came as a result of the former speaking from the point of view of the egocentric self whilst Zenji Sama spoke from that of the Lord of the House and so the latter's teaching cannot only be understood—it can be accepted and applied.

20th. February.

Every day since my last entry (February 3rd.) Americans have been coming here. They are determined not to leave me alone with the Japanese again under any circumstances or so they have said. Many have come for the whole day every Sunday. They keep me company; they come to ceremonies; they come to meditate; they want to form a meditation club. Zenji Sama is overjoyed and it is so wonderful to have people to talk to. They have been bringing me food and medical supplies; above all, they have been bringing me love.

Jim is still not speaking to me but I suppose that cannot be helped. He is working in the kitchen. They are blaming me for the way he is behaving; I barely know him. All I have done is obey an order to ordain him. Maybe I should have done a better job; I should have tried to teach him in a different way perhaps. I must remember that it is I that is always at fault if the pupil does not learn.

10th. March.

Constant stream of foreign visitors, day in and day out. I am hardly ever in the little box room, which is a blessing, and Zenji Sama is even more overjoyed than before. He is now talking almost of having a foreign temple. He is actually beginning to like the idea of finding a small place for me to have because, he says, then the foreigners will have a definite place to go to if anything ever happens to him.

My health has greatly improved but a couple of the American doctors are very concerned about this little room that I am in. They actually spoke to Rev. Hajime about it and just now I heard I am to be moved to what is virtually an outsize cupboard on the other side of the corridor. If I keep the doors open I can see the sun coming in through the windows on the other side of the corridor so at least it will be all right for the Spring, Summer and Autumn. I'm not sure what it will be like in the Winter.

The two doctors were really furious with Jim. They seem to think that he is one of the most selfish people they have ever met but, well . . . what can I do?

He doesn't worry me. If he *wants* to *be* selfish he will have to *be* selfish. I cannot stop him. There is nothing I can do. It takes as long as it takes for someone to convert; *I* found that out last year. There is no way of speeding it up.

My health is greatly improved though. It is so wonderful to feel strong again. I will never be able to thank these Americans enough for what they have done for me. They more or less took someone who was on the edge of death and brought them back to life again. Just before I left the base, on the 2nd. of February, the husband there said to me, "If you ever leave Japan come to America. Please help us with what you have learned here. We

feel sure that you can." I promised him I would. It is a promise
I will keep.

We have not had much time for translations since Rev.
Hajime has had his new job. Administration takes up his time
to a tremendous extent but we have managed to get most of the
ceremonies translated; funeral, wedding and all the things that
will really matter if I ever become a full parish priest as well as
quite a lot of legal stuff that I will need to know. I get the feeling that I am going to need these things fairly soon, especially
since Zenji Sama is so interested in having a temple for foreigners.

8th. April.

We began Jūkai to-day. Rev. Hajime wants Jim to go to
Jūkai; he wants to try to resolve the difficulties between us. He
called him in to see him and told him exactly what he thought
of his selfishness, which didn't have much effect; then he told
him that, unless he did something about it, he would never be
able to go any higher than a bottom-grade junior trainee. This
had some effect and he agreed to come to me and see if there
was any way in which we could work things out.

I have long been beyond caring whether we ever work it out
or not. He has spelled trouble for me from the moment of his
arrival. Anyway, we had tea together and that was it. Rev.
Hajime called me to his room.

"It is Zenji Sama's wish that you should go up the ranks
now that you have got as far as Transmission and have your
own disciple. The next rank is Kessei."

"Don't I have to do Zuisse first?"

"Yes, you *should* do Zuisse first but, you see, you are not a
Japanese and you are not a man. You may have the *rank* of
Zuisse but you may *not* do the ceremony."

"Then I don't think that I'm terribly interested in the rank,"
I said.

"It is necessary that you do it. It is necessary also that you
fight the prejudice against women here."

"Whatever for?"

"For the sake of Japanese women," he said. "Surely that is the least you could do for them?"

"I thought you were against all this sort of thing? I thought you approved of everything that happens to women?"

"I am not any longer sure that what they are doing is right or wrong. I look at you and I look at my wife. In you I see something magnificent and free; I have never met a woman who can think as you think so I wonder about educating women. In my wife I can see that the same things you have are there had she been given the right to use them. I wonder, have men done wrong? To-morrow there will come to this temple the head of all the women priests in this country. She wants to see you. She wants you to try and fight for the right to do Zuisse so that all women may do it. She thinks that you, a foreigner, and the favourite of the archbishop, have a better chance of doing it than has anyone else and, once you have done it, all can do it."

"I see. If that is your wish then that is what I will do." I bowed and left him.

9th. April.

Rev. Myotsu came to-day together with several of the girls from the women's office of the priesthood. We discussed the plight of women for a long time and I discovered the many wonderful things that she has done to help them, not least of which was her going to the administration and, finally, to the Japanese parliament itself to fight for their rights when the war had ended; how she had won for them once more that which they had had in the twelfth century and which the Tokugawas had taken away in the sixteenth, the right to do Transmission. And now she was also trying to win the right to do the congratulatory ceremony of graduation, called Zuisse, at the head temples. All the other higher ceremonies were open to men and women equally; but this one, recognition of graduation by the Emperor was, as yet, not. A woman may be a full priest, complete with certificates, but may *not* graduate publicly. As I listened to her I was fascinated by her courage. Here was a kindred spirit, someone who had suffered the agonies that I had suffered and who was willing to fight on. She told me of another woman in Tokyo who had been in a similar position to me in another of the great temples and who had fought on alone and had succeeded. She renewed my spirit and gave me encouragement. I know it's going to be tough but I'm well now. I'll help her all I can.

I had a long talk with Jim after this. I told him what Rev. Myotsu had told me and the way in which we would be able to help the women if we really tried; he agreed that, whether we like each other or not, whether we get on well or not, we should at least pull together for the sake of others and so it was decided that, when I went on after Zuisse to the higher ranks of the priesthood, he should become my Chief Junior at my ceremony of Kessei.

23rd. April.

To-day I entered Tokubetsu Sōdō so that I can get a Sei degree (roughly equivalent to a Christian Doctor of Divinity). I hear I already have a first.

10th. May.

Since my last entry the foreigners have continued to come as much as ever. I told them that I am to do my Zuisse in the morning and they were overjoyed. Several wished to wait and stay in the temple in order to see it.

At six o'clock this evening I was taken to the special guest hall, dressed in the red kesa and slippers of the graduating priest, to spend the night in the abbot's guest room.

11th. May.

This morning I was taken to the Shrine of the Founders of the temple before the actual ceremony and then trouble struck. Everyone that I could see seemed to be complaining about my doing the ceremony. There was to be one other person who was to do it with me, a young man from another temple, who seemed to rather like the idea of having me with him but everyone said it would be degrading for him to do it with a woman.

The author after her Zuisse ceremony.

Just before the ceremony was due to start I was asked if I would wait to do mine later on. Some sixth sense told me not to and I insisted on doing it together with the young man. I could feel the fury in all the men standing there but I fought on. I was going to do that ceremony; I was not going to wait for I knew there was going to be no second chance if I did.

Standing in the centre of the hall with the two rows of priests on either side of me was like standing in an empty street with shuttered windows waiting for a gun-fight. No-one wanted to look out. No-one wanted to see. No-one wanted to accept; and I didn't care for I *knew* I was right. *I went on!* I listened to the offertory, I heard myself proclaimed priest, I heard the young man proclaimed priest and I didn't care about the chauvinism and the narrowness and the meanness all round me for I had done right.

When I returned to the special guest department in which I had spent the night the certificates that we were to receive were read out but mine was not the normal certificate. It did not say that I had graduated. To my amazement the Director read out a certificate which said that I had been nominated by Zenji Sama to become the Buddhist Bishop of London. I didn't know quite what to do. I didn't know whether I should say, "This is all wrong. I don't want the job. I want the other certificate," whether to be pleased, sorry or startled. I just didn't know what to do. I sat there numb. I had got all this way and what had I got? Was it better or worse? Was it wise or not? Was it *real* or not? Was anything in this place where people lived by trickery worth having?[4,35] And then the Iron Man inside me smiled quietly and said, "It doesn't matter. You are you, always were and always will be. Sit still within your own heart. Care not for what goes on externally."[39]

After the reading I went round to all the different officers of the temple to thank them, as was the custom, but most of them were in such a bad temper over it that I didn't even get a curt nod from many. I received my graduation certificate by post; at the last minute prejudice had intervened to refuse to present it publicly.[45]

12th. May.

Zenji Sama sent for me this morning. He has decided to give me my own temple so that I shall be able to rest more and look after the foreign guests properly. It seems that there is too much hatred of the foreigners here, especially the great numbers in which they are now coming. He wants me to consolidate them so that I may turn them into a firm body that cannot be broken. He has found for me, he said, through Rev. Hajime, a tiny, very old temple. It is extremely poor; the priest who was there before me died of starvation but at least it will be mine. No-one can interfere with me there; that will be wonderful.

He also asked me if I was willing for Jim to officially enter the Meditation Hall here for he has been sitting outside all this time. Something inside me said no and I told him so. I could not give him any reason why. I just knew that it was the right thing to do.

He nodded. "I think you are wise," he said. "I, too, do not yet think that he is fit. I find myself wondering what to believe. We have both seen him, you and I. I think it is well that he does not enter my Meditation Hall; not, at any rate, until you are happy about it."

"I hope that one day he will be able to enter it, Zenji Sama."

He looked at me. "One day all beings must be able to enter it."

"Yes, Zenji Sama."

"To-morrow I want you to go and see your new temple. If you like it let me know. Come back, get your things and stay there, at least temporarily, for I want you to be able to do the ceremonies of Kessei. Before I am dead I want to see you legally able to teach."

"Yes, Zenji Sama, but please don't speak of death."

He smiled. "I am not so young. Now go and leave me."

I bowed and left him.

13th. May.

Rev. Hajime and I journeyed all the way down to see the temple this morning. It took many hours but it was worth doing. It is quite close to Rev. Hajime's own temple; that is about twenty miles away on the other side of a mountain range. It is very small and very derelict but, to me, it looked like Buckingham Palace. It will be mine and mine alone; and here I can rest and help my American friends. Odd that they think I'm teaching them; they do but I don't.

I worked and worked at cleaning the temple up a bit (it was in an awful mess) and I met the town council and a lot of other people and they seemed to like me and I liked them.

We spent the night in the house of one of Rev. Hajime's friends.

14th. May.

We travelled back to Tokyo to-day and I went to see Zenji Sama.

"It's the most beautiful place I've ever seen, Zenji Sama. Thank you for letting me have it."

He smiled gently. "It is time you had it for you are ready and worthy to prepare for the great ceremonies of Kessei, becoming a teacher; and for that you must train your Chief Junior, Jim. He will give you a lot of hard work and a lot of pain." He smiled sadly.

"I'll try all I can, Zenji Sama. I can't tell you anything more than that."

"Go down and get the temple ready. It will need much preparation. By about November it should be ready for the ceremonies and I will send Jim to you just as soon as you are ready for him."

"Do I *have* to go and leave you, Zenji Sama?"

He smiled. "Listen. You have gone through more of a hell here than anybody I know and you've come out of it because you did what had to be done without fear. That could be because I am here or it could be because somebody else is here, I don't know, but you need, above all, to be able to make your way now for yourself completely alone. You have to *choose* whether you want to go on from here and the only way you can do that is to go and be completely alone for a time. If you like, this temple will become your Bo Tree. Sit beneath it, grow, flourish, learn and study in detail. When you are ready, hoist the flag of Kessei that all may come to test, to understand and to be sure."

I bowed. "Thank you, Zenji Sama. I swear to you you shall not lose your faith in me."

A wistful look came over his face. "You say that now but the time *could* come . . . . .[46] At all times you will have to choose which way you will go, that which is contrary to my teaching or according to it. There are only volunteers in Buddhism. This you must know by now. Go now and let me know when you are ready to hoist the flag of Kessei."

"Sayonara, Zenji Sama."

"Sayonara, Jiyu."

We bowed.

This afternoon, having packed what I could that would be of use to me, and with a bed that Zenji Sama has ordered to be mine (a set of large cushions) I was put on the train, with the help of several friends, to go to my new temple.

Here ends the Story of the Trainee.

Book III.
The Parish Priest.

Book III.
The Parish Priest.

16th. May.

I arrived at the station nearest to my temple round three in the afternoon and was met by Rev. Hajime's wife. It was a little worrying meeting her again, after what had happened on our previous acquaintance, but she seemed very friendly and anxious to help; I must admit I was very glad of her aid. She had a taxi waiting at the station and we set off for the village together. It was impossible for the taxi to go up the very narrow village lanes, which are really only suitable for small ox-carts, and so, after the taxi had got stuck at the top end of one of them, we decided that it would be best to get out and carry my cases and the rest of my luggage to the temple. The temple itself is very old, very, very old, about two hundred and fifty years, and that, for an unattended wooden building, means that it is in a bad state of repair as I said earlier; but it doesn't really matter so very much; it is actually mine to rest in. The fact that the doors don't lock and the roof leaks isn't so very important; what is really important is that I shall be able to get better alone; at last be able to rest.

The local town council, as well as the temple council, came to greet me and it was obvious from the beginning that one of them, a woman, was determined that I should spend most of my time in her house rather than live in my own temple. I decided that I was going to discourage this and made it very clear that, however kind her offers of staying in her house were, I had every intention of staying in the temple itself and nowhere else. I hope this didn't annoy her but really there is nothing else to do. My bed and a number of other things had already been sent on before me and delivered, for some reason, to this woman's house. I was, however, able, with the assistance of an ox-cart, to take everything to the temple. There I began to unpack. It was somewhat disconcerting to see every "child" in the village that was under the age of twenty-one staring in through the windows watching me but I suppose this was to be expected. I mentioned the matter to Rev. Hajime's wife and she suggested we put up the wooden shutters. For May it is very hot, and this is a hotter part of the country than Tokyo, so putting up the shutters was not a terribly good idea but at least we got rid of the audience. Now I have to hope that if I have my windows open at night I don't get an audience staring in. It is also a little disconcerting that there is no fence or wall around the temple. The other two temples in the village have walls but mine doesn't. I hope I shall be safe here; I don't see why I shouldn't be though; after all, they've got nothing against me as far as I know. One of the bigger problems is the fact that there is only one light bulb in the whole building; this has to be carried on an incredibly long cord from place to place. As soon as I can I must get the electricity fixed properly.

17th. May.

I spent a wonderful night just sleeping; it was so marvellous to be able to get up when I felt like it. Unfortunately I was disturbed this morning by the good woman from down the road. Her name is Mrs. Suzuki and she wanted to be certain that I was all right. I assured her that I was and that the one thing that I needed to do more than anything else was rest. Rev. Hajime's wife had explained this to her before leaving me yesterday but she had to come to make certain for herself. It was very kind of her but I did so want a very long sleep.

After talking with Mrs. Suzuki for most of the morning (most of the time I'd hoped to be working on cleaning up the place) I was able to start sweeping and cleaning. Only one room has mats and that is the one where the altar is; presumably I have to live around the altar but, with time, I will mend up the other rooms. They need mats and the walls need some attention;

part of the roofing needs attention too, since it seems to be sagging, but it won't take very long.

18th. May.

I went to the nearest city to-day to do some shopping. On my return I found the entire village council sitting on the temple steps. I was told by the mayor that no priest, in fact no-one in the village, ever went to the city without telling him. He had to know where everyone was; since I had gone I should at least have brought back a present for every member of the council including him. I thought this was peculiar and so made a 'phone call to Rev. Hajime's wife who, after chuckling a little about it, informed me that it was the normal procedure in places where the system was still completely feudal such as the mountain villages. I asked her how it was possible that things could be so modern in Tokyo and she said that feudalism still existed even there and, if I were to go to the smaller cities, I would find them about twenty to thirty years behind the average city in the West as well as feudal. If I went to the larger towns I would find them about fifty years behind; in the villages or smaller towns I would continue to step back in time until, in the mountain villages, I would be somewhere in the thirteenth century. I wonder how I shall get on in this sort of a society; and yet it's rather fascinating. I've never seen anything like it before. I've heard of feudalism, I've read about it, but I wonder how many people ever have the opportunity of living in it?

19th. May.

A publisher friend of mine from Tokyo came to see me this morning. He was rather concerned about the fact that the bathroom here is falling down and so is completely unusable. Almost the entire house from just beyond the door that leads to the actual Hondō is in a state of such dilapidation as to be literally collapsing. He has decided to donate a bathroom and the whole of a porch, including a covered walkway to the well outside. This last will be of great value in bad weather. How very kind he is.

I wrote a letter to Rev. Hajime telling him of this and also of the fears that Jim has had with regard to one of the junior disciplinarians in the temple in Tokyo. I do wish he would do his own dirty work.

20th. May.

I was required to assist at a funeral to-day. It is the custom to pay something like two hundred yen a funeral; the equivalent of about two shillings. Small wonder that many of the priests find it impossible to earn a living when they have families and have to take other work. All three of the other local priests work in various ways. But the funeral itself was totally different from the ones that I have participated in in Tokyo up to now. In fact it was so different that I felt I needed to record it here. We all went to the home of the bereaved family and there performed a ceremony for the dead whilst the family members prepared the body. No-one here is needed as an undertaker although all funerals are arranged by undertakers in Tokyo. The body was placed in the kowtow position in a large wicker basket which the family manufactured for themselves; it was dressed in a white kimono with the head shaved like a priest's for a Buddhist funeral is, of course, a ceremony of ordination to the priesthood. Holding a rosary in its hands in the basket, the body was covered with a white cloth over the top of which was laid a gold brocade kesa signifying the fact that the person was indeed a full priest. The following day another, larger ceremony was held, the ceremony of ordination. When it was over everyone went in procession to the cemetery carrying the wreaths. The four chief mourners bore the body in its wicker basket on two poles. In front of the place of cremation were three large stones, one upon which the celebrant stood, one which was used as an altar and one upon which the basket was laid prior to being burned. There was another short ceremony and then the basket was taken to a pit a few feet away and placed on top of a bag of charcoal; another bag of charcoal was placed on top of the body. When the burning had got under way everyone went back to the house where the ceremonies had been held and settled down to a large meal. It is required by custom that every member of the priesthood shall drink otherwise the dead cannot be happy in the heavenly world to which they have gone. It seems that unless the priest is willing to drink the dead can have no joy in the Western Paradise. It didn't take very long for me to learn how this type of drinking was done to prevent excess. Everyone is provided with an incredibly small cup; one sips at it and constantly passes it round to others. If one is careful one consumes no more than a very minute quantity of alcohol but, even so, it is not a custom that I much like although, whilst here, I have no alternative but to go along with it.

I received a letter from Rev. Hajime to-day saying that he has started sending in the papers for my Kessei to the administration.

21st. May.

I heard this morning, by a very roundabout route, that my mother is dead. Apparently she died last year on December 3rd. Because my brother feared that I would give the money she has left to the Buddhists (he is very anti-Buddhist) the fact that she had died was not told to me. Indeed, he had told his lawyers that he did not know where to find me although he knew this to be a lie. I would not have known of her death if I hadn't written to a friend in London saying that I hadn't heard from my mother for a long time. He had asked his mother, who lived quite close to mine, to see how my mother was. It is a terrible way to learn of a mother's death. I am indeed paying a heavy price for doing what I believe to be right for me.

22nd. May.

I received a letter from the lawyers who are acting for me on behalf of my deceased mother—my friend had contacted them. It seems I have no alternative but to start legal proceedings. I wrote to the lawyers to tell them that all I want from the estate is some pictures and two photographs; one of my father and one of my mother. I don't really want anything else.

3rd. June.

I received a card from Rev. Hajime wishing me well in my new home. It was good to have so kind a thought.

6th. June.

Another letter came from Rev. Hajime this morning. He told me of many things that are happening, including the fact that Jim has a bad cold. He also told me that any money that is put into the box outside the temple is legally mine. With regard to the letters I wrote about the junior disciplinarian he says he will have to be very careful in case they cause problems with Zenji Sama; he could be very angry with the young man concerned; I have written to Rev. Hajime to tell him to do everything to prevent such problems. He told me something else too; that the parishioners here want me to teach English to their children. That should be fun. It will certainly be a change from the sort of people I've been teaching in Tokyo; all I ever got out of the girls there were giggles.

10th. June.

I have reclaimed three of the rooms. It is now possible for me to have a private room behind the main altar; this was originally the guest room. It took a lot of cleaning up but it's good to have a private room. I've also cleaned out and mended the indoor toilet so the whole place is beginning to take shape as a little home. It's hard work but I can do it steadily at a slow pace. I wonder though how I shall be able to get the whole place ready in time for Kessei; I've got to have every room livable in by then.

13th. June.

Received another letter of encouragement from Rev. Hajime. It really does help to have someone occasionally write and tell you to keep at it when you're cleaning up a place in the mess this is. I'm very grateful to him for these stray letters.

18th. June.

Another letter from Rev. Hajime requiring me to fill in all sorts of documents with regard to my history, almost life story, so that he can send everything to the Administration Section for my Kessei. It's amazing the amount of things they want to know; some of them seem so unnecessary and everything has to be done out in triplicate. I then have to collect seals from all sorts of people including the mayor of this village. Because this is a feudal system no-one can even do personal ceremonies without getting the mayor's permission. So I have to get his seals on the papers first, then take them to the local city and get the boss of the city's seals and then send them to Tokyo where they get sealed again by the administration. What a system!

1st. July.

It is getting very hot here but, all things considered, everything is going really well. The only slight problem is that I have arranged to take my baths in Mrs. Suzuki's house. Unfortunately this has made her very happy and some of the other villagers very angry. I shall have to arrange to bath in other houses or there'll be jealousy. Anyway I'll have my own bathroom soon. I've got used to visiting the villagers and going to their homes to recite the Scriptures. They're really a very friendly collection of people, very gentle and very kind. They're just a farming community with the usual mean elements but, on the whole, they're very sincere. Their meanness is, I suppose, reasonable. After all, being a farmer in this sort of area isn't exactly being a rich man.

I had another card from Rev. Hajime who was very sad to hear of my mother's death. He told me that it is perfectly all right for me to conduct the Segaki ceremonies for OBon. He also told me some rather interesting things. There is absolutely no difference in the rank of a male or female priest but still only men may perform the congratulatory ceremony of Zuisse, graduation recognised by the Emperor. I can wear colored robes and a golden rakusu after doing Kessei as the men do because it has been decided that I am to be given a first Kyoshi, or first class degree, as a result of the training I've already done in the Tokyo temple.[48] This means that I can also become the priest of the highest rank of temple if anyone ever wants to appoint me. I'm really very fortunate to have been able to study in so important a temple.

6th. July.

More papers arrived from Tokyo requiring seals. I seem to spend so much of my time in the local city collecting them. I wonder how many more they'll need?

10th. July.

A young man named Andy arrived this morning. He's come all the way from Tokyo; Rev. Hajime has had him in the temple there for a few days prior to sending him down to me. It seems that he's heard about me from somewhere and very much wants to help with getting the things ready for Kessei. It's very kind of him. He's an extremely good handyman and this means that a lot of the carpentry that I couldn't otherwise have done very well by myself will now be done properly. I'm really very grateful to Rev. Hajime for having sent him.

23rd. July.

I heard from my lawyers to-day. My brother is going to contest my mother's will every inch of the way. There seems to be no alternative but to fight. It's terrible that his relations with me have become this bitter but the worst news of the day is that Zenji Sama has collapsed. Apparently he just folded over in the Hondō and was carried back to his room; he hasn't moved since. The doctors say he has diabetes but it sounds more like a stroke to me. Rev. Hajime wrote to tell me that I shall be the last person Zenji Sama will ever Transmit personally.

The news of Zenji Sama's collapse has hit me so very hard; I wouldn't have believed that anything could have done so, not even my mother's and father's deaths have affected me as this has. There is that between Zenji Sama and I that is so exquisite that just the thought of his being harmed in any way, even by a natural illness, is as a mortal blow to myself.

24th. July.

Now that I am so much better and the temple is in pretty good condition, all things considered, I have decided to start a definite schedule of ceremonies for morning and evening together with periods of meditation. Andy loves the idea and we're hard at it. The temple itself is beginning to look very beautiful. Of course it's not got the gold brocade and the gold carvings of the other temples here but that doesn't matter. It looks really good just as it is and I know we're going to make a success of the place. Zenji Sama wanted somewhere for the foreigners and, if we work hard, we'll have one; the first person to come has been Andy. At a later date Jim will presumably come too but, in the meantime, Andy and I can get on.

A number of newspaper reporters turned up to-day thanks to Rev. Ichirō who has just come down to his own temple and has discovered that I am here. It seems that the man is determined to extract every bit of publicity he possibly can out of me and any other unfortunate foreigner he happens to come across.

The parishioners are constantly bringing us vegetables and bags of rice, giving us help in many directions, telling us where to get things and how to get them. One of the kindest things was to take me up the mountain behind this temple and show me some of the more dangerous insects and plants around here so as to make sure that no-one who comes to stay with us gets hurt.

Another letter came from Rev. Hajime telling me that my cousin's house in London is acceptable as a temple. Because of the certificate I was given when I did my Zuisse I found myself priest of a non-existent temple; it was then required of me that I find a place so as to turn it into an existing temple! The only place I could think of was my cousin's house. Some people from the administration went to England on a business trip, paid a visit to the house and approved it. So I am now not only Bishop of London but have a "palace" which isn't my own and a "cathedral" which isn't there.

Rev. Hajime wanted to know if I was willing for Jim to enter the Meditation Hall in the Tokyo temple properly and I have at last agreed that he should. I hope he may be worthy of it. It is a terrible thing to enter the Meditation Hall and be insincere.

29th. July.

The letter I wrote to the Emperor came back to-day duly translated. Apparently the original has already been sent off. I also got another card from Rev. Hajime saying that Jim has entered the Meditation Hall. It is good to know that he has at last done it although he will only be in Tokyo for a couple more days before he comes here to help me. The weather is getting very hot. The locals now just sit around and watch the rice ripen. I suppose there isn't very much else to do.

1st. August.

I received a card this morning to say that Jim will be arriving some time to-day together with the odd-eyed white cat (it has one gold eye and one blue one) that has been his companion for the last two months in the temple in Tokyo. There's only one real problem and that is that he's coming to the station close to Rev. Hajime's temple and both Rev. Hajime and his wife are insisting that, since I am meeting him, I must spend the night in Rev. Hajime's temple with him. I don't really want to do that at all. Rev. Hajime also tells me that unless I'm willing to help him in his temple for the OBon festival on the 17th. of August he is not willing to help me with any further translations.

10th. August.

Jim has been here for almost ten days and he and Andy aren't getting along any too well. Andy is a rather straightforward, old-fashioned young man and a lot younger than Jim is. I hope there aren't too many complications as a result of this. To-day Jim wanted to officially enter this temple. He said he'd never been allowed to do the formal entry into the temple in Tokyo, that is, make the formal walk to the front gate and wait there to be admitted. Both Andy and I felt that this was a bit of play-acting on his part, for his words didn't ring particularly true to either of us, but we decided that the kindest thing would be to let him go ahead and do it if he really wanted to. He made the formal walk to the front gate and stood outside it for an hour waiting to be admitted. One of the villagers saw him and, wondering what we were doing, came and scolded me for being cruel to him.

12th. August.

Received another card from Tokyo requiring information as to the exact area of the ground on which my cousin's house in London stands; apparently this has to be noted before the building can be formally regarded as a temple by the authorities here. They also wish to know if I am willing for the name they have suggested to be put upon the certificate. I agreed.

Several Americans have come to the temple in Tokyo. Rev. Hajime is telling them all to come down here.

I had a long discussion with Jim over many things concerning his past life and am becoming increasingly concerned at what it has been like. I feel desperately sorry for him but I cannot help wondering if he is not perhaps hiding in the priesthood from the fact that he doesn't, at the moment, know how to live life in any way other than to run away from it.

13th. August.

At three o'clock this morning we started the OBon festival for the village. The bell of the largest temple rang and I and the two priests from the other temples went around to officially open the altar in each house in the village. Visiting each house in turn, we recited Scriptures and offered incense on the family altar and were provided with refreshments; always beer. Consider the fact that there are something like one hundred and seventy-eight houses here, that it takes from three in the morning until about two or three in the afternoon to get them all done and one is offered beer in each; the state one is in when the ceremonies are over is a little difficult to describe. I very soon discovered that I must be very careful not to drink more than a sip in each house;

this annoyed the villagers but certainly saved me a lot of problems. The other two priests didn't seem to be so worried and one
of them, I'm afraid, got very much the worse for wear.

15th. August.

Segaki ceremonies in my own temple took place to-day and
I was very grateful for the help of both Andy and Jim in the per-
formance of them. It was the first time I had been celebrant at a
big ceremony and, although I had learned how to do it along
with all the other ceremonial when in the temple in Tokyo, it
was a totally different thing to be doing such a ceremony completely alone for the first time with no Japanese assistance. Jim
caused me quite a few problems by constantly ogling various
female members of the congregation and a couple of the town
council members complained. I must do something about him.
He really is very worrying.

16th. August.

Apparently Jim has gone round the village saying that he
feels he ought to have a temple such as this and asking the villagers if they would take a vote as to who they would prefer,
him or me. One of them actually wrote to Rev. Hajime to tell
him about this and see if it was possible to have him; Rev.
Hajime wrote back to say that not only is he not qualified, he is
just barely a newly-made member of the priesthood, not having
even done his Chief Junior, let alone his Transmission. It's
going to be almost impossible to run this temple if I am to have
someone like this living in it with me, constantly upsetting the
villagers, yet I have no alternative but to keep him here for he
is legally my disciple and thus my responsibility. There are
times when I think that Zenji Sama has complicated my kōan
very much for me; and times when I think that maybe I was the
one who complicated it for myself; I didn't *have* to ordain him.

17th. August.

Against my better judgement I went to help at Rev.
Hajime's temple to-day together with Jim. I told Rev. Hajime

many of the difficulties that are the result of having Jim in the temple with me but there seems to be nothing that can be done about it. He *is* legally my disciple. There were so many Segaki ceremonies; we did something like forty this first day and, at the end of them, Rev. Hajime gave everyone a big feast. There were twenty or thirty other people helping at the ceremonies with us for Rev. Hajime's is a very important temple. As usual there was much saké drinking when all the work was over. I'm sorry to say that Rev. Hajime got very drunk and fell asleep beside the table.

19th. August.

We have been doing ceremonies in Rev. Hajime's temple solidly for two days. I am almost reciting the "Kanromon" in my sleep but I made some money for doing it; a thousand yen for each day's work which is something like a pound. Having been fed well we all went home. It was good to get back to my own temple and find that Andy had looked after it well whilst I was gone. There is really nothing like having your own bed in your own house to sleep in although I must say that Rev. Hajime's wife was very kind during the past two days. She showed none of the signs of hatred, sullenness and temper she exhibited last year. Perhaps it was just because I was living in her house and she was worried over my being ill. Let's hope it was that.

20th. August.

Received a very short card from Rev. Hajime to say that he's safely back in the temple in Tokyo and is missing both Jim and I very much; he is sending all the foreigners he can to be with us here. This means that there'll be quite a few here for my Kessei. Jim asked me many questions to-day. Like me, during my own training, he is wondering why the wall is still there but his questions seemed insincere.[49]

"Is it wrong to search for the absolute?" he asked.

"Yes," I replied. "When I asked this question of Rev. Hajime he said that the reason why the wall was still there was because I was still young in spirituality."

"If it is wrong to search for Truth what am I doing here?" he asked.

"You know, I asked the very same question," I replied, "and do you know the answer I got?"

"I have no idea," he said, already seeming disinterested.

"Well, the English he used was very bad; the meaning came out as 'Go on, go on, always *going* on, always *becoming* Buddha.' His actual words were, 'After going on we shall be reaching there.'"

"You've often mentioned that you don't get happiness out of meditation but you do get absolute peace," said Andy. "What is peace?"

"Again the only answer I can give to that is the one that Zenji Sama himself gave me, 'Peace is everywhere if we meditate properly.' It's the way we live that makes a place peaceful. It's not something that we can find; it's something that we ourselves create from within."

"Have you found it?" he asked.

"Yes," I replied, "but not in a way you can understand. All the mess in the world goes on just as it has done but it doesn't affect me any longer. That's all. There is no stress or strain if we do everything naturally; there is no mental struggle, worry or trouble. That is what it means to be Buddha."

"Can one really do it?"

"It is possible but it has to be worked at every hour of the day and night. Peace is not something you get permanently and don't have to train to maintain afterwards, believing that it's going to be yours forever without any work on your part. You have to do a lot of work on yourself to be able to keep it."

"Do you think we could set aside a specific time each day for some questions and discussions of this sort?" asked Andy.

"Certainly. I don't see why not. In any case I've got to train Jim for his Chief Junior. It's a good idea."

And we left it at that. Gradually our schedule is beginning to form. We have our meditation three times a day, our Morning and Evening Service; we work on mending the house and now we're going to have our questions and discussions. It looks as though this is going to turn into a real, live temple.

21st. August.

This morning, after we'd finished working, Jim said to me, "Can you start teaching me now for my Chief Junior?" I tried not to show that I was hesitant but something in me was not too happy about the idea.

"All right," I said, after a couple of minutes pause, "I'll show you what you have to do for the actual ceremony."

We spent an hour and a half rehearsing then he said, "What about the questions and answers?"

"Have you ever seen a Chief Junior ceremony?" I asked.

"No," he replied.

"Do you know the sort of questions that they're likely to ask you?"

"No."

"The best thing I can do then is find some for you. Because it wasn't possible for me to do my own Chief Junior ceremony in the Hondō like everyone else, since I was a woman and a foreigner, I had a ceremony in Zenji Sama's own room after which he gave me the certificate. I only had two people there as well as Zenji Sama; one was my Benji and the other Rev. Hajime. Let me find you some questions with their answers. Do you want them?"

"Please." Both he and Andy seemed very eager.

I found the verse that is usually recited by the Benji at the beginning of the questioning and ends with the sentence, "The Emperor could not understand these answers so Bodhidharma crossed the river and went to sit facing the wall in Shōrinji for nine years."

"My answer to this poem," I said, "was the following, 'When we see a leaf fall from a tree we can know that it is Autumn.' My Benji replied, 'We must not be muddled by the changing of the four seasons.' 'Every sight is the same Autumn,' I answered. 'You say Autumn,' he said, 'but you are making a mistake in that, in seeing the flowers blooming and the leaves falling, you are thinking them to be the real sight of the Truth.'

'Be still and you will know it.' 'Congratulations,' he said. 'Thank you,' was the reply. 'Unclear. Please teach me,' said another. 'Please listen carefully; they never ever change their colours.' 'The real presence of Autumn is that they never change their colours,' he challenged. 'Still you do not know the eternal sight that is told by our ancestors.' 'Congratulations,' he said. 'Thank you,' was the reply."

When I finished speaking both Jim and Andy were silent. Then Jim said, "Isn't it customary for people to take these questions and answers from a book?"

I said, "Sometimes. In many cases here in Japan they are prepared from a book; however, some are still done completely spontaneously. Wouldn't you like to do it that way?"

"I don't know that I can," he replied. "I don't know that I can speak Japanese well enough."

"Well, we can always do it from a book. Many people do."

We left it there, deciding that, nearer the time, we could rehearse him from one of the chapters of the special book. He can, as have many Chief Juniors before him, do it by this method.[50]

1st. September.

The house is almost completely in order now; we have even got a living room and two bedrooms. We went round, all three of us together, begging disused, old mats and furniture from people here; finally we have a little home together. It's so wonderful to have something of our own; at any rate *I* think it is. I sometimes wonder if it's good enough for the other two but it is certainly marvelous as far as I'm concerned. I don't know when they will start work on the new bathroom but, when it is finished, the temple will be complete.

5th. September.

Andy had to return to Tokyo to-day. It was rather unfortunate but there wasn't very much he could do about it so we wished him good luck. I look forward to seeing him as soon as he can come back again.

6th. September.

To-day three reporters arrived from a magazine which is reputed to be the worst in the country. I absolutely refused to see them for I knew that the only news they ever printed was sensational and distorted. Unfortunately they insisted on standing outside the door, pounding on it, for something like two to three hours; Jim got very worried. Then one of them put his fist through the glass in the top of the door. This terrified Jim so much that he started panicking. I suggested he went out via a back window and over the neighbour's wall to the house next door. This he did. By now the reporters were yelling obscenities; it was remarkable to me that none of the villagers seemed to be around to hear until I remembered that they were all in the fields harvesting the rice. There was no-one around to help me so I sat down to meditate. In another couple of hours it was too dark for the reporters to stay outside any longer. They went away threatening to come back in the morning.

Jim returned and I visited the local policeman. He wanted to know why I had refused to see the reporters and I told him bluntly that I felt that there *was* such a thing as privacy in this world to which I was entitled as were those with me. He told me that, if I wished to stay in Japan, I would have to think differently, there being no such thing as privacy for a foreigner. He did, however, agree to come back in the morning if the reporters caused us any more problems. They did indeed come back in the morning and I *still* refused to see them. They went off threatening to visit the local town council.[51]

9th. September.

I received a card from Rev. Hajime telling me how impressed he was with Andy who, he felt, had become an extremely earnest young man whilst being in my temple. Well, all we've done here is hard work and meditation. Just that and nothing more.

There seem to be two main factions in the village. One is run by Mrs. Suzuki who met me when I first came here and the other, which seems to comprise the majority of the villagers, by a woman who lives on the other side of this temple. Such situations are very difficult for a priest coming to a new village; I should be beyond involvement with either side but it is obvious that there are political factions even in so small a community as this and I will have to be careful that I do not tread on the corns of either side. I have agreed to bath in other houses on alternate nights so as not to cause jealousy with the rest of the villagers.

25th. September.

I received a long letter from Rev. Hajime to-day concerning the Kessei arrangements. My special robes have been ordered and the number of children for the procession has been fixed at somewhere around fifty. There is such a lot to be done; making sure that there are enough people to come and prepare the feasts for all the priests who will have to be here; making certain that I have enough beds for everyone; booking the two choirs, one from Rev. Hajime's temple and another from the local town, to sing in the procession. It is really amazing what a lot has to be done. The Chinese abbot has sent me a thousand dollars to pay all the expenses since I have no money of my own and no means of completing my Kessei without financial assistance. The Japanese here will give none although the cost of a new priest's Kessei is normally bourne by his parishioners.[52]

3rd. October.

The money for the new bathroom, vestibule and covered walkway to the well arrived to-day and a number of the villagers came to start work on it. They estimate that it will take about a month to finish; they are also getting me an electric pump for the well. Apparently my publisher friend has given a hundred and thirty thousand yen for all of this. It is indeed a wonderful present. Rev. Hajime wrote to say that the money has already been deposited to his account ready to be given to the villagers as soon as the work is finished.

4th. October.

At the discussion to-day Jim said to me, "During meditation this morning I seemed to almost disappear with everything around me but I was so afraid that I stopped myself. I was afraid of what might happen. Ought I to meditate in my room instead of in the Meditation Hall or is it better not to? I want to meditate during the day in my room in any case." Again his voice did not sound sincere.

"The only answer I can give you," I replied, "is the one that they gave me when I made exactly the same request. 'We must be in the Zendō whenever others are there.' You can do it in your own room at any other time if you wish."

"What does that mean?" he asked.

"It means what it sounds like. If you have some spare time by all means go ahead and meditate. Use any spare time you've got but you should know that when it's a work period we should all work together; when it's a meditation period we should all meditate together. That's the way they taught it to me. Do you remember I told you once about what happened when I was in the garden weeding and I wanted to go off and weed by myself?"

"Oh, yes," he said, "but that . . . that was a different thing. That was you."

I said, "No, it's not different. You and I are identically the same. You shouldn't go off by yourself. Why do you consider yourself different?"

"Well . . . ," and his voice trailed off. Suddenly he changed the subject. "What happened to that young disciplinarian you wrote the letters about?"

"I don't know," I answered. "I think he was given a different job in the temple. I don't know anything more about it."

"Perhaps he liked punishing people or beating them up when they were bigger than he was," he said. "Maybe it makes him feel bigger than he is."

"According to Rev. Hajime," I replied, "it's not right to use the kyosaku on anyone if they're sitting correctly and it's wrong for people to talk and lecture when others are sitting; but, as he told me, there are many traditions in that temple we were in Tokyo so, well . . . it's a bit like a large boarding school. According to Rev. Hajime we should be allowed to sit quietly without being disturbed by anything."

"What's that got to do with dealing with him?"

"With who?" I asked.

"That young disciplinarian," he replied.

"Nothing," I answered.

"Well, are they going to deal with him?"

"Why are you so anxious that they should deal with him?" I asked. "You mustn't be vindictive."

"Oh, so now you're going to become holy."

I got up and went to my room. On the way I noticed that the building of the bathroom was getting well under way. The far wall, which had fallen down entirely, has now been completely replaced and the vestibule is almost finished. How very pleasant to have so beautiful a bathroom.

5th. October.

I received another card from Rev. Hajime to say that my robes are finished and he has had a specially good red one made. He also seems to have got a bad cold. The date of my Kessei has been fixed for November 28th.

18th. October.

To-day several village women came to discuss the arrangements for the Kessei procession and to tell me of the children who will be the Chigo-san. They also wanted to arrange many things with regard to the food and we decided how much it was to cost for the entire three days of ceremonies; something like two hundred pounds or the equivalent of two hundred thousand yen.[53]

20th. October.

Rev. Hajime wrote to say that he will be arriving on the 29th. of October so as to be able to discuss many things with the villagers with regard to my Kessei.

23rd. October.

Again Jim and I were having a discussion. I feel that I am doing a really atrocious job of teaching him.

He said to me, "When shall we reach perfection? That's really what I want. To be complete. To be free to do as I wish."

I answered, "We are never ever complete, without responsibility for eternity."

"That's awful and it's wrong."

"No, it isn't," I said, "and you must learn not to disobey my teaching. You must listen. If you don't you will not be fit to become a Chief Junior."

"Well, if perfection and freedom to do as I like are not going to come for eternity what am I doing here?"

"You are here to do the very best you can at all times and in all places. That's all there is; to do the very best one can. Dōgen Zenji himself said, 'Always we must be disturbed by the Truth.' If we are satisfied with the state we are in, if we are complete, then we are never going to learn anything and we are certainly never going to train ourselves for the training itself is that which matters."

"Humph," he sat silent for some time, then spoke again. "You know, I've been happier here these last few weeks than ever before in my whole life, in spite of the hell of Sesshin that they put me through up in Tokyo. Odd as it may seem I was just beginning to find it advantageous around the fifth day."

"It's a hard road to enlightenment," I said, "but, according to Zenji Sama, it is right under our feet. You and I had some sort of experience but there are many who don't have any."

He sat silent again staring into space. Then he spoke slowly. "How do you explain that to the world?"

"To live simply and normally, if there is no doubt, is enlightenment itself. Rev. Hajime told me that and I now know it to be a fact for myself."

Again there was a long pause before he spoke. "I'm beginning to think that we sit facing a wall and are beaten to make us realise what fools we are."

"Enlightenment is eternity," I answered. "We should awaken to it every moment wherever we are."

"I think that enlightenment is to understand and know that we are free in a way that cannot be expressed in words," he said, "and to be able to do whatsoever we wish with that freedom, to do exactly what we like."

"According to Dōgen Zenji, according to Zenji Sama and according to my own experience," I replied, "we can realise enlightenment through the course of our daily life. We cannot tell of it in words or know it through intellection; only through changing our attitude of mind and, thus radically changing our behaviour, do we understand it directly."

Again a long silence. Then he spoke. "We must always go on then? I am sometimes very ashamed of myself for sitting down and going nowhere for so many years and for hurting so many people."

"In Japanese, 'fusei,' as they call it, is the first step in the training of a Bodhisattva."

"What is 'fusei?'"

"Not to be pleased with the self," I replied. "I took the four Bodhisattva vows in London, and again in Malaysia, after I found Buddhism as a child. I so wanted to share my joy with everyone. Do you know what the Bodhisattva vows are?"

"No," he answered.

"The version I took goes like this, 'I promise to abstain from all that will make further bad karma. I promise to strive for the enlightenment of all beings.' I like that translation rather better than the one usually used. I thought that you'd already taken the Bodhisattva vows?"

"Well, I did that thing back home but I honestly didn't know what it was that I did."

"You know, that affair worries me. I wonder if you really were ordained or not."

"Why worry? You've done or re-done it. It's proper now."

"Let's hope it is," I said.

We had to leave it there for some guests had arrived and I had to do a ceremony for them.

29th. October.

Rev. Hajime came early this morning and spent the entire day. He explained many things to me; how to decorate the altars, how to arrange the rooms for the ceremonies, the order with regard to which the ceremonies should be carried out. I wrote everything down carefully. He was overjoyed with the way in which we had mended the temple and the amount of work that had been done on getting a congregation. He felt that the temple was a totally different building from the one he had originally seen.

When he had gone Jim sat silent and a little sullen, looking at me rather strangely. "You realise that he is in love with you, don't you?" he said.

I couldn't quite believe that I'd heard what I thought I had.

"You're mad," I said. "He's a priest and so am I. What are you talking about?"

"You don't have to be that innocent with me," he said, sneering.

"I am being neither innocent nor guilty. I just do not know what it is you speak of."

"All right," he said, "but I'm glad to know that you are not in love with him. I think it is a blessing for your sake."

I just shook my head, walked to my room and that was it for the day.

2nd. November.

There was trouble again between the villagers and Mrs. Suzuki since they feel she is trying to hog my company. I assured them that I intended to go round to see them all equally and peace was once again restored.

The bathroom is finished and is truly magnificent. For the first time since coming here we were able to turn on a tap and not have to use the pump. It makes such a difference with regard to the cleaning as does the fact that there is now a covered walkway to the well and sink. It's amazing how we miss these little, simple things. We think of them as being our normal rights and only appreciate them when we have not had them for a time. One can never realise how helpful they are if one isn't suddenly faced one day with being without them. That's one of the great advantages of Zen training. It takes everything away from you and all you have is the one mat on which you live, two meters long by a meter wide, the two cupboards behind it in which to keep your clothes, books and bed, the space on top of the cupboard for your food bowls and the place underneath the one mat for your shoes. You learn to live in that small amount of space and you learn that that's all a human being really needs; and it's so appreciated when you get a bit more. How delicious is water. How beautiful it is to be able to keep clean in one's own house.[54]

5th. November.

An unusual letter arrived this morning from the Director of the temple in Tokyo. It was written in Japanese and there was a translation with it from Rev. Hajime. It simply congratulated me on doing my Kessei and told me that he, the Director, was happy and willing to send the four or five trainees I had asked to come to it. He also told me how much Zenji Sama is looking forward to seeing me again and how much he himself is looking forward to seeing me too. It is the first time that he has written to me and it looks as though he's really sincerely interested in what I am doing. Perhaps, when I go back after this ceremony, there will be others from whom I can learn as well as Rev. Hajime. That will make such a difference.

11th. November.

The finishing touches are being put on the Kessei ceremony arrangements. A long letter came from Rev. Hajime explaining the last few things, plus a tremendous bundle of official documents that I again have to seal and take to the mayor and then to the officials in the city before sending them back to Tokyo. I seem to have been doing nothing but get seals for the last three months.

Rev. Hajime tells me that, although there will be many people who will object to the fact that I am wearing a red robe for some of the ceremonies, I should, nevertheless, wear it. Women can go all the way up the ranks of the priesthood but prejudicial customs still remain; he wants me, as does Zenji Sama, to fight these prejudices for the sake of all the women in Japan. I suppose it is a wonderful opportunity to be in the spearhead of such things but I really have no personal interest in them. I found what I came looking for. Just I do that, however, which has to be done. If it is the will of Zenji Sama that I fight prejudice then it is my will also.

I hear that the Administrative Section has sent the temple certificates for my cousin's house in London.

16th. November.

I received a card from Rev. Hajime to say that Zenji Sama is sending me a hossu for use at the ceremonies as a present to me personally along with a bamboo sword, the sword of Manjusri, to raise the rank of my temple and show that I have the right to teach. I hear that it is the first time that he has ever sent such things to a woman and the first time that anything of the sort has been sent to a foreigner. The temple in Tokyo is sending me a gold brocade cover for the altar.

Rev. Ichirō has finally left Japan to go to his new post.

18th. November.

I received another card from Rev. Hajime to say that he and the Director are buying many presents to give to those who are coming here for the Kessei ceremonies since many great priests intend to come. I have only invited twenty-five of my friends but it looks as though far more than that are going to turn up.

26th. November.

The guests started arriving to-day. I have borrowed many futons for them and most will spend the night in the big clubhouse in the temple garden which will eventually become the Meditation Hall. I do not know what time most of the people I have invited will arrive; the ones who got here to-day I do not know at all. At the moment there are many people in the temple busy making food. It is like running a hotel. It's amazing that the floors of this old building are able to stand up to the weight of so many people.

27th. November.

There are already fifty-four priests in the temple. The Kessei flag flies above the roof to tell everyone that I am ready to accept their challenge, to debate with them and to prove that I am a priest and teacher. The rehearsals for the ceremonies start to-day. I gave Jim to the five junior trainees who I had arranged to come from the temple in Tokyo; they can teach him the book version of doing the Chief Junior ceremony. This is a common practice. He does not feel he knows the Japanese language well enough to do it differently.

At about five o'clock this evening the priest whom Zenji Sama has selected to represent him arrived and was greeted by a great beating of drums and ringing of bells which many of the priests have brought with them. I have borrowed a large drum from the village and also have a number of small bells. Zenji Sama is still completely paralyzed down the entire left side of his body but the doctors are still insisting that he has diabetes. These people and their fear of losing face; if they say one has a specific disease they may not change the diagnosis even when they are wrong. I sincerely hope that I am never seriously ill in this country.

After the formal entry of Zenji Sama's representative we had the Nyudo no Hai ceremony at which Jim officially entered the temple as Chief Junior. This was followed by the formal tea ceremony. Rev. Hajime, Rev. Jirō, who has come as the official lecturer, and I sat at the far end of the hall. The rest of the priests were grouped in two rows facing each other on either side. The formal tea was brought and then Rev. Hajime read out the names of those who would take an active part in the running of the temple for the days of Kessei. He also gave a long talk on why I, a woman and a foreigner, was being allowed to have such rank as this in a Japanese temple. He explained that many women in Japan were eligible to do the ceremonies but afraid to because of Japanese custom. They should see that there was one who was unafraid in spite of the many difficulties. He wished everyone to know that I was doing the ceremonies at the wish of Zenji Sama, the Archbishop. We then drank the cups of tea we had been holding, each taking the same amount of sips exactly together so that we all set the cups down at the same time. When the tea ceremony was over we went to bed. The house is so full of people.

28th. November.

The really important ceremonies of Kessei started to-day. The waking-up bell went at two in the morning; everyone rose and went to meditation and Morning Service then cleaned the house and gardens. The villagers have built a huge ramp, as an extension to the front of the temple, to take the weight of so many extra people. After breakfast (we had formal breakfast in the club-hall) I was taken to the mayor's house where I took a formal bath and prepared for the procession. Thirty priests and fifty children formed up for the procession outside the mayor's house and I, in my red and gold robes, walked under a great red umbrella, carried by one of the members of the town council, from the mayor's house to the temple. At the front of the procession went the two choirs ringing small silver bells as they sang. The fifty children wore gold crowns and elaborate, cloth-of-gold costumes, thus representing the royal children who brought lotus blossoms to the Buddha on the day of his enlightenment; each carried a lotus blossom.[55] After every three children walked one of the priests. The procession stretched for something like two miles. On arrival at the temple-gate my assistant, who was one of the chief priests of the big temple in Tokyo sent specially for the purpose by Zenji Sama, one of his own assistants and very important, handed me the incense as I said the formal words, "Whilst I live the gate of this temple shall never be closed to any living thing." This is known as 'the formal opening of the gate.'[56] Then, to the thunder of drums, I entered the temple and walked to the main altar where I dedicated myself to the service of the village, all living things and

"Whilst I live the gate of this temple shall never be closed to any living thing."

"As I stood upon the altar there was no difference between me and he who stood in front questioning me for we all sat upon the altar of the lotus together . . ."

The author with the Chigo-san, or royal children,
and guests in celebration of her Kessei.

the teachings of the Buddhas and Patriarchs. Next I asked for the
spiritual guidance of Zenji Sama without which I shall be useless for no priest is capable of anything unless his master[57] helps
him. I then went to my room to change from the red and gold of
the chief priest to the purple of the priest who is to be questioned
upon the altar to see if he is indeed the living Buddha.

As I stood before the altar, saying the prayer that all priests
must say before they mount it, "The white clouds are still above
the altar; I pray that He[58] Who teaches me shall help me now,"
I knew that Zenji Sama[59] was there with me and always would
be no matter what clouds may one day hide him from my sight.

The questions came in a language-style that is difficult even
for those who speak Japanese—imagine an average Englishman
trying to speak Chaucerian English—yet the answers came easily. As I stood upon the altar there was no difference between
me and he who stood in front questioning me for we all sat upon
the altar of the lotus together and all trained together in the
same way. Whether I answered in English or Japanese did not
matter for our spirits were one. The words were of no importance—there was only the meditation within which one stands

upon the altar—that beautiful meditation in which there is no disturbance—in which the white clouds are still.

I heard the sound of the Shōmei striking the wooden block. I heard the words pronounced, "I proclaim that this is well and truly Buddha; that these answers have been well and truly given." I had not seen the huge audience. There had been but Zenji Sama and I in that hall and we two had been one; all others had been aspects of the two of us and we had been aspects of them and of Him. I saw Zenji Sama's representative smile softly as I offered incense and thanked Zenji Sama for being with me—at that moment I knew a joy even deeper than that of Transmission. Speeches of congratulation were then made by all the important people and my assistant read congratulatory telegrams from all over Japan.

We had lunch and then the ceremony of Chief Junior took place. The other juniors had rehearsed Jim very well and the ceremony was a success. He is now a Chief Junior and I a full priest. Everyone attended the large feast and I was called to the club-hall to thank all the people of the village who had helped me; they were having a big feast too. The priests drank much but it didn't matter any longer; these things were of no importance. I was extraordinarily exhausted but I felt that I must take time to write this. Such a day must never be forgotten.

Andy was there and so were several people whom I knew from the American bases. They took photographs and were happy for *their* priest had made it; *their* priest had been accepted—she was not only a foreigner—she was also a female.

29th. November.

Everyone got up at three o'clock this morning. We had meditation, Morning Service and breakfast and then all the guests left. I took down the Kessei flag—the red, yellow, green, white and purple flag of the full priest which I may fly now whenever I wish. Anyone may come and debate with me. Oh, what a glory and an honour it is to be a Buddhist priest.

30th. November.

Andy, Jim and I were so exhausted we just didn't get up until noon. This was probably very bad but we really were terribly tired.

2nd. December.

Rev. Hajime wrote to say that he was very pleased with my Kessei and that everyone in the Tokyo temple felt that I had done it excellently. He said that everyone thought it was wonderful. He said one thing that concerned me somewhat. He feels that Jim is not exactly my best friend and that perhaps he should have an old temple of his own somewhere else. He thinks he may always make problems for me in the village since he is very jealous, always trying to take what others have. For some reason he is of the opinion that I am going to Transmit him. I never said I would and he is certainly not ready for it.

Zenji Sama is getting peeved because I have not returned to the temple in Tokyo yet. He sent me word that Sesshin is going on there and asked bluntly, "Don't you want to be with me?" I am always with him even if he cannot sit in the Meditation Hall physically with me. I will go to Tokyo as soon as I can. There is no cessation of training whatever one's rank in the priesthood; Sesshin is not just for junior trainees.

12th. December.

Jim was staring moodily out of the window instead of being bright and attentive at our discussion this morning. Suddenly he said, "Isn't there a danger of becoming apathetic if one just accepts things without fighting them?"

"Your understanding is only intellectual," I said. "It's no good doing it that way. You must understand through your own experience for yourself. You shouldn't try to rush things."

"I wasn't aware that I was rushing things," he answered. "You've misunderstood what I was saying. I wasn't complaining; only saying that the Buddha seems to have abandoned the method we are using for a more peaceful one. You say that realisation is possible by this method."

"You are always trying to rush things," I replied. "You must
understand everything from your own experience as I did. Your
experience is not yet very deep."

"It's not that much shallower than yours."

"I have been in Buddhism since I was very young," I replied. "You have only been in it a matter of a few months."

"Well, I intend to do Transmission before I go," he said.

"Are you going?" I asked.

"It seems you're not willing to keep me! It's your duty,
though. You ordained me and the temple in Tokyo sends you
money."

"I can't support you financially. I can barely keep myself.
You don't seem to realise that I don't have that kind of money.
It took everything I'd got to do these Kessei ceremonies."

"I thought it was expensive. I don't know why you did it.
We could have lived on the money from Malaysia."

"I had an opportunity which will not come again. The
money that came from Malaysia was not for living on; only for
these ceremonies," I answered.

There was a long silence during which he again stared out
of the window. "Don't you find it rather frightening at times to
realise that you cannot do what is expected of you?" he asked,
"you are not a master if you cannot keep me."

It was my turn to be silent then I said, "The country of the
Buddhas will be established gradually. Until that time all we
have to do is keep going. Gyate, gyate; go on, go on, always
going on, always *becoming* Buddha. Our present civilisation is
founded on greed, on killing and plundering. It's wrong, a mistake. I believe that we need to establish a different type of civilisation run along the lines that the Buddha laid down, based on
his doctrine; a doctrine which teaches that greed, killing and
plundering are wrong. One day there will be a civilisation under
the protection of the Buddhas and Bodhisattvas. My duty is to
train myself and, when the opportunity arises to establish that
civilisation, to do everything I can. That is all I am going to do,

all I can do and all I'm going to try to do. Just train myself and, in being ready, exhibit the world of the Buddhas in my own life style that others may want to copy. The kingdom of the Buddhas can only be established by people like us. So we're the ones that have to do the training in order to bring about the civilisation of the Buddhas. We must change ourselves if we would change the world for *we* are the world."

There was another long silence. "Kanzeon has a thousand arms and a thousand eyes. Which one is the true eye? Which one is the true arm?" he asked.

"All is one," I said. My voice was very still.

"Since enlightenment is here and now, in all things, and all we have to do is get rid of self, what is the use of asking questions in the Hondō? There is nothing to be asked."

Again my voice was very still. "You are thinking too shallowly," I said.

"The simplest things are always the most difficult to do. That is why so few people are enlightened I suppose."

"You are thinking of enlightenment too narrowly," I replied. "You must think of it on a much wider scale than this. It must embrace everything at all times and in all places."

"When are you going to Transmit me?" he asked.

I was silent and rose to leave the room but he came behind me.

"I *want* to be Transmitted!"

"I will write to Rev. Hajime," I said and left him.

13th. December.

Jim was again staring moodily out of the window. The sun was very wintry and it has indeed become very cold in the last few days. Suddenly he glared as he looked up at me.

"You know, if you don't Transmit me, I can always tell people that Rev. Hajime likes you perhaps more than he should. They'll stretch it from there."

I stood still. It was as if everything inside me stood still; my spirit, my mind, everything and I and Zenji Sama and the temple stood still—a solid oneness.

"Yes," I said, "you could say that."

"So—will you Transmit me?"

"Only if Rev. Hajime thinks it's a good idea."

I walked on past him to my room. A card and letter arrived from Rev. Hajime. In them he applauded my idea to allow Jim to return to his own country. He then said that a Transmission ceremony has its own built-in safeguards. I know that a Transmission ceremony for those who are not ready to be Transmitted remains but a ceremony. Just that and nothing more. The secret teaching is never written down, only given in the middle of the ceremony at the master's discretion. One can only be *Transmitted* if one is *ready* to be Transmitted. That which happens at a Transmission ceremony can only be understood when the two spirits are willing and ready to meet in mid-air. I still see no reason to Transmit Jim. A priest must be single-minded yet practical.

25th. December.

I received a card from Zenji Sama to-day, together with one from the Director. They both say they are looking forward to seeing me on the 30th. of the month, ready for the New Year celebrations; they want me back to look after the Foreign Section which is growing rapidly. The head of all the women priests in Tokyo also wishes to see me. They tell me that Jim has been booked on a ship. It will sail at four o'clock on the 30th.

Andy cooked Christmas dinner. It was rather fun having Christmas dinner in our own house. It was very simple; just some fried vegetables and pancakes, but it was our dinner in our house. How I love such simple things.

26th. December.

Rev. Hajime wrote to say that it would not be possible to get silks for Jim's proposed Transmission in time for him to write them before leaving. I have no doubt there will be consequences.

29th. December.

Jim, Andy and I returned to Tokyo this morning. Jim leaves to-morrow. Andy stayed the night in the Guest Section of the

Tokyo temple. It seems that the same "friend" in London who wrote to Rev. Jones to tell him not to ordain me when in Malaysia has now written to Zenji Sama to say that, as I am a woman, I should not be allowed to return to England to teach. The only people whom he is willing to welcome there as teachers will be Japanese men. Zenji Sama is furious about this. He thinks that I have misled him in saying that I taught Buddhism in England. I have assured him that I have not lied to him in any way but he says he must make certain by writing to other people in England to check what I have said. It is terrible that Zenji Sama, so sick and ill, should be worried by such silly things. How is it possible that people like this man in England can call themselves Buddhists?[60]

30th. December.

Jim left this afternoon. Just before he left Zenji Sama sent me the letters that my so-called friend in London has sent him. This man is terrified that I will go back to England and teach. Whilst I was away he wrote to Zenji Sama asking for a teacher of Zen to be sent to England and Zenji Sama said that I would be ready this December. This was what prompted the letter saying I shouldn't be sent, that I wouldn't be accepted; now Zenji Sama is terribly muddled. He doesn't know who to believe. He gave me the letters to read since, in Buddhism, if someone speaks against another, the person spoken against must always be told so that he may know his enemies and teach them better Buddhism. I sincerely hope that whomsoever Zenji Sama writes to in England to clarify the situation does not make it worse through misunderstanding his motives.

After saying good-bye to Jim I returned to the temple where I found a large number of trainees very glad and anxious to see me. I have been moved from where I was living before and am now beside the Director whom, it seems, I am to be assistant to. It will be indeed very helpful to have the post of assistant to the Director as well as looking after all the foreign guests. What an opportunity to learn! A really wonderful new year lies ahead of us. Certainly the trainees were all glad to see me back again. It's amazing what a difference it makes when Rev. Ichirō isn't here.[61] It's like being in a totally different world.

We all had a party. Several of the others were convinced that I must be very unhappy at the departure of Jim and insisted on doing everything they could for me.

31st. December.

The last day of the old year—perhaps the greatest year of my life. No, that isn't true. I don't know which is the greatest; the year I was Transmitted, the year of my great kenshō or this year, the year of my Kessei; they have been three such wonderful years. It's as though I was reborn when I had my kenshō; after that I became alive for the first time in the whole of my life.

Towards eleven o'clock this evening we all went to the great hall to bow to Zenji Sama. We bowed to his empty chair; the saddest thing I have seen is his empty chair. As we were leaving the hall someone beckoned and I was taken to his private room where he lay in bed, completely unable to move. I thanked him for his help and for the wonderful year; he told me he had seen the photographs of my Kessei and was overjoyed. We talked for a few moments and then I had to go.

1st. January.

After the New Year ceremonies I went again to see Zenji Sama to wish him a happy New Year and a speedy recovery. Those of us who were his real disciples were allowed to have breakfast in his private guest room but it was not the same as when he is there; there was an empty space at the top of the room by the toko-no-ma. Now the formal New Year celebrations are over and we are relaxing. We are drinking the New Year wine, waiting for a year in which Zenji Sama is ill, in which I have been taken under the wing of the Director. My room is beside the Director's, as I said, and two rooms away from that of Rev. Hajime. I am in the administration block, quite close to the main door, so that I shall be readily available for the foreign guests.

10th. January.

Apparently Zenji Sama did write to someone in England to check my so-called friend's comment that a woman cannot teach Buddhism. To-day a letter came for me, as well as one for Zenji Sama, which made him absolutely furious. It said that, although I can teach Buddhism, and have taught it for a good many years, there is just no room at the moment for another school of Buddhism in England since they are well satisfied with the Rinzai school. I was afraid that if Zenji Sama wrote he might make matters worse. There is so much sectarianism and fear of competition in Britain in spite of protestations to the contrary. Quite reasonably Zenji Sama is thinking that there is a genuine attempt to prevent our school of Zen being spread in my native country, especially in view of the fact that he was asked for a teacher in the first letter. Unfortunately everybody here has to have their letters read if their master is present and Zenji Sama demanded to see the letter that came for me. This said that the writer knew exactly what a rōshi was and obviously *our* Zen's type of rōshi was totally different from that of Rinzai. He stated that the word 'rōshi' clearly has two utterly different meanings in Rinzai and in our school of Zen and that the British know the Rinzai well. He maintains that in Rinzai it means a very rare flower of long years of enlightened effort, matured by five or ten years' work after the Transmission is granted. He also assured me that the fact that someone is a rōshi is *never* published aloud[62] and that there are never any exams, degrees and ceremonies. A rōshi, he said, must have attained a whole series of large scale satori and have been further trained to teach. Only then can such a man take sanzen or use kōans for his pupils. He concluded that in England they have met four such men in twenty years and one other who is more of our school but is also Rinzai trained. Thus, he informed me, the term as used in our temple has obviously a very different meaning from that of Rinzai.

It was hopeless for me to say that I didn't want to translate this letter for Zenji Sama because of his illness. It was equally hopeless for me to try and translate it differently. Rev. Hajime was with me and, noting my hesitation, took it and translated it word for word as it had actually been written. I hid my eyes from Zenji Sama's grieved face. Then, quite simply, he said that obviously no-one in England understood *any* school of Buddhism at all if they suffered from the idea that satori was gained piecemeal and that the Rinzai school had the monopoly. He dictated a long letter which he ordered me to write to England. I took it down and went back to my room where I wrote it out. It was obvious that it could not be sent for it would be completely misunderstood. It was equally obvious that there was no way, at the moment, in which this matter could be sorted out so, in desperation, I went back to Zenji Sama alone.

"Zenji Sama," I said, "please forgive me. I have no right to go against your wishes but may I respectfully suggest that this letter is not sent?"

"Why?" He was still very angry.

"Because I don't think it will be understood. May I ask Zenji Sama what it was he actually wrote in his letter of inquiry to this person?"

"Yes," he said. "I asked him what criminal activity you had been up to prior to coming here that made it necessary for you to hide in a monastery and not be able to return to England."

I gulped. "I see," I said.

"I also said that I had named you as my direct disciple, as one of my Dharma Heirs, and that you have the title of Rōshi because you have earned it. At a later date you will receive the certificate of sanzen from the Administration Branch."

"Did you write it in English?"

"Rev. Hajime translated it," he replied.

"I see," I said.

There was a long pause whilst his girl assistant brought in tea for he obviously didn't want to talk whilst she was there. When she had put down the tea things and gone away, with a few pleasantries having been muttered to her, he said, "If you think this reply is unwise what do you suggest I write? You know the British. You are one of them. You should therefore know what it is safe to write and what it is not."

I said, "As brief a letter as possible would be the best, Zenji Sama, and I would be very grateful if you did not ask me to write it. For obvious reasons it is not what I should do. I have spoken of this matter with another Briton and he suggested this."

"But I want you to do all my foreign correspondence."

"Zenji Sama, there are so many priests here. Rev. Hajime is good at English now. Why don't you let him do it? It would be much better if you had him rather than me."

He thought for a moment. "Yes, perhaps you are right," he said. "I understand what you mean."

He rang his bell to call for Rev. Hajime. When he arrived he said, "I want you to write a letter."

Rev. Hajime looked worried. "Yes?" he said.

"I want you to write to this man in England and tell him that he obviously understands nothing whatsoever about true Zen."

"May I suggest something, Zenji Sama," Rev. Hajime ventured.

"Yes."

"Might we say, 'I have read your comments with regard to our school of Zen. It seems that you, a layman, know more of what a rōshi is than does an Archbishop of Zen. Under the circumstances there is no need for any further communication between us.'"

"Yes, that is excellent! That is exactly what I wanted to say," replied Zenji Sama. "Send it!"[63]

I knew what this letter would do and I knew that I had no power to do anything to prevent its being sent. I did not dare again tell Zenji Sama that it was unwise.

He looked at me. "Do you wish to say anything?"

"No, Zenji Sama."

"You perhaps still think the letter is unwise?"

"At this juncture I think any letter is unwise, Zenji Sama."

"That is because you are afraid. There is such a thing as Fūgen; you cannot always live in Kanzeon. Kanzeon is passive; she allows everything to happen; Fūgen is active and moves when he must move. The duty of Fūgen is to teach. These people obviously do not understand Buddhism at all and I must teach them."

"Zenji Sama, there may be some terrible consequences to me as a result of this."

"You are my direct disciple. As such, it is your duty to bear those consequences."

The meeting was obviously over. I bowed. "Yes, Zenji Sama," I said as I rose and left the room.

I have noticed in the last day or two some difficulty with my physical sitting in the Meditation Hall. It's as though the top of my left thigh is larger than it should be and is causing me great pain in twisting itself into the lotus position. It's probably just the cold and nothing more. I'd best forget about it.

20th. January.

We have had foreigners coming to the temple every week-end now since the big New Year celebration. It has really been very enjoyable to have English-speaking people with me. They usually come on Saturdays, stay overnight, hear lectures and practice meditation. We decided that, for this weekend, we would have a full-scale Sesshin which would last two days, Saturday and Sunday.

We settled down in the laymen's Meditation Hall; there was a lot of squirming on the part of those who couldn't sit properly but, on the whole, it went extraordinarily well. Rev. Hajime came to see how we were doing and went off to report very happily to Zenji Sama.

30th. January.

As a result of the Sesshin a lot of people have decided that they want to meet regularly as a Zazenkai, or meditation club; to have a complete day of meditation, a complete day away from their bases; to be quiet and discuss the ways of the Buddhas. Up to now the people who came were different each week. Now we will have regulars. Rev. Hajime was a bit worried. He wanted to know whether the people who are going to come regularly are loyal to Japan or America. I found this extraordinarily odd and asked him what he meant.

He said, "This is Japanese Buddhism not American Buddhism. How can they learn Japanese Buddhism?" I couldn't quite believe what I had heard so I asked him to repeat what he'd said.

Then I said, "But Buddhism is beyond nationalities."

"Then you should find your own form. You should not be copying us."

"Doubtless when I am in England I will find my own form but, whilst I am in Japan, I must do it the way that the Japanese do. What does it matter whether they are loyal to Japan or to America? They are Buddhists first and Americans second just as I am a Buddhist first and a Briton second. I'm not a Japanese."

"Then you are different from us."

"Yes," I said, "and I am also the same. Remember all is one and all is different."

"How dare you try to teach me!"

"Rev. Hajime, what's wrong with you?"

"I am of the Gassan line; you are of the Manzan. We are different lines. Why *should* I teach you?"

"Well, if you don't want to, you don't have to."

"You are more interested in those Americans than you are in me."

"I am a priest who is doing her job; if you will excuse me I will get on with it," and I left him.

31st. January.

It seems that the letters that came from England have become known throughout the entire senior community. It is a great shame for everyone was quite obviously determined to try to fully accept both me and the foreigners who are coming here. In this place there are absolutely no secrets; it's just like living in each other's pockets from one end of the buildings to the other. There is no way in which there can be anything of the nature of privacy. The contents of the letters are known and the whole place is seething with disgust. Those who had reluctantly agreed with Zenji Sama to co-operate in really accepting me and the other foreigners in the temple are now openly saying that they were right in being reluctant; those who were eager to accept me are sad and wondering, feeling almost that I have let them down, their faith badly shaken. I wonder what it is I have done to earn such treatment from my fellow Britons? I know that some of them were extraordinarily jealous of me when I was invited to Japan but I cannot—I cannot understand how they can carry jealousy this far; if indeed it is jealousy. I just don't understand what is going on there; my mind boggles.

2nd. February.

To-day we had bean throwing; this year it was totally different. Although there was much snow it was tremendous fun. I was helping in one of the side-shows in which people could win things; old-time Japanese fair prizes, imitation cherry-blossom branches on the ends of which were fastened good luck charms; nothing very elaborate. I thoroughly enjoyed helping look after the stall. We started at about eight in the morning and finished somewhere round dusk. The stall was just a platform with four poles holding a tarpaulin over the top together with a little counter that we rigged up. It was very cold but it was so good to be with all the junior trainees. Fortunately they have not, as yet, been affected by this business in England and are just as anxious and happy and pleased to see me as they were when I got back from my own temple. I felt rather sorry for one old grandfather, with his small granddaughter, who kept paying out ten yen to see if he could win one of the prizes for the child; he kept drawing the wrong numbers out of a large box of pieces of paper. In the end, when the others weren't looking, although he had again drawn one that wasn't worth anything, I gave the child a prize and she and her grandfather went away happily together. After all, she was only three. It isn't good to make a child of that age unhappy.

6th. February.

To my surprise I was informed this morning by Rev. Hajime, in a somewhat disgruntled tone, that I am to go to the chapter meetings of the officers every day to explain and discuss the foreign business of the temple. Zenji Sama has decided that everyone must know what is happening with the foreigners whether they want to or not and he is insisting that I attend the chapter meeting in order to discuss with the officers what I intend to do and what rooms I shall need to use. When I got to the chapter room there were some quiet grumblings in the background about my not being an officer of the temple, that I should not be there and had no right to be there. I decided not to hear them. It seems the safest thing.

I explained, when all the others had finished their business, what the Foreign Section was doing and what I proposed to do with it. The information was received in absolute silence. The Director drank his tea, doing little more than stare into his cup. The rest of the officers did much the same thing. When I had finished they did not even say thank you. On the whole it was a bit like drinking tea in a mortuary. Anyway, I complied with Zenji Sama's requirements.

8th. February.

The Director informed me this morning that I will be officially assisting him at the ceremony for the Buddha's death which is to be held for the temple children in the main hall. He asked me if I had studied the duties of an assistant and I said yes.

"Good," he said. "Do you realise that no woman has ever yet assisted at a ceremony in the main temple?"

"Yes," I replied.

"Do you realise that there will be many who will criticise you for doing it?"

"Yes," I said.

"Then come with me."

I went to my room and changed into my robes, my special ceremonial ones, and went back to his room. He was still sitting quietly at his desk.

"Well?"

"What do you wish me to do?" I said.

"It is the duty of my assistant to get my robes and get me ready for the ceremony. Haven't you ever done that for Rev. Hajime?"

"Uh, I've got him his robes, yes, but I've . . . I've certainly not dressed him."

He smiled. "I don't mean from scratch. Just the koromo and kesa." His voice held a hint of great amusement.

"Which ones do you wish to wear, Rev. Director?"

"I shall wear red and a gold brocade kesa."

"Do you need a tatte-mōsu?"

"No."

"Do you need a hossu?"

"Yes."

"And you will need a mat?"

"Correct, and *you* carry the mat."

I got the necessary things and assisted him to dress.

"In the morning," he said, "I wish you to make certain that I am awake as soon as the rising bell rings. You should also bring a plum in sugared water and a cup of tea to my bed."

"Very well," I replied.

"Then you should get my robes ready, light the incense in my room, make certain that the candles are burning on my private altar and then go with me to the Meditation Hall. I have already changed your seat so that you are sitting opposite me. Do you realise that you will also be sitting opposite the chief disciplinarian?"

"Yes," I said.

"It doesn't worry you?"

"No, why should it?"

He smiled. "Good. There seems to be no problem." Then he said, "I don't know how people will react to your being my full assistant and, you know, I don't really care. Zenji Sama is extremely ill. I was once his Chief Junior. Now I am the Director of his temple. That makes me, to some extent, your elder brother. As this is so, and our father is no longer well enough to be with us at all times, I have told him that I will take you under my wing whilst I remain within this temple."

"What do you mean, 'whilst you remain within this temple?'"

"One day Zenji Sama will die. As soon as that happens, or perhaps within a very short time of it, I shall have to leave here. You should know that, at that time, there will be no room for you at all here for the next abbot is not in our line."[64]

"I see."

"You should be prepared, at all times, to leave here as indeed I am. Your certificates and papers should always be within your trainee's box."

"At all times I am in all places as are you. Why does one need to worry about certificates and papers?"

He smiled. "You and I do not need to worry about them but the world outside does and, from what I can see of your friends in London, they are going to worry very much. With the ideal comes the actual. Do not *pretend* to be holy; do that which has to be done for the good of all. Now let us go to the ceremony."

I lit the incense, placed it upon the sambō and, together, we left the room.

9th. February.

As soon as the bell rang this morning I went to the Director's room. I'd noticed that he had a dimming switch on the light over his bed and I put this on so that the light should come on gradually and not disturb him too greatly at the beginning.

He blinked up at me and smiled. "There," he said, "is the makings of the perfect assistant; an assistant that understands that the chief priest whom he assists has feelings." I looked down.

"Have you brought my sugar plum?"

"I have forgotten."

He smiled wickedly. "You see, you didn't think it through enough. You were thoughtful in one thing but not in others. You have to be thoughtful in all ways at all times.[65] Thus is Kanzeon."

"Forgive me, Reverend Director." I left the room immediately to get the plum, sugar and tea. On my return he had already dressed. I set the cups down in front of him and got his robes ready. He watched me whilst he drank. I had already lit the incense and candle upon his altar. He walked to it and bowed, then turned to me and said, "Let's hurry. We mustn't be late."

I followed him to the Meditation Hall and sat opposite him for the first time. I was glad not to be sitting opposite Zenji Sama's empty seat for it would have constantly reminded me that he was ill. It was very kind of the Director to have my seat changed. I can guess the reasons why.

After we had had breakfast and I had given instructions to the junior trainee, who is also on the Director's staff, to clean the room and arrange the new flowers on his private altar, it was time to go to another ceremony; a very big one. I got the Director's robes ready, made sure that everything was correct in the hall and set off in procession with the other trainees. The Director had already gone to Zenji Sama's lodging ahead of us for the ceremony was so important that his procession had to start from there. It was not until I got to Zenji Sama's house that I realised I had forgotten to bring the tatte-mōsu. The bells were ringing, everyone was waiting, including the important guests, and I had forgotten something! In desperation I fled back along the corridor. It is almost a mile and a half from Zenji Sama's house to the administration block where the Director and I have our rooms. I hurriedly found the tatte-mōsu and flew back to Zenji Sama's house. Kneeling down before I opened the door, and endeavouring not to look puffed, I bowed to the guests inside. To my relief the other assistant who was to help me at the ceremony had made tea and the guests and the Director and everyone else were happily drinking it. The Director's eyes twinkled as I came in but otherwise his face showed no sign of anything.[65] I carefully dressed him and we went to the ceremony which went extraordinarily well.

When it was over and I was back in his room, putting his robes away, he said, "It is said that no assistant knows how to do his job until he has made a dire mistake in the presence of the Emperor. Let's have some tea."

I made tea and we drank it together. I had noticed that my leg was still giving me some trouble and I asked him if it was possible for me to pay a visit to a doctor.

"Of course," he said.

"I think it's only a pulled muscle, Reverend Director. I don't think it can be anything more than that. It just feels extraordinarily stiff and is extremely difficult to twist up in meditation. I think if I have it looked at nothing more serious will come of it."

"Go ahead," he said. "I'm going to rest for a couple of hours anyway. I am rather tired."

I looked at him. He was obviously very old.

"Thank you, Reverend Director," I said and went off to see the doctor who told me that there was absolutely nothing wrong. So I must just forget about it. It's not important.

I have been so busy looking after the Director and writing up the translations that Rev. Hajime and I have already done in the past that I have not had time to report everything that has been happening in this diary.

18th. February.

It is really wonderful to have so much to do; performing ceremonies, going to meditation, looking after the Director, making sure that the assistant cleans his rooms properly (he has a suite of four as well as a balcony and a beautiful garden) and making certain that everything is done to keep his robes clean and mended. There is a tremendous amount of teaching that he gives every time I walk into his room. We were celebrating an important ceremony to-day, one of a whole collection of memorial ceremonies since it was his ceremonial duty day;[66] there were something like forty of them. Just before it he turned to me and said, "By doing ceremonial we can see that meditation is in all things, in all work, in all places. As we walk round in the nenge, always clockwise, always going in one direction, never going backwards, always going on, we can understand the 'Hannyashingyō.' As we stand still to recite the Scriptures we can know that, whether we are lying down, standing up or

232 · THE WILD, WHITE GOOSE

sitting still, that which is within us can be still and complete. Always the movements and the stillness are one thing; always the going, going, going on. Sometimes a priest places incense on the altar and sometimes he smells a cabbage in the pot. Sometimes he sits in the Meditation Hall and sometimes he goes to the toilet. Whatever he does must be a religious act; an act of a Buddha; for all work is the work of a Buddha. If he can see any difference between the secular and the sacred then he does not understand Buddhism at all. We can know this by how flustered he gets when he assists at a ceremony. If others frighten him, if the form of the ceremony is all that matters, if what counts is doing the ceremony exactly right as opposed to *doing* the ceremony, allowing it to do itself, if he is in any way embarrassed, he does not understand the ceremony. He who works from his centre, he who lives within his centre and radiates therefrom, can do all ceremonies without doing ceremonies and all ceremonies are needed. All of everyday life is a ceremony of gratitude. Do you understand me?"

"Yes, Reverend Director."

"You do," he said. "I watched you this morning. There were several people who were grumbling under their breath, hissing at you for not standing correctly or not holding the incense correctly or not putting it absolutely straight in the bowl. And I noticed what you did. Everytime you made the gasshō, put to rights what they had complained about and, when they had nothing to complain about, you made the gasshō and did nothing more than just stand or sit. That is to live from the centre. I am pleased with you."

"Yes, Reverend Director." I bowed and the procession started again.

19th. February.

I went to my first important outside ceremony to-day. It was a funeral at which the Director was the celebrant. I had never before seen how a Zen ceremony in an upper-class house was celebrated. It was necessary to take all the funeral and ceremonial furniture from the temple itself to set up the equivalent of a full-scale temple in the house of the dead. I did not know of this. I did not realise that, in the cities, there is such big business in funeral halls with very expensive, beautiful mortuaries and crematoria. I had only ever seen the pit into which the local farmers, after laying out their dead, burned them up. But here, in a magnificent coffin, enclosed in a carved carriage with bamboo and cloth-of-gold screens, the dead was placed upon a high altar which had been erected in the main guest room of the house. In front of it were more elaborate wood carvings all of which were borrowed from the undertaker; great carved lanterns, dragons holding lanterns. The dead was indeed the Buddha upon the altar! A kyokuroku had been brought from the temple, as well as the necessary bells, gongs and drums. Six other priests, myself as the Director's assistant and the Director conducted the funeral. When it was over a magnificent hearse, decorated in black and gold with a canopy over the top held up by four golden dragons, came to take the dead to the crematorium and two junior trainees were dispatched to recite the Scriptures whilst the body was burned. After the departure of the hearse there was a great feast in the house where we had performed the funeral. I am extraordinarily pleased to discover that the Director does not drink. He does what I do; takes three sips and says that if that isn't enough to get somebody to heaven he doesn't know what will be. I am relieved to find that there are people in existence in this priesthood who do not give way to parish pressures as do some of the priests that I have met.[67]

20th. February.

I have so much work to do now that it's beginning to be impossible for me to look after the foreigners but it is wonderful to be so busy. I am learning so much about ceremonial; I didn't realise there was so much to learn. Every day I find something new. Every day there are different types of ceremonies and the Director and Rev. Hajime say that I am the perfect assistant because I instinctively know what to do and, if I make a mistake, it is obvious to no-one; I can rectify the errors as I go along. However there is one problem. When these outside

ceremonies are over there tends to be . . . it's as if I were a conversation piece. I don't know what they would normally talk
about at big funeral meals but I become such a matter of discussion for being a "strange, rare thing, a foreign priest," that I
feel I am almost being made a public show of. To his credit the
Director talks about normal temple business, the dead, and the
funeral and treats me as if I were an ordinary assistant but some
of the other temple officers obviously like to take me along
because it is very, very enjoyable to have a conversation piece
whilst they get drunk. I wonder, do such people regard me
really as a priest or even as a human being?[67] But then, what the
heck does it matter what they regard me as? I *know* I am both.

The Director's teaching on this was good when I asked him
about it. "Let them go on as they are; the state of *their* training is
the state of *their* training. You are in *your* state of training. Do not
criticise the state they are in. Just do your own training which
may, for the time being, mean being a conversation piece."

25th. February.

I was sent for by Zenji Sama to-day. He was lying back in bed
moving the one hand that he still has the use of. His eyes were
closed and he was looking much older than I remember him.

"I want you to become my foreign secretary," he said. "I
want you to do all the foreign business that I have; to deal with
all the letters that come."

"Zenji Sama, I can't always translate them properly. I don't
know Japanese well enough."

"You can always get Rev. Hajime to help you but I want
you to write the letters. I do not want to make mistakes with
foreigners. You told me it was perhaps best if I hadn't written
any letters to London. I am thinking that I could have made a
big mistake, that what you said was right, and so I will trust
your judgement from now on. I want you, and you alone, to
write letters. After you have told me what is in them and I have
told you my wishes I want you to write all the foreign letters."

"Zenji Sama, that is such a big thing. I . . . I could be dealing with really important foreign people. This temple is the

royal temple. We frequently have government members come here, cabinet ministers. The Emperor comes twice a year. Besides, I have written some really silly letters to London myself over what has happened—I frequently make mistakes like that—but I was so angry[68] because they had caused you to worry when you were so ill. I shouldn't have written the letters I did. Considering all this, I don't think I'm capable of doing so important a job."

"I think you are, for you know how important it is; I think you are the right person and I want you to do it. I also want the entire temple to know that, whatever is said in London, whatever is said *anywhere*, whatever anyone may think, *I* trust you. You are my true disciple and always have been; *I* trust my *true* disciple. This is my wish. Do not cross me in it."

"No, Zenji Sama, I will obey your wish but I truly wonder if I am capable of doing that which you feel I should do."

"Whilst you have such thoughts you are capable. Leave me now. I am very tired."

"Yes, Zenji Sama." I bowed and left him.

26th. February.

When the opportunity arose I told the Director of Zenji Sama's wish. He said, "Zenji Sama is very clever. By trusting you thus absolutely no-one here can doubt your integrity with regard to the affair in London but you may find that such favour will cause you great problems later on, especially as soon as Zenji Sama is dead. Remember my warning. Whilst *I* am here you will be safe; when I am not here go quickly. Under no circumstances stay here when I am not here."

"Yes, Reverend Director. There are some other things I have to tell you about. The Americans want me to go down to their bases at least twice a week to lecture. May I do this? It's going to mean that I shan't be able to attend you so much."

"It will be good for you to get out a bit with your own people; it will be good for you to get some Western food. I do not want you ill again as you were before. It will be good for you to go there. How long do you think it will take you each day?"

"Well, it will probably take me an afternoon and evening twice a week. Is that all right?"

"Yes. In any case you must learn to teach; the sooner the better."

I thanked him and went away to make the necessary arrangements.

28th. February.

At the chapter meeting this morning I was informed by the chief guest master, the treasurer and the disciplinarian that I must keep records of all the foreigners that come to the temple. They want a properly organised department for the foreigners since this is what Zenji Sama also wishes. He called them all to him yesterday and told them that an absolutely new and complete department is to be set up. There must be no difference between its status and that of the other departments of the temple. He has also given instructions for me to buy the necessary equipment for the office. I asked if there was a specific way in which the records were to be kept and was told, "As we keep ours," so I presume that I had better study the ancient business methods of the Chikoryō quickly otherwise I will make some bad mistakes, employing modern ways in a Middle Ages setting.

3rd. March.

To-day I was able to get the various items of office equipment together; the main office gave me the necessary cash from the temple funds. Unfortunately, when it arrived, there was no place to put it. It seems that the person in charge of allocating rooms does not want the Foreign Section to be set up and so is unwilling to give out a room for the purpose. The reason he has given to Zenji Sama is that there are no spare rooms in the temple. All the things are waiting in one of the halls. Some seniors really do make problems here.[67]

4th. March.

Rev. Hajime has arranged for me to share the Treasury in which he works. He has to be out of it for a large part of the day and he says that someone is needed to guard the safe. By so doing he has been able to get all my office equipment at least into a room and out of the corridor and hall in which it was standing. I wouldn't have thought that such a safe as his needed guarding! It is huge. I don't think I've ever seen one as big or as old. My desk has been placed in front of it and I sit there, officially guarding the safe, in fact doing the Foreign Guest Department work and listening for the Director's calls from the next door room whenever he wants me.

My leg is a bit odd; I started limping to-day. Maybe I should go and see another doctor. It is getting quite difficult to sit.

10th. March.

The Empress arrived to-day. She comes twice a year to pray for her ancestors. All the head temples in the country have shrines such as this and the Imperial family goes to each one in turn to pray for their relatives.

I had just come back from visiting one of the bases when the chief guest master came up to me and said, "Quickly, you must go to Zenji Sama's guest department. It is very important." Unfortunately he didn't explain why. The only thing he said was, as we went along, "You really must meet this lady. It is very important that you meet her." Just as I got to the steps that led up to Zenji Sama's guest department I saw a large concourse of priests and ladies and, in the centre, one middle-aged one who looked rather kind and who was obviously the person concerned. She smiled at me as I came up to her and, since no-one seemed to be willing to introduce us, I held out my hand. She shook it with great glee, obviously enjoying herself and thoroughly pleased with the fact that I had offered to shake hands with her. I noticed that everyone seemed to be startled but, since nobody explained who she was, I felt that I had done the right thing and, to my delight, she began speaking in English, telling me how glad she was that I was there and hoping to see me again on her next visit. She passed on and I joined the crowd that was with her.

When I got back to my room the Director paid me a visit.

"I want you to shake hands with me," he said.

I looked a little startled but agreed. "May I ask why, Reverend Director?" I asked.

"You shook the hand of the Empress of Japan. No living person has touched that hand other than the Emperor. You do not realise what a great thing you have done."

"Really? I'm awfully sorry. Somebody should have explained to me who she was." I had barely got these words out when my door opened and the entire staff of officers appeared, formed a queue behind the Director and, each in turn, required me to shake hands with them; behind them came a huge queue of junior trainees. Ah well, I suppose shaking the hand of him or her who shook the hand is the next best thing to shaking the hand.

11th. March.

There are many arrangements going on at the moment for a great celebration to be held next year. At the chapter meeting this morning we were told that a whole new branch of the temple is to be opened to deal with it. There have been people working on this for the past ten years but now they are to have a large, complete staff and a whole new set of offices. The temple staff is going to be very swollen. It will be interesting to see what new priests come. I am told that my part will be to look after the Director as usual as well as all the foreigners who may attend.

18th. March.

Now that I am sitting in the Treasury most of my spare time Rev. Hajime has much more time for translating with me than he had before and we have got going again on many of the things that we had not, as yet, been able to finish. Apart from this, work continues as usual with me looking after the Director, his household affairs, assisting him at all ceremonies, going off to lecture and teach and looking after the foreigners. I really don't get much time to write this diary.

20th. March.

Things have gone so awfully well since January; I have been able to learn a tremendous amount. I thought everything was going too well to last. This morning a letter came for Zenji Sama from that "friend" of mine in England. I don't know what it is that I have done to deserve such friends; his behaviour really does make me wonder.[67] After apologising to Zenji Sama for having written about me in the way he had, he then said how ashamed he was that Zenji Sama had checked out his words with another person; however, as is usual with this man's letters, he can never prevent himself from being vitriolic. He went on to say even worse things about me than he had before. He explained that in Europe they are accustomed to think of a rōshi as an enlightened *man*, an absolute master of the Dharma and a teacher of *very* high standing. The British, he said, know from experience that few of these men are likely to be found and he stated that all those who come to England from Japan confirm this. For this reason he was startled to be told that "Rev. Miss Kennett" was a rōshi. He told Zenji Sama that I could certainly return to England at any time for I am English and there is also certainly nothing to stop me teaching Buddhism, as do other ladies in Europe. He ended by saying that he had no desire to quarrel with me and that if he was unhappy it was because of the way I had been made the messenger of information which he felt should have been addressed personally to himself.

I had completely forgotten about that "information." It had happened within months of my coming to Japan. I had been required by the Administration Department to explain to this man that he had been ordained as a lay Buddhist and not as a priest. This was reasonable since he had never been in a training monastery but there had been a misunderstanding at his Reception Ceremony. It had never occurred to me that he would blame me and carry this matter around in his mind for such a long time. The authorities had told him he could come to Japan to be trained as a priest, they had apologised for the mistake, and here he was still blaming me for the fact that I had been required to write him the letter explaining it since the authorities could not write English.

After Zenji Sama had read this letter and talked to me about it I said, "Zenji Sama, please don't ask me to have *anything* to do with answering letters to this man. Obviously anything I say, anything I do, is going to be held in evidence against me. Whatever I try to do to help him he is going to misunderstand; whatever I write is going to be misinterpreted. I see no point whatsoever in perpetuating this sort of misery. Please, Zenji Sama, let us not even reply to this letter. I don't think it deserves a reply.[67] I don't think it *needs* one."

"I understand," he said. "If I have a reply to this letter I will get Rev. Hajime to make it but know that I still want you to be my foreign secretary in all matters other than this."

"Thank you, Zenji Sama," and I left him.

21st. March.

To-day a letter came for *me* from my so-called friend. He is really angry over the way in which I was required to be the messenger of what he considers private information. I thought at the time that the Administration Department should not have used me for the job but they haven't got anyone who speaks English well and, to make matters worse, no-one who really knows him. As they said, it was reasonable for them to think that I, as his friend, would be the best person to break the news to him as gently as possible and I certainly did try to do that. Anyway, after telling me about all this and giving me a lot of information on his own history in Buddhism, he did at least have the decency to say that what had happened was not my fault. He wanted to know who it was that had required information as to his qualifications as a priest but I felt that this was not a matter that I should discuss with him. After all, such a thing as that is best left in the limbo to which it belongs. He pointed out that he didn't think that any further monasteries were needed in England because of the economic problems and then, as usual, went off into his usual tirade. It seems that there is no way in which he can prevent himself complaining to me because Zenji

Sama has made me one of his heirs. He said that he was not happy about my being described as a rōshi, explaining that in Britain they have come to expect a great deal from anyone given such a description:– absolute mastery of the Dharma, a high degree of enlightenment, and being an "exceptional" person altogether. To most Western Buddhists, he said, this is not a matter of either priestly degrees or anything comparable. He cited the example of a lay rōshi who had recently passed his way who had a high reputation, higher than most clerical ones. He informed me that the present trend even among many Buddhists in Japan seems to be moving away altogether from the temples and the priesthood according to all reports, including official ones.

He then said that he was glad I had given him a cat a few years ago. I don't know. I came here to do something about *me*; I didn't come here to be able to go back and convert the world. As I knew when I came here, if I could convert *me* I'd be happy. I've no desire to go back to England; I've no desire to go *anywhere*. All I want to do is stay here with Zenji Sama and train to the best of my ability; and these people keep behaving as though I am about to take over their little tin-pot organisations.[67] This man is the one who wrote to Zenji Sama in the first place requiring someone to come to England. Zenji Sama offered me and now he hears that there is no room for any further teachers in London. What this man really means is that there is no room for me; but then, maybe I knew that long ago when the war[69] ended and so many young people like me had no place to live, no place to go, other than abroad. I sometimes think that the crime my generation committed was coming back from the war.[70]

I have been required to make preparations for the foreigners here for Jūkai. It will mean a lot of work and I must admit I'm looking forward to it. Zenji Sama is sending many, many letters to me to translate and so my time is completely filled. I suppose I ought to reply to this man's letter. I don't know that I can; not, at any rate, in a way that will help him for his mind is completely closed to me.[71]

My leg seems to be giving me greater difficulties.

Late this evening I sat down to draft a reply to the letter that came this morning. I felt I must make an attempt. I probably didn't say the things I have said at all in the way in which I should have said them. I asked the Director before I did it how I should reply and he said, "Even the most enlightened man has difficulty at times in doing such things as this. Just do the very best you can and, whatever you say to him, do it with love in your heart. Do not do it with any intention of hurting. The art of being Fūgen is to love the creator of karma whilst he is reaping its fruit. To have respect for him as the Buddha who, never-the-less, must take the consequences of his actions. In so doing, and *only* in so doing, can the person learn the true purpose of karmic consequence which is to teach and not to punish." With this in mind I sat down to write the letter.

Halfway through it the Director came to my room and said, "Hold still within the centre or you will not be able to speak the Truth; you must reply to this as you replied to the questions upon the altar of the lotus. When men cut off a limb from the Buddha, or beat him, always his place must be calm and still and filled with the heavenly deities." He then left me and I wrote the letter as best I could. I told my friend that I felt that what he had written was rather brutal and there seemed to be quite a lot of hostility in his words towards our school of Zen; certainly this is how Zenji Sama feels. I cannot remember the exact words I used; I do not doubt that I made a lot of mistakes in that letter.

There are few people, I suppose, in existence who can understand that I really love England very deeply. To know that Buddhism there is so gravely misunderstood makes me long to return to teach the peace and joy that I have learned here, but this is not going to be possible if mistrust is going to be sown from one end of the country to the other by people like this man.[67] The Americans are constantly telling me that when I leave here there will always be a home for me in America; per-haps I should consider this as a possibility. If I were to go to England, as things are, Buddhism could be torn to pieces.[72]

9th. April.

We started Jūkai this morning. There are a number of foreigners attending and I have had to spend a lot of time explaining the various ceremonies to them. They seem to have some objections, however, to ceremonial; they feel that it is not as important as is doing meditation. I explained to them what the Director had explained to me about the use of ceremonial, moving meditation, and finding their centre within themselves, finding that all activity is meditation, but it is obvious that they do not know it in their hearts yet and some of them do not even believe me.

16th. April.

The old chief lecturer who I had found so wonderful and who welcomed me when I first came here left this morning and a new one arrived this afternoon. The first thing he did was praise me to my face after he had sent for me. He then told me that other foreigners were not as I was. *I* had understood the wonder and the beauty of Japanese religion, which was true religion, but other foreigners didn't understand it at all. He had met many of them. I explained to him that we were going to have a lot of foreigners here and he became angry.

"I do not think that is good," he said. "Having one is one thing, having a number is different. In any case, how can foreigners understand our religion completely? Foreigners are not as we are."

I wondered if I was misunderstanding his words so I begged to be excused. I *could* have misunderstood him. After all, my Japanese is not nearly as perfect as it might be. I sincerely *hope* I misunderstood him.

21st. April.

Another letter came to-day in reply to the one I had sent; it would really have been better if I hadn't replied. Zenji Sama sent for me. It seems he knows of the other letters that I have received and is furious that I had somehow circumvented his finding out what had been written; I only did it so as not to worry him. I don't know who it is that has snitched to him. I know that there are other people who keep letters from him when they feel that there are things that will hurt him. There must still be someone here who is determined either to discredit me in his eyes or to harm him.[73] I hope against hope that it is not the latter.

I did not want to translate the letter for him and I explained to him that it was a private one to myself but he insisted on hearing it and sent for Rev. Hajime. As usual my "friend" had completely misinterpreted and misunderstood what I had said. The letter was just full of frustrated greed and envy over my being in the temple. One paragraph was particularly telling. He said that the difference between a nun and a priestess is purely academic in the West. He mentioned that there is one nun, "of a sort," living in England and that she has to live alone as she cannot live in any of the monastic houses now established. The Bikkuni order, he explained, is regarded in Theravada, the prevailing stream of thought among British Buddhists, as being extinct. Nuns are therefore treated as lay-women. He went on to remind me that priests and priestesses are suspect in English Buddhist circles anyhow,[74] since they think that the word is really a misnomer in Buddhism and many people have spent many years denying the existence of such people in the Buddhist fold.

When Zenji Sama heard this I thought he was going to have another stroke and both Rev. Hajime and I were horrified.

"We shouldn't have translated it for him," I gasped.

Rev. Hajime said, "We had no alternative. He insisted on hearing."

But Zenji Sama was all right. "If that is what he thinks," he said, "then he is denying me who made him a Buddhist. He is saying that I, as a priest, am not a priest." He turned his eyes full on me; they were terrifying. "If he wishes to follow such thoughts, if he wishes to follow such beliefs, I forbid you ever again, whilst I live, to write to him, speak to him or have anything whatsoever to do with him. Do you understand me?"

"Yes, Zenji Sama. I understand you."

I was very frightened for I was sure that he would die on the spot.

"I forbid you to have anything to do with him," he repeated, "ever! Not merely whilst I live. Forever! Do you understand that?"

"Yes, Zenji Sama."

There was a long silence. I was grieved by the terrible suffering in his face. I didn't know what to do or say and then suddenly inspiration came.

"Zenji Sama, to-day or to-morrow—I'm not sure which for I am waiting for a telegram—there is a young Chinese girl coming here to become my disciple. She will be your grand-disciple. I will bring her to see you as soon as she comes."

The pain vanished from his face. "A young girl to become my grand-disciple?"

"Yes, Zenji Sama."

"Ah, you mean my grand-disciple?"

"Yes."

"That is good news. Bring her to me as soon as she comes."

I bowed. "Is there anything I can do for you, Zenji Sama?"

"No. Do not reply to that letter," and he closed his eyes. Rev. Hajime and I bowed. We both left him.

On the way back through Zenji Sama's house the chief assistant became extremely angry with me for upsetting Zenji Sama so much.

"If someone hadn't told him that I had had these letters he would not have been upset," I said. "There are things you withhold from him. How is it that he could have learned of these letters?" He looked uncomfortable. "You have access to him at all times," I said. "There is only one way in which he could have got that information."

To his credit the assistant looked even more uncomfortable and, if it had been possible for him to blush, I think he would have done so, but he turned away and made no further comment. I've probably made an enemy.[75] Ah well, at this stage it doesn't make much difference. He had obviously told Zenji

Sama about the letters. I must remember that he is no friend of
mine and certainly no friend of Zenji Sama.[67, 76]

22nd. April.

I received a letter from the parishioners of my temple to-day
requiring me to come back for some ceremonies. The Chinese girl
arrives some time this afternoon. I must go to the port to meet her.

23rd. April.

After spending the night here, the Chinese girl, whose name
is Andrea, went with me to my own temple. The journey
seemed long and tiring although we went on the new express
train. When I got out I found that my leg was causing me more
trouble than usual. What did it was probably just sitting in one
position for so long a time.

6th. May.

I sent telegrams to the temple in Tokyo to tell them that I
was ordaining Andrea this morning. I took her to see Zenji Sama
on the 22nd., just after she arrived. He was overjoyed, all smiles
and happy, but I must really make sure that I shield him from
any more shocks of the sort caused by the letters from England.
Whilst Zenji Sama lives I will never write to those people again
whatever happens; such worry for him is just too cruel.

The ordination was attended by some friends of mine one of
whom had been in the Tokyo temple with me during my first
year and has now returned to his own temple; he is now married.
Andy came down from Tokyo specially to be a witness. Just as
we were about to do the actual ordination ceremony Andrea had
second thoughts; she wasn't sure if she wanted to go through
with it. After a few minutes she decided that she did and we
went ahead.

7th. May.

I told Andy about the problems in England since he is a fellow Briton. He looked somewhat concerned but said he didn't
think it was worth worrying about; he then went back to Tokyo.

10th. May.

I telephoned Rev. Hajime from the only local call-box which happens to be, of all places, in the wine store and was somewhat appalled to hear that Andy, on returning to Tokyo, had gone to see him and said that what was happening in England was my fault and that, by writing the letters I had, I had caused the problems with the people concerned. He is blaming me completely for having written the letters and for not having persuaded Zenji Sama to make no replies at all. He seems to have forgotten that the letters originated in England, not with me. Rev. Hajime is now in a very strange frame of mind; he doesn't know who to trust. I wonder sometimes if people understand fully what it is they do. Rev. Hajime blew up on the 'phone. He wanted to know how it was possible for one Englishman to speak against another Englishman in such a way to a foreigner, for no Japanese, however badly he had behaved, would ever be spoken against by another Japanese to an out-sider; and no *Buddhist* would ever do so either; he was shocked and surprised at Andy. I suppose all these problems come out of the differences of national attitudes of mind to others. Is talk-ing against others, I wonder, a British national trait? What a ter-rible thought; and yet I *am* beginning to wonder. But why should this man in England, and now Andy, want to harm *me*? It makes no sense; I barely know them. The Japanese have this wonderful feeling of nationality, of family, of belonging. Any-one who speaks against one Japanese speaks against the whole Japanese nation; anyone who speaks against an Englishman is merely speaking against one individual. It is a pity that the peo-ple who make all these troubles in England have no compre-hension of what it is that they do over here.

The other thing I heard was that someone is spreading a rumour in the temple to the effect that I'm in bed with someone. I wonder who? It's a pity they haven't got something better to do than gossip.[77] I've got so much work; even if I wanted to get into bed with somebody I wouldn't have the energy to do it.

11th. May.

I had a card from Rev. Hajime this morning; he was very kind. He said that an unclean mirror cannot reflect a true picture; I must be careful not to be blinded by the dust that people throw or I shall not see the reflection clearly. It is a good warning. I will remember to watch out. It was kind of him to send me the card.

There were three memorial ceremonies to-day. It's amazing how much I have learned whilst being with the Director. It really helped. I can be celebrant so much more efficiently now.

14th. May.

There are distinct disadvantages in having a lot of money. Andrea is the daughter of a Chinese millionaire and she seems to think that she can buy enlightenment with cash. Her main interest at the moment is visiting the nearest big city for presents for her family and new clothes for herself. I explained to her that a priest's duty is solely to wear robes and nothing more but she doesn't seem to understand what being a member of the priesthood is. I now wonder very much about why the person who sent her to me, a Chinese priest of high standing, recommended her as a perfect person to enter the priesthood. I am really worried. I doubt if she will make it past the very early stages of her training.[78] Certainly she shows no other signs at the moment. What shall I tell Zenji Sama? The news will upset him very much.

19th. May.

A card came from Rev. Hajime to-day. He told me that the Administration Department is sending me a special certificate in English to prove that I am a priest for as, and when, I may need it. This is because of the letter from England concerning nuns and priestesses. I am sure it will be very useful. They are also sending me a copy in Japanese.

One of the priests in this area comes to visit me frequently and is helping very much financially by inviting me to outside ceremonies. It is very kind of him to do so much. Andy arrived this morning. The certificates I had been promised also arrived.

25th. May.

A card came from Rev. Hajime to say that I am expected back in Tokyo on the 31st. Zenji Sama is, at present, at a spa not far from here and wants to see me. The only way that he could get another doctor to look at him was by going away from Tokyo as if cured. He became officially ill again at the spa and a new doctor has diagnosed a stroke. Now he can be treated for what is really wrong with him without causing the first doctor to lose face. What a system! I sincerely hope I never fall seriously ill here. There were many outside ceremonies in the village to-day.

30th. May.

Some friends of mine from Kyoto came to see me to-day. It was good to have them here. Unfortunately there are so few trains that connect with the two buses a day leaving this village; we were only able to spend a few hours together.

14th. June.

A card came from Rev. Hajime. He said that Zenji Sama is now deeply concerned at having been so angry with me for not showing him the letters; he says he completely understands my reason. Another letter has come for Zenji Sama from the person he wrote to in England concerning me. Rev. Hajime's card said that this letter from England has caused Zenji Sama much concern. Apparently part of it proves that my opinion was right; that he is refusing to allow our school of Zen to be spread in London. He said that when I come back to the temple he wants to know all about it. I don't know "all about it," and, if I did, I don't know that it would be wise to tell him. Why can't he let this confounded mess sink into the limbo to which it belongs and leave it there? It would make much more sense than constantly stirring it up. They tell me I must know that mud exists but not stir it up: just grow lotus blossoms in it. The lotus roots are in the mud but the stem and the blossom rise out of it. If the stirring continues surely this mess is only going to get worse. What am I doing, criticising Zenji Sama? Whatever he does is *right*. I must keep the mirror clean; I am becoming the worst of all trainees. I must let others go on and do my own training; just that and nothing more.

17th. June.

Another letter from Rev. Hajime. Just before I left to come here I carefully packed everything in my room. With the exception of three boxes and a basket containing clothes that I will need when in the Tokyo temple, I have arranged for everything to come here. Some friends of mine, connected with the British authorities, are coming to spend a few days with me and will bring the things with them in their car. It occurred to me that if, as the Director says, it could be dangerous for me in the Tokyo temple when both he and Zenji Sama are away, it might be advisable for me to be down here much of the time until Zenji Sama returns and this means that I'll need many of my things. By leaving just the bare necessities in the Tokyo temple I shall be able to come here and work efficiently whensoever I wish. With regard to the mess in England, Rev. Hajime said something very sad; he said that human beings are really selfish animals, but that they want to dream of perfection. When they speak hatred and evil they are dreaming of perfection. He concluded that I should remember what he said to me when he saw me first, "Be very careful or we will break your heart." That applies now to my own country as well as here. His English was a little quaint but somehow it gave the letter added poignancy. He sent me a couple of hundred envelopes and some special stationery that has been printed for the Foreign Section as well as my office files and told me to do the work for the Foreign Department from here and look after my new disciple. I know that he is warning me to stay away whilst Zenji Sama is not in the temple. Perhaps I somehow knew instinctively that Zenji Sama was going to go away; perhaps that was really why I packed my things as I did. Oh, what silly things people do! Whyever can't they love and accept each other?

20th. June.

It is getting extraordinarily hot here. Andy, I and my other British friends from Tokyo are busy putting up a wall around the temple. It is going to cost us thirty thousand yen the villagers tell me. I can't help feeling that if we had bought the materials ourselves it would have cost a lot less.

30th. June.

We have finished the wall but the villagers are refusing to allow us to put up a gate for "fear of the foreigners inside." They think we will make it into some sort of fortress and they themselves won't be able to get in to get near their statue of Kanzeon. It is no use our trying to explain to them that this is not so; that all we want is to be able to close the gate at night and feel safe from people who put their hands through doors that are only made of paper and bamboo. I'm not at all sure how we are going to deal with this problem but I know we will have to.

4th. July.

Another card came from Rev. Hajime. Zenji Sama, who has now returned to Tokyo, is still getting letters from this man in England. According to Rev. Hajime, he asked why I didn't go back to England, and said I should go back there soon. Rev. Hajime has discussed the situation in London with the Vice-Abbot whom I have met on one or two occasions. He has rather different opinions on the subject from Zenji Sama, according to Rev. Hajime, but the latter did not tell me what they were. Somehow Zenji Sama's alleged comments do not ring true. Something in me finds it difficult to believe what Rev. Hajime said about him. Zenji Sama has always implied that he wants me here until his death.

We are continuing our schedule here as usual, working hard at our meditation and Morning Service and having our discussions. Andrea is causing some problems, still insisting on being out most of the day sightseeing and not doing very much in the way of genuine training.

9th. July.

I received a card from Rev. Hajime in reply to one I had sent concerning the difficulties with the village over the gate. According to Rev. Hajime, if he explains to the villagers what I have asked him to, which is simply what I set down earlier in this diary, viz. that we need a gate so as to be able to feel completely private and safe at night, everyone's feelings here will be hurt. It is useless for me to try to explain to him that it is not the villagers of whom I am afraid. The people I have to be careful of are the sort who came from that magazine last year; they printed an article about me none of which is true for they never met me. The photographs they had were acquired from Mrs. Suzuki, photographs I had given her. The article said that I am setting up a great new sect of Buddhism to be run by foreigners, a foreign temple, here in the west of Japan. This has infuriated the officers in the temple in Tokyo who say that I am trying to set myself above Zenji Sama. Zenji Sama is deeply hurt by the whole affair for he knows the true story; he knows that I do not want to be here; so does the Director. This sort of thing is going to go on as long as I have no means of keeping people of an unsavory[79] character out of here.

I telephoned Rev. Hajime to see if there was any way in which we could sue the magazine concerned but he says there isn't. After I had told him I realised that he was right. Suing them, like everything else, could only make the matter worse. What a blessing is meditation. Without it I could not survive.[80]

12th. July.

I have been trying to teach Andrea for days but she refuses to listen to anything I have to say. She quite obviously believes more in Shin Buddhism than she does in Zen which, after all, is what she was brought up in, and I have suggested that it might be as well if she goes back to Shin rather than stay with us. It would make a lot more sense.

Andy has been helping much with the carpentry. The house, apart from sections of the roof, is now in extraordinarily good condition. My leg is still causing me much trouble. To sit for forty minutes now is almost agony. Andy denies everything Rev. Hajime says he said. Who the hell[81] am I to believe?

19th. July.

Another card from Rev. Hajime asking me to teach English to some of his villagers. I have agreed to do so. He complained bitterly that I have not written him any letters since the one in which I asked about the gate. I really haven't written to him because I didn't want to cause him problems. This mess in England is quite enough for him to put up with; Zenji Sama seems to be constantly complaining about it; the other officers are at him concerning it with regard to me. If people don't see letters coming through the post from me they're not going to be able to ask what it is I'm talking to him about. If I write to him . . . . . well . . . . . there's the danger of rumour too. I don't want to give wrong impressions. I don't want to worry anyone. These are my affairs, not his.

20th. July.

I heard of two young people I know who are coming from England to visit Japan. I telephoned Rev. Hajime to ask if it would be possible for them to stay in the Tokyo temple. They are coming, it seems, to check me out on behalf of the person whom Zenji Sama wrote to in London! I felt there were some misunderstandings on the 'phone, however. It is sometimes extraordinarily difficult to explain things in the Japanese language, there being no absolute equivalent to, or even approximation of, some British terms. I tried to explain clearly but it was obvious that Rev. Hajime did not understand me. Again and again I tried to explain to him but, in the end, he said he must hang up because the 'phone call was costing too much money. Part of me wondered if the misunderstanding was deliberate; what a wicked thought to have! Of course not. I *must* stop this.

31st. July.

A letter came from Rev. Hajime to say that he has been made Vice-Director. There are rumours running about the temple that his advancement first to Treasurer and now to Vice-Director is due to the fact that he taught me, Zenji Sama's pet. Because of this Zenji Sama is pulling him up the ladder.

There has been a grave mistake over the occupation of the young couple coming from England; because of it they are going to be treated as if they are V.I.P.'s rather than ordinary guests. I must rectify this quickly. I must make it clear that there is a mistake otherwise I shall be in very great trouble. I *knew* Rev. Hajime had misunderstood me on the 'phone.

I wrote a letter to Rev. Hajime to this effect, trying once again to explain matters clearly. I can only hope this clarifies the situation.

1st. August.

Zenji Sama is demanding my return at once. A peremptory telephone call came to the village call-box and Zenji Sama's assistant didn't mind how long he had to wait on the other end for me to be called there. He said that Zenji Sama wanted me at once. I explained my difficulty with physical sitting, that I did not understand what was wrong with my leg; he implied that I didn't want to be with Zenji Sama. I agreed to return on the seventh.

4th. August.

A card came from Rev. Hajime asking me to meet him at his temple to-morrow. He wants to talk of what has been going on in London, especially about the "friends" that I have there. I have told him I will come.

5th. August.

I went to Rev. Hajime's temple this morning. His wife was neither friendly nor unfriendly and, after we had had some tea in the general living room, Rev. Hajime settled down to discuss the things he wrote about yesterday. I explained to him again, very carefully, what I tried to explain in my last letter but he was obviously in no mood to listen. He became very angry and said, "So you have told us that these people are much more important than they are!"

"No," I said, "I have tried to explain to you that their occupation does not fall into any exact category that you have in Japan. It is higher than one description and lower than another, something in between. You Japanese insist on putting everything into pigeon-holes which must fit exactly. We don't."

"Then we have laid on all these elaborate arrangements for nothing," he said. "These people are not important or influential. What use are they to us?"

"They can help clarify the letters received from England concerning me."

"That only helps you. Why should we welcome them if they have no influence in high places to help us?"

I got up. "I think I'll go back to my own temple, Rev. Hajime. I see no point in staying here."

"You had better come back to Tokyo quickly or there will be great trouble for you."

"Why?" I said.

"Because Zenji Sama can have your visa cancelled at any time since he is your sponsor. Without a sponsor you cannot stay here and you will certainly get no-one else to sponsor you if Zenji Sama decides to withdraw his support."

"Why are you behaving like this?" I asked.

"There are many rumours because I have helped you. I do not like these rumours. I do not like it said that I have become Vice-Director because I know you."

"It isn't true and you know it," I replied. "Why do you worry about such silly things?"

"What do you mean, 'such silly things?'"

"Whenever I have worried about things like that in the past you've told me not to worry about them."

"So you presume to teach me again?"

"No, Rev. Hajime. Please let me go back to my temple."

"You have gravely misled us with regard to these two people from England."

"I have told you the truth as best I can. If I have misled you I am sorry but it is not my fault that you have made elaborate arrangements for welcoming them, nor is it my fault that they are not influential enough for you. I told you the truth. I told you they were both higher and lower than you thought; that they were something in between the two. If you can't understand that, and act accordingly, then there's not much I can do to help you. They can clarify the letters from London if they will, that is all."

I said good-bye to his wife and went home.

7th. August.

I returned to Tokyo this morning together with Andrea who has decided to go back to Malaysia; she says that Zen is not going to give her what she had hoped for. Her idea of Zen, it seems, is that all she should have to do is sit in meditation for hours on end, be waited on, do nothing else and—behold, she would be in heaven! I'm afraid the Buddhas and Patriarchs don't make life that simple; it's much more complicated than that. I applaud her intention to leave Japan.

8th. August.

I went to the port to-day to meet the young couple from England. It was good to see them again. I took them back to the temple in the car that Zenji Sama had provided. As soon as we arrived Zenji Sama sent word that he wanted to see them at once. He was overjoyed as they walked in. He looked up at me from the bed, trying to rise, saying, "Now I will hear the truth. Now I will know." Something clutched at my heart for fear he would again be disappointed. I do so not want that for him.

He asked them about the letters from London. They were very obviously non-committal; they did not want to speak in front of me. Zenji Sama hid his disappointment and, after having tea with them, turned to me and said, "Anything in the temple they want they are to have. Do you understand me?" I could feel his disappointment but his compassion was boundless.

"Yes, Zenji Sama," I replied.

"Good," he said and lay back in bed. "I am tired now. Please leave me."

I bowed. "Thank you, Zenji Sama."

As we were getting up to go the wife turned to him and said in English, "We have very wonderful monks in England. We have one who has been ordained in every Buddhist sect in existence so that he will be able to bring all the Truth together. He knows every teaching and practice. We do not believe in sectarianism in England."

Zenji Sama gave me a strange look, obviously requiring an interpretation. I made no reply but a university professor friend of mine, who had come from Kyoto and who spoke excellent English, translated for him. The old man gave me a long look, then seemed to heave himself up in the bed. "You know," he said, "*anyone* who meditates runs the risk of being grabbed by the Cosmic Buddha. You should remember that."

The professor translated this into English. "What does he mean?" I was asked.

"He means," I said, "that what you have said indicates that meditation is not much practised in England. What matters most to you is the study of doctrines, Scriptures, practices, debating and lectures. He wishes to point out that bringing all the schools of teaching together is not nearly as important as meditation."

Zenji Sama asked the professor what I had said and he told him. The old man said, "He who meditates runs the risk of being grabbed by the Cosmic Buddha. If you do not wish to know the *Truth* of Buddhism just study the Scriptures and doctrines, lecture and read books. Do *not* meditate. But, if you meditate, know that you *will* be grabbed by the Cosmic Buddha. The Cosmic Buddha *is*."

The professor looked at me and I almost imperceptibly shook my head. There was no point in interpreting that. Zenji Sama looked at me, smiled softly, the professor and I bowed, and all of us left the room. As we went out the girl assistant said, "Don't forget what Zenji Sama said. They may have *anything* they wish in this temple."

10th. August.

One of the two guests from England, the wife, is causing some problems because she cannot sit properly. She insists that she must have chairs to sit on; she cannot sit on the floor. I can appreciate how difficult this is for someone with a chronic physical disability but the fact remains that *she* wanted to come here; I see no way in which the rules can be deliberately waived for her even if she is *not* able to sit on the floor comfortably. Both she and her husband made so many waves this morning that I didn't quite know what to do.

The Director had arranged several special ceremonies for their benefit. Such an unprecedented honour for a guest has been unknown before now in this temple and the officers are grumbling loudly. They feel that these two are receiving far more honour than they should. It was unfortunate that the wife, halfway through one of these special ceremonies, got up saying she was going to leave because the floor was too uncomfortable for her to sit on. When I suggested that she should not do so since the Director had been kind enough to arrange the ceremonies in their honour she said, "Then I must sit in that chair over there," and made for the celebrant's chair which was in the middle of the Hondō. I could hardly believe my eyes. A couple of my friends watched with faint amusement as I charged across the hall to prevent what was obviously going to be a catastrophe.

My own difficulty with physical sitting is growing much worse but I have no alternative but to try and sit. I pointed this out to the wife but it didn't seem to have much effect.

The Director called me to his room shortly afterwards and said, "I think it is well if your young friends and you visit the Vice-Abbot in his temple. I have arranged an air-conditioned car for the three of you."

I knew that what he really meant was that these two were causing too much trouble. When the husband insisted on finding his maps in his suitcase before he got into the car, no matter how much that car was costing the temple by being kept waiting, I saw the Director's smothered disgust and exasperation. I bowed to him and asked him to forgive me. He smiled gently and said, "Not your fault." I got the pair into the car and we drove off. I heaved such a sigh of relief.

I can only guess what the other officers in the temple will be saying now. What a reputation England is going to get here! First all those letters and now this.

17th. August.

The couple from England and I went over to Rev. Hajime's temple this morning. He had asked us to go because of the OBon festival and he wanted me to assist at the ceremonies. When they were all over we had dinner together and Rev. Hajime had a long talk with us. He explained much to the two with me concerning my 'fight' for women's rights in Japan. To his very great surprise they were not happy about it. They obviously did not consider that such a thing was either necessary or wise.

We all went to bed late but Rev. Hajime called me to his room again when the others had retired. "You know," he said, "I'm wondering very much about these two. Why was it that they wanted to be treated as ordinary members of the Buddhist Church here?"

"I thought I had warned you, Rev. Hajime, as I tried to warn Zenji Sama, that in England the Buddhist Church is thought of in a totally different way from what it is here. They want to be treated as ordinary members of the Buddhist Church *as they know it*. Their exact words in their letters to me were that they wanted to be treated as if they were 'monks in training' but they don't know what 'monks in training' are. And if we treat them as such they're going to be very worried, very frightened and very upset."

"But they *said* they wanted that. Maybe that is what is wrong." He was staring out of the window and across the balcony outside his room. "You know, I think the best thing we can do is to mirror them."

"Rev. Hajime, that will be terrible. That will cause unbelievable problems and equally unbelievable trouble!"

"Nonsense! They're very sincere people. I think it will work."

"Well, I don't."

"Look, unless you show them their pride—and they are incredibly proud, just listen to what they were saying this evening—unless you show them their pride while they are young they are never going to know that they possess it."

"Rev. Hajime, if you make me 'mirror monk'[82] you will really destroy me in England."

"No, I won't. They will understand. And don't argue with me."

I sighed. "There seems to be no way in which I can induce you to understand this," I said, "so the best thing I can do is just hope and go on."

"You'll find I'm right," he said, patted me on the shoulder and, as we bowed and said good-night, whispered, "Don't be afraid. It will work."

I went to bed with very considerable misgiving.

18th. August.

Rev. Hajime went ahead with his intention of trying to treat the couple as if they were an ordinary pair of monastic trainees. He set me up at every turn, yelled and screamed at me, pointed at me with the finger of, "Look how proud she is." Everything I did was wrong; however many times I bowed I was wrong; whatever I tried to do I was wrong. I knew that it was all done to show them themselves but they did not comprehend this. The wife got more and more disgusted with me. Finally, since their misunderstanding was causing them to become incredibly hard, I told them exactly what we were trying to do.

The wife turned away in disgust. "I knew there was something wrong with you all along. That is why the letters were sent from London. Now we have the proof of it from your teacher's own lips. He himself is saying how proud and ambitious you are."

I turned to Rev. Hajime. "I told you it wouldn't work; I told you they wouldn't understand it. The only time you can mirror another person is when he is truly seeking the Way and undergoing monastic training as *we* understand it."

Rev. Hajime looked worried, very worried. "Perhaps I have done wrong," he said.

The husband instantly came in, "Of course you haven't done wrong to show us what she's really like. That's what we came over here for. Now we can go back to England and explain quite clearly that it was wrong for us to even consider her in the first place—and definitely unnecessary for us to take the trouble of coming all this way to do so."

Rev. Hajime's face was consternation itself. "But . . . ," he was about to go on but I got up, walked to the door and walked out. I walked and walked through the town, up the hills, finally to the mountains beyond them. I must have walked for something like three miles. A beautiful mountain stretched in front of me on top of which was a small Kanzeon temple. I have never climbed a mountain in my life before to-day; to-day I went up one. It wasn't too difficult. The little temple was deserted. I lay down on the floor and stared at its ceiling—a ceiling that was rotting from disuse—on mats that were rotting for lack of cash to mend them for no-one, apart from the town council, has the repair and care of this temple and there is never any money available for it. After an hour or so I sat up and looked out over the balcony. The panorama was magnificent— Lake Biwa in one direction, more mountains in another, the sea in a third. My own temple was not visible but it was somewhere between the mountains and the sea.

I stayed there for a long, long time meditating. When it began to get dusk I realised that it would be very dangerous to stay there any longer for I would have no means of finding my way down the scarcely marked path and, although the weather was hot, although it was August, it was likely to get pretty cold. I carefully picked my way down to the town and, instead of going back to Rev. Hajime's temple, went back to my own one. Fortunately there was still one bus left. I caught it with about five minutes to spare.

When I got home I found the couple there. They had apparently forced the door to get in and had a letter with them from Rev. Hajime. I really didn't want to talk to either of them; I didn't want to be bothered with them or anything else. I had gone to Japan to do something about me. I'd found my peace and quiet and was happy. And here was this bunch of idiots[67] yelping and screaming against my going back to England when I hadn't asked to and didn't want to; I'd made it quite clear that I'd never thought about it and was not at all happy at the suggestion. They were telling me that I couldn't go back to something I didn't want to go back to and they were jumping up and down like a pair of baboons in case I did. I am beginning to really understand the value of all those beatings in the Zendō; they teach you to be at peace when the world breaks out in idiocy.

I took the note from Rev. Hajime to my room. It was very simple. He said he was very sorry for letting me get angry and he wanted us to have a talk with the couple. He thought I had better not change my mind about throwing them out, for not to change my mind was good for both me and others. He concluded by saying that he would expect me at the temple we were supposed to be helping at this evening as I had promised.

I'd forgotten that particular temple. I folded the note and went to the temple leaving the couple there. The other bus back to the town where he lived had not yet gone; it was the one I had just come over on. I boarded it and went to the temple. The ceremonies went as usual. Rev. Hajime asked me to be his personal assistant and I agreed. He then asked if I would like to stay the night in his temple.

"Not particularly," I said.

"Where will you go then? There is no way back to-night; there is absolutely no other bus."

"I can walk."

"It's more than twenty miles. You can't walk it in the dark. Besides it would be dangerous."

"I see."

"Please stay the night in my house."

Something in me said, "What the heck, why don't you? There's no point in making a big thing out of this. You told him it wouldn't work—he didn't believe you. How could he? He doesn't know the nature of the British as you do; he doesn't know their outlook on life. And how the heck were that couple to know that what he was doing was mirroring when they don't know Zen teaching methods any more than you did when you first came here? You knew that they couldn't understand what was happening; you knew that he hadn't explained it to them. What took place was bound to be the result of what he did."

And the other side of me argued, "Yes, that's true. But if he'd listened to me, if he'd understood that they couldn't understand it, then this situation would never have arisen."

I went back with him. His wife was very kind and I stayed the night there.

19th. August.

I went back to my own temple this morning. The couple were very standoffish, very cold. I went round doing my work, attending to the necessary business of the temple, seeing the village officials who usually come once a day, arranging ceremonies, getting on with looking after the everyday spiritual life of the village as a parish priest should. In the evening, after we had fired up the bath, I sat in the little living room reading a book. The young couple were bathing together and talking rather loudly. It is extraordinarily difficult in rooms that are only made of paper and bamboo—one doesn't *want* to listen but one *can't* help overhearing. Admittedly there was glass on these doors (the ones to the bathroom) but that didn't help matters very much. I had no alternative but to hear what was being said.

The wife was telling the husband that they should go away as soon as possible—go off to Kyoto to their other friends. Obviously I was no good; I never would be any good. What Rev. Hajime had said was quite true. I was incredibly proud and ambitious and, as such, unfit to be a teacher of Buddhism. If I couldn't put up with the fact that they were going away, if I couldn't "take it," as she put it, then that was just too bad. That was what they must do. They had come on a wild goose chase; they should never have come.

I listened helplessly then finally said in a clear, loud voice, "You should know that I can hear what you are saying. I'm sorry but I cannot help it."

20th. August.

The husband asked me to go with him to the local city to-
day. He was the one of the two I had known best in England and
he is still in two minds as to whether what he heard in Rev.
Hajime's temple was true or what I had said it was—a means of
teaching—lateral teaching. I explained it to him again, as best I
could, but he was obviously not convinced. He told me that he
had decided to come out with me by himself because he wanted
to talk about it without his wife being there, she being much
more interested in the Rinzai school and therefore inclined to
look for flaws in our methods. He wanted to give our school a
fair chance but it was quite clear that this could not be; the damage done by Rev. Hajime's mirroring was just too great. His
faith in my words was just not strong enough.

We returned to the temple and the wife, whom he and several others in England in recent years have regarded as being
fairly good at Buddhism, made it quite clear that she neither
believed nor trusted me and, above all, that she didn't like me.
We went to bed but I could sense that they slept uneasily.

28th. August.

There has been an uneasy truce for the last eight days. We
have gone about our business, they reading books and meditating, me doing my ceremonies, meditating and getting on with
the running of the temple. They are not too happy about ceremonies but they come to some of them.

Segaki took place to-day. Some villagers did not come because of the argument there has been over the gate—not that that
matters very much. Those who came were the ones who had had
dead relatives this year and, really, Segaki is only for them. The
fact that it is frequently turned into a public show, or public holiday, has got nothing to do with actual Buddhist teaching.

During the Segaki ceremonies we remembered a dead girl-
friend of the husband. He had been particularly fond of this girl
before his marriage and she had died of cancer. I had gone to the
funeral with him in England and his wife had gone too. She hadn't
been happy at the funeral; she was furious that he was having a

Segaki ceremony celebrated for the dead girl. She refused to offer incense or prayers. Something in me winced horribly. How is it possible that one can remain jealous of the dead?

Anyway, when the ceremony was over, they started packing their things. Tomorrow they are going to friends in Kyoto.

29th. August.

I and the couple went in the car of a friend of mine from here to Kyoto. My friend, a young Japanese, wanted to show us many of the beautiful sights in Kyoto but the couple were in too great a hurry to get to their friends and away from me to appreciate what was being done for them. This angered my friend considerably; he thought they were being incredibly rude. He wanted to take them to several parks on the way but they didn't want to go. He lost his temper and took them to one. This added to the tensions in the car very considerably. It also didn't help my friend's driving which has never at any time been particularly good. He parked the car on top of a ravine so that they could see the magnificent view. They refused to look. This put him in so furious a temper that he put the car in first gear instead of reverse and we almost shot over the edge of the cliff. One blessing at least came out of this. The pair in the back kept quiet until we got to Kyoto.

30th. August.

To-day has been *so* wonderful. Absolutely no-one here—no villagers and not that couple! I know this is bad Buddhism but I am still human. It's funny but I'm getting to the state when I don't *want* to see anybody or know anybody. I know that's *awfully* bad Buddhism; I know it's the Arahant ideal; I know I'm becoming a very bad trainee but, so help me, people are as ungrateful as all hell and they all know it! Why the heck have I got to be the one and only saint in existence? What am I saying? I must double my efforts at meditation; how easy it is to fall out of training. Just listen to my words.

31st. August.

I'm thoroughly ashamed of the way I felt yesterday. It was a terrible way to be. I rang Rev. Hajime and told him and he told me that Zen masters feel that way sometimes. The important thing is that it doesn't last for longer than a few minutes with them. I told him that it must have lasted for most of the night and he said, "How do you know? You were asleep. As to the way you felt, remember that a Zen master is a human being not a god. Shakyamuni Buddha had feelings all his life. Zen masters can weep in spite of stupid Western ideas to the contrary. Even saints feel relief when the tortures inflicted on their bodies cease. You felt relief when this couple left your house; that was all."

There were many outside ceremonies to-day. The priest from the local temple who has been helping me so much invited me to help celebrate Segaki at his temple and I went along. It was really very enjoyable.

A 'phone call came from Tokyo to the local call-box late in the evening to tell me that Zenji Sama's cat has died. Strange that Zenji Sama's old disciple should have rung me up to tell me that. He thought it strange too. He said that Zenji Sama had expressed the wish that I should know.

3rd. September.

A letter came from Rev. Hajime. It was odd because it was sent special delivery and I found myself wondering what could be so important that it needed this type of expensive postage. He asked me how I was getting on in the incredibly hot weather that we are having now and then said that Zenji Sama is still thinking the same thoughts as before with regard to England. He wants to talk with me about the subject when he will see me next. Zenji Sama seems to dislike the idea that I stay in Japan for such a long time when there is so much trouble going on in England. He feels that the two people—the one who first wrote to him and the one he wrote to—are not Buddhists for they are fighting so very much, longing to be powerful and being jealous of each other. Rev. Hajime then asked me to tell him the exact schedule of the young couple who came from England when they return to the Tokyo temple. He enclosed three letters for them which had been opened because of the temple's innocence of English and asked me not to blame anyone for this.

I felt concerned for I knew that the couple would not understand the reasons why the letters had been opened. I have explained so many times that there is no way in which one can have secrets in a temple such as the one in Tokyo but still foreigners cannot understand that, if they stay there, their letters are bound to be opened. I suppose Zenji Sama's hope is that I will return to England and convert the people there. If I can manage to completely convert me I will have done something pretty wonderful. In order to be converted one has to want to be converted. As things are, I don't know of anyone in England whom I knew in the old days who *truly* wants enlightenment. They all talk about it, they all say how wonderful it is but I don't think any of them have any idea of what is involved in having it. They think of it as living in a state of bliss; I know that it brings peace and joy but—*no* happiness of the type they are imagining. A Zen master knows grief in a way that few ever know it. "He who meditates gets grabbed by the Cosmic Buddha;" said Zenji Sama, "don't meditate if you do not want this to happen," to which my heart replied, "When ignorance is bliss 'tis folly to be wise." Certainly this would seem to be true in the case of the couple now in Kyoto. I must make Zenji Sama understand this.

I'm still having much difficulty with physical sitting. It is getting worse and worse. It has got to a state where I can only twist up one leg; the other one seems to refuse to move. I must really see the doctor again.

13th. September.

I returned to Tokyo. The fact that Zenji Sama had deliberately had me 'phoned to explain about the death of his cat gave me much cause for thought. I went round the village before leaving and found a small, male kitten. I took it with me when I returned. On arrival I went straight to Zenji Sama's room and said, "I have brought you a kitten, Zenji Sama."

His eyes were closed but I knew they were smiling. "Thank you," he said. "I knew you would."

I put it on the bed and his one good hand searched for it. The little creature snuggled round in the bed clothes and cuddled up close to him. Zenji Sama's face broke out in a big smile. "Thank you," he said. "It is so wonderful to have something warm and alive to feel." It wasn't a very pretty kitten—it was the only one I could get at such short notice. It was a very plain tabby as cats go but it made all the difference to Zenji Sama.

When I left the room his assistants were fuming. Whatever had I brought that thing for to give them extra work? "I brought it," I said, "because I knew that Zenji Sama wanted it and I also knew that I was the only one who would get it for him," and I left them.

I should have bowed to these two but I didn't; something in me absolutely refused to.[83] I am reminded of a conversation I had with the Director on one occasion in which I asked him how I should behave towards people who obviously were not exhibiting the Buddha Nature at all times and he said, "Where the Buddha is not do not linger." I asked him what he meant and he said, "If you linger much when the Buddha Nature is not evident you'll be tempted to fall into error, to live from the ego-centric 'I' in the presence of the egocentric 'I.' There is no alternative to this happening occasionally but the more often it takes place the more you will get out of the habit of exhibiting your own Buddha Nature at all times. If such people cannot catch the Lord at the moment It flashes it is best not to linger in their company for a million years may pass before they will look—and you have not got that much time to spare."

I know that Zenji Sama is very ill; I know it must be incredibly hard work looking after him for everything must be done for him. But "with the ideal comes the actual;" with the Zen master comes the lonely old priest, denied a wife and children because of his calling. And now, close to death, he obviously longs sometimes for something warm and alive that he can touch and feel without people giving him a bad reputation; and a little kitten is perfect for the job.

How is it possible that people who have been looking after him for so long can be so blind to this simple necessity? How is it possible that they can understand so little of the True Mind of Kanzeon? [84]

1st. October.

The young couple from England were due at the Vice-Abbot's temple to-day and he and I, and a large number of important Japanese, met them on the station nearest to the temple. The Vice-Abbot has decided to go ahead with all the plans he had made for them originally, treating them as though they were genuinely V.I.P.'s with great influence in government and other circles. Apparently, if he did not do so, after making the arrangements, he would lose face with all the important local people. But it is obvious that the person who is going to take the blame for this, after the couple have gone, is me. The fact that I tried to explain the situation, that I tried to explain it *exactly*, is neither here nor there. This couple just did not fall into the exact category that the Japanese wanted them to and the fault, since blame must be laid somewhere, is going to be mine.

2nd. October.

The couple came back to Tokyo to-day to say good-bye to Zenji Sama. He struggled to sit up in bed for it was obvious that he still wanted to hear the words from their own lips that I had done nothing wrong in England and could return there whenever I wished. Assurances in letters, it seems, are of no use to him. He must hear it from people in person. And the obvious sectarianism that is going on in British Buddhism is just too unbelievable for him, beyond his comprehension; Buddhists do not quarrel. Here he had two live people. From them he was still hoping to hear the truth.

He continued to struggle to sit up, finally gave up and asked the university professor, who had again come from Kyoto, to interpret so that he could be sure of the answers from someone other than me, "Can she return?" he said.

The husband looked a little uncomfortable and then said, "I'm afraid your school of Zen, as I have seen it here, would be thoroughly unacceptable in Britain. The means of testing people by the use of the mirror monk which has been explained to me and this business of constant beatings during meditation would be completely unacceptable. Other schools of Buddhism obviously have much better methods—much better actual teaching methods. The fact that you are none too interested in the Scriptures is also worrying. I am sorry, there is simply no way that I can see this school being accepted in Britain."

Zenji Sama tried to hide the pain in his face and said, "Can she not return to England?"

"There is no legal barrier to her return," said the husband.

"She was very unhappy there," said the wife.

I was startled by this for she had not known me for very long or particularly well in England; although I had had the ups and downs common to all people of the war generation—the ups and downs of the unwanted and unneeded—the fact remains that I had had a good many happy times in England. If I hadn't I would not have stayed to the age I did there.

Zenji Sama was silent. Then he said quite quietly, "Goodbye," turned to me and said, "Take them to the port;" he then turned his face to the wall. I bowed and left him.

I took the couple to the port and they went off on the first part of their journey which would take them, via Russia, back to England. A typhoon is due in this particular area of Japan tonight. I hope their ship gets safely away from it. The typhoons here can be really nasty.

On my return to the temple I was sent for by Zenji Sama. I sat on the floor beside his bed and for a long time he didn't speak. Then he said, "As long as I live I want you to stay in Japan. Will you do so?"

"Yes, Zenji Sama," I said.

"As long as I live I never want to hear another word about England."

"Yes, Zenji Sama."

"As long as I live I do not want to hear that you have written to anyone in England whatsoever nor that you have at any time communicated with any Briton whatsoever. If you are my disciple you will obey this my order."

I was appalled for I have friends—friends whom I occasionally visit. I wanted to tell him this but I didn't for I knew that he was in no mood to listen. I kept silent.

He put out his one good hand and touched me on the shoulder. "You will have to think of Japan as your country from now on," he said. "Can you do that?"

"I will try, Zenji Sama."

It must have been the touch of his hand that caused it for my voice started to catch as I said, "Please get well soon. I want you back in the Zendō."

His lovely smile burst out again. "Thank you for that feeling," he said, "but you and I are always in the same Zendō, you know that. Go and leave me now." I bowed and left him.

3rd. October.

I was asked to have tea in Zenji Sama's room with some of the senior officers. Zenji Sama had obviously been upset by something or other. It was very difficult to know what it was; then the new senior lecturer started talking. He said nothing directly; just that it was obvious that a lot of the people who came from foreign countries were not exactly of the best type. They were people that their own countries didn't want to keep; otherwise they wouldn't have come. What he was trying to get over to the other officers was quite clear—that there was something wrong with me, that I had done something; that was why I had fled to Japan, why I had run away to enter a monastery, to hide from my past. This was the whole purpose of my coming.

Zenji Sama said nothing for some time. Then suddenly he burst out at me, "Why did you come? What have you done?"

"I have done nothing, Zenji Sama. You may check with the police throughout the world; you may check with my friends; you may check with whoever you wish—I have done nothing wrong."

"Why is it that only such bad foreigners come to this country?" This from the lecturer.

"The Reverend Lecturer is right. Why is it that only bad ones come here?"

"They are not all bad, Zenji Sama. There is much misunderstanding, that is all. What is needed is much love, much compassion, much understanding on *both* sides. They who come here are trying to deal with something of which they know nothing. You are trying to deal with something of which you know nothing. How can you blame them? I do not understand you. First I am told that I am not to see or communicate with any of my fellow Britons when I have done nothing wrong. Now I am told that all my fellow Britons are bad and, by implication, so am I."

I could feel my anger rising and yet, even with the anger, I could feel the complete peace inside below it. My meditation was holding me still. This saved me for I anchored it in the peace within Zenji Sama himself but the quarrel was there hanging above us like a cloud. The lecturer continued to make snide comments. I sat completely silent, moved my legs as best I could into the meditation position and just sat there meditating. The lecturer hadn't noticed; Zenji Sama had. He put his one good hand into the meditation position over his abdomen on top of the bedclothes. The lecturer went on. I took no notice.

Presently Zenji Sama opened his eyes and said, "Well, that was an interesting conversation. Good-morning." We left him.

On returning to my room I found some papers from the Japanese government on my desk. They were application forms for becoming a Japanese citizen. This afternoon I visited the British Consulate and asked what would happen to my British citizenship if I were to become a Japanese. Was it possible to have dual nationality? Apparently in Japan it is not.

On my return to the temple everyone I met looked at me oddly. The quarrel (if quarrel it can be called) between Zenji Sama and myself had been blown out of all proportion to what it actually had been by everyone in the temple. It would seem that the new lecturer really does hate foreigners. Apparently something happened to his temple during the war; it lost most of its money and lands in the reshuffle of temple wealth that was undertaken by the American government during the occupation and he is determined that every Briton, every American, everybody, in fact, who is not a Japanese, shall pay for it.

As I walked past one of the office doors I heard a hissed comment, "Foreigners are lower than animals!" I hurried by and went to my room. I need to think. Above all I need to know if I *want* to be a Japanese. I will go down to my own temple to-morrow.

4th. October.

I moved everything that I could—that I had left and would not be likely to need—from the temple in Tokyo to my own temple to-day. I shipped these things and intended to follow. I was about to go through the door when an order came over the intercom for me to go to Zenji Sama at once. Normally I always go to see him before I leave the temple but I had no intention of doing so on this occasion. I went to his room. The chief lecturer was sitting there. Zenji Sama was obviously suffering great pain; it was equally obvious that it was pain of mind. He spoke to me in a voice that was grating strangely.

"Some of the officers here think that I was wrong to Transmit you," he said. "They tell me I have done great wrong in having a foreigner in the temple; that you have brought some atrociously bad foreigners here. This last pair were unbelievable. I need to know once and for all if you are properly Transmitted or if I did wrong—if you were unfit, unready. I order you to go to Kyoto where lives the greatest living saint of our school. He is old, he has the same illness that I have, but he can confirm or deny your Transmission. You will go and see him. You will take him this letter from me. When I get his answer," and he looked around at the assembled officers, "I will abide by whatsoever that answer is and so will you. Now go."

I took the letter he gave me and went. The train to Kyoto left around five this afternoon. I shall arrive there early tomorrow morning.

5th. October.

I visited the priest that Zenji Sama had sent me to; his temple was miles out in the country beyond the outskirts of Kyoto. He was lying in an upstairs room; nothing of him seemed alive except his eyes and one hand. The situation of himself and Zenji Sama was so alike I was immediately struck by it. I had handed the letter that Zenji Sama had given me to the assistant who had taken it up and read it to him. I was then taken upstairs to see him.

The old man looked at me for a long, long time. His eyes looked straight through me and all through me. They were incredibly beautiful eyes; they radiated a peace that I have only seen once before, on the night of my Transmission. Something within me answered the look and I *loved* him. He held up his one good hand in the gasshō and I gasshōed back with both of mine. He turned to the assistant and said, "Hajime-cun[85] used to be one of my junior trainees when I was in Tokyo at the same temple where her Zenji Sama now lives." The assistant bowed. The old priest then said in a totally different voice, "Write to Zenji Sama, 'I have seen. I am happy.'" He turned back to me, flooded me once again with his look and said, "Return to Zenji Sama soon. He will be waiting," closed his eyes and the interview was over. The assistant said he would write to Zenji Sama.

I went back to my own temple and telephoned Rev. Hajime. I told him all that had happened and that a letter would be sent from this old priest to Zenji Sama.

My difficulty with physical sitting is getting worse and worse. It is almost impossible for me now to even sit on a chair. The only thing I can do comfortably is lie flat. The will-power it is taking to keep this thing from breaking me is quite unbelievable. There seems to be no doctor available and, if there were, none of those I have seen seem to know what is wrong so why should anyone else? I *must* be imagining it.

6th. October.

A letter came from Rev. Hajime to say that Zenji Sama is already beginning to change his mind with regard to foreigners.

After I left he exploded even more about the type of foreigner he was getting and the fact that he could get no proof with regard to me from my fellow Britons. But the fact that I am away from him is upsetting him greatly and he is longing for me to come back.

Rev. Hajime made one comment that was surprising—that the old priest I had visited had become genuinely useless. I wonder if that is because he called him Hajime-cun—that little boy Hajime?[86] I indeed hope that there is not a darker reason—that the officers are not going to go round saying that because he has approved of my Transmission he is now old and useless; it is so difficult to live amongst people who are determined to believe ill of you.[87] More and more it occurs to me that the sanest thing I can do is go to America when Zenji Sama dies and not stay here at all. There is no point in running risks with such people as those I have encountered from England. I suppose I was no threat to them while I was just lecturing on Buddhism in London. But what threat can I be now? All I have done is work on *me*. I never intended to go back and take over their organisations. I've got enough problems dealing with me.

Many ceremonies took place this afternoon and Andy arrived. I still wonder about whether he did make accusations about me to Rev. Hajime but have said nothing more. If it is his nature to talk about others behind their backs that is up to him; he is helping mend the temple—just that and nothing more. If he does not wish to understand or learn real Buddhism that, too, is up to him—just that and nothing more. He is busy mending the front steps.

9th. October.

Another letter came from Rev. Hajime. It seems I am to be given the official title of Director's Assistant and Foreign Guest Hall Master as well as the official rank of a Junior Officer of the temple in Tokyo. This is Zenji Sama's order. The letter says that I should not expect any of the privileges of being a junior officer however.[88] I shall probably get paid as one but I must not expect anything else. The certificate stating that I am a junior officer has already been posted on the temple notice-board. It is both Rev. Hajime's and Zenji Sama's opinion that, whatever rank they give me, the other officers in the temple will refuse to acknowledge it. The letter ends with an interesting comment to the effect that the cat that I brought to Zenji Sama was very effective.

The letter orders me to return to Tokyo but the difficulty with my left leg is now so bad that I do not intend to go. There would be no point whatsoever since I cannot obey the rules by going to the Meditation Hall and doing everything else that is required of me. To go back in the state I am in physically would be most unwise.

A letter came to-day from the British young couple who are now once more in London. The husband is reaffirming what he said originally—that our school of Zen is just not suitable for England. He said that he had given much thought to the many things we talked about since returning home. It seems he now feels that he was absolutely right in advising me against returning as a teacher in the near future. It is not only a question of the person that Zenji Sama wrote to and the one who had originally written to him. He simply cannot think that our school of Zen as he saw it is for export to Britain. He says that whatever the rights of beating, this method would just not be tolerated, whether under Zen or any other label. Then he commented on the question of testing which he says I put forward as an alternative, saying that, apart from anything else, it seemed to him that this is not a method of tuition but only of examination. Other schools of Buddhism, he says, seem to have more definite methods of actual instruction than this. He concludes by saying that he is sorry to sound so negative but must tell me frankly how it strikes him and hopes that I will believe he writes as a true friend to say that I myself still have personal problems to overcome as my teacher very well knows. My "fights" with the ecclesiastical machine, it would seem, are not exactly conducive to the peace of mind I need, according to his analysis. He then offers to stand ready to advise or help me in any further way, now or in the future.

I went over to Rev. Hajime's temple with this letter and blew up.[89] After all, if it had not been for his intention to try and force this couple to study Zen as if they were junior trainees, presuming that they were just as serious, instead of realising that they were a pair of dilettantes, none of this would have happened and Zenji Sama would have been saved much misery. Zenji Sama and he were always talking of the trust that must exist between master and disciple—so why did they not trust me over what was written from London? Why keep on about 'proof?' Proof of *what*? I had been made the scape-goat in too many situations here. I needed to make a stand. Nowhere in Buddhism does it say that one must put up with this sort of thing and say nothing.

I exploded for some time, ending with the fact that I do not intend to do anything further about the female priests' rank in Japan. They must do it for themselves. I have never seen such an ungrateful bunch! Most of them are furious over my being in the head temple in Tokyo and give me no backing-up in what I try to do for them; most of them are furious because I'm in a temple with a bunch of men and they cannot enter it; most of them are saying that I'm up to heaven alone knows what there when I'm doing my best to train in Buddhism. From here on they can all help themselves—I don't care a damn[81] for any of them! I ended by walking out of the house and wandering round the streets before going home.

10th. October.
Rang Rev. Hajime to apologise for yesterday. He was very kind and invited me to his house to-morrow for dinner.

11th. October.
Something strange happened to-day. On the way to Rev. Hajime's temple I was thinking of Zenji Sama, thinking of what I had promised him—to stay with him until his death—when I suddenly knew something for certain inside myself. I had been thrown into a somewhat odd state of mind over the papers that I found on my desk concerning Japanese citizenship. I had been

disquieted by them. "Is it really possible for a Briton to become a Japanese?" has been going through my mind for a long time. Zenji Sama obviously believes so; so do quite a few others. Why should I remain different from everyone else around me? Such a thing was wrong, utterly wrong.

I was about halfway down the main street which, at that time of the evening, was almost deserted when I suddenly realised that Japan and England were one and the same. I have known it for a long time—ever since my great kenshō—but this was a specific thing that hit home, as it were, in the same place but from a different angle. I realised it in a way that flooded my whole body and mind and, for the first time since starting my wanderings some fifteen years previously, I felt that I had a physical resting place. I quickened my pace, determined to tell Rev. Hajime that I was going to go ahead with the change of citizenship; to tell him again I was sorry about my previous visit. The British affair was such a trivial thing.

At the door of his house I overheard his wife say to him, "Why do you keep on inviting that foreigner here? She's not one of us and never will be."

"It is Zenji Sama's wish not mine," he replied, "it is he who wants foreigners."

I stopped dead in my tracks. The vision of the oneness was gone. As long as I live there will be a difference between a Briton and a Japanese, not in my mind but in theirs. It was then that I knew that I would not become a Japanese citizen—not because I could not but because the Japanese would not really let me.

I stood there for a full ten minutes on the doorstep before entering. When I did everyone in the house was smiling a welcome. They wanted me to stay the night but I refused. I said I must return to my own temple and went off to catch the last bus.

The Chinese abbot has always offered me a place to live and study any time I want it. To-night I wrote him a letter saying that I will gladly accept his offer.[90] It seems the wisest plan. I am not ready to go to the West; I doubt if I ever will be.

20th. October.

A card came from Rev. Hajime to say that the officers of the temple in Tokyo insist I must either cancel all my studies or give up being an officer. I cannot study and be an officer at the same time. They have been very much against the fact that I was put into Tokubetsu-sōdō, or special training, which also carries with it the right to get a Sei-kyoshi degree, something which is the equivalent of a Doctor of Divinity in Buddhism. I was put in for this during the Spring before last and have been studying for it steadily ever since. Now, it seems, the officers are willing to fly in the face of Zenji Sama's orders and say that I must either stop all my studies and lose the possibility of my degree or give up the right to be an officer of the temple. It does not seem to matter that Zenji Sama is giving the orders. Now that he is so sick I am beginning to appreciate fully what it was that the Director told me. If anything happens to him I will indeed be in difficulties. I'm extremely relieved that I have written to the abbot in Malaysia.

I wrote to Zenji Sama to tell him what the officers are try-ing to do. I realise this will make trouble but, if I discontinue my studies or refuse to be an officer, he will be infuriated. It is best he knows what is going on.

30th. October.

Rev. Hajime sent me a long letter to-day. In it he thanked me for telling him of the great wrong that he did with the peo-ple who came from England concerning me. He had no inten-tion of doing such a thing at all. It was all done by his ignorance of the difference between Britons and Japanese, and he begs my pardon and asks my forgiveness. He said that he accepts all that I have said and does not want to repeat such a grave mistake.[91] The letter I sent to Zenji Sama has apparently caused consider-able problems with the officers. Zenji Sama is determined that I shall do both—studies and be a junior officer. The Director has decided the following:– if I want to finish my Tokubetsu-sōdō and get my Sei-kyoshi I will merely get the certificate of being a junior officer. It is the only way he can persuade the rest of the officers to do what Zenji Sama has said.

Then he mentioned that I also told Zenji Sama I will be leaving in order to go to Malaysia. Zenji Sama is not happy about it but the certificates proving that I have been here will be sent from the Administration Department. They want my reasons for going to Malaysia in writing. I am to do my Sei-kyoshi examination next April. Apparently the degree will be given automatically if I pass. He asks me to be careful of my health.

I suppose this is the best compromise possible. After all, from the previous letter nobody intended treating me as an officer anyway, although Zenji Sama says I am one. So, if they are going to give me the certificate plus the cash, make sure I do the job, blame me when it goes wrong but give me none of the glory and, at the same time allow me to get my Sei-kyoshi degree, I am doing better than I could have hoped for. It just isn't worthwhile hitting one's head against a brick wall with such people.[87]

6th. November.

A card came from Rev. Hajime. The Administration Office says I need no extra certificates. The first-class Kyoshi I already have is all I need and the Sei-kyoshi I will get next year. They are not willing to give any other certificates whatever Zenji Sama may order. He then said that he has completely lost his courage and confidence to help me. After what has happened with this affair in London he has become afraid of doing something wrong and asked me not to expect anything from him.

Well, if British Buddhist politicians set out to destroy me they certainly seem to be doing a pretty good job in the worldly sense. The only thing that is so wonderful is the peace within me. They can destroy my reputation, destroy my body, cause me to starve to death—I suppose they could conceivably get me thrown out of the Tokyo temple—but there is one thing they can never harm and that is my inner peace. Truly the old Zen story of the monk who comes home and finds everything in his house stolen is a true one. The monk even gives the thief his clothes and, after the latter has gone, looks at the moon and says, "If only I could have given him that wonderful moon." Oh, if only I could give England the peace that is within me.

7th. November.
A 'phone call from Tokyo to-day. Zenji Sama has ordered me back at once. I did not go.

15th. November.
My difficulty with physical sitting has reached an all-time peak. I can no longer even sleep.

16th. November.
There were many, many ceremonies in the temple to-day. I somehow managed to sit on the floor for them. The thing that made it possible was what can only be described as eternal meditation; this I found during the beatings in Tokyo. One sits still whilst everything else goes on round one, whilst all the craziness and idiocy and pain and horror continues—all one does is sit, anchored and still with peace and joy within and the smile, as it were, within one's guts.

I was looking for that smile for so many years. How wonderful indeed it is to have found it. How much I want to share it and how impossible it is to make other people understand.

29th. November.
Zenji Sama is furious. He demanded over the 'phone—they had to actually hold the instrument to his own mouth—that I return at once. Whenever anyone else rings up now I take no notice; when he speaks I hear. I shall return to Tokyo to-morrow.

I have noticed over the past few months how my distrust of everyone other than Zenji Sama is growing. It is very worrying to note this—very worrying indeed. I find myself wondering much about it. But, whenever Zenji Sama himself speaks, there is no problem; only when the others do. I must watch this; it is very bad.

30th. November.

I returned to Tokyo to-day and Zenji Sama immediately called me to his room. He informed me that he wants me to gather and look after all the foreigners that have been coming during the past year. He wants a grand Taikai with them for the New Year and he wants me to get all their classes going again. He said it was very important to him. He was very kind and very gentle; I agreed to do as he wished. He also told me that one of his other disciples is going to England soon to study at London University and he asked me to help him with regard to getting his visa from the British Consulate. His name is Rev. Isaburo.

1st. December.

Sesshin started to-day. It is physically impossible for me to sit. I really do not know what to do.

2nd. December.

The officers are grumbling loudly because I cannot sit. I begged that I may take a chair into the Meditation Hall but they would not permit it. I went in and sat in agony for something like two hours.

I am organising the Foreign Section as best I can through the newspapers. It is indeed fortunate that, as a result of the problems with the newspapers in the past, at least one reporter has become a very good friend of mine as have a couple of radio announcers. They are giving much help simply by telling people through their various media that the temple will be open to all who have been here before for the New Year celebrations.

I seem to be beginning to gain weight.

8th. December.

Sesshin ended to-day. I have sat at least two hours every day during the week. I'm not at all sure how.

9th. December.

I hope to stay with a friend of mine in Tokyo for a couple of days. I want to think out what happened at Rev. Hajime's temple alone. I need to think some more on this business of becoming a Japanese. I know I can never do it but there is so much I need to explain to myself.

12th. December.

I returned from my friend's house this morning. I got back very early—about five in the morning for breakfast. To my amazement I discovered that I was speaking Japanese with an English accent and using a lot of the grammar wrongly. This startled many in the temple considerably but not nearly as much as when I walked into the Meditation Hall carrying a knife, fork and plate instead of a pair of chopsticks and a begging bowl for breakfast. Later, in his room, the Director asked me about it. We were waiting for the start of the many ceremonies that took place to-day.

"It is impossible for me to become a Japanese," I said, "for none of you will ever let me do it."

He sat down slowly and eyed me thoughtfully. "What happened when you were in your temple?" he asked and I told him. He was silent for a long time then he started to make tea. When he had finished he said, "Tell me how you feel."

"Numb," I replied. "I knew that moment in the main street near Rev. Hajime's temple that I could do what you want and become a Japanese. I was even eager to do it. I knew for a few brief minutes that all was really one—I know it still. I know that racial differences do not matter in the least for they are the delusion of mankind; and, after hearing Rev. Hajime's wife's remarks and his answer, I know that delusion, even in the priesthood, is compounded by greed and obedience to superiors."

[92] "How can I answer that question? Only you know the workings of your own heart. I know that there is much prejudice here against me because I am a foreigner and a woman. Only two or three days ago, when I returned here and went to do Nyudo no Hai in the Meditation Hall, another trainee who was doing it with me (a boy of seventeen) was handed the incense stick instead of me although I am a junior officer of the temple. Zenji Sama heard about it and got angry, stopped

the ceremony and ordered the incense to be handed to me. How do you think I felt? And do you think that Zenji Sama's stopping the ceremony changed the prejudiced minds here one iota? All that came out of this incident was a deeper despisation of me and a lot of false, external smiles. The so-called equality of women in our school of Zen is something to which lip service is given and nothing more. There have been a million such incidents as the one of the incense stick and I have ignored them as Zenji Sama told me to. You have tried repeatedly to induce me to become a Japanese, even telling me that the colour of my skin was changing. Do you remember? But for what? Am I of political value to this temple? Is it because you feel sorry for me over what has happened in England? I know that many foreigners are merely used by Japanese temples for publicity purposes. This temple did that with me until I refused to see any more newspapermen and Zenji Sama backed me up. Then what happened? Stories about me were told behind my back to both the newspapers and magazines which have caused untold unhappiness to my friends and relatives. What am I supposed to learn from all this? When I was a junior here I repeatedly asked to be sent to the women's monastery not far from where my own temple is so as to avoid the problem of being a woman in a men's temple but no-one took any notice of my request; and everyone still goes on complaining about my being here. You say that all is one, and I know that it is in a way that I could never have known it when I was in England, but the delusion of Japan, and of this temple, is so great that no practical use can come of the knowledge as things are. Look at the way you Japanese treat the Koreans who have been for centuries in Japan. I am told they're not even allowed the right of citizenship although they know of no other country than this. They cannot attend Japanese schools, vote or get work other than that of a menial nature; and they are descended from the Royal Korean potters. You carried them off from Korea hundreds of years ago.[93] No country in the world is as racist as is Japan! The Negroes of America think they have a rough time; they should try living here!"

I was out of breath. It was as if all the injustices of the past few years were oozing out of me like the pus from a boil. The Director was staring at me in amazement for he had never heard me make so long a speech. Then he said, "You are not in the women's temple because Zenji Sama thinks it is good for both your training and ours that you stay here. If the trainees here, either young or old, or senior officers are prejudiced against women, and foreigners in particular, maybe they can see their delusion as a result of your misfortune and learn compassion."

"And what of me?" I said. "What am I supposed to learn?"

"Strength to stand against the stupidity of the world. You will need it when you return to the West.[94] The prejudice, as you have found out from your so-called friends in London, is no less elsewhere than it is here. It is just that here it is a lot more concentrated. Why did you imagine that the Buddhists of England would welcome you when you return?"

"I thought you wanted me to be a Japanese? What has that got to do with my returning to England?"

"If you had not overheard that conversation between Rev. Hajime and his wife there would probably never have been any necessity for you to return to England."

[92] "I see. In other words I was to stay here after what had happened in London without ever *knowing* how people really felt about me and foreigners in general. I was always to think that anti-foreign comments that I heard, or thought I heard, were imagined. I was to be a creature that was a cut above the Koreans because I was of use to the temple but of whom no-one could forget that I possessed two round eyes and a long nose. That is Japanese Buddhism—and I've just had some examples of British Buddhism! I find myself wondering what would happen if the Buddha were to return to the world now. I find myself wondering if there is anyone in existence who knows really what he taught. Do you realise that in forcing me to stay here, instead of letting me go to the women's monastery, you have made me the object of the jealousy of every female trainee in this country? Am I to understand that Zenji Sama wishes this so as to show the women priests their mean nature; or to show

them that they are jealous? What do you think I am, a saint? Believe me, I am human and I came here to do something about myself because I *knew* I was human; I did not come in order to lead and teach others either directly or indirectly as a result of being a sort of guinea-pig to show others their faults. It seems that I am to be an eternal mirror monk; but that job isn't forced on anyone else here."

He sighed. "Long ago I taught you the 'Sandōkai'—'With the ideal comes the actual like a box and its lid.' It seems you are still, to a certain extent, stuck with the ideal. You *must* know that it exists—of course you must know that it exists. If you don't you can never understand true Buddhism. As I told you a long time ago, however, understanding—enlightenment—whatever you like to call it—does not bring happiness, only the kokoro konashiku—the great grief—out of which comes the all embracing all-acceptance and selfless love of Shakyamuni Buddha, the actual, which unites it with the ideal. You must *know* the ideal; you must *accept* the actual. Only thus can you help others and yourself. Things are as they are because of the greed, hate and delusion of the world. The only people we can do anything about are ourselves. Here in this temple we have the opportunity of being true Bodhisattvas; to be mirrors of the Truth to all our fellow trainees so that they may see that which exists within themselves is the greatest of all callings."

"And if I go to America how does that particular teaching help the oppressed Negroes and other minority groups there?" I asked. "Am I to tell them that things are as they are and that they must learn to accept them?"

"As things are now, have they any alternative?" he replied. "The only certain cure for such a situation is self-knowledge and, as each of us does something about himself, so does the day of help for these unfortunate people draw nearer. We have to do something about ourselves in order to help them. They have to do something about themselves in order to help us."

95 "Please listen to me, Reverend Director. Zenji Sama seems to be playing God, and he is not God, and neither am I.

So help me, please. I am merely a woman who is trying to do the best she can."

"That is all Zenji Sama wants of you or anyone else. This temple is a small world which mirrors the great world outside. In it, as you yourself once wrote, can be found every type of human being, from the saint to the sinner, and every vice as well as every virtue. 'With the ideal comes the actual like a box and its lid.' The greatest teaching this temple can give is that of all-acceptance which is the understanding that all is one and all is different. You know that both Japan and Britain are identical. You also know that they are different."

"I shall never become a Japanese citizen. I am British and I shall always remain so."

The Hondō bell started to ring for the first ceremony and I went to fetch his robes from the cupboard and light the incense since he was to be the celebrant. I turned back towards him.

"You have said that I am the best assistant you have ever had. Was that, too, because Zenji Sama ordered you to have me?"

"I obey the orders of my superiors without question as does Rev. Hajime whose conversation you overheard. There is such a thing as too great a sincerity in training and you are suffering from it. For example, you have upset the washerwoman here because your mending of the embroidery on my robes is better than hers is and I prefer it. You would do well to strive more for the actual in some respects than for the ideal."

"But that makes rubbish of Buddhism."

"Sometimes I raise the eyebrows of old Shakyamuni Buddha and sometimes I do not. There are times when it is prudent not to be Buddha and times when it is prudent to be Buddha. Remember the words of Dōgen Zenji. 'It is not wise to tell your dreams[96] to the foolish.'"

The bells of the Hondō, Zendō and the long corridor were answering each other as they rang down for the celebrant's procession and the Director and I left his room to go to the Hondō.

"Kane areba hatō, hō hibekeba saidō," he said. "'If the bell is ringing you must put on your robes.' When Zenji Sama dies another will ring the bell."

"I have heard whisperings that the Vice-Abbot will not want the previous abbot's disciples," I said.

"A bell rings according as it is struck and we answer it in the same way. The 'all is one' and the 'all is different' manifest themselves in all things at all times and in different ways."

We were already in the Ceremony Hall and had to leave it there. There were something like thirty ceremonies.

15th. December.

There are four-hundred people coming for the New Year celebrations and I've arranged for six assistants to come and help me. Three of them are friends of Andy's. One is a Yugoslav girl who speaks good English; two are Japanese who speak reasonable English; two more are friends of mine from one of the American bases and Andy himself. They will all spend some time here, help run and organise the Grand Taikai.

23rd. December.

I have been invited to spend Christmas at the British Consulate.

25th. December.

I went to a party and Christmas dinner at the British Consulate to-day after getting permission to do so from Zenji Sama. It was very enjoyable to have a British meal once again and to be with my fellow Britons. I asked Zenji Sama if I could go because of his prohibition with regard to England and he said that, provided I was only with government officials, he had no objections. What he does not want me to do is have any contact with people connected with British Buddhism.

When I got home in the evening, feeling very happy and with a large slab of Christmas cake for the cold days to come, Zenji Sama's assistant was standing near the door together with the chief lecturer. They both scolded me for having been out to a party. Apparently Zenji Sama had told them; and the lecturer said that I was no Buddhist since I was enjoying Christmas.

29th. December.

A large number of people are due to come early on the thirty-first so I arranged for the six assistants to get here to-day. I told the chapter; some were happy, others not. There were the usual grumbles. The great hall has at last been finished and Zenji Sama ordered the Director to be celebrant for the opening ceremony in it. This meant that I was the first person to carry out the duties of priest's assistant there.

31st. December.

Early this morning we started preparing the temple for the guests, marking passages with coloured ribbons so that the people would know how to get to their rooms. This was necessary since most of them speak no Japanese. It was a lot of work and by noon we were very tired. I went to inspect everything after lunch and found that all our work had been undone, ribbons taken down, cushions, beds and eating utensils put away. Apparently some of the junior trainees had been told by the senior lecturer that we were messing up the temple. I went to see Zenji Sama and he rang for the senior lecturer, told him to mind his own business, and then I and my six assistants had to re-do all our work—getting all the tables ready, getting all the rooms ready, putting out the cushions and beds once more. It was really a bit much!

I probably shall not have time to write about what happened to-day until long after it is over for the whole celebration is going to take until this time to-morrow and I shall certainly have no further time for writing to-day. I and the assistants are now waiting for the guests to arrive.

1st. January.

It is six in the evening and I have been asleep since about three this afternoon. I didn't get to bed until then and am really feeling knocked out. More than the expected four-hundred foreign guests arrived and they all made large contributions to the temple to help with the cost of the new hall which, although finished, is far from paid for. The ceremonies were identically the same as they have been every other New Year with one important difference. I not only had to look after and co-ordinate the arrangements for all the guests, shepherding them from room to room and from ceremony to ceremony, I also had to assist the Director at all the ceremonies themselves since he was the celebrant. This meant that I was not off my feet from about five in the afternoon until twelve noon to-day; and, as soon as the foreign guests left at nine o'clock this morning, I had to look after the Director's private guests until three this afternoon.

The foreign guests on the whole were extraordinarily well behaved. Most of them, of course, came for recreation, to enjoy their New Year, a fact which greatly annoyed some of the older priests here. But they were really very well behaved and everyone thoroughly enjoyed the day. Many of them, however, did not want to have mochi for breakfast this morning and the temple authorities were very angry when they found that most of the food was being wasted.

I had apparently just got to bed when an announcement was made on the intercom that I must clean up the mess that the guests had left behind them. Fortunately all my six assistants were so dead tired, having had so much to do, that none of us heard the announcement and some of the junior trainees cleaned up. I must be sure to find out who and thank them for it was indeed very kind.

2nd. January.

The 'phone doesn't seem to stop ringing to-day. The number of people who are congratulating the Director for the New Year is unbelievable. I am constantly answering the 'phone. Also, many people who were here last night are wanting to come to the various classes for foreigners that Zenji Sama wishes me to arrange.

One of my duties as the Director's assistant is to bring the celebration wine to the guests who come to see him and I shall be sitting most of these next two or three days in the Director's private room for this purpose.

Halfway through this morning the Director told me not to let any more guests in since he needed a rest. I went into his inner room—not the one that he uses as a bedroom but the one just in front of it and prepared a day-bed for him close to his kotatsu. I was about to go when I had a feeling that he wanted to talk to me; I very much wanted to talk to him so I lingered a little.

"What is it?" he asked.

"Reverend Director, the belief in the West is that Zen masters are super-human; they must have no feelings whatsoever. When the sort of things that have happened with me in England occur Zen masters are not supposed to be disturbed by them in the least nor are they supposed to do anything about them. I am supposed to be Zenji Sama's direct descendant and, of course, that means, as far as the British are concerned, that none of this sort of thing should touch me in the least, nor should I be concerned about it. But I am concerned and, to a certain extent, I'm hurt by it. I suppose that means that I am no good, that Zenji Sama did not properly Transmit me."

The Director looked at me for a moment and then said, "There is no such thing as a Zen master that is super-human. All Zen masters have feelings; every living thing has feelings. And what those people are up to in England is enough to ruin a saint. There have been many legends that have grown up in Zen. You should know that all Zen masters were, and are, human as was the Buddha Himself. All were born, all have to die. The only difference between them and ordinary people is that they have found peace within themselves and so can put up with the behaviour of people such as those who came here recently whilst still feeling somewhat hurt by it."

"Knowing what sort of stupidity sometimes exists in the world, why did Zenji Sama so insist on checking this affair out in England? What was the cause of it all? He receives a letter asking for a Zen teacher. It must have been obvious, after he got the second letter, that the person who wrote it didn't like me and definitely didn't want me. His villification at times makes him sound almost crazy. Then Zenji Sama digs up this hornet's nest. What was the purpose of it?"

The old Director sat up and looked at me sadly. "Zenji Sama is old; he is very sick. He has not got long for this world. In many respects you are his favourite disciple, the one upon whom he pins most of his hopes for the things that he's always wanted to do—the opening up to the Truth of foreign countries and the continuation of his line there. The disappointment to him was incredible when that letter came from England. He wanted to find out if you had in any way lied to him. And I think there was another reason; the amount of pressure being put upon him by certain people here, both in this temple and outside it, because he had a foreigner and a woman in the temple itself. He wanted to be able to vindicate you in the eyes of everyone so that, when you leave here, there is no way in which anyone can point the finger of suspicion at you."

"Why couldn't he have trusted me?"

"That is an unreasonable statement. Have you ever thought of what the pressures are like for him here?"

"I can guess."

"Then forgive him. All he was trying to do was make certain that true Zen could be spread in the West from an irreproachable source. It is not possible to do this if the vessel that spreads it has any faults or weaknesses. You know what this temple is like. It is a veritable hotbed of intrigue, scandal-mongering and genuine spirituality."

"I'll grant that. I'll grant that there's certainly far more spirituality here than I've found elsewhere—of the real variety; and certainly far more scandal."

"Zenji Sama wanted the safety of your reputation.[97] He wanted to be certain that *nothing* could harm you on your return to the West as I said. He wanted to prove to everyone the unassailability of your reputation whilst he was still alive and strong enough to fight."

"As it is he's proved nothing."

"I think he's proved quite a lot. He was forced to have you checked by the greatest living Zen master—you went to Kyoto, he saw you and completely and utterly approved of Zenji Sama's Transmission of you. I saw the letter that was sent.

There is not a single person in the whole of this country that can point a finger at you and say that you are not a true Dharma Heir of Zenji Sama.[98] So he can die in peace; that others are willing to accept you or not no longer matters, it is of no importance. Even if you can never return to England, and at the moment he is determined that you shall never do so, wherever you go you will teach true Zen. Whether it is as a priest or as an ordinary human being there is no way in which you *cannot* teach true Zen."

"Reverend Director, I've still got human faults and failings; I still get annoyed with people like those from England."

"And so you should. How else will they be cured? A Zen master is not a quiet nincompoop who goes around saying everyone has the right to beat him up, ill-treat him or slander him. Remember, where the Buddha is not do not linger; where the Buddha is do not stay. A Zen master does that which has to be done. He does not sit upon a throne, worshipped, a perfect specimen. He is a human being who knows what has to be done and does it. People like the couple who came from England get the sort of Zen masters they deserve, the variety at whose feet they can worship but who can teach them absolutely nothing. Wherever *you* go you will always be able to teach those who are *really* looking. There is no way that you can avoid it, absolutely no way, for you exhibit the signs of enlightenment without knowing it and all those who exhibit them, without fear or favour, without worrying as to whether they will be *seen* to be Zen masters, are *true* Zen masters. You know how to show sympathy, benevolence, tenderness, charity. Why do you think it was that Zenji Sama telephoned you about his cat? He knew that there was only one person in the whole of Japan who would understand his need and to whom he was really close enough to mention it. He had tried everyone here and been told that there was no such thing as a tom-kitten in existence in the whole of Tokyo. He is a bedridden invalid. Do you realise that he had to telephone all the way to the west of the country to get someone to hear that he was lonely? You didn't consider whether the officers here would be happy about it; you found a kitten and brought it to him. You didn't consider the effects of this upon yourself; you didn't check as to whether it would be wise for you politically to bring it; you brought the kitten and you gave it to him; and you took the consequences from the officers. He who gives comfort in such ways understands tenderness and sympathy; by such signs as these we know the Zen master. He is warm flesh and blood with great influence over others because of his great love for all living things. Sitting still and magnificent like a stone Buddha upon a throne is useless. A Zen master is someone who is alive, real, vibrant and unafraid. You exhibit all these traits. You were certified to exhibit them by the greatest living Zen master. Whatever the world may do to you, you are Zenji Sama's true heir."

I was silent for there was nothing whatsoever that I could say. Then he said, "Zenji Sama wants you to write one more letter to the couple in England to try and explain to them what Rev. Hajime was doing with regard to the mirroring."

"Reverend Director, they're not going to understand."

"Never mind. Try."

"But what's the point?"

"Don't argue with me. It is your duty to keep on trying, there is *never* a limit to trying, just that and nothing more. Don't quarrel about it; don't argue about it; do it."

"Yes, Reverend Director. But, you know, this business has left a nasty taste. There's something almost like a shadow that lurks between—no, not between, *near* Zenji Sama and I as a result of this mistrust."

"It will go and the trust between you will be all the more magnificent because of it. Many true disciples 'quarrel'[99] thus with their masters once and later know that the quarrels never took place. Go and leave me now. I am very tired."

I said, "Even as I 'quarrelled' I knew in the depths of me that there was *no* quarrel." He nodded.

I left him and went to my room to write the letter. Again I tried to explain many things to the British couple as clearly as possible but something in me just isn't in this. I don't feel that those two are ever going to understand if I explain from now 'til doomsday.[100]

3rd. January.

Still dozens of people coming for the New Year; still I am plying them with New Year wine. It's rather enjoyable being with the Director all the time during this period. He is so pleasant to be with and so obviously wants to teach at all times; he makes his every movement a meditation.

When I got back to my room this evening I found Rev. Hajime sitting on the opposite side of my desk looking concerned.

"What's wrong?" I asked.

"Oh, if it's not one thing it's another," he said. His voice was almost a groan.

"What now?" I asked.

"It's one of the girls[101] who works here. She's pregnant."

"Really?" I said. I didn't want to sound terribly interested or uninterested. I felt that it was really not my business.

"Yes. She says that one of the trainees here is the father."

"Oh?" I said.

"She says she got pregnant by this young man because I refused to give her my body. It is the first time such a thing has happened in six hundred years."

I said nothing.

"She said that because I would not give her my body she went ahead and got somebody else so that she could imagine it was me."

"Is this girl a member of the priesthood?" I asked.

"No," he said. "She's just an employee."

"We should be grateful for small mercies,"[100] I said.

"Do you think I was wrong?" he asked.

"Wrong about what?"

"Wrong in not giving her my body when she so desired it; wrong to let this happen."

"That's a peculiar argument. Supposing you *had* given her your body; she might have been pregnant by you and your family life would have been ruined. Really, Rev. Hajime, this is a daft conversation!"

He leaned back against the wall. "Yes, you're right. Forgive me. This whole business has shaken me considerably."

"I can see that."

"Would *you* have a talk with her?" He had risen, his hand on the door, and was turning back to look at me.

"What for?"

"Because you are older than she is and I think you might be able to get some sense into her head. She wants to abort the baby."

"I'll certainly try and stop her doing that. If there's one thing that would be wrong it would be that."

"Why?" he asked.

"Because I've yet to find any woman who has had an abortion who hasn't regretted it terribly afterwards."[102]

"Have a talk to her," he said. "I'll arrange it sometime. Good-night," and he left the room.

4th. January.

There have been many, many ceremonies to-day. The Director teaches me every time he does a ceremony. The slightest thing I do wrong he corrects in so gentle and perfect a way that I can learn at every moment.

I did quite a lot of translating after lunch with Rev. Hajime, continuing with the works we've already been working on. Late in the afternoon the Director called me into his room. "Your Sei-kyoshi is coming up this year," he said. "You will get the questions soon."

"But I haven't read any particular books. Well—yes, I have—I've read an awful lot, but shouldn't I be getting specific tutorials or something from someone?"

"You've been working with me for over a year. That is more than most people ever get for a Sei-kyoshi!" He had an impish, wicked grin on his face as was usual during such conversations. "If you can't turn what you've learned from me into the answers for a successful Sei-kyoshi examination then you just aren't fit to have a Sei-kyoshi."

"I see. Where is the examination going to be held?"

"You'll be given the questions and you'll be able to do them in your own time whenever you wish."

"But I'll be able to crib!"

"No, you won't. It's impossible to crib from books on Sei-kyoshi questions. What you have to write is what you *know* by *experience*, not what you've read. You'll find out what I mean when you see the questions."

"Well, how do I know I can do it?"

"You can do it. Don't argue with me. And go to bed. I'm tired!"

"But it's only five in the afternoon!"

"Oh, yes, so it is. Oh well, I'll go to bed anyway. Good-night," and he disappeared into his inner-room.

6th. January.

For the last few weeks the difficulty with my leg has eased somewhat. It's still extraordinarily difficult to move but the pain is no longer there. I went along to the local Western hospital for some tests.

8th. January.

Came out of hospital to-day; the doctors were unable to find anything wrong with me. This leg really is worrying. I am not sure if it is the top of the leg that is causing the trouble or the bottom of my torso where it joins the thigh.

23rd. January.

There have been so many foreigners coming to this temple that I've had no time whatsoever to write anything since my last entry. The amount of work that I now have is quite incredible. As a result of my going to see the old Zen master in Kyoto, there have been no further comments whatsoever with regard to whether Zenji Sama did right or wrong in Transmitting me. Those who previously got angry about it and wanted proof are now extremely silent—too silent, I feel. I know there is some-thing brewing with them but there is no way that I can put a fin-ger on it and I know that it will not actually expose itself until Zenji Sama is dead. The rest are accepting me happily and gladly, far more so than they ever did before. On the whole it's extraordinarily enjoyable to be here. I do not see Zenji Sama very much; his assistants are making it more and more difficult for me to get near him but I am doing what he wants done. Although some of the other officers are furious because I am attending the officers' chapter meetings and refuse to acknowledge me or gasshō to me, I am carrying out Zenji Sama's wishes to the best of my ability and it doesn't worry me any longer if others are happy about what I am doing; nor does it matter whether they think of me as a fellow officer or not.

A letter came from the British couple to-day. It merely gave me the news of what is happening in England and no comments whatsoever on the letter that I had written to them. As I knew when I wrote it, the thing was a lost cause.[100] I'll take the opportunity of going to Malaysia, possibly to stay there, for I certainly do not now want to stay forever in Japan. There would be no point to my doing so. In many respects I have truly become a monk—I have no home whatsoever. Admittedly I carry a British passport but that is all.

24th. January.

A letter came from the Chinese abbot to-day promising me a ticket to Malaysia in August; he wants me for at least three months. He was extremely kind. He said that, after all I had gone through here and in recognition of the qualifications I have earned, he has decided to give me a really enjoyable holiday. He has booked me a first-class cabin on a cruise ship since he wants me to get a real rest. It is incredibly kind of him.

25th. January.

I have almost no time whatsoever to write this diary because of the tremendous number of foreigners that are still coming here. I am lecturing almost every day.

Zenji Sama is complaining that I do not see him enough. Several flowers arrived in my room on several occasions and I was just unable to go and see him for lack of time; I did manage to go one day only to be turned back by the assistants. I went to the garden outside his room, tapped on the window and heard his voice call. I opened the window and went in. The smile he gave me was full of joy. "You came," he said.

"I've been trying to come for a long time, Zenji Sama, but it's extraordinarily difficult to get in here. And when I do come it's almost impossible for me to see you alone. Is it possible that I *could* see you alone sometimes without your assistants? There is so much I want to talk to you about."

He didn't reply. He said instead, "I want many foreigners to come here for bean throwing. You are guarding them all for me? You are keeping them all safe?"

"I am doing my best, Zenji Sama. It isn't always easy but I'm doing my best."

"Good," he said.

"May I see you alone sometimes, Zenji Sama? To-day is such a joy!"

"I will think about it," he said. "Look after my foreigners; look after them all."

"Yes, Zenji Sama."

His hand dropped back on the bed and he closed his eyes. I left him before his assistants could find out that I had got to his room unannounced.

29th. January.

Have been arranging, through the newspapers and radio, for the foreigners to come for bean throwing. It will take place, as usual, on the second of February. And now, I suppose, my 'phone will start ringing, as it did just before Christmas, and there will again be hundreds of applications.

2nd. February.

We had bean throwing to-day. A hundred and eighty foreigners came for the ceremony and two of them won the right to throw beans. It was very enjoyable to watch but I am so tired I have no time to set down the details. It was different last year when I had time and could describe everything. Having done it once, however, it doesn't need to be done again. In this diary the described events of one year will remind me of all the years in time to come.

3rd. February.

Started to cram for my Sei-kyoshi exam—it's probably a bit stupid but I decided I'd go through all the books again that I have been told to study in the past three years. I shall also read all others I can lay my hands on in the Library and Archives.

3rd. March.

No time to write this diary before to-day since I have been studying non-stop in addition to attending many ceremonies and giving lectures. The Director gives me no teaching in words; just to watch him every moment that I am with him is an unbelievably good lecture.

I started the Jūkai classes for the foreigners to-day. At least eight people wish to be officially received as full Buddhists. Of the four-hundred that came for the New Year some sixty to eighty come regularly each week to five different classes. Out of the above-mentioned, eight wish to become full Buddhists and, eventually, some say they will become full priests. It is really wonderful news for Zenji Sama. I went to see him and told him all about it. It was as if the sun shone from his face. He said he will arrange the many things that will be needed to make it possible for the eight to do Jūkai. He thinks that unless *he* makes the arrangements there will be no room for them to meditate in, no way in which they can get meals and no place for them to sleep. He promised he would help me with all this and I left him.

Halfway down the corridor I went back again. In spite of the assistants, in spite of everything, I returned.

"Zenji Sama," I said, "would you give me the right to order the rooms and other things for the foreigners' Jūkai?"

"Why?" he asked.

"Because other people may pretend that you didn't say that the foreigners could come or that you forgot to make the arrangements. If I say that *you* have given me the authority to book the rooms and the food no-one will dispute my word. I am sure of it."

He smiled. "Go ahead," he said.

"Thank you, Zenji Sama," I replied and left him.

9th. April.

The foreigners came to-day for Jūkai. The Guest Office, however, refused to let me have any rooms for them to sleep in and I was forced to go and see Zenji Sama again this morning. I told him that the office was refusing to allow the foreigners to stay in the temple for the nights of Jūkai although I had told them that Zenji Sama had given his permission for them to do so.

Zenji Sama nodded his head sadly. "Very well," he said, "send for the chief guest master."

I told the assistant and the chief guest master arrived.

"I have instructed Jiyu to use my chief guest room for the foreign guests who will be here during Jūkai," he said. "That guest room is to become the Zendō for all foreigners in this temple. Since I can no longer sit in it with my guests it is wasted space. The foreigners may thus have it for their Zendō without taking any space usually available to others. Do you understand?"

A gasp of horror came from the chief guest master. "But, Zenji Sama, that is your private guest room!"

"Yes," he replied. "I am aware of the fact but you say there are no spare rooms in the temple. I shall be moving into my new private house on the other side of the temple soon—the house that has been specially built for me by a friend. That means that this house will be completely empty and I am giving at least two of its rooms to Jiyu to use for these eight foreigners—so that she may teach them, lecture to them and prepare them. I want them to become my disciples before I die. I want all eight of them and, when I am dead, Jiyu will look after them for me."

The chief guest master glared at me but could not argue.

"What about the food, Zenji Sama?" I asked.

"The kitchen will provide food for these guests."

"What about payment?" cried the chief guest master.

"Jiyu has already arranged that. They will pay the same as do all the Japanese guests who come here."

The chief guest master bowed. "Very well, Zenji Sama." He swept out of the room.

"Thank you, Zenji Sama," I said and bowed.

"It will be good to have my disciples in the room beside me," he said, "I will be able to feel their closeness. Bring them to see me often. I want to see them at least once a day."

"Yes, Zenji Sama."

I went away and made the necessary preparations for the guests to move into their new accommodation. I had an incredible amount of difficulty in getting beds to put in the room. Finally, however, after a lot of argument, I succeeded.

It is truly amazing how much the foreigners are getting out of this particular Jūkai. When I went to bed to-night—and I slept in the same room that they did—the feeling of joy and anticipation was so real, so wonderful, so different from the jaded[103] feeling that one frequently gets from the Japanese.

13th. April.

This is the last day of Jūkai. There are something like four-thousand other guests in the temple but, as far as the eight foreigners and I are concerned, close as we are in this huge and magnificent set of guest rooms, close to Zenji Sama, it has been a very, very wonderful time.

Zenji Sama sent for us again to-day. He wanted us all to have a final tea with him before the eight went back to their bases. One of them was very disgruntled during tea and Zenji Sama, who had been propped up in bed, beckoned me over with his good hand and asked what was wrong.

"Well, Zenji Sama, he feels that there's been too much tea-drinking and too many cream cakes in here with you. He says he came here to be disciplined and we have not disciplined him." I felt that it was unwise not to tell the truth.

The old man's face crinkled into a slightly wicked, impish grin. "Give me that dish of cream cakes," he said.

"I beg your pardon, Zenji Sama?"

"Don't argue. Give them to me."

I gave him the dish. He held it with his one good hand while I supported the other side for fear that he should drop it.

"Call him here," he said.

I spoke to the young man concerned, asking him to come over to Zenji Sama's bed.

"My friend," he said, looking the young man straight in the eye, "I want you to eat this whole dish of cream cakes."

The young man stared at me. "What's he talking about?" he said.

"I think his meaning is this," I replied. "You are saying you came here to be disciplined and you are complaining that you weren't disciplined. But discipline doesn't have to be what we want it to be."

He stared at me again. "You mean . . . ."

"I mean this—discipline can be having to sit and eat cream cakes and drink tea; or it can mean being beaten in the Meditation Hall. Discipline is discipline. It does not necessarily take the form that we want it to take."

The young man took the dish of cream cakes, put it on the floor, walked to the door and stalked out. Zenji Sama's chuckle followed him.

15th. April.

The great festival for which they have been preparing for the past ten years started to-day. Over twenty-thousand Japanese from all over the country are attending the five-day celebrations. I have to attend the Director at all the ceremonies.

20th. April.

My Sei-kyoshi examination questions came to-day. They are as follows:– 1. The priest Jizō said, "When we do not know we have everything." 2. Jōsai Daishi said, "Everyone is the vessel of the Dharma and every day is the best day." 3. In the "Tenzo-kyōkun" there are three minds, pleasant, old and great. 4. Explain the opinion of Dōgen Zenji on our daily life. 5. Add nothing and break nothing. Explain this. 6. What is the history of the way to explain the doctrine of our school of Zen a) on the eve of a funeral, b) at a memorial ceremony?

I considered these questions for some time. I decided that, for the next two days, I will do nothing but meditate.

22nd. April.

Having meditated most of the time since my last entry I started writing the actual papers to-day. The Director was very kind in giving me the two days off to meditate as well as the time in which to write now. I am recording the answers to the questions here since it will be easy for me to translate them into Japanese from this diary. They are as follows:–

1. The Chinese "Book of the Regulations of the Zen Monastery" says, "Sacred or common, monks are endowed with such a power as penetrates the whole universe." The German philosopher Eckhart said that a man shall become truly free and as pure as the day he was born when he has nothing, wants nothing and knows nothing. Therefore, if a man knows he is enlightened, he is not for he still clings to the knowledge of knowing. We are only conscious of what good health is when we have not got it. When a man is joyful, loving and generous at all times, without wishing to know why, he is enlightened. We are only conscious of needing to know something when we do not know. Therefore, not to know is not to need, and not to need, know or have is to manifest the True Self which is that which is most familiar to us since the True Self needs nothing adding to Itself and nothing taking away from It.

2. The Dharma is inestimable and all-pervading for all life is a manifestation thereof but most people are prevented from showing their true Buddha Nature because they clutch their own opinions and so produce the artificial "self" which desires instead of accepts. Thus the true "self," or Dharma Nature, Buddha Nature, which accepts all and does not want, have or know anything is hidden. But we are part God and part animal and the two parts cannot be separated. The selfish "self" and the Dharma Nature are one. The God-Nature, Dharma Nature, is the accepting part whilst the animal-nature is the selfish one.

The True Vessel of the Dharma is he who works to help both self and others. In so doing his animal-nature is transcended thus transforming inadequacy, externalised as greed, into adequacy, externalised as acceptance of all things. Thus he is always at peace. If a man has such a mind every moment is ever changing, ever constant, kaleidoscopic. Dōgen taught that those who make use of every moment in this way, adequate within themselves, find every day to be the best they have ever lived.

3. The three minds are not three but one, each interacting upon the other, for the mind of gratitude, or joy, is exemplified in the mind of love by the mind of generosity which shows itself in its immobility and impartiality. So there are not three minds but three aspects of the One Mind. If there were three minds the mind would be divided against itself and the trainee would be constantly asking himself with what mind did he do each act. Since there is nothing from the first, however, this One Mind becomes illusion when it is clutched at—it can only be understood when we do not search for it, when we are joyful, loving and generous. Therefore the mind of the true trainee is intangible to himself but tangible to others—he is only conscious of doing that which has to be done. He does not know with the ordinary mind when he is enlightened; he always knows when he is not.

4. Zen is the experiencing of the Buddha Mind and so Dōgen made no special effort to provide a means for analysing theoretical reality. To Dōgen, "to be able to say" and "not to be able to say" are self-identical. He therefore regarded training as the supreme work of the trainee. According to him one should not just *know* Buddhism but *become* Buddhism. Finding that discriminating intellect did not resolve his doubts he found a solution through the unification of training and experience; contradictions can only be truly resolved through Zen action. His realisation that "the Mind itself is the Buddha" enabled him to break the religious impasse reached by the Tendai and Shingon doctrines of "the body itself becoming Buddha." He insisted that training must be carried out without relaxation even in a degenerate age. He found deep meaning in unremitting

effort to realise eternal truth with his whole personality. He asserted that there was no difference between training and enlightenment and emphasized non-duality. So Zazen is not just sitting but training based on enlightenment. Dōgen's Zazen, therefore, is not a means to an end but an end in itself. It enfolds no gain and no expectation. It is a way of living in one's True Self. Consequently there is no wish to become Buddha and no striving with a kōan. Since training is enlightenment there is no end to training even after understanding has been reached. But Dōgen did not believe only in sitting. He purified and permeated daily work with the basic spirit of Zen for daily work is true Buddhism. He taught that Buddhism lives and works in daily activity. For those who make use of every moment every day is a good day. Such Zazen, without "thought," frees us from the duality of body and mind and removes the delusion that we and the Buddhas are separated. It enables us to realise the unity of all things.

5. It says in the "Genjo-kōan" that if birds separate themselves from the sky or fish separate themselves from water they die for fish live by water and birds by the sky just as the sky lives by the birds and the water by the fish. The order of things must be accepted as it is with no attempt to change it. Yet change is constant in the birds, the sky, the fish and the water and all accept the change within themselves and do not notice it because the change is familiar and usual to them. If we feel the need for something to be added we have not found the True Self for the True Self is complete and needs nothing. Conversely, if there is the need to break something we have not found the True Self for therein there is nothing to be broken.[104]

I will do the sixth to-morrow. I am very tired.

23rd. April.

Too tired to do the sixth answer in English first so told it to Rev. Hajime who helped me turn my bad Japanese into better.

29th. April.

I sent in the papers as soon as they were all translated and to-day I received the certificate of my Sei-kyoshi from the

Administration Section. Apparently my answers, though short, were quite satisfactory. The Director says the real examination took place earlier; I had been seen *living* the answers to my questions and so passed.

30th. April.

I was invited this morning to have coffee at the British Consulate along with some other British people in the area. Ever since my telling the Consul that I was thinking of becoming a Japanese citizen I have been invited to various functions, dinners and parties. The Consul has made it quite clear that he is not at all happy about the idea of my becoming a Japanese citizen.

When I got back to the temple the Director sent for me. He wanted me to mend one of his robes that had been somewhat damaged and, as I sat on the floor sewing, he said, "The kōan appears naturally in daily life. You now know well what your kōan is."

"Yes, Reverend Director. It's the fact that I'm a foreigner and a female at the wrong time and in the wrong place."

"That isn't good Zen—'wrong time and wrong place.' It is always the right time and the right place."

"I beg your pardon. You are correct."

He smiled. "You are handling that part of the kōan, being foreign and female, extraordinarily well. I hope you realise that."

"I am doing that which has to be done."

"Correct. That is the way in which the kōan always has to be handled. In the early stages it is very easy. We always think our first kenshō is so huge—the kenshō that makes it possible for us to be *truly* [105] Transmitted. But it is after Transmission that the *real* kōan really appears. The problem with Rinzai-ists is that they believe that once they have solved the three-hundred odd real (as they call it) kōans that other people have solved then they are fully enlightened. But they have never, in most cases, learned how to deal with, solve, their own *real* kōan. This is the problem with Rinzai. *We* know that the kōan goes on forever and the deeper one meditates the more one understands the self, the better one is at dealing with, solving, that particular kōan. For example, you could not have dealt with what has happened in England three or four years ago; it would have broken you. In many respects to be able to stay completely sane when everybody else is acting insanely around you is the greatest and most important sign of enlightenment. The sane man in a mad world is the enlightened man—which doesn't alter the fact, of course, that when the world is mad the sane man is in grave danger."

" 'In the country of the blind the one-eyed man is king,' " I said.

"Tell me about that," he said.

"Oh, it's a story by a famous writer concerning a man who finds himself in a strange valley in which everyone is blind and where those who have sight are regarded as deformed. The man thinks that because he has sight he will be able to help everyone and become their leader but he ends by becoming their slave as well as being blinded in trying to escape."

The Director smiled. "It is a good story and a very Zen one. You should remember to be very careful how you go with the Truth within your heart. There are times when it is absolutely necessary to behave like an ordinary human being; and to be insane in the presence of the mad. That is why it is said that the Dharma Treasure is he who has realised the Truth and behaves as an ordinary man. He who goes around like a stone Buddha, sitting on pedestals waiting for people to worship him as a Zen master, is in grave danger for one day he will be proved to be inadequate and will end up very dead. That is what went wrong with Christ, you know. In the country of the blind he did not know that the one-eyed man was in great danger—if he threw his weight around because he could see. He should have kept his sight to himself, silently within, and done his teaching according to the Zen method—just doing that which has to be done at all times, being sane when everybody else is insane but not forcing his sanity on other people."

"Then you think that the way in which I have handled this affair with regard to the young couple from England is right, completely right?"

"You didn't allow them to play games with you; you didn't allow them to play games with us. You have done nothing wrong and you know you have done nothing wrong. You have something they have not and, as they are, will never have. This is to have something indeed. But don't try and force it down their throats."

"Reverend Director, what am I to do? I feel that Zenji Sama still wants me to go back to England."

"Zenji Sama wants you to be able to act effectively and efficiently wherever you are. It is true he *had* hoped you would go to England but, now that he knows what the situation is like there, as he has said, he wants you to have nothing whatsoever to do with England at least whilst he lives. And he certainly doesn't want you to leave Japan—neither do I. As I've told you, I've never had such a good assistant. Do you know what you really need?" he added with a grin.

"No."

"More confidence in you. It's the problem of most women. They don't have enough confidence in themselves. You need a bit more confidence and a bit more pride—just that and nothing more. You know the Truth. Don't be afraid of going ahead and doing what you believe to be right. And, above all, don't be pulled off centre by silly idiots who tell you they know what a Zen master is. If they do, bow to them, congratulate them, tell them *you* don't know, that they know more than you do and walk on by. That's all I have to say to you on that. Don't bother with them. And remember that he who can keep sane when the world is insane is the Zen master. You kept sane when everything here was going crazy. You never doubted Zenji Sama even when you were hurt by him and, in his heart of hearts, he never doubted you."

"Thank you, Reverend Director. It's been a great comfort talking to you."

He smiled. "Your friends at the Consulate are inviting you a lot lately."

"Yes," I said.

"Is it because we suggested that you should become a Japanese?"

"Possibly, but I hope it's because they want my company. I'm swollen-headed enough, and lonely enough, to hope that."

"That is a human thought. It is good that a Zen master retains human thoughts. Too many of them go off the rails and become isolated, icy-cold, hermits almost, distant stars to be worshipped because they enjoy the worship, because they are afraid to let it be known that they are still human. The true Zen master is a very *human* being. Good-night."

"Good-night, Reverend Director." I bowed and softly closed the door as I left the room.

1st. May.

I had a long talk to-day with the girl who got herself pregnant. I pointed out to her that a woman who has her child aborted always remembers within her heart that she has destroyed that which is part of her own self. I have met many girls in my life who have had abortions and not one of them has ever been completely happy again. I tried to convey all this to her. I finished by saying that if she had the child, and had no home for it, I would be willing to adopt it since I have some money in England and no-one to leave it to; I am the last of my family and have no living relatives. She said she would think about this.

2nd. May.

I was disgusted to hear a rumour circulating round the temple to the effect that I have been in bed with someone. It is so bad that I went off to see Zenji Sama. Zenji Sama was furious about it too. Someone had already told him.

"What am I to believe?" he said. "I know that you and Rev. Hajime are often together; I know that you and the Director are often together. Why do you worry me so much?"

"Zenji Sama, you should not have a woman in this temple. It is not fair to you and it is certainly not fair to me."

"How can I be certain about these rumours?" The old man twisted on the bed.

"I will get you proof, Zenji Sama, but I'm deeply hurt that you cannot believe my words."[106]

He turned over as best he could and did not answer.

As I stood up I said, "If you cannot trust me there is no point in my staying here. Good-bye, Zenji Sama," and I left the room.[106, 100]

I went to the local Western hospital and asked if I could see a woman doctor. They told me there was a German woman doctor living in Tokyo who had been there during the war. I went to see her.

"What's wrong?" she asked.

"Doctor, I've got a very strange request of you."

"Yes?" she said.

"There's a rumour circulating about me that I'm in bed with somebody and, in all my life, I've never been in bed with anyone. I am as much a virgin now as when I was born. Can you examine me and write a certificate of proof as to whether or not my hymen is intact?"

She looked straight at me. "Who's been saying this?"

"Oh, somebody or other where I live. I don't know who the heck's been saying it."

"It's a pity they've got nothing better to do than gossip," she said. "Come on in."

She took me into her surgery and examined me, then said, "It is obvious that you have never been touched by anyone in all your life. I will write you a certificate to that effect."

"What is your fee, doctor?"

"Nonsense! Nothing. It's the least one woman can do for another under circumstances such as these. But you should come and see me more often. You don't look at all well."

"I don't think that is terribly surprising. I've got a most peculiar thing going on at the top of my left leg; I wish I knew what it was. And I also seem to be putting on weight at an enormous speed. I will come again if I may."

"Please do."

"I haven't really gone to doctors much because—well, I don't seem to get—perhaps it's that I can't talk to them well enough in Japanese—I don't know—but they don't seem to be able to find anything wrong with me. I went into the local foreign hospital for three days of tests and they could find nothing wrong. But this thing at the top of my thigh still causes me incredible problems. I don't *think* I'm imagining it."

She examined me. "One thing is certain," she said, "something seems to be going very wrong with your glands. Look at the weight you're putting on."

"I know. It's very worrying."

"Come and see me frequently." She smiled as we went to the door. "I'll try and look after you."

"Thanks," I said and left her.

When I returned to the temple I packed what was left of my things and then went to bed for it was already bedtime. In the morning I will go to the officers' chapter for the last time.

3rd. May.

I went to the officers' chapter meeting and, before anyone had time to say anything whatsoever, I put the certificate of my virginity on the table in front of the Director.

"Here is proof that I have never been in bed with anyone in all my life," I said, "and I challenge whoever it is that said that I have to come forward and tell me who I have been in bed with." There was absolute silence in the room.

"Whoever wants to accuse me, come out and do so." There was still silence. I rose. "I thank you all for having me here these past few years," I said. "I shall be going to Malaysia soon. Good-bye." I bowed, left the room and went back to my own.

Within minutes the Director was in my room. "Jiyu San, don't go."

"Reverend Director, there is no point in this. There's a limit and I have reached it."

"Who do you think has been making up this tale?" he asked.

"I wish I knew." My voice was grating.

"It is not a man," he said.

"*Not* a man?"

"If I were asked to make a guess I'd say it was a woman. Whom have you upset here?"

"The only women here are the employees. There aren't any actual women members of the priesthood other than the one that lives in Zenji Sama's house. She hates my guts but I don't think she hates me enough to do this."

He was thoughtful for a time. "Maybe," he said.

"Who am I supposed to be in bed with? What's the actual rumour, Reverend Director?"

"You'll find it hard to believe but the majority of them think that you're in bed with Zenji Sama. He's the first choice. I presume I must be the second and Rev. Hajime the third."

"That's unbelievable—and it's sick! Zenji Sama is as ill as he can be—he can't even stand, he can't even move."

"Don't expect logic from idiots."

"Ohhhhh." I sat down. "Reverend Director, please help me. What on earth are they going to get out of this, whoever this person is?"

"Jealousy is said to be the prevailing trait of women in Japan. Everyone here is convinced that you suffer from it to exactly the same extent as a Japanese."

"I see. But what's *this* woman going to get out of it? Does *she* want to get into bed, whoever she is, with Zenji Sama?"

"No, but she wants to ruin you, to discredit you."

"And what's the temple getting out of it?"

"How many times am I to tell you of the political factions in Japanese religion? Zenji Sama's faction is waning; he is dying. His enemies are gathering ready to pick his bones if they can. Why on earth did you suffer from the idea that we were a bunch of saints here? We're not! Saints are rare anywhere. How many have you got in your country?"

"To my knowledge, none. We've been stupid enough to believe that they all exist over here."

"Exactly. Just as the Japanese have been stupid enough to believe in the past that they all exist in the West. It's high time you started using your common sense. There are no more saints here than there are there—either in our church or in the Christian—but saints exist. You have met them. You have met Zenji Sama; you met the one in Kyoto."

"And I've met you, Reverend Director."

"Don't call me that!"

"I'm sorry. Reverend Director, the way I handled this particular aspect of the kōan was totally different from the way in which the old Zen master handled it. You remember the story? Somebody says he's the father of a child and all he says is, 'Is that so?' as they hand the child to him. And, when they come to collect it, having found out it isn't his, and to apologise to him, all he says is, 'Is that so?' I'm not really very good. I should be able to handle kōans on that level."

"Listen. Too many people misunderstand that type of kōan. For a man, that was the way to handle that particular kōan. For a woman, the way you have handled it is the correct and only way. A man will always be given the benefit of the doubt by his fellows but a woman never. Therefore, when a woman has to handle this particular kōan, she needs to have proof of her innocence. You have proof which, incidentally, is no longer proof."

"What are you talking about?"

"That certificate was dated yesterday." His face was impish.

"Reverend Director, please!"

"However hard we try there will always be people who will be able to make something out of nothing. Don't worry about them. *You* know that you are completely innocent; *I* know that you are completely innocent; everyone here who really matters knows that you're completely innocent. The problems are being caused by two people. It's the old saying that you have quoted to me several times:– empty cans make the most rattle."

"I'm still going off to Malaysia, Reverend Director."

"I can't stop you but I hope that you come back. I think you will. Zenji Sama needs you."

"As I feel at the moment I don't want to ever see Zenji Sama again."[100, 106]

"Ah, the 'quarrel' continues." He rose. "I am going to miss you. I want you back. Remember that."

"I'm going to my temple to-day, Reverend Director."

"Have a good journey." He bowed and left me.

I picked up my one small case, looked at the other two that I'd packed and then decided 'no.' I would leave a few things; I put them in the cupboard. I went off, caught the train and arrived at my temple late this evening.

4th. May.

It was as well I came down for there have been many cere-monies. I've been continuing to mend the temple—there are all sorts of things that still need to be done. There were quite a number of letters here also. A large number of the foreigners from Tokyo want to come down for part of the Summer. Since I had already told them to give me at least a fortnight's notice before coming, none of them have turned up when I wasn't here. I answered most of the letters but found it impossible to sit because of the difficulty with the top of my leg again.

3rd. June.

I had a letter from Rev. Hajime this morning enclosing the ticket which has come for me from the Chinese abbot. He also told me that Andy is leaving Japan.

16th. June.

I have had so much to do; there has been no point in trying to write this diary. Just I am recording a letter that came from Rev. Hajime this morning. There was no particular news in it—he obviously wanted to talk to someone for a few moments. He said that he was so busy that he had no time to think—but he still had time to write that!

The difficulty with physical sitting seems to be decreasing a little again. I wish I knew what's wrong with me.

20th. June.

Another letter from Rev. Hajime. It seems that Rev. Isaburo, who went to England and whose visa I helped to obtain from the British Consulate, has been causing quite a few problems there. Instead of doing what he'd said he was going to do, study at London University, he told people that he was officially the Buddhist Bishop of London sent by our school of Zen. This caused an uproar. Now he is back in Tokyo. I really do not intend to get involved in this mess. Rev. Hajime says that when Rev. Isaburo comes to the Tokyo temple (apparently he is keeping well away from it at the moment) he will be able to tell me more about the affair. I don't *want* to know about it—ever! But I expect I'll be forced to listen.

Rev. Hajime also said that the Tokyo temple's university wants me to lecture on Zen in English. Something inside me tells me I should go back; they want me in July. But, unless I make it quite clear that people are to stop assing about with silly rumours, I will always have problems. I feel the time has come to make a stand.

26th. June.

I've not answered any of Rev. Hajime's letters which is perhaps the reason why another one came this morning. This one was rather remarkable. After asking me how I was (the first time anyone has been that polite since I've been in the Tokyo temple) Rev. Hajime told me that the Director did not intend to say or do anything concerning the accusation made against me. He also informed me that the Director is ordering me to return to the temple at once. He says I had told him I would not return unless I was invited but the Director says he is ordering me back. The disciplinarian, according to Rev. Hajime, says that he has never had anything against me; someone has apparently implied that he has. I wonder who that was?

Now, Rev. Hajime says, everything is fine. If I return to the temple I shall be treated as an officer except in one respect— the others will still not permit me to be celebrant at Morning Service. I am to have all the responsibility, all the worry, all the cash, do night-watch, fill in all the forms—everything except this. In spite of the fact that I have been celebrant both at graduation and other times this is the one thing that the chief lecturer will not agree to my doing. I think I will stay here.

2nd. August.

We've been working hard and the temple is now magnificent. I've even got a garden started. I got a pond marked out and I intend to have fish in it at a later date—if I ever come back from Malaysia. It's been rather fun planting all the trees and shrubs.

A letter came from Rev. Hajime, brought by one of the villagers who has just visited the Tokyo temple. Rev. Hajime says that the girl who became pregnant went to a doctor, together with the Director, and had her child aborted. The letter went on to say that she is feeling very sad and that he is very sorry for having asked me to help her. He asks me to forget about this matter. Forget about it? I had offered the child a home. It's as well I had made no actual plans. And what an age to abort at! Six months—that child could see.

17th. August.

The local priest at whose temple I have been helping lately has given me so much work to do that I really haven't had nearly as much time for looking after the village affairs as perhaps I should have done. The village wants me to do several lectures this summer for the old people.

Rev. Hajime telephoned to require that I help at his temple for Segaki. I did so and lost the last bus back but his wife refused to allow me to stay in the temple for the night. I walked back. I'm really extremely tired and my leg is causing a lot of trouble; fortunately, however, not when I am walking.

20th. August.

A very strange card from Rev. Hajime. He said that I had not written and offered to give me a big party if I did not want to see him again. Then he asked if I did or didn't want to see him and concluded that it seemed I did not. Therefore he will give me a party before I go. It is up to me, he ended.

Whatever is wrong with the man?

29th. August.

Another card from Rev. Hajime. I made a gold brocade kesa for the Director some time ago and now I receive a card from Rev. Hajime saying that the Director is very pleased with the kesa. Rev. Hajime also says he is shocked at some of the comments that I reported to him once—made by some of the villagers here. He wants to hear about them. I wonder why he is bringing up all this back stuff? Is it as an inducement to get me going in soap-opera conversation with him again? He's going the wrong way about getting me to write.

An American arrived from Tokyo to look after my temple whilst I am in Malaysia.

28th. September.

I returned to Tokyo this morning since my ship sails on the thirtieth. Something in me wanted to see Zenji Sama; something in me equally said, "Why the heck should I bother?" I sat in my old room,[107] grouching to myself about this, when the Director came hurrying in.

"Jiyu San, Jiyu San, Zenji Sama will *have* to see you. You can't go off without seeing him." His smile was impish, roguish.

"Reverend Director, do I *have* to?"

"Yes, you *do* have to! Come on. I'll come with you."

He took me by the arm and hurried me along the corridors to Zenji Sama's new house in which he is at last installed. Zenji Sama writhed in an effort to rise on his one elbow.

"Jiyu San, it is good to see you."

I *thought* there was something between us—a hurtfulness, a barrier, a loneliness—I don't know what it was. And then I *knew* it wasn't there; that I was imagining it.

"Hello, Zenji Sama," I said. "I'm going off to-day."

"Yes," he said.

I bowed. Neither of us said good-bye. Something told me I was wrong to go. I had promised to stay with him until his death.[108] I left the room.

When I got back to my room the Director looked at me intently. "While I am here you will always be welcome. Just I want you to remember that."

He then did something very strange. He put his arms round me and hugged me, then stood back. "You do not respond at all," he said.

"Did you think I would?"

"It is good for me to know such things, specially when people ask questions," and he left the room.

29th. September.

Spent most of the day going round to various places in the Tokyo area dealing with affairs that I have to attend to, making arrangements for the various foreigners who wish to come to the temple to wait until they hear from me, cancelling classes.

30th. September.

The ship sailed this evening at about eight and I have time to write this. At around five in the evening I went to the Kōshakudai (the great entrance door in front of the kitchen) and there stood, dressed for a journey with all the junior trainees lined up in two rows on either side. And then of all people, the chief lecturer turned up. Since he was the ranking senior Rev. Hajime and the Director approached him to do the official farewell ceremony. The lecturer bridled.

"Why should I?" he snapped. "I have nothing to do with her."

The Director's eyes became a little steely. "You will *do* the ceremony," he said.

"But you are senior to me."

"*I* am not here now," and the Director turned on his heel and walked away.

The lecturer looked at the assembled company, none of whom were officially hearing anything; he looked at me; then he did the farewell ceremony.

I went off by car, with two friends of mine, to the ship. At about six this evening twenty of my trainee friends turned up on board together with three bottles of pink champagne and there was a party in my cabin. Everyone toasted me; it was obvious that every one of the juniors was upset at my going. There was not one of them who had not heard of the virginity certificate and several congratulated me on having gone to get it.

The girl who had been pregnant was there too but there was something rather horrible about her; she obviously now hates my guts. I really don't know very much about how to handle women.

Rev. Hajime said something very odd. He was drinking the pink champagne rather too quickly and spluttering as a result. Then he said to me, "That young couple that came from England—the wife was really very jealous of you. How long have you been in love with her husband?" I couldn't believe what I was hearing.

"What *are* you talking about?" I said. "I've never been in love with him at all. I only know the man from attending lectures." But Rev. Hajime had already forgotten what he said—too deep in his cups.

One of his daughters was there. She has become extraordinarily friendly with the girl who had the abortion. The two were whispering quietly in a corner, chewing on a box of sweets that an elderly lady had brought me as a present and the elderly lady was getting annoyed about it.

Then the announcement came, "All ashore that's going ashore," and everyone left. They waited on the dock and, as the ship slipped into the night, cheered and threw streamers. Rev. Hajime was too drunk to do anything. His daughter and the girl were talking to each other seated on a bollard and the junior trainees were having great fun throwing the streamers to me. All things considered, a great send-off.

14th. October.

I have had no time to write until now. The Chinese abbot had arranged lectures for me in almost every major city in Malaysia and, as soon as I had finished, there were hundreds of young Chinese who wanted to talk and get advice on various subjects. I am amazed at how much I seem to really know. I have lectured at four different universities. I now have a few days off. I start again on October 20th.

A letter came to-day from Rev. Hajime. I had written to the Director of the Tokyo temple and to the Trainees' Club chairman thanking them for many things and telling them why I felt I did not wish to return. Apparently Rev. Hajime does not want to translate either of the letters for them. Instead he wants me to come back. He says that the parishioners of my temple also want me back. More than half of them voted for me to stay in the parish although I was originally supposed to only be there for three years. This is unusual since most Japanese do not have much interest in religion nowadays. He also said that he is losing his courage to continue to be a priest although he knows he will be one for the rest of his days. I can guess how he feels considering the political machinations that go on in that Tokyo temple. When in Japan I had asked him if the Vice-Abbot would be willing to be my guarantor after Zenji Sama's death, always presuming, of course, that the authorities *really* want the Foreign Section to continue in the temple. The last few months prior to my going down to my own temple made it quite clear that a number of them were really beginning to get interested in the foreigners. Rev. Hajime says the Vice-Abbot hasn't yet decided.

20th. October.

The Chinese abbot went with me to the local immigration office to-day. Although he would very much like me to stay here in Malaysia it seems physically impossible for me to do so under the existing law. The Malaysian government's new policy is that absolutely no-one who has not been living here for ten years or more can ever become a permanent resident of the country. It's all part of their new policy to make sure that they get rid of all foreign religions[109] within as short a time as possible. All the Christian missionaries are to be out of the country and their schools closed within the next ten years. This means that there is no way in which I can take on the temple that the abbot would like me to have here. It's rather unfortunate for I would have liked to have stayed with him. He has been so

extraordinarily kind and so obviously understands real Buddhism. He reminds me of a young form of Zenji Sama. How
much I miss Zenji Sama.

The Chinese are going to print the lectures I have been giving together with questions and answers which were included in
the seminars.

Only one thing has marred this tour. The Chinese abbot
took me for two days to a temple high on one of the hills.
Unfortunately the priest there was obviously very afraid of
women and treated me very badly. I shouldn't have done it but
I got into a huff; probably because I was so tired. I got out of it
very quickly but I must remember to keep my training going in
every situation, remember what the Director said, remember
what Zenji Sama said—and remember that the enlightened man
has feelings! It is important to remember that the enlightened
man is human at all times.

2nd. November.

Another letter from Rev. Hajime; not a very helpful letter.
He said that I am not expected to return to the temple in Tokyo.
If I do return I should not expect to be treated particularly well.
The Vice-Abbot has said nothing yet concerning his willing-
ness to be my sponsor.

There was one ray of good news; Zenji Sama is extremely
pleased that I sent him a card and letter. Rev. Hajime says, however, that Zenji Sama has no reply for me. The Trainees' Club
chairman has not answered either. Rev. Hajime again reiterated
that the village is expecting me back; he then went on to say
that the Director is not at all interested in the foreigners and
does not want the Foreign Section to continue.[110] In addition to
this, the Junior Officers' Club have refused to have any women
in it whatsoever.

Rev. Hajime ended his letter by saying that his private opinion is that if I want to come back to Japan and work for the foreigners who are here I had better do it outside the Tokyo temple,
in my own temple, otherwise I will always have to feel miserable.

I wonder. Is this letter temple politics or is it Zenji Sama's will? The only way I shall know is if I meditate deeply and act accordingly. I can trust no-one's words;[111] the only thing I have to trust is my own heart and, so help me, whilst I live, that's all I will ever trust again.

3rd. November.

I spent most of the day in meditation; then I wrote a letter to Zenji Sama. I told him that I was listening to no opinions other than those of my own heart; that I had written a book; that I will return if he requires me to look after his foreigners; that he himself should let me know if he wishes me to return; that he should not communicate with me through a third person; how much I miss him.

23rd. November.

A letter came from Rev. Hajime this morning together with one from the Director. Rev. Hajime's was very interesting. It was itemized very simply and, after saying that he had received my letter (I hadn't written him one), said that:– 1) He will come to see me at the ship on my arrival at Yokohama and bring someone else with him to help bring me back to the temple. 2) I should bring the presents I have for Zenji Sama. 3) Since it is now Winter they will bring my Winter clothes to the ship. 4) My room waits for me. 5) The Vice-Abbot says that I should come back to the temple quickly. 6) Concerning his last letter, he has found that some parts of it are changed but he wants to talk about this when I come back.

The Director's letter said that he is glad to hear that I am well and successful in Malaysia and he is sorry for not writing for a long time. He feels that it is up to me whether I come back to the temple. He offered no suggestions with regard to the presents I have for Zenji Sama.

The two letters seem at variance[110] but obviously someone read my letter to Zenji Sama; it is also obvious that the prevarication that has been going on has been stomped on by Zenji Sama. My heart was right when it decided not to listen to the swayings and the runnings back and forth of Rev. Hajime's comments; I was right to go over his head directly to Zenji Sama himself. From now on I will never again go through Rev. Hajime for anything for it is obvious that he is too busy sitting on both sides of the political fence for me to be able to trust him in matters between myself and Zenji Sama. Every day I think how wonderful it will be to be with Zenji Sama again. I should never have left him.[112]

3rd. December.

We went to Singapore to catch the boat for my return to Japan. I will stay with Zenji Sama until his death as I promised; then I will leave Japan or live in my temple, whichever is the most advisable at the time. This is my decision. I am extremely tired. My brain is reeling from too many lectures and meeting too many people but I have ten days on this ship and should be able to rest. We call at Hong Kong on the way and I will be able to visit some friends.

It has been a wonderful visit; I know that I have true friends in the priesthood in Malaysia. I know that they would love to have me in their country if the governmental authorities made it possible but there is no way in which this can be arranged as yet. In a few years' time the situation may be different. At least I am *wanted* here. All that has to be changed are government regulations, not anti-foreign feeling.

My body is swelling terribly. I don't know if it is from eating Chinese food, living in the heat of Malaysia or the result of what is wrong with the top of my leg. I have a feeling that the two last are interrelated but I cannot be certain.

5th. December.

I have been unable to sleep for two nights as a result of having overworked during these last three months. I went to see the ship's doctor who gave me some tablets. Perhaps to-night I shall sleep.

10th. December.

I have been sleeping well. All I needed to do was relax and get my nerves wound down from the overwork.

When we arrived at Yokohama Rev. Hajime and Zenji Sama's own private chief assistant—his new one, not the old one—were waiting for me on the docks. I was taken back to the temple and there informed that I was to have dinner with the senior officers to-night by order of Zenji Sama. He had arranged a special party for me with them. I had brought quite a number of presents with me but not enough for all the senior officers; this caused considerable problems at the party. Several officers were very angry because they didn't all get something equally good. This business of giving presents every time one goes somewhere is not only extraordinarily expensive but, to my mind, extremely unnecessary. The party, on the whole, was not much of a success; the chief lecturer saw to that. He is obviously furious that I have returned but there is nothing that he can do about it.

Zenji Sama sent word that the foreigners who used to come are to be notified at once since he wants them all for New Year. He intends to get out of bed and be carried to the Hondō to talk to them; he feels this may be the last time he will ever see them. I am glad that I have returned. Although I am still hurt in a strange sort of way over this business of his checking everything out concerning me, there is something between him and I that nothing can harm—ever.

I asked Rev. Hajime, when the party was over, why it was that there was a new chief assistant in Zenji Sama's house. His answer was that the previous one had become infatuated by one of the girl-priests who had been temporarily staying here. Zenji Sama had found out about it and become extremely angry. One day the chief assistant was missing and so was the girl, leaving behind the assistant's wife and baby. Apparently it hurt Zenji Sama very, very greatly. I can well believe that it has.

Zenji Sama sent for me as soon as the party was over. "I hear that the Chinese are printing a book of your lectures," he said.

"Yes, Zenji Sama."

"They are to be printed here too."

"May I rewrite them, Zenji Sama, to make them better?"

"Yes."

"Zenji Sama, you have always said that I was not to write any books because of the way in which the average Westerner who comes here goes away and writes books and articles without ever having learned properly."

"I want your book." His tone was slightly angry.

"Yes, Zenji Sama."

"I want copies of everything you have translated with Rev. Hajime. I want them printed."

"Yes, Zenji Sama. I am *glad* to be home."

A big smile broke out on his face. "You never went away."

25th. December.

It has been extremely hard work getting all the foreigners together but, thanks once again to the newspapers and radio, it has been possible.

To-day I again had Christmas dinner at the British Consulate. One of the first 'phone calls I got after my return from Malaysia was from the Consul's wife saying she would like me to come over. We had a very enjoyable party and a very enjoyable Christmas dinner. Now I am back in the temple and I suppose I have another year ahead of me—and a year after that and a year after that—of living with prejudice and trying to help the foreigners as best I can—and being near Zenji Sama.

31st. December.

It was not possible for me to get any assistants from outside this year. The chief lecturer refused to allow them in and I was not able to get to Zenji Sama to explain this to him. So I arranged that four or five friends of mine amongst the junior trainees should help instead. They can't speak English but they're willing to try and understand what the foreigners say to them.

We have been getting the temple ready most of the day. Only two-hundred visitors are expected this year. Zenji Sama complained bitterly when I told him a few days ago that two-hundred was all we were going to have. He said that it was my fault that there were so few; if I had not been away for such a long time there would have been many, many more.

1st. January.

I don't know how I looked after those two-hundred last night. The chief lecturer refused to allow me to have all five assistants and I found myself with only two to deal with all the beds, meals and attendance at ceremonies as well as looking after the Director at the ceremonies as his assistant. When everything was over at six o'clock this morning I came back to my room hoping to rest but the chief lecturer refused to allow me to do so. I had got to clean up the temple from the foreigners and no-one was to assist me. However, the Director wanted me to look after the celebration wine for his New Year guests; the chief lecturer was screaming that I'd got to clean up the temple. I suggested they talk to each other. The Director won.

My difficulty with physical sitting was incredible to-day. I could not sit at all and the size of my body is becoming frightening.

2nd. January.

I didn't go anywhere near the Meditation Hall this morning; I slept right through all the bells; my body flatly refused to do anything else. I looked after the guests in the Director's guest hall; hundreds of them came, as they did last year, and at least six of them suggested again that I become a Japanese. I made no comment.

3rd. January.

This is the last day for the New Year guests to come to offer their congratulations. I really am not sorry. I am so very tired.

4th. January.

I have two lectures to give to-day at one of the American bases. Many foreigners have booked to stay for weekends or other periods here and there are also tour groups that I must take round the temple. Taking people round the grounds and buildings has always been one of my jobs. I really do need to get someone to help me; the job is getting a bit too big in some respects. All Zenji Sama's foreign letters come to me; he still insists that I answer them all. As soon as they are written I take them to him for his approval and signature; he often says, "I trust you, send them off." I wish he wouldn't do that; I want him to read everything I write.

10th. January.

I went into the temple hospital to-day for tests to find out what is making me get so fat but they can find absolutely nothing. They've decided I am to stay in for a couple of weeks to see if they can get my weight down. They say that I am imagining what is wrong with my leg.

2nd. February.

Bean throwing again. A huge crowd of foreigners—at least one of them won the right to throw beans.

10th. February.

So many ceremonies. I just don't know which way to look—so much work, so many outside lectures. Some of the trainees here don't believe that I give lectures, they think I am socialising, so I asked the Director if he would come to one with me but he refused. Instead he says he will send one of the juniors sometime.

18th. February.

This morning, after we had finished all the ceremonies and just before lunch, Rev. Hajime called me to his room.

"What is it with you British?" he asked.

"What do you mean?" I said.

"Well, after you had boarded the ship to go to Malaysia last year, a letter came from Andy saying that it was you that had caused all the problems in London; that if you hadn't egged

Zenji Sama on to write and check out the situation there none of the unpleasantness would have arisen."

"Rev. Hajime, I do *not* intend to get involved in that mess again. From now on I know *nothing* about it and never will know anything about it."

"I cannot understand the minds of you British. Why should he do this?"

"I cannot understand a lot of things; just I do the best I can to the utmost of my ability."

"Andy is certainly no friend of yours."

"Really?"

"He doesn't seem to be any friend of ours either. He wrote some disgusting things about the other temple he's been staying at not far from here. I am thoroughly disgusted with the whole affair!"

"What did he say?" I couldn't help my curiosity at this.

"He said that he was convinced that our school of Zen is no good whatsoever[113] and he's going off to join somebody he's found in India who is a real master—somebody called a Maharishi."

"I see."

"You're not disturbed by that?"

"Rev. Hajime, *I'm not* interested."

"Oh, well, if you're not interested why should I waste my time with you?"

"I promised Zenji Sama I would have nothing more to do with what is going on in England. Whilst he lives I won't do so and I am only staying here whilst he lives."

"Then why do you keep going to the British Consulate? It annoys him considerably."

"The British authorities invite me to their functions because I still hold a British passport and Zenji Sama agreed to this. Some of the officials are also very good friends of mine."

"Then you are going to become a Japanese?"

"No, I am not. I am doing that which has to be done."

He stared at me oddly. "We should continue our translations sometime," he said.

"I agree," I replied and left him.

21st. February.

Again, after all the morning ceremonies were over and I was trying to sit back for a few minutes peace and quiet in my room, Rev. Hajime came to see me.

"It's about that man, that disciple of Zenji Sama's who went to England," he said.

"Yes?" I said.

"There are letters that need to be written."

"Yes?" I said.

"It needs to be explained quite clearly to the British that it was not our idea that he should go there and proclaim himself to be Bishop of London. It is necessary that they should know he went there officially as a student."

"I see."

"You will write the letters?"

"I would rather you didn't ask me to. I have promised Zenji Sama I will not get involved with what is going on in British Buddhism. I intend to stick to that promise."

An American friend of mine was sitting in my room at the time. He had come a few minutes earlier and intended to spend the next week in the temple. After Rev. Hajime had gone he asked me about our conversation. I explained the situation with Zenji Sama as well as what had happened in England.

"You know," I said, "there's one thing I can't understand and that is the willingness of the British to be so gullible with regard to foreigners, and Orientals in particular. People of their own nation in Buddhism they frequently treat like dirt; an Oriental as God Almighty. You know, in many respects they are exactly the opposite of the Japanese. The Japanese trust no-one unless he's Japanese and the British trust no-one unless he's foreign."

My friend looked at me thoughtfully. "I'm glad this Bishop affair happened to the British and not to the Americans," he said. "I always thought *we* were the most gullible people on earth. I'm glad to know we're not."

1st. March.

I was putting away the Director's robes in the afternoon after all the day's ceremonies were finished when he turned to me and said, "How do you view the way in which the kōan expresses itself in daily life?"

"The whole of existence is the kōan," I said.

"Explain that."

"From all directions come flying objects. The only person who makes it from here to there is the one who goes straight on regardless and the 'from here to there' is still."

He nodded. "I had noticed," he said.

"Noticed?" I answered.

"Yes, I had noticed. Nothing deters you. You now take no notice of any of the quarrels that go on; you take no notice of any of the discussions for or against foreigners; you arrange everything that Zenji Sama requires you to arrange; you do not ask if others are pleased or displeased. You do everything to the best of your ability. You are not pulled off centre by what is happening in England nor by what is happening here."

"What are you trying to tell me, Reverend Director?"

"That yours is a dangerous and a magnificent course."

"It is the only course open to me."

"Of course," he replied. "*Living* life is a dangerous occupation; most people just exist, fearing to *live*. How to *live* is what you came here to learn; to find the courage to live and to be completely peaceful while you do it. It will not be long now before you receive the certificate from the Administration Section proving that you have the right to teach."

"Really?"

"Not long," he replied.

"I see."

He smiled. "You show no more interest in that, and no more disinterest in it, than you do in the affairs of London or the affairs of this temple."

"They have nothing to do with me. My concern is to do my training to the very best of my ability—just that and nothing more."

He bowed, took my hands in between his and gasshōed them to his forehead. I left him.

21st. March.

Too many ceremonies for me to be able to write about anything!

25th. March.

Went to some outside ceremonies to-day and then down to one of the American bases, taking with me one of the Director's other assistants. The assistant didn't quite believe what he saw, and when I got back this evening it was obvious that he was furious about it for he had discovered, and indeed reported, that I had not been playing games down on the base but doing genuine teaching. I am amazed that I hadn't thought of this particular form of idiocy before. Apparently it has been the current belief in the entire temple that I do literally nothing when I go out except enjoy myself. They should try it sometime! As I walked into the Director's office three juniors were sitting there muttering together and I couldn't help overhearing their conversation. It was to the effect that a Japanese could do the job on the American bases just as well as I could and they should make arrangements to make sure that one of them got it. So the next thing is that they are going to try and take over my job with the Americans. They're welcome to it if they want it; I'm not in competition with anyone.

30th. March.

There was a strange atmosphere in the temple to-day. I don't know what it indicates but it worries me. *Later.* Someone told me that Zenji Sama has become blind.

1st. April.

At the officers' chapter this morning it was decided that there is to be a big shake-up of all the junior officers in the temple. According to the senior lecturer those working for Zenji Sama have been with him for too long. They are all to be changed. The only one who will be left with him is the girl who has nursed him throughout his illness. Since she is Zenji Sama's private employee they cannot touch her. She is viciously anti me. The lecturer also said that I have been with the Director too long—that is to be changed too. This is a very serious matter for Zenji Sama. It means that he will have to get used to a whole new set of people; people who are not his own Transmitted disciples. It means that the person who has always cooked his food in the kitchen—the food that he has enjoyed so much—one of the few pleasures left to him, will be changed also; and it means that I shall no longer have the Director.

When the meeting was over, the Director came to see me together with the chief disciplinarian. The latter thanked me for the three years that I have worked with the Director and said that, in many ways, he's extremely sorry about the reshuffle but there is no way in which he can fight the chief lecturer's decision.

After he had left the room the Director, who was drinking tea on the other side of my desk, said to me, "It is as well that you have learned to walk straight and without fear for now you must be really brave and walk alone."

"This whole thing was aimed at me, wasn't it?"[100] I said.

"You should not think such wicked thoughts. They are not good."

"Forgive me, Reverend Director. You are right; I am wrong."

"Guard the foreigners well," he said, looked at me for a long time, then, as I got up to open the door for him, he embraced me once more, stood back and said, "Still absolutely no response. Magnificent. I was right," and he went to his room.

2nd. April.

A large group of foreigners came to-day. I was shocked at the way in which the Guest Department reacted towards them. They would not allow them to have any cushions to sit on and the meals that had been arranged were deliberately cancelled. The Director must have suspected this sort of thing which is why he gave me the warning he did yesterday. I thought of going to see Zenji Sama but, instead, made excuses to the foreigners and got things together as best I could. I'm going to sit still for a day or two and see what happens.

5th. April.

I received a letter from a Japanese gentleman who wanted me to correspond with an English friend of his who is interested in learning about our school of Zen. After much thought, for I do not intend to break my promise to Zenji Sama, I wrote to him to say that if his friend writes to ask for instruction I will place the letter before Zenji Sama.

9th. April.

Sesshin for the foreign laymen started this morning. The Director watched us and wanted to come but it was obvious that he did not dare to. The chief lecturer walked by the door and made some very rude comments about the foreigners who were sitting there. Fortunately none of them could understand his Japanese; I hope they couldn't!

17th. April.

I found a flower in my room to-day. It had been put there by an old washer-woman[114] who was leaving the room as I entered. She looked at me and said, "Zenji Sama."

I remembered this old woman from a long time ago. She has always been very kind and very self-effacing.

I went immediately to Zenji Sama's house. I went in via the window rather than go through the room where his new assistants were.

"Jiyu," he said, "I am becoming deaf as well as blind."

"That sometimes happens, Zenji Sama." I raised my voice so as to make sure that he could hear me.

"But, if I am deaf as well as blind, I am useless. You realise that I started going blind whilst you were in Malaysia?"

I had heard rumours but this was the first time they had been confirmed. He had not seemed particularly blind when I visited him on my return.

"If I am blind, paralyzed and deaf what use am I?" he said.

"Zenji Sama, you mustn't talk like that. You finished writing a book only a few weeks ago. You must start another."

"A Zen master should only live whilst he is useful."

"Zenji Sama, ..."

"A snail carries his house with him wherever he goes and he dies within his own house. That is the Lord."[115]

The door was rudely opened by someone I didn't know. "What are you doing here?" he demanded.

"I came because Zenji Sama sent for me."

"You have no right here. Leave at once."

Zenji Sama's voice came from a long way off. "Guard my foreign disciples."

"Yes, Zenji Sama."

"Get out of here," said the assistant. I bowed to Zenji Sama[116] and left the room.

22nd. April.

It was late in the evening. I was finishing off the accounts since the new treasurer has demanded a complete audit of all the books of the Foreign Section. He wants to make certain that I have not embezzled any of the cash that the foreigners have given. It would be a little difficult to embezzle anything since I have to pay everything in every month and have the books signed regularly on the thirty-first by the treasurer himself who also checks all the bills and expenditures.

I had almost finished when that old disciple of Zenji Sama's, the one I have seen once or twice before, came very softly into the room with one of the members of the Tokubetsu Sōdō who has been studying with me and who has always seemed to be very quiet, as if off in the distance somewhere. The two sat down on the floor and bowed. Then the old disciple said, "Guard Zenji Sama's foreign disciples. Guard them well. You have written the book that Zenji Sama wanted?"

"Well, I've done most of it—yes, but it isn't printed yet."

"Let me have the manuscript." I found it and gave it to him. "What about the manuscripts of the things that you have been translating with Rev. Hajime?"

"So far only one of them has been written up properly—that is the 'Kyōjukaimon.'"

"Let me have the manuscript." I gave it to him. "What about the lectures you have been giving to the foreigners?"

"Well, we have been printing them on a Gestetner for the last year and a half. I've been writing them up."

"Let me have them. I will turn them into a book."

I gave him the manuscripts and he put them in his sleeve after carefully folding them. Then he said, "To-morrow your Tokubetsu Sōdō will end. You will be officially graduated as having the right to teach although you will not yet have your teaching certificate, only that of having finished Tokubetsu Sōdō. It is Zenji Sama's wish that you attend the graduation ceremony."

"Thank you," I said.

Just as he got to the door he turned and said, "Zenji Sama's cat is dead."

"I will remember," I replied. He bowed, so did the young man with him, and I was left alone.

I telephoned to a friend of mine whose cat I knew had recently had kittens. She has promised me a beautiful black one for to-morrow.

23rd. April.

I am not at all sure of what has happened to-day. I do not want to make any sort of judgement on it. At the officers' chapter this morning the Shūryo Shiki, or graduation ceremony, was announced but the actual time of it was not given. I therefore asked Rev. Hajime what time it would take place but he said he didn't know; he would tell me when he did. I was still working on the accounts for the Treasury. Lunchtime came. After lunch I went to the Director's room to ask him some questions concerning foreign matters. I also asked what time the Shūryo Shiki was to take place.

"It took place this morning," he said.

"But Zenji Sama wanted me to attend it. He sent his eldest disciple last night to tell me so."

The Director looked amazed and then called Rev. Hajime. Rev. Hajime got angry. "She's got no right to do a Shūryo Shiki," he said, "no right at all! Why should she be allowed to do it and be a junior officer at the same time? No-one else has the right. Why should she?"

The Director said nothing but rang his bell for his new assistant. "Tell the chief disciplinarian," he said, "to set up the main hall for another Shūryo Shiki. Jiyu San has not yet been officially graduated and it seems there was some mistake this morning. She should have been included in the ceremony."

Half an hour later I entered the Ceremony Hall to officially receive the certificate of having completed Tokubetsu Sōdō. The certificate had a blotch on it. As I learned afterwards, the Records Department was furious at having had to write it out.

20th. May.

Charles, a very old friend of mine from America who also knew me in England, visited the temple to-day and is staying the night. He was very concerned when he discovered that I had not contacted him although he had been in Japan for some time. To tell the truth although I had known he was there I had made no attempt to contact him for one very good reason: he had gone to Kyoto immediately upon his arrival and, knowing the situation prevailing there, thanks to the British couple, I had not wished to contact him for fear I should cause him embarrassment or problems.

I explained this to him together with what had happened in England as a result of the man who had originally written for a teacher. He looked deeply concerned.

"But surely they would welcome *anyone* who is legally permitted to teach, who is a real teacher?" he said.

I gave a laugh—not a very nice one; I couldn't help it. "I'll show you exactly how anxious they are to have a real, live teacher," I said. "Read these," and I showed him the originals of the letters that had come from both my so-called British friends.

He read them and became very sad and silent for a long time. Then he said, "If you do leave here where will you go?"

"Probably to my temple," I said. "I have nowhere else to go."

"You can always come to America. There are thousands of us who'd love to have you over there." Then he stopped and looked at me thoughtfully. "But what would you come on?" he said. "Of course, you have no cash."

I smiled rather ruefully. "Do you realise that from one week's end to another I have barely enough cash to get me down to my own temple?" I said. "Do you realise that I wouldn't have the money to scrape together for the fare to get any further than that? That's what's so funny about this affair in England; I literally haven't the cash to get there. And these people are yelling and screaming that I'm about to go back and take over."

"How much is it going to cost to stay the night here?" he asked.

"Oh, it's only a thousand yen," I said.

"Come on, let me give you a lot more than that."

"I can't."

"Why not?"

"Because the legal charge for staying here is a thousand yen a night."

"Well, let me give *you* something."

"Whilst I work here as the guest master for the foreigners I work here as guest master for the foreigners. The charge is a thousand yen a night."

He sighed. "Well, it was nice seeing you again."

"Yes," I said, "you and I have been like ships that pass in the night for a good many years. We meet in a country, we wave to each other—'Hello, good to see you, good-bye'—and that's it."

He nodded. "You're the only person I've ever known like that."

"Oh, well, maybe it's just my way." I stretched.

Rev. Hajime knocked on the door. He had got some beer and wanted us to have a drink with him. We both did.

I got the room next-door to mine ready for Charles, complete with a mosquito net, and warned him to get inside it as quickly as possible since the mosquitos are wily and sit on the outside of the net waiting to push inside when you lift it up—to get in with you.

When I told him this he said, "Ah, they've got it all figured out, have they?" That was that.

21st. May.

This morning I took Charles to the main entrance and wished him well on the next stage of his journey; he is going back to America. I had a feeling that he was turning round to see if I was watching him but I wasn't; I just continued on my way back to my room. It was nice seeing Charles. I wonder where and when I shall see him again?

31st. May.

I have had so much work to do with the foreigners there's just been no time to write anything. I have stopped going to the Meditation Hall because the atmosphere has become so strange. I go to the foreigners' Meditation Hall instead for we still have the right to use Zenji Sama's big guest rooms in his old house. There I and the foreigners meditate together. It is bad to be cutting ourselves off like this but I cannot expose them to the hostility that I feel exists. It is obvious that the people gaining power here do not want foreigners. I wish Zenji Sama would let me take them away. *I* know that all is one but it does not seem possible that some here will ever find this out.[100] Zenji Sama is dying and the abbot-to-be is a member of a different line; but we are all one in the Buddha Nature and whatever people may do, whatever may happen, I will see as a manifestation of that.

1st. June.

One of the foreigners who has been here for a very long time got into a furious temper to-day. It was primarily my fault;

I know that. I went to his house to apologise but he refused to listen; indeed he refused to see me. I should not have told him of the hostility here with regard to foreigners. That was what caused it all. But I was so lonely; I wanted to tell *someone* about what was happening and why we were in the foreign Meditation Hall instead of being in the big one with everyone else as we should have been and, indeed, would have been had Zenji Sama still been in full control of the temple. His deafness has resulted in some amazing things here.

But the young man wouldn't listen and there was no way I could make him. He had gone off, like a knight on a white horse, after I had told him of the situation, to see the chief lecturer. And the chief lecturer had more or less told him it was not his business which, of course, was to be expected. I blame myself completely. If I had told him nothing this would never have happened.[117] I must remember, a priest has no friends in the worldly sense whatsoever, and no-one in whom he can confide other than his own Buddha Nature for, if he tries to confide in anyone or tries to make a friend of anyone, then he appears to be insufficient within himself and the person he confides in is eventually going to turn upon him.[100]

Another foreigner here, a young man who, it seems, has jumped his ship in Yokohama, has been causing problems with the lecturer. During the work periods he has not been completely dressed as the lecturer feels he should have been. Apparently he had his sleeves rolled up; I have told him he cannot do this. He says that he will do exactly as he wishes.

I have to go out this afternoon to a ceremony. I hope I shall be all right; I don't feel any too well.

4th. June.

I am back in the Tokyo temple after being away for three days. I don't remember going to the ceremony that I mentioned in my last entry; I don't terribly much remember anything. What I do remember is finding myself this morning in the house of a friend in the very rich district of Tokyo where most of the foreigners live. My friend told me that I had been there for the past three days. I do not remember why.

I 'phoned to a doctor friend of mine on one of the American bases or, rather, I didn't 'phone him, the friend who was with me the other day, George, did. George and the doctor, Fred, took me off to a Tokyo hotel and then brought me back here. George had a long talk with Rev. Hajime. He wanted to know what it was that was actually going on; he too had noticed the atrocious treatment of the foreigners. He did not tell me what Rev. Hajime said to him but he urged me to go to my own temple as soon as possible. I shall leave to-morrow.

12th. June.

Most of the foreigners who would have attended Sesshin at the Tokyo temple are coming here, including twelve from an American college that are spending their Summer term here in Japan.

19th. June.

I am extremely tired from all the work with the foreigners. Being completely alone here makes it very difficult. The young man who was staying in the temple, the one who had jumped ship, is coming down to-morrow to help me. That will at least be something.

We have started sending out newsletters to all the foreigners. He helped me with them just before I came away and it seems that we shall now have a newsletter each month. It will keep everyone together and benefit those who cannot get here.

30th. June.

I received a card from Rev. Hajime this morning. It was a strange card. He says that I wrote to him but I do not remember what about. He says that all has been arranged. He asked me to go to his temple on the fifth of next month since he is going to have a party for viewing the beautiful flowers in his garden. I wonder what he's talking about?

1st. July.

A letter came from Rev. Hajime—indeed a very strange letter. He writes that he thought that Zenji Sama was willing to allow me to do all things there but he does not allow me to do so. Because of the reaction not only there but throughout our entire school of Zen he says that Zenji Sama does not want foreigners at the risk of bad reactions in our school of Zen.[118] He reports that he has never seen Zenji Sama in such a hot temper before and that, if I cancel all my "requirements," there is no problem. He ends by saying he does not like to write this letter but he must; he is very sad to have to tell me such things.

Zenji Sama would never say such a thing about the foreigners. I do not *believe* that that is what he said. I *know* he said none of it. Sitting still and listening within my heart I know this letter is a lie.[119]

I do not want to go to the party at Rev. Hajime's house.

Another Sesshin begins here to-day. Another college professor from America, who has a class presently studying in Japan, is bringing something like thirty people here. Three friends of mine from the American bases are coming to help. That, at least, will be something. The priest from the neighbouring temple who has always been kind is also coming to help. There is so much work. I could so do with a permanent assistant.

8th. August.

Another card from Rev. Hajime to say that he has not yet seen the Vice-Abbot but is still asking him if he will be my sponsor when Zenji Sama is dead. I have not answered the card.

13th. August.

OBon began to-day. I am exhausted from going round to open all the houses. My leg is causing me problems again and now, to add to it, every now and then I get a strange dizziness that hit me those three days when I was in Tokyo.[120] Whatever it is that is wrong, it's not imagined; this thing's real. My body has put on sixty pounds.[121] You can't do that sort of thing through imagination!

15th. August.

The young man who had jumped ship is leaving us to-day. I was somewhat surprised to learn that Rev. Hajime had told him to go through the books I had left in the Tokyo temple and find the ones I wanted brought down here. He had read through most of the private papers that I had left in one of those books and was surprised at some of the teachings of Zen. These teachings are only given to people who are ready to have them. It was obvious that they had disturbed and worried him.[122] I told him that he should not have read them but it did not help. He left to-day in a very peculiar state of mind.

17th. August.

I went to help at Rev. Hajime's temple to-day for the OBon festival. I knew that if I refused there would be trouble and it was just not worth it. When the ceremonies were over Rev. Hajime said to me, "That young man who missed his ship says that your brain is unhealthy."[122]

"Really?" I said.

"Yes. He read some papers of yours; he was very concerned about them."

"The papers that he read are the private ones given at Transmission. He read them because you permitted him to do so when you told him to look through my books."

"I don't think that's what he was talking about."

"That is what he told me. If he says my brain is unhealthy then the deep teachings of Zen are unhealthy."

Rev. Hajime considered me for some time then broke into a grin. "Anyway, what does it matter? We are together; I intend to get drunk to-night."

"Go ahead," I said, went to the room in which I was to stay and shut the door.

19th. August.

A couple of people came from Kyoto to-day saying that they have been recommended to me as the only person who is at present running a temple for foreigners in this country.[123] I couldn't help feeling that they were rather peculiar but they had good references—I checked them—and so I didn't argue.

They had been in the temple some hours when I felt the necessity to ring the gongs—I didn't know why but something in me said, "Ring the gongs every hour on the hour." Ringing the gongs is something that is frequently done when somebody who is unfit to be in a temple is in it. It is done by priests to make certain that they keep their minds in meditation no matter what distractions are around them. I saw it used much when I was in Malaysia. There was one temple where the priest was doing it constantly—every hour on the hour—because of the large numbers of people who wandered through the temple imagining that if they rubbed their rosaries sufficiently something magical would happen with the Buddhas and Patriarchs. Now here was I with something warning me that I needed to do it; so I did it. It certainly helps to keep one's mind fully in the meditative situation.

28th. August.

Segaki was held at my temple. Hundreds of people came, both foreign and Japanese. It's amazing how these ceremonies have picked up since I have been living here full-time—truly amazing. The fees for the ceremonies have gone up too. I didn't ask for them to be put up; the parishioners did it of their own free will. From something like ten yen a funeral they have gone up to two or three thousand.

The couple who have been staying here for the past ten days went back to Kyoto to collect their things. In spite of the peculiar atmosphere that they give off, they have behaved quite well and have certainly seemed to try to follow the curriculum of the temple.

29th. August.

The couple came back to-day. As soon as they entered the temple the same thing came over me—the necessity for ringing the gong. So I'm ringing it.

My difficulty with physical sitting is excessive. I tried using a chair for meditation.

2nd. September.

I had a letter from Rev. Hajime to-day saying that the Vice-Abbot is willing to take up my visa guarantee. It also said that the Director is expecting me back in the temple. I suspect that the lecturer is missing otherwise that comment wouldn't have been written. The letter ended by asking if I was all right. Yes, he hasn't heard from me since the 17th. of August and he's not likely to.

6th. September.

A card came from Rev. Hajime. It said that the lecturer and several other officers are completely against my having any assistance if I come back to the temple. They are also saying that I may not bath in any of the temple baths because I am a foreigner and a woman. They are not willing for me to do any ceremonies either. The Director is powerless against them; Zenji Sama is sinking fast. I can talk to no living thing about this for the response I would get would be the same as that of the young man whom I upset in Tokyo. As I said earlier, a priest has absolutely no friends. He must be completely sufficient within himself. The only things in which I can confide are the pages of this diary and that which is within my heart. I record— just that and nothing more.

I have been ringing the gongs every hour. To-day I knew the reason why. I accidentally overheard something from one of the couple staying here which I had not meant to hear but could not help hearing. It was to the effect that the general opinion in Kyoto, thanks to the couple who came from England, is that people only come to my temple when nobody else will accept them because they are no good. So that is why I've got this pair. I suspect that for some reason they have been thrown out of several temples. I must be careful that they do no harm to any of my people from Tokyo. It's the old problem—Rinzai against our school. I'm getting so bored with religious politics.

8th. September.

A very short note from Rev. Hajime to say that he is enclosing one from the Director and that the Vice-Abbot is waiting to see me when I return to Tokyo. The Director's letter was interesting considering what Rev. Hajime wrote on his last card. He said that, if I continue for a long time to be in the Zendō and the Hondō every morning in the Tokyo temple, all the things that were denied to me at our last meeting will eventually be given. He ended by saying that he respects me and is expecting me there. He does not agree to send any of my things that are left in the temple to me at this time.

I am not going to listen to either him or Rev. Hajime; they swing from one side to the other like monkeys in a tree. I will only listen to my own heart and to Zenji Sama who speaks to it directly. The Director knows well the physical difficulty I am having with sitting at the moment; it is physically impossible for me to be in the Hondō and Zendō with my leg as it is. I have been forced to sit on a chair at the Sesshins here and I am finding more and more how wonderful it is to be in meditation at all times. One can have one's mind in that state at every minute of the day, not specifically just when one is sitting down in a specific place.[124] This I now know well. I found it out long ago when I had so much work looking after the foreigners. Under no circumstances am I returning to Tokyo at the moment.

Apart from my difficulty with physical sitting, there is also the fact that, if I move quickly, I become very dizzy; especially so if I try to walk fast. My body is huge—it has now put on almost seventy pounds. I don't know what's wrong with me but I know that something is. The doctors say there isn't anything. It would be physically impossible for me to rush round the Tokyo temple as I am. I have got to be clear-headed when I walk; when I go down a staircase I mustn't fall down because of dizziness. If I were to try to go quickly when the bells ring I would collapse.

I telephoned the temple and told them this. I don't think they believed me.

The couple from Kyoto have finally shown their colours. It seems that they have been thrown out, as I suspected earlier, of every temple that admits foreigners; my temple, according to Kyoto, will take anyone. What happened this morning with the couple made it imperative that *I* throw them out. I found them copulating in front of the main altar. They said that Zen gives you the right to be completely free, to do whatsoever you wish; so they were copulating in front of the main altar. I did not know that such disgust could arise in me. I told them to get out at once but they made no move to do so. I threatened to call the local police and, after some considerable delay, they packed their bags and went. I cleaned the temple completely from one end to the other and did a purification ceremony. Now a great peace is with me for there is no-one here—just me, the statue of Kanzeon and, of course, as always, Zenji Sama.

I do wish I could move more quickly. It is so inconvenient not to be able to hurry round and get on with things. When cleaning the temple I had to sit down eight or nine times because of the dizziness.

20th. September.

Another letter from Rev. Hajime. He tells me that he is coming down on the 23rd. of this month and wants to visit me on the 26th. It is interesting that he wishes to visit me here; he has done that so very seldom.

The Vice-Abbot, it seems, has become very careful about foreigners. According to Rev. Hajime this is because of some "disgusting things" that he has heard concerning them. He says he wants to talk to me about this when he comes here. He also says that, after hearing comments of certain of the officers there with regard to foreigners, he thinks I had better not return there. If I do so I will find far more difficulties and feel much more unhappy than I was before. Instead of returning there he feels I should be able to work more effectively in my own temple or some other place. I may use the name of the betsuin of the Tokyo temple if I wish.

I must consult my heart and know if this is Zenji Sama's wish or Rev. Hajime's.[125]

21st. September.

Many of the foreigners who have come here tell me that it is very important that we rebuild this temple so as to make it big enough for everyone. It is a good idea. They say they will collect the money.

26th. September.

Rev. Hajime came to my temple to-day. What he had to tell me was disturbing. It seems that the couple I was forced to throw out had spent some time in a temple belonging to one of the disciples of the Vice-Abbot and had done identically the same thing there that they did here. Apparently they have been copulating in front of the altar of every temple they stayed in. This has caused considerable disgust at foreigners throughout the country. This was all I needed to "help" the Foreign Section at the moment!

28th. September.

Short note from Rev. Hajime telling me that a friend of his will supply the wood for the rebuilding of my temple at a very moderate price.

30th. September.

I went to the 'phone booth in the wine store to-day to answer a peremptory call to return from the temple in Tokyo. I had to hurry in order to get there and almost collapsed on the floor of the wine shop after arriving. I *must* remember—I cannot move quickly any longer.

I don't know about going back to the Tokyo temple. I need to know Zenji Sama's wishes.

6th. October.

Another letter came from Rev. Hajime. It tells me he has been hesitating to write this letter. On the 4th. he reports that he

saw Zenji Sama and read to him the letter that I had sent him.
The Director and the treasurer were present. He says that he has
not the courage to tell me what Zenji Sama said. He asks what
I have done with him; he cannot understand it. He says he will
tell me the details when he sees me next. He ends by stating that
there is now no hope for me to return there unless I become
extremely miserable. About my finances, he will arrange for me
to receive them in my temple. He hopes I am always well.

I half believe it and half not. I feel sure there is nothing
wrong between Zenji Sama and I, never has been and never will
be. I *must* believe this.

8th. October.

Another 'phone call ordering me to return to Tokyo at once.
I said that I was too ill.

9th. October.

Another letter from Rev. Hajime. The letter said that the
Director wants to talk to several of the officers before I come
back to Tokyo. Between these peremptory calls to return and
the letters telling me not to the only thing I can do is sit still.
This is indeed the Bo tree. When all the powers of Mara attack
you from all directions there is but one thing to do—sit absolutely still; and *ground* oneself.

10th. October.

Another letter from Rev. Hajime. He said that a statue left
behind here is a present to me. He also said that the young man
who left it now denies that he said I had an unhealthy mind.
When Rev. Hajime came here I asked for details about this and
he said that this particular young man, together with the one that
I upset during the Summer, had had a discussion on the subject.
Now I have it on paper that it never happened! I no longer care
whether it did or didn't. I no longer care *who* is telling lies!

Rev. Hajime says that he is going to make sure that I get
sufficient cash to be able to continue here. He also says that the
Director does not want Zenji Sama's cat.

Rev. Hajime went on to say that I should get some sort of work, any sort I feel like, so as to be able to support myself. He also wants to know if I still want the robes that I ordered. Why shouldn't I? I am a priest and I always will be.

This evening I dreamt, or imagined, I do not know which, that a 'phone call came. This time it was a woman's voice and I recognised it as that of the old washerwoman who has brought me flowers from Zenji Sama. The only thing she said was, "Zenji Sama has a lily for you." I will return to Tokyo to-morrow.

11th. October.

I don't know how I did it but I returned to Tokyo this morning. I went to see a doctor because I was in such great pain. It wasn't merely difficulty with physical sitting any longer; it was genuine, terrible pain. But he said he could find nothing wrong. I had arranged to have lunch at the British Consulate and then go on to stay with friends in the evening. I was very much afraid of going back to the temple in Tokyo; however, after lunch, something said that I must. I started to the station but the pain was so great I decided against it. I telephoned the temple and got straight through to Zenji Sama's house. I explained to Zenji Sama that I was on my way but was stopping off at a doctor's surgery to try and find out what was wrong. Zenji Sama was incredibly kind.

I got to a friend's house and found that it was impossible to keep any food within me. Having vomited severely I felt a lot better. I then wrote this. I will try and go back to Tokyo after all. I feel as if Zenji Sama is trying to reach out to me urgently.

28th. October.

I was taken to hospital from my friend's house at two in the morning of the 12th. Now I am waiting to be operated on. It seems that I have a large growth, which may or may not be malignant, and which must be removed as soon as possible. This is what has been causing the trouble with my leg.[126]

Rev. Hajime was standing at the foot of the bed. The temple had been telephoned to say that I had been taken to hospital.

This afternoon, whilst they were trying to X-ray me, I collapsed. They were trying to induce me to stand up; finally they had to lay me flat for the X-rays. They tell me there are many complications not least of which is the fact that my bowels have been inoperative for several days. They hope to be able to operate on the 31st.

31st. October.

Rev. Hajime and Rev. Tarō came to see me to-day. They are to stay here during the operation. This is by order of both Zenji Sama and the Director. With them is the elderly lady who has been a good friend to me and at whose house I have sometimes stayed. She is Japanese and she will be staying throughout the night. The hospital authorities are not pleased about this for I am not in a Japanese hospital, where such things are encouraged, but a foreign one. The operation takes place to-night.

Rev. Hajime brought me an omiage—a folded paper with words written upon it and ten thousand yen inside it. It came from Zenji Sama saying, according to Rev. Hajime, "Get well soon. This is to help you pay the bill." Rev. Hajime tells me that Zenji Sama wants to know the instant I am out of danger.

4th. November.

I had not thought it possible that one could feel so ill. Early in the morning of the 1st., when the effects of the anaesthetic had more or less worn off, the events of the night—an unbelievable night—gradually become clear. The operation took place at seven o'clock in the evening. Around two-thirty in the morning I can remember waking up; the Western doctor at the foot of my bed telling me that it was all out; Rev. Hajime and Rev. Tarō had gone home, the lady from Tokyo was standing by my bed. There was a sound in my ears of a rushing wind, a great beating of wings.

They kept it from me until to-day—Zenji Sama died as I came out of the anaesthetic just after he heard that I was out of danger.

Rev. Hajime, Rev. Tarō and the Director all sat at the foot of my bed this afternoon. Rev. Hajime was peculiarly silent.

Then he said, "It was as if he was determined not to die before he knew that you were going to live." I said nothing. "You should realise that he gave his life that you might have yours." Again I said nothing. The Director came up to me and put his hand on mine. "Get well soon," he said. "The foreigners are waiting for you." Rev. Tarō smiled and waved.

Later. I left hospital to-day. I tried and tried to go yesterday because that was the day on which they held Zenji Sama's funeral but the doctors wouldn't let me. It is rumoured that, since I am not a Christian, I cannot have free hospital treatment.[127] I really should have gone to a Buddhist hospital. I am extremely weak but I cannot afford to stay here any longer at fifty-thousand yen a day. As it is, I do not see how I will ever be able to pay this bill.[127]

One of the kindest people I know of is the British Consul who has agreed to take me into his house, the consular residence, until I am strong enough to go about again by myself. Both he and his wife are among the most compassionate people I have ever met.

When I got to the hospital door there were no taxis available and no-one seemed particularly willing to try and find one for me. One of the doctors happened by who knows me from the Consulate and lent me one of the British Embassy cars. And so, instead of having to try and catch a taxi on a busy road, I went to the British Consulate in an embassy car.

18th. November.

I have been in the Consulate ever since I left the hospital. In addition to the hospitality of the Consul and his wife I was invited to attend several social gatherings held at houses of the British community here. I also conducted a ceremony at the Cenotaph on the eleventh for all the British war-dead who happened to be Buddhists.

I was shocked on arrival at the Tokyo temple this morning to find it almost completely empty. There are but sixty trainees left out of the original two-hundred and thirty; and thirty of the sixty are officers. I had barely arrived in the temple when I heard the bells and gongs ringing for a ceremony. Although I am having to use a stick in order to walk I made my way to the Ceremony Hall. They were holding a memorial ceremony for Zenji Sama. It was the first time I have been able to offer incense to his memory.

I got back to my room but the new Abbot (the former Vice-Abbot), the now Zenji Sama I supposed, suggested that I went to his old temple in the mountains. It is very quiet, very peaceful; it also has sulphur spring baths which he felt would help me get better quickly.

1st. December.

It was very cold up in the mountains but it was worth going. Rev. Hajime sent me a card on the 24th. to say that the new Zenji Sama wants me to stay in the temple and look after the foreigners. He said that he was very busy and that I should stay in the temple in the mountains for a little longer but it was obvious that I could not. I returned to-day. The new Chief Abbot, the new Zenji Sama, had his Shinzan, or ceremony of officially entering the temple, to-day. It was magnificent—utterly magnificent. I do not think I have seen anything as magnificent as this before but I could not enjoy it for my heart was with *my* Zenji Sama—I know that's bad Zen but a large part of me wants to die and be with him.

3rd. December.

A letter came for the new Chief Abbot from the man who started all the trouble in England. I was asked to answer it. The letter said that from Hawaii he had learned of the death of the Chief Abbot on the first of November and he is sorry to hear this. He offers his condolences to the new Chief Abbot and all those who were close to the late Chief Abbot. He writes that he was told that Zenji Sama was ill for some time and also blind so it must have been what they term in the West, 'a happy release from suffering.' He says that he is advised that the new Zenji Sama has taken over as the Chief Abbot and wishes him a long and happy term of office. He reports that he has the card which the new Chief Abbot gave him, which is framed and hangs on the wall and there is also the small green kesa to remind the writer of him. He concludes that it seems a long time since the new Chief Abbot was in London and that he would find changes in London Buddhism now: it is growing well, he assures him, and promises to become a very live movement in the future.

Can't this man let Zenji Sama's bones grow cold before he tries to find someone else to use, to suck up to?[100, 128] How long is he to continue in his evil path?[129]

15th. December.

Thanks to the chief lecturer no more foreigners are to come to this temple. According to the new Chief Abbot he is not willing to risk having any more foreigners here if it is going to upset people to the extent it's upsetting the chief lecturer. The chief lecturer himself is going round saying that foreigners are only animals—that's all they ever have been and all they ever will be; he has arranged matters in such a way that all foreigners are being excluded from the temple. There is no longer a single disciple of *my* Zenji Sama left living here.

I was about to go and finish my packing when the Director's door opened very softly and in came Zenji Sama's old disciple; the one who has come to me on several occasions before. He held a package in his hand. "These are for you, Jiyu San," he said. "They are the kesa Zenji Sama wore at your Transmission and the kimono he wore under his own ordination robe as well as another. They are yours." He bowed and disappeared.

This evening I stayed with a friend of mine whose dog was dying and who wanted me to make the decision to have it put to sleep for her. Since the dog had already shredded its tongue from the agony of a tumour I arranged for the vet to come to the house and performed the necessary ceremony over the dying animal. My friend was in a very bad emotional state and I stayed with her for the rest of the night. I telephoned the temple to say where I was.

16th. December.

To-day I went to lunch with a British friend and paid as much as I could of my hospital bill. The Chinese abbot has sent me a thousand Malaysian dollars towards it but, since I had been in the hospital for almost a month, this did not begin to cover the cost. My friend was not at all nice.

"If you couldn't pay you should have gone to a Japanese hospital. It was your idea to join the Buddhists not ours. Why should we keep you free in the luxury of *our* hospital?"

He pronounced the first half of the word 'Buddhists' as one would pronounce 'bud.' I had told him that the new officials of the Tokyo temple were refusing me any financial assistance towards the bill since they thought it extortionate; they wouldn't even lend me the money; the remainder of the bill was something like a million yen.

"Why should we help you?" he repeated.

"I hear that, if I had been a Christian, there would have been no bill. The wife of a C. of E. parson here was given free hospitalisation and free air passage home when she was ill recently.[127] Are Buddhists so different?"

My host's wife was obviously very embarrassed but he took no notice.

"Why should we do that for you? Have you ever helped Britons as the Christians here do? I see no signs of the Buddhists doing anything." He was walking about, pacing with annoyance.

"The Tokyo temple has had many Britons under its roof."

"Did they get free food?"

"Frequently."

"Huh!"

I said nothing. To continue such a conversation would have been pointless. We ate lunch in an embarrassed silence. I excused myself as soon as possible. The wife was very distressed.

This evening a parson friend of mine from the local Christian Church brought his car and we took everything to my temple. The Treasury has given me my office furniture. The neighbours had a meal ready for us when we arrived.

Here ends the Story of the Parish Priest.

Book IV.
The Eternal Bo Tree.

The author sitting in front of the Kanzeon statue on the main altar in the Ceremony Hall at Unpukuji, her temple in Mie Prefecture.

Book IV.
The Eternal Bo Tree.

17th. December.[130]

I have been sitting alone in meditation for most of the day. As I watched the statue of Kanzeon I could have sworn that I saw her hands move and I heard again, loud and clear, the beating of the wings; they have been beating and beating every day since I have come out of hospital. I saw the hands move, I heard the beating of the wings, and something inside me turned and said, 'yes.' A full acceptance and a full obedience. The meaning of 'gyate, gyate' which is eternal meditation. One call, one answer and the two are one.

Dark shadows flit across the corners of my eyes. They have done this for some weeks now; ever since the operation. It is as if death is stalking me, greedy for its lost prey, flashing past. I am still very weak and must spend much time resting. I feel the wings trying to lift me: I am a baby eagle, trying to rise from its nest on a high mountain, knowing that it is only a matter of a few weeks before it must fly away for ever. And yet this is not a leaving of this world but an entering into it; a leaving of the nest. I am still unable to stand fully upright and it is with great difficulty that I descend staircases although I have no difficulty whatsoever in climbing them. The wings practice their flight during my sleep, pleasantly anticipating the freedom of the open sky in the full strength of adulthood, fanning themselves softly, pulsing with thrilling life. I am utterly alone in this temple with no means of communication with the outside world except the telephone in the wine shop. I am content. It is glorious to be alone as I am now. Great surges of strength rush

359

through me and the wings beat faster. I can never cease to give thanks for the indestructibility which I know to be mine.

18th. December.

Letter from a friend in Kyoto asking if there is anything she can do to help me. She has heard of my operation. I have asked her if she can come here for a short time. The letter has been coming since the twenty-third of November. I wonder why it took so long?

25th. December.

Have been basking in the joy of being here ever since my arrival. The wings fan themselves wherever I go; a great surge of joy rushes through me and I soar into the sky. Zenji Sama is for ever here, closer than he ever was in life. I bought myself a few delicacies for my Christmas dinner and a tiny bottle of champagne. Zenji Sama, Kanzeon and I spent Christmas to-gether—and it was FUN. I have a tiny television set and spent a happy hour watching it. No grand party or dinner at the British Consulate this year; not even the invitation.

26th. December.

I dreamt of great, soaring mountains and a high eagle's nest perched in a cranny; a blue sky that stretched to eternity. Al-though I am alone, as the world understands the term, I am so full, so utterly complete. Night comes; the glory of the universe is mine. That I can get up so seldom does not matter. I seem to have had a slight relapse since coming here.

31st. December.

All day the drums of the Shinto shrine on top of the hill behind my temple have sounded the knell of the old year. It is now almost midnight and the villagers are flocking to the shrine.

1st. January.

Midnight has struck and the new fire has been kindled on the hill. The gate to my temple stands wide open and wine is upon the altar for all who wish to toast the New Year. I drink to a new life on my forty-fourth birthday which is to-day. I sounded the temple bell here one hundred and eight times, one for each sin that a Buddhist can commit. It is the first time since the war that a bell has sounded across the paddy fields and mountains from this temple. The last bell was taken to make into war munitions. Harry arrived whilst I was ringing the new one. This new bell, although small, rang out loud and clear. I am very tired; the wings fan softly; I will go to bed.

Later. Some villagers came to congratulate me both on the new bell and for the New Year. I am very tired and very happy. I will stay here until the wings carry me to where I must go. A leaf goes wherever the wind blows it—it does not disobey the wind.

A card came from Rev. Hajime wishing me a happy birthday and a happy New Year. He asked how I was and hoped that I was enjoying myself. He also said something I never thought I'd hear him say—he said that he now realised that my temple is very useful for me. I wonder why he never realised it before?

A letter also came from one of the English-speaking newspapers offering me the opportunity of writing for them once a week for the next month and then once a fortnight thereafter as their religious correspondent. They are going to pay me six thousand yen an article. It will certainly help my finances, especially if anything goes wrong with my being paid by the temple in Tokyo.

Harry, who has been the newsletter editor, is now going to write the newsletter from here. He will be staying with me until July. He had heard how ill I had been in Tokyo and has come down to look after me. It is indeed very kind of him to do so. He insists that I lie still. For the first time we thought of turning the newsletter into something more than just a chatty communication. I've not mentioned it before in this diary because I didn't consider it important; up to now it has just been a letter that was sent out to people who have been in the Foreign Section for some years, wanted to know how each other were doing and get some information on the group in general. Now, however, we are going to send with it at least one Buddhist article a month—a sort of lecture—as well as give news of everyone.

We have sent out lectures in the past but it's the first time that the newsletter will incorporate them as part of itself. It will certainly keep the foreigners together much more. At the moment, with everyone so scattered, it's the only way I can think of doing what Zenji Sama wanted.

2nd. January.

"Whyever did it take so long for the doctors to find out what was really wrong with you?"

Harry asked me this as we were having coffee this morning. I was a little worried as to how to answer, since I didn't really want to alarm him, but he was obviously unwilling to be put off.

"Tell me about it," he said. "Why was it?"

"I really don't know," I replied, "except that—well, here in Japan things are all—fixed. For example, the doctors took innumerable X-rays but each time, and always for the same reasons, believed nothing was wrong. I am a foreigner and so rather bigger than most Japanese. The shadow of the growth on the X-rays was so big that the doctors always believed there was a flaw in the film. No Japanese would have a growth that big so it wasn't possible for me to have one."

He stared at me appalled. "But how could they *all* think that it was a dud film?" he asked. "How could *all* the films be dud?"

"I know it doesn't make very much sense but that's exactly what happened, exactly the problem—the doctors didn't believe in a growth that big and so they didn't think anything was wrong."

He was silent for a long time. "I'm not satisfied with that for an answer," he said.

"Whether you are satisfied or not is up to you. It's the only answer I can give you for it is the only answer I know; it is the reason they gave me—that and the fact that the growth was hidden under my intestines which made X-raying difficult."

"How do the doctors feel about it now? Aren't they rather ashamed of themselves?"

"Harry, can't we change the subject?"

"No. Look at you; you're not well yet; you should still be under a doctor's care."

"I can't afford it, Harry. Not at the prices they charge here; it's impossible—I can't *afford* it. Forget about it. I shall be all right."

"But there should be some sort of after-care—I mean—how do you *know* you're going to be all right?"

"I'll be all right. Stop worrying."

"I don't know what to do." He got up, paced round my little living room, walked into the Hondō, stared out of the main door and came back into the living room again. "Listen," he said, "you've got to see more doctors; you've got to make sure that this thing is completely finished."

"Harry, it costs three thousand yen just to sit in the doctor's room; just for use of the *room*, let alone seeing the doctor. Then there's three thousand yen for the use of the instruments and three thousand yen for the fact that the receptionist looks after you—I can't *afford* that sort of money. I haven't got it—if I die then I must die—there's the long and short of it—now forget about the thing, will you? If you don't, I'll have to ask you to leave me."

He sighed. "Then at least let me try and get the British authorities to help."

"No, Harry, don't. If you do they'll only tell you what I've more or less been told by friends whenever they've mentioned cash to the British authorities. None of the latter will ever help you financially in a foreign country. You've got to get that firmly through your head. The only way they'll do it is if they deport you and then you pay them back after you get home. Now stop it, will you? Why don't we get down to some work on the newsletter? After all, if we are going to send out a big one we should get on with it."

"All right," he said, "if that is what you really want to do. What shall we write about?" We were silent for a long time; then he said, "Why not write about our new bell and the new life we are going to live here? I want to include a lot of news. I think we should be much more careful about who we let in."

"What do you mean, 'careful about who we let in?'"

"Well, in that Tokyo temple you had to take everybody that came but here you can choose who you'll have. It often occurred to me, watching that bunch, that some of them should see a psychiatrist not a priest. I think we should make it a requirement that anyone who comes *specifically* from a foreign country to Japan to study Zen should be checked out to see if he's a bit queer in the head."

"That's a funny comment to make."

"Look, out of all the people who have come to Japan *specially* to study Zen, I've met exactly three (of which you are one) that were not a bit odd. All the rest had come in order to flee from something. It's the reason why they've made such a mess of things with the Japanese."

"Some of the people who come over do create trouble for the Japanese; but not all of them by a very long way. My personal estimate would only be about two to three percent, but that is quite enough to show—and be remembered. I don't like breaking the Precepts by speaking against my fellow foreigners even if some of them—well—aren't exactly out of the top drawer and are running away from life."

"Whether you like it or not I'm going to talk about this in the newsletter. People should be checked out with great care. We should make sure that they are of good character before they come here. You're living here alone, you know. You're in bed, an invalid, for much of the day. Such people could place you in considerable difficulties."

"They've done that for a long time—a very long time."[131]

"I'm also going to put in something about the sort of things we need. You know, we need a much bigger bell than that one out there."

"But I'm happy with that bell."

"Yeah, but we'll need a bigger one. And we need to mend the Meditation Hall—we need to do such a lot of work."

"All right, Harry. You go ahead, you write the newsletter, you write all your news."

"Will you write the article?"

"If you want me to. I'll write about our new bell. I'll call it "The Song of the Bell." After all, it is a New Year."

"You don't really want to talk about nasty things at all, do you?" he said. "You don't want to talk about this business of what happened in the hospital, you don't want to talk about any of it."

"Harry, forget it. It's all in the past. None of it matters—don't you realise that? Absolutely *none of it* matters."

"But, I mean, supposing they did all this—deliberately, to harm you?"

"So,—they didn't harm me. What are you worrying about?"

"Supposing they had?"

"Oh, Harry, shut up. They haven't. What people do, whether they do it for good reasons or bad reasons—there's no point in discussing it. Good or bad reasons are of no importance to anybody. One's own training is all that matters and this shows in our reactions to the behaviour of others. Do that which has to be done and stop bothering about others' motives."

"I wish you'd explain that to me more fully."

"I will, but I can see the mayor and some other people coming and I've got to do a memorial service for them. Now be a good chap and help me with the ceremony."

He sighed. "I shall come back to this."

"All right," I said, "but enough for to-day."

3rd. January.

I was sitting by the window watching the Winter sunshine, feeling the gentle fanning of the strength that is fast returning to me, when Harry went back to the conversation of yesterday; this time from a totally different tack. He wanted to know why the other trainees in the Tokyo temple seemed to be so utterly cold-blooded with regard to my illness.

"You know, Harry," I said, "there are a lot of mistakes in Zen training, not least of which is the idea of many people that a Zen master, Zen priest, must be beyond human feelings. True Zen teaches that a priest has human feelings, always has had them, always will have them and always must have them.

People seek for wisdom first, instead of compassion and, as a result, Zen is frequently learned, both in this country and in the West, as something which is cold, starry, distant; completely lacking in compassion and love; something to be experienced alone rather than lived with other people. When I was entering the Meditation Hall as a new trainee, and all the newspaper reporters and the like were causing problems,[131] the priest who was standing with me, the one who was to lead me round the Meditation Hall, was standing there almost as though he'd dug a hole, jumped inside it and pulled the earth over the top of himself. It was unfortunate—a grave misunderstanding of Zen, but it does so often happen. Time and time again I get letters from people who say they're studying Zen; they talk of having no concern for anything other than their meditation, their Sesshins and how many kōans they have solved. But other people *are part of* their kōan, their all-important training. They forget about the heart of Kanzeon completely; and that's what training is all about. They come to Zen to seek wisdom, to gain power, instead of training themselves to be worthy of wisdom when they have become compassionate. Zenji Sama worried about such people. The most important teaching of Buddhism is the expression of compassion and love for within them lies true wisdom. Zen training is the search for wisdom within compassion and love; without these two, compassion and love, Buddhism falls to pieces. A Zen master is not someone who is icy cold, isolated in order to find his own perfection so that he may sink into it; he trains himself so that he may be able to show wisdom through the expression of compassion and love.

"You know, I'm putting this very badly but the best way I can describe it is by that old story of the Zen priest who'd been meditating for twenty years, thanks to the patronage of an old woman. At the end of the twenty years the old woman paid a prostitute to visit the priest, embrace him and then ask, "What now?" According to the story, when the prostitute had done this, the old priest said, "An old pine tree grows on a barren rock; nowhere is there any warmth." The old woman was so furious when the prostitute reported this to her that she burned the old priest's house down. When asked why, the old woman said, "He didn't have to evince passion but he should have understood compassion enough to know how to teach and help the prostitute in her situation." He should have known, in other words, compassion and love whilst, at the same time, not giving in to the desire of the prostitute. But he had no compassion, he had no love and, in consequence, he had no *real* wisdom because wisdom is expressed in compassion and love. I suppose what I'm trying to explain to you is this. The sort of thing that goes on in those big temples where they train Buddhist priests—the sort of thing that went on in that temple in Tokyo—is something that is tailored, if you like, for young men who are going to become members of an organised, hereditary priesthood. They learn to live within the system in much the same way as one learns to live in a boarding school. When things got difficult one either deliberately managed not to be present or else learned how to become 'invisible' by digging a non-existent hole. Many of the Buddhist priests 'dig holes' all the time in those big temples; so do Christian priests and so do thousands of people I know, especially Westerners who come to study Zen. In fact, they think that that sort of detachment is the be-all and end-all of Zen training—completely detached from the world. But Zen training is *not* to be detached in that way from the world; it is to be *concerned* in the world but not *involved* in it so that it overwhelms you. You *have* to be concerned in the world but you must *not* be overwhelmed by it otherwise you can't act. So many of these people are afraid. They think that if they do not spend all their time in formal meditation then they will never be able to be completely detached from worldly affairs. However, if they were in *true* meditation, which *requires* no formality although it may use it, there would be no problem because worldly affairs couldn't affect them anyway. That was the wonderful thing I found out. You can be concerned about the world but not affected by it. You can act but be completely unharmed. That was the terrific lesson I learned, thanks to what went on in the Tokyo temple. It didn't matter how badly they seemed to treat me or how unconcerned they were—I found the peace I went looking for and I discovered how to keep it *and* act completely within their system—for that matter within any system. That temple is just a small world where everything is magnified a thousand times compared to similar situations in the world outside. That the priest I was with at my admission did not wish to be involved was not my problem; it was his."

"What could he have done?" asked Harry.

"I don't know; I am not him."

"You give me such strange answers," he said.

"Harry, listen. I don't want to sound swollen-headed but I have great difficulty in thinking any longer as the world thinks because the world understands involvement from the point of view of what I used to call 'soap-opera.' I understand concern and involvement from a totally different angle. You remember I told you a long time ago about all the mess that went on in England as a result of the couple that came over and the person who wrote letters asking for a Buddhist priest and then said he didn't want one if it was going to be me? Well, in the beginning that sort of thing mattered and it hurt; and then it didn't matter at all and I could continue to work perfectly without any problem whatsoever. Those who want to believe and those who don't, don't matter. What does matter is that *I* do my own training and am still willing to try and help anyone who wants help. An awful lot of people in temples don't understand what the principle of training is; to be concerned but not overwhelmed. And the more one meditates, the deeper one goes into meditation, the less is the danger of being overwhelmed. But this stage cannot be reached by never coming out of the temple; one needs more than formal meditation for this. Every act must be a meditation too; one must not appear as a plaster saint. You'll see what I mean as I get better at trying to explain what I'm talking about."

He shook his head. "In a way I know what you're trying to say but I have great difficulty in understanding how such people can behave like this—people who are supposed to be priests."

"Harry, stop trying to think of them as saints; they're not. They're people who are doing the best they can as they are— you're suffering from the idea that there are thousands of saints in the Buddhist Church when there aren't. Young men who are in this priesthood are there because their fathers were there before them—at any rate, most of them are. In the old days in Buddhism people went into the priesthood because they felt the 'call,' if you like. Nowadays the majority of Japanese go in because it's a hereditary priesthood and, if they don't become priests, their families will lose the temples. This means that we've got a totally different type of person from what we had hundreds of years ago. The type that went in because they wanted to really do something about themselves are very, very few in number now. I met about three or four in the temple in Tokyo amongst the actual junior trainees. Look, I've got to get on with doing a lot of things. Why don't we go back to this conversation later?"

"All right," he said. "I want to go into the village anyway."

4th. January.

When I was working for the Christian Church I found politics everywhere (religious politics) and a large number of people who were trying to live moral lives, as they understood the term 'moral.' Here in the Buddhist Church I have found politics everywhere (religious politics) and a large number of people who are trying to live moral lives. But I have found something else too—I have found at least five saints that I know of—at least five people whom I would call saints—and twelve more who are on the way. When you think about it that's not at all bad.

I know I was talking to Harry yesterday about people who go into the priesthood because their fathers did but, in all the years I worked for the Christian Church, I never found anyone who had got as far in religion as have the five I've met here or the twelve who are following in their footsteps.

5th. January.

"Those young men who come into the monastery because their temples belong to their families," said Harry after we sat down to coffee this morning, "what sort of kōans did they have? If you're supposed to have a natural kōan when you come into the monastery, and they're just coming in because their parents were in the priesthood, whatever *is* their kōan?"

"I would imagine it is just the fact that their parents were in the priesthood," I replied. I knew that I was smiling wanly but I couldn't help it.

"What do you mean?" he said.

"Well, for me, if I had got to go into a job, whether I wanted to or not, because it was the only way in which I could keep the roof over my family's head, and I was interested in doing something else, I think I would have a pretty *big* kōan. It is said that the kōan arises naturally in daily life and I *know* that it does. Certainly, as I see it, having to become a trainee in a place like the Tokyo temple, if I really didn't *feel* like doing it, or hadn't got the inclination, would be, to me, a very, very big kōan."

"What can you tell me about the natural kōan?" he asked. "For some people it seems to be so much bigger than others."

"The size of the natural kōan is in ratio to the time it has been possessed and the spiritual development of the person concerned," I said. "Many people seem to have their present kōans created when they are very young, some at birth or even before. What on earth am I here for? Whatever is the use of life? A person who is constantly being told that she is facing death, as I was as a small child, finds herself wondering—is there anywhere in this whole world where there is joy? What's the reason for it all? That's what it came down to. And, because I'd had it such a long time, it was all that much more powerful. Most youngsters have a healthy, lively childhood; I spent my first five years, according to my mother,[132] in hospital—so I needed to find a reason for living early; a lot of other people don't seem to need to. They just have the normal problems that come as a result of growing up. Many people get their natural kōan at puberty; others later still. But the size of that kōan, its immediacy, is exactly in ratio to the amount of time that they've possessed it and how urgent it is to do something about it, i.e. their spiritual development."

"Does that mean," asked Harry, "that if one's kōan isn't so big the understanding that one gets isn't so big?"

"There's an old saying—'big misunderstanding, big understanding; medium misunderstanding, medium understanding; little misunderstanding, little understanding.' But, you know, you shouldn't try to think of enlightenment in such terms—because it *is* enlightenment you're thinking of."

"I didn't say enlightenment because I know you don't like people to use the word," he said.

"I know, but you're thinking it and that's what matters. Enlightenment is one and undivided. It's not something that you get piecemeal. They were always bashing this into my head in the Tokyo temple and I know it to be completely true. Enlightenment is enlightenment. That you have a big glimpse or a little glimpse doesn't alter the fact that you *see*: that you *understand*. You should remember that."

I got up from the table to wash the coffee things and Harry followed me out to the kitchen. "Why don't you let me do that?" he asked.

"If you wish," I said.

He looked at me. "You neither try to stop me doing things nor encourage me to do them. You should go back to bed."

"We must each do our own training in the best way we can."

He shook his head, took the coffee things from me and washed them up.

6th. January.

Harry has been asking me a lot of questions about the attitude of mind of my friend in England with regard to my returning. I still have to rest on the bed most of the day and he spends much of his time sitting beside me.

"You are from New Zealand, aren't you?" I said.

"Yes," he said. "I really can't understand what is going on; I really and truly can't. Every time I've gone to England people

have been so—supercilious, I suppose, is the word—to me because I'm from the Colonies. I've got to the state when I don't
want to go to England and now I hear of what happened to
you—I don't know what to believe—you're one of them, not a
Colonial."

"There's something you should understand about England,
Harry. I and others have been of this opinion for many years.
The English haven't yet got over the effects of having had the
Colonies; of having had the Empire. And, as the husband of that
British couple said when he was staying here, the British will
never forgive me for going native. Look at me—I am wearing
the robes of the local priesthood and I've got a shaven head.
There's no crime quite as bad as going native in the minds of
the generation above mine and they are the ones in control.

People in England are perfectly happy with Orientals and
foreigners teaching Buddhism because—well—they're someone from whom they can learn as dilettantes. But, if one of their
number takes that learning seriously, if one of their number
really wants to do the job completely, if he truly *believes* in
what he is doing, then he's in great trouble. You can admire
these things if you are British, you can enjoy them, you can
dabble in them, you can participate in them, but you mustn't
believe in them. You see I *believe* in Buddhism, I don't dabble
in it. That is the 'crime' I have committed and why I probably
cannot return to England. I have 'gone native' as far as the
British are concerned."

"Do you realise what you're saying?"

"Yes. Yes, I fully realise what I'm saying. I'm saying that
as long as I live I will probably never be able to return permanently to England. And, you know, in many respects
you're in the same situation. You are from New Zealand.
Admittedly your parents *left* England and went there but they,
if you like, went native too; they left England and became
Colonials. There is no crime quite that big in the mind of some
Britons. I'm not explaining this very well; and I don't particularly understand the mind-attitude behind it. It's very un-
Buddhist. You know, I can remember as a child at school what

used to happen on Empire Day. Everybody had to go down to the big hall and stand in front of the map of the world on which all the bits of the Empire were marked in in red; it went the whole length of the room. We used to sing the Empire songs and be proud of ourselves because we were the mother nation of the Empire. We were almost taught to look down on the Colonies. They were places that hadn't yet got *our* culture, that must at least be fifty years behind us in understanding. Nations who weren't in the Empire were regarded as being thousands of years behind us, living in the dark middle-ages of stupidity and heathenism.

"I can remember when I was about ten looking out over the sea and wondering what on earth Paris was like; wondering if the French lived in trees. That sounds ridiculous but it's a fact. We were brainwashed that way. One day, years later, I got the curiosity bug and started travelling—and I discovered that the rest of the world did pretty well—just as well as we did—in fact, many did an awful lot better. But, in making that discovery, I put myself outside the pale enclosing my former acquaintances; I was cut off from them because I had recognised that other people were equal with the British. It's a grave crime to commit in the minds of some, you know, the recognition that other people are human. But, Harry, why talk about these silly, useless things? One day I shall leave Japan and it won't be very long from now—I know that. And, when I go, I probably shan't go back to England."

"Where will you go?"

"I don't know."

"How about coming to New Zealand?"

"I'll go wherever the wind blows me. And I'll tell you something else; wherever I go I shall not be ashamed of my priest's robe or my shaven head. I shall wear them proudly until I'm dead, whether people think I've gone native or whether they don't, because what I told you was the truth—I *believe* in what I'm doing and I don't care two hoots whether other people like it or lump it. I found what I came looking for and I'm overjoyed."

"You know, I've been watching you closely. It seems as though there are great surges of life rising up in you every now and then."

"Harry," I stretched myself, "you shouldn't ask questions about some things—just they happen. You do your own training. Right?"

He gave me a queer look. "All right," he said, "if that's the way you want it."

7th. January.

According to Dōgen one should never tell one's dreams to the foolish. After talking to Harry yesterday I wondered if I should tell him about the fanning wings and the black shadows; the latter still flit across the corners of my eyes. I don't think I should; I don't think he'd understand them. It's very difficult to answer his questions for he is in the state I was in some years ago. It is like trying to teach someone to swim from the opposite bank of a river. All you can do is tell them to dive in and encourage them to keep going until they reach you. I just don't know how to answer him in a way that will satisfy. If I tell him the truth he won't believe me. I so want to share what I have with him and I know that he isn't ready.

11th. January.

Harry was asking me about the way in which drugs are being used to get Zen experience over in the West. I heard a little about this when I was in the Tokyo temple but nobody took very much notice of it.

"Do you really think you can get the same experience through drugs?" he asked. "Because, if so, it would be well worth doing."

"I can tell you this, Harry," I said. "From my experience of drugs when they were used on me in hospital—and they used a lot whenever they operated on me—I found that the effect of the drugs wears off. Maybe you *can* get a feeling of well-being as a result of taking these drugs—psychedelics or whatever— but the effect is going to wear off; the feeling of well-being is *not* going to be permanent. On the other hand, that which one gets as a result of training oneself in Zen *is* permanent. So long as you keep up your training, so long as you always do your meditation, so long as you live within the Precepts of the Buddhas and do that which has to be done, you will *always* have the magnificent and wonderful peace that I can guarantee you comes as a result of studying Zen. And that peace requires no stimulation other than actual meditation.

"From what you tell me of these drugs they are extremely expensive and I suspect they would be very, very dangerous to the human body; I have yet to find any drug that doesn't have *some* side-effects and many are serious. But meditation has no side-effects whatsoever of a detrimental variety. The only thing meditation does is make you incredibly healthy."

"What about you? What about that illness?"

"That's got nothing to do with it. According to the doctors I had been ill in that particular area for a good many years; the growth had just lain there undetected. I know for certain that if it had not been for the peace of mind brought about by meditation that growth would have killed me. Exactly the same thing killed both my mother and my grandmother. It's out now. The doctors are wondering how on earth it was possible for me to put up with the incredible pain of the last year or so of it without any medication whatsoever. If I hadn't been meditating I couldn't have stood it; and it was my inner strength, faith, if you like, the peace within me, that made it possible for me to go through the operation although by then I had no confidence whatsoever in those performing it. You see I didn't care whether I lived or died—it didn't matter for I was at peace with the universe. There was nothing that could possibly be added to or taken away from me. Since greed for neither life nor death entered into it I was doing that which had to be done. There were people in that hospital who had to be given pain killers for days and weeks after their operations but I was up and walking the next night and out in four days after mine. People are still wondering how and why."

"But you *do* need after-care and I want to get you some."

"Oh, stop whining about after-care. I can't afford it. The best after-care I can give myself is to meditate like mad. You'll see—I'll get better."

"But you can't even stand upright yet. You have to rest most of the day."

"Miracles don't happen overnight. I'll manage. I've been thinking of digging a pond in the garden. It will be nice to have a goldfish pond and that will give my stomach muscles the necessary exercise."

He looked appalled. "You'll hurt yourself."

"No, I won't; I'll be fine."

He went into the kitchen to cook lunch and the post arrived; with it came a letter from that man in England who started all the trouble so long ago—the one who first wrote for a Buddhist priest. As usual the letter was extremely rude. I suppose some people just never learn.

13th. January.

A card came from Rev. Hajime. It said that he was terribly busy but on the ninth he talked to the new Zenji Sama, together with his new staff, about the Foreign Section. Apparently they've still not made up their minds as to whether they want foreigners. He said that they want me to go on with my work here and that they do not object to sending cash for this from the temple itself. Well, at least we shan't starve and I will look after the foreigners as best I can here.

30th. January.

Another letter came from Rev. Hajime to-day. He said that he was still extremely busy and that the Patriarch had died on the nineteenth. It is *so* sad—first that wonderful old priest I visited in Kyoto, then Zenji Sama, then the Zenji Sama of the other great Zen temple of our school, then the Vice-Abbot Elect of the temple in Tokyo and now the Patriarch—all five, the five great saints of which I spoke—dead in the space of a few weeks. The twelve who are coming up are much too young to take over yet. I am very much afraid of what may happen for the people whom I know will now take over the top positions are politicians. They have not the spiritual calibre of those five.

Rev. Hajime's letter continued to say that the current generation of officers is becoming younger but that he is not sure that the change is better or worse. He may well say that.

It seems I am to get three thousand yen a month for the next three months and ten thousand yen a month from April.

Rev. Hajime says that the new Zenji Sama is not concerned about (interested in) having foreigners in the procession at his Jōdō ceremony which will take place the day after *my* Zenji Sama's state funeral.

The letter ended on a rather sad note. Rev. Hajime wrote that he was in a very difficult situation concerning the debts of the Tokyo temple and how to pay them. He indicated that it was difficult for him to explain this in a letter. Whilst Zenji Sama was alive Rev. Hajime was for a time the temple treasurer and he arranged many loans, to make the building of the new Hondō possible, by order of Zenji Sama. I suspect that he is now being blamed for having done so. I cannot help feeling that this is just another political move. I hope that no harm may actually come to him although I am deeply worried by his obvious involvement in politics—it grows worse daily. He has always vacillated from one side to the other. One day foreigners and women would be wonderful and the next not worth knowing depending on whether or not Zenji Sama was in residence. On the days when Zenji Sama was there Rev. Hajime thought that the foreigners and I were important; on the days when Zenji Sama was away Rev. Hajime thought us a damned nuisance and said so. Whenever I asked him about his ambivalence he said that his change of mind was caused by his drinking. There is something in me that really winces when I am with a person who licks the boots of whoever is in power. I feel it to be so dangerous for him spiritually. I wonder sometimes what exactly will happen to him. I have seen him change so much throughout the years from a wonderful, truly spiritual person to something that—no, I won't say it, I mustn't say it, I mustn't even think it.[133]

Harry was sitting in the window seat looking a bit moody and I asked him what was wrong. I was lying on the bed.

"I don't know," he said. "Knowing what you had to put up with in that temple I can't understand why the heck you ever stayed there."

"That's because you don't know the nature of discipleship," I replied. "If you did you would understand it."

"Tell me," he said.

"A disciple is someone who truly believes in his master. But it's more than belief. I don't know exactly how to put this, Harry, but I promised Zenji Sama I'd stay with him until he was dead. I did just that. I promised him I would guard his foreigners. I am doing that, too, to the best of my ability. Discipleship, you see, entails obedience, however unusual may be the circumstances and the requests of the master, because that which the master passes on to a disciple is so exquisite, so wonderful—I can't explain this to you. You'd have to go into full-time training to do Transmission and become one with the master as I became one with Zenji Sama."

"But you never had any physical contact with Zenji Sama."

"Of course not. Discipleship doesn't require physical contact. What are you talking about?"

"Well then—is it like *spiritual* love?"

"Oh, it goes far beyond spiritual love—far, far beyond that. It's a willingness to do anything that is asked of one, the willingness to go through hell if necessary and come out the other side."

"Isn't it very dangerous to have that sort of a belief in someone?"

"It can be—yes, it can go wrong. But if you truly believe that all men are the possessors of the Buddha Nature, if you truly believe that the master who is in front of you possesses the Buddha Nature, there's absolutely no danger. You don't seem to understand very much about Buddhism although you've been with me so long. You don't seem to realise that you have to really *believe*; you have to have real faith. This is a religion; it's not a way of life. There are so many ideas floating around; that you can get enlightenment by means of drugs and the like.

People meditate in order to be able to do better work, to be in possession of this or that, but such desires come out of greed because they feel basically inadequate. They are not the 'ends' of Zen. If you would truly study you have to really *believe* that there is something greater than yourself and that you can find it within you. You have to go and find the best person possible and learn from him or her; and you have to completely and utterly trust them when you do it. When you believe in your greater self you are at peace with you and you get rid of the inadequacies I spoke of. You need no drugs; you are competent at work; you possess yourself completely. But the loss of inadequacies is a side effect of enlightenment; it should not be confused with it although it is one of its signs."

"Tell me more," he said.

"Unless you can see the master as the incarnation of Shakyamuni Buddha, unless you can see every single thing as possessing the Buddha Nature, as I told you, you are never going to understand Buddhism. And when you do see your master as being the incarnation of Shakyamuni Buddha, when you see his Buddha Nature in front of you at the moment of Transmission, when you *know* that you share that Buddha Nature with him and with all things, in spite of the fact that everything is different and each thing is individual as it is and yet one within that Buddha Nature, then it doesn't matter two hoots what goes on around you; you stay with it permanently; you are always there and always at peace. What the world does is the world's private problem—it can't harm you once you find this place. Whyever would you walk out on the Buddha once you have found Him? If you have *truly* found Him you are always in heaven. What the world is like is the world's problem, not yours. Your problem is that you do the best you can at all times; that at every minute of the day you work like mad on your own training to make yourself worthy of the master whom you have found.

"You have to love the master in such a way that whatever he asks no sacrifice is too great, no duty too small, too insignificant; you must do it to the very best of your ability at all times however menial it may seem to the world or however great. I'm not explaining this very well. You have to experience it to know it. Unless you are willing to give that sort of obedience, to show that sort of sincerity in training, you're never really going to find the peace and freedom, the immaculacy of Zen, you're never going to find what I suppose you would call enlightenment—understanding, peace-of-mind—I don't care what you call it. I was willing to follow Zenji Sama to heaven or hell because wherever he was was a greater place than heaven. And now, thanks to him, I am always in that place because he showed me how to find it. And so I give thanks to him every day of the week, and to all the other Buddhas and Patriarchs before him for they showed him how to find that place so that he could lead me. And, you know, I so want to take everyone else there but I can't unless they want to go; the only way they can go is if they have the same sincerity and obedience that I gave to Zenji Sama."

"Are you telling me that I've got to take a master if I would find it?"

"Unless you are willing to learn, unless you are willing to be humble enough to believe that there are things you don't know and that there are things you can learn from other people, unless you are willing to look at everything around you and learn from it at all times, you are never going to know the peace of Zen. So long as you suffer from the idea—that is a master or that is not; that is a teacher, that is not; that is a Buddha, that is not; so long as you live in these opposites you will never know the peace of anything. For everything in existence *is* Zenji Sama; everything stands within Zenji Sama's eyes as it does in those of all the Buddhas and Patriarchs before him and in those of the Cosmic Buddha. When you look at the Zenji Sama that is around you with gratitude in your heart for its very existence, no matter how it may behave towards you, then you'll understand Zen."

"What *are* you talking about?"

"Zenji Sama exists everywhere; Shakyamuni Buddha exists everywhere. I stayed in that temple because the way in which people behaved, what they did or didn't do, was of no importance. What *I* did was what mattered; my reactions, how I behaved as a result of what they were doing, was what mattered. As Dōgen rightly points out, 'It is not the truth or falsity of the teaching that matters but the truth or falsity (sincerity) of the training of the trainee.' If the trainee is really sincere in his training he can always find the truth even when what the world regards as devils surround him. He must be willing to lay his life on the line if he would be reborn in the world of the Buddhas and Patriarchs."

"Then a master isn't necessary. All I need do is suffer."

"A master is *always* necessary. *Everything* is the master. Suffering is unnecessary."

"I don't know what the hell you're talking about!" He jumped up and paced the room.

"Sit still in the place where you're asking the question and you'll hear what I'm trying to say," I said. "Stop looking for *specific* masters; stop worrying about external things; stop worrying about what people did and what people didn't do. Just stay still inside and listen to the voice of the Lord of the House."

"I'm going in to meditate." He walked into the Hondō and sat down.

I really am very bad at teaching people; I know what I'm trying to say but I don't seem very good at getting it over.

1st. February.

We started work on the next newsletter. It is a great help having Harry here but I do find it very difficult trying to teach him. He asks so many questions. The answers I know but I don't know how to get them over. And, quite truthfully, all I really want to do is bask in the glory of the peace inside myself. Yet I am pleasantly disturbed by the beating of the wings. I suspect they are trying to tell me that I should not just sit here and bask; I have a feeling they want to take me somewhere and I know that I don't terribly much want to go. It is so peaceful— and yet there is an urgency in the wings, a fanning, a growing strength—the beauty of the endless blue sky that I see every night beckoning me as did the sea when I was so young. It's as if all the mystery of life and the joy of being born again were new every moment. This time it is not just the world I shall cross when I take wing; limitless space and limitless time are mine.

12th. February.

"I still don't understand this business of the master and disciple," said Harry this morning.

"What don't you understand?" I asked.

"Well, did all the trainees in the temple have the same feeling for Zenji Sama that you did?"

"I really wouldn't know; I'm not them."

"Don't give me an answer like that—it doesn't help. I need to know . . . ." He was getting annoyed.

"Listen, Harry, I was Zenji Sama's own private disciple, the person whom he himself ordained and Transmitted and whom he licensed as a full priest. That made a special relationship between him and I. Surely you can understand that?"

"Yes. But didn't that relationship exist between all the other trainees and him?"

"Oh, no. You've got to understand that most of them came from other temples. Their masters ordained them and then sent them to Zenji Sama to be educated. As I said, that Tokyo temple is like a big school; people are sent there to be educated in Buddhism."

"Then presumably the other trainees would have a similar relationship with their masters to what you had with Zenji Sama."

"I would hope they would—I would really hope they would but I do not know."

"Do you think they would have done as much for their masters as you did for Zenji Sama?"

"If they were true disciples there is no limit to what they would do—because, you see, the master and the disciple are one, completely and utterly one. They may be different in time; one may have been born physically at an earlier time to the other; but they are reborn every moment that they look upon each other; every second of the day and night they are one life that is constantly arising, going to bed, sitting down, sleeping, walking, eating; it is the same one life that belongs to Shakyamuni Buddha. Shakyamuni Buddha is not dead."

"I'm still stuck."

"How?"

"Well—I can't understand why the temples should have been the way they are. What you've described I know you went through because I was there."

"You need to understand the difference between now and olden times. Long ago people went to monasteries solely because they wanted to do something about themselves and they chose a suitable priest with whom to study—the best one they could find. When they had learned all they could from him, and had found the Truth within themselves, they received the Transmission and that was it. In Japan, around 1600, the priesthood's function was changed by the government, since it feared the power of the priests, and most of the temples were then only used as funeral registries. A hundred years or so ago the priests were allowed to marry and the temples became hereditary; like it or lump it, the youngsters born to the families living in those temples had to study for the priesthood in order to keep the temple in the family as I told you. This meant that a lot of the youngsters who came, a lot of the youngsters who come to-day too, did so because it's a job; because there is no other way they can keep the roof over the heads of their relatives. They don't come particularly to do something about themselves; idealistically they may believe it but that is about as far as it gets for some of them. They come in order to learn the job of being a priest, a profession, go back and do that job. The number of people in that Tokyo temple who had come to genuinely do something about themselves seemed to be remarkably few.[60] And it's not just *that* temple; it's true all over the country— every Zen temple in existence is in the same boat.[134]

"But there *are* people who come to genuinely do something about themselves—I met at least a dozen when I was in that temple and they were all doing pretty well. As I've told you

before, I also met at least five saints all of whom are now dead
unfortunately. But others will come up—you'll see."

"How did the others there, the ones who were the professional priests, react towards the ones who were trying to do
something about themselves?"

I smiled ruefully. "They thought them pretty odd.[134] You
know, it's like every other profession—worldliness, assisted by
time, has done an amazing amount of damage. It's a sort of ero-
sion; the world gets in gradually. First it's some little thing that
the government agrees to do in return for something that the
priests want done; then it's another little thing here and another
little thing there—'If we alter the curriculum thus, then we can
make the government happy;' or 'If we agree to do such and
such then we can make this or that official happy;' before you
know it you've got a whole bureaucracy running your monastery
and all religion has flown out of the window. Zenji Sama tried
valiantly to prevent that from happening. He did pretty well but
the bureaucrats won in the end, at least temporarily; until
another such as he arises."

"How do you know?"

"I used to watch him fight them; I knew the misery that it
was for him; the officials always trying to force him to give in
to what they wanted. The temple seemed at times to be almost
divided into two sections—the bunch that ran the administration, that dealt with all the bureaucratic stuff, and those who
were teaching religion. I'm not trying to say that the bureaucrats weren't really religious; in their way they were. I'm not
trying to say that the 'holier-than-thou' bunch, as they sometimes seemed to become, that were trying to run the educational
side, were better either. But it is true to say that if you want
something more than a tree underneath which to teach you're
always going to have to agree to do something that the world
wants done; you are always going to have to take time out from
your teaching to spend with suspicious government officials. If
you're happy with just a tree you can *know* the Truth without
worrying about houses, taxes and the like but you may still need
licenses and permits just to open your mouth in some countries.

Then there are patrons. A patron who's giving you food may only want you to teach what he wants to hear. If you look after, and do everything for, yourself you have the right to believe what you wish but you may not have the right to say it to others without a government permit; and then in troupe the bureaucrats, suspicions and all, dragging behind them psychiatrists to test your sanity and heaven alone knows what else if you don't make sense as they understand the word. And when you gain help from officials, emperors, presidents, as soon as you have corporations, the truth is frequently scattered to the four winds. If I ever do go back to the West I shall try and do what Zenji Sama himself wanted to do without any such things as corporations and the like. But I don't know of any country that would let me be completely free in that way; I would probably be arrested for vagrancy.

"Dōgen Zenji refused to compromise his teachings which is why he had such a hard job to keep a monastery together. It was not until a few years before his death that he became abbot of a big temple. He spent almost all his life organising small communities up and down the country and refusing to take what could at best be regarded as bribes from emperors and the like because he was afraid of what would happen to the purity of his teaching. That's the way I want to do it when I leave here. I'm often appalled by the compromises I've been forced to make just to be able to do *anything* in this particular temple. Do you know what happens every time I try to ordain somebody? First I have to get the mayor's permission, then I have to get the agreement of several of the priests in the area, then go to the prefectural administrator in the next-door city and then to the administration in Tokyo. None of these people turn up at the ceremony (the people I ordain are foreigners in whom they have no interest) but all have to be placated or there is trouble. When I've got the seals from this lot, which cost the earth in time, presents and fees, I *may* be permitted to have a disciple; everyone wants a finger in the pie and money for the non-existent work that most of them do. It's so absolutely contrary to everything that was originally true

Buddhism. Such customs are things we don't have to carry across the sea when we leave here.

"Zenji Sama was quite right when he said that an awful lot of traditions have grown up in our school of Zen and, indeed, throughout the whole of Buddhism—traditions that are utterly useless, a complete waste of time. All that is needed in Buddhism is a master who has been truly Transmitted, a disciple and a tree underneath which to sit."

It was already eleven o'clock in the morning and I knew that I had a memorial ceremony at twelve after which there would be the customary banquet so I had to get Harry to make his own lunch whilst I got ready for the ceremony.

20th. February.

A letter came to-day from a married couple that want our help in order to enter a temple here. Harry asked me where I thought was suitable.

"Absolutely nowhere," I said, "if they want to go together."

"You're not surely advocating that they separate?"[135]

"I'm advocating that they separate whilst they are in training in temples, yes—for one very good reason. If they both go to a male temple the wife won't be allowed to train properly because she'll be a female in a man's world, a lay female than which there is nothing lower; she will always be on the fringe of things, treated a bit like a third-class kitchen maid. If they go to a woman's temple they won't let the husband in the door and he's going to be miserable. The obvious answer is for one to go to a woman's temple and the other to go to a man's. They should make a definite decision to do this for a period of a month or two at a time, come back together again and then go off to the temple for another month or two if they want to. So help me, I wouldn't recommend *any* married couple to go to a Japanese temple together. It would be extremely unkind to both sides. I hate having to suggest that they separate but, honestly, I don't know what else to do. I saw so many people hurt in that Tokyo temple; I don't want it to happen again."

Harry sighed. "We'd best put that in the newsletter, then, because this is about the eighth letter we've had asking about arrangements for married couples. How do you feel about them coming here?"

"There should be some way in which married couples can train together but there's something in me that says that the marriage itself is always going to be a barrier to actual training."

"Whyever should it be?"

"I think it's got to do with the *Japanese* attitude to the master-disciple relationship and the fact that a marriage is itself a unity. It's like putting a third party into the marriage—a master. A truly *married* couple has to have a unity of spirit just as the master and disciple have to have a unity of spirit. A married couple in training for the priesthood here in Japan would be a bit like having a religious triangle. Lay couples just coming in now and then are, of course, a different matter. I've seen so much happen just with Rev. Hajime—he's got his wife in his temple (she's officially a 'nun with hair')—and the Buddhist priesthood; the priesthood is always getting in the way of his marriage—he goes off to the Tokyo temple, for example, to be a lecturer and leaves his wife behind since she cannot enter a male temple and, even if she could, would be so low in rank that the marriage would be ruined. He's married to his job; the wife's duty is solely to produce young. It is an extremely unhappy situation for any woman; I wouldn't want it if I were married and I would certainly not marry a *Japanese* Buddhist priest under the circumstances. The Buddhist priesthood here, as of now, has no room for matrimony. One day, many years from now, I'll try to work out how it's possible for married couples to train together in a monastery but this is certainly not the country and I certainly don't know enough yet to be able to do it."

"All right," said Harry, "we'll tell them all this in the newsletter."

This afternoon we did a lot more work on the mending of the temple. The new high altar on which we started work some time ago will soon be finished. One of the local priests has brought along a friend of his, who is a professional carpenter, to help with it. We're also going to widen the temple itself by building a new front on it. It's about time it had some new front walls. There have been almost no repairs done on this place at all for two-hundred and fifty years.

27th. February.

"The other day you said that what other people did didn't matter; what does matter is our reactions to what they do."

"Yes?"

"Do you think any of the things that were done to you in the early days when you were in the Tokyo temple were done deliberately in order to get you to react in specific ways?"

"You mean were they manipulative to get me to specific states of awareness? Is that what you're talking about?"

"Yes."

"No, I don't believe it at all. No true Zen master, no true Zen trainee, ever manipulates anybody. The kōan arises *naturally* in daily life; we don't *need* to give it any false assistance. We don't *need* to manipulate anything to create the kōan. The seeming use of manipulation has been the objection of many to Rinzai for years for they think it is the setting up of an artificial situation. However, in *true* Rinzai and Sōtō this is not the case. In Rinzai you are given a kōan which should, of course, agree with your natural kōan. Some say that when you've gone through all three-hundred odd of the official kōans you are *officially* enlightened but this is not so with a *real* master. The kōan arises *naturally* in daily life. A *true* master, whether Rinzai or Sōtō, uses the situations as they arise, for they are *natural* kōans, along with the traditional ones, for you are with him to learn how to live *naturally* at peace. Everything the trainee does tells the master something about the trainee. The master notes these things and uses them to point the way for the trainee to his *naturally True* state. That which arose *naturally* for me in the Tokyo temple was the fact that I was a woman and a foreigner in a Japanese man's temple. It was a natural problem, given the culture here, a natural kōan; it needed no manipulation whatsoever. The kōan arose every day of the week, every minute, every hour. It continues to arise now but I know exactly what to do with it. Through it I solved the real kōan, belief in me, faith in my own Buddha Nature. This is to solve the kōan of everyday life which contains all kōans. Once the barrier of the opposites is broken for one situation it remains so for all others provided one keeps up one's training. To solve the kōan of everyday life is to understand the Truth of Buddhism and to live completely at peace without doubt. You'll have to find that which is *your* natural kōan and learn to deal with it, then you will live naturally and at peace without doubt—you will bathe, if you like, in your Buddha Nature in this world; you will *rejoice* in living in it, regarding Samsara as a beautiful playground in which you can help all living things as well as yourself, in which you can show them how to enjoy their lives because you yourself are the living proof that the Lord of the House can be found within this world. In other words, you will have learned to handle the kōan of everyday life. A manipulated situation is not natural; when you leave it you will not be able to behave naturally and normally in situations that *do* arise naturally. You will always have to live in a manipulative, or manipulated, situation. I don't have to tell you the terrible dangers that would arise from that. I don't have to talk to you of the horrible dangers of tyrants who manipulate thousands of people. Just think of what it would be like if you had a person who manipulated his disciples. They would be automatons in his hands; he could be a complete and utter tyrant. They would never, in fact, be free at any time or in any place. At *all* times one must learn to handle one's own kōan for *oneself*; all the master ever does is point the way.

"No, I can assure you that none of the stuff that was done with me in Tokyo was done deliberately from the point of view of manipulation. It may or may not have been done deliberately in order to hurt me. But who cares? From where I am now it doesn't matter two hoots as I told you the other day. But I *do* know that it was not done to manipulate me."

29th. February.

A card came from Rev. Hajime. He tells me that if I do not come to Zenji Sama's state funeral in April he will buy some red roses for me which will be put upon the altar. He also tells me that a British friend came to collect some of the things that I had left behind. He is very kindly going to bring them down here when he visits me in a week or two's time.

1st. March.

Harry has been working on the newsletter. He has collected a lot more news than I would ever have dreamed of putting in, including the fact that the mayor and town council have decided to put a completely new roof on the entire temple. It's about time! Part of the old one fell in the first year I was here; I remember having to have it repaired at my own expense.

He's also written about married couples since we had that discussion the other day. I'm a little worried about what he wrote—that and a couple of other things. I'll record them here just in case they are ever talked about at a later date.

> 1. If you are a married couple we advise that you separate and go to different temples after you arrive here. We hate to suggest that you separate but Japan can be a crucible which can melt down the strongest Western marriage simply because of the Japanese attitude to women. Jiyu Rōshi has spent more of her time healing broken marriages than she cares to remember. Since this attitude to women is simply Japanese custom and has nothing to do with Buddhism it is a pity to harm both your marriage and your faith. It upsets the husband to see his wife underprivileged and excites jealousy in the wife to see her husband getting preferential treatment. There is also the fact that many temples dislike having married couples and may refuse to take you because of this.

That's not strictly what I told him. Anyway it's what he wrote. The second warning he gave was concerning invitations to Japan. I quote,

2. Be very careful how you accept invitations from Japanese in foreign countries to visit Japan. Please do not misunderstand us. Most invitations are sincerely meant but some are not and we know of at least three people who gave up excellent posts in their own countries to enter temples only to find that they were not really expected to come when they got here or else were expected to stay for only a very short time. We all know the expression, 'Come and stay sometime,' which all of us have used from time to time in our own countries, knowing full well that the invitation was extended to be polite and not meant to be taken seriously. We get the feeling that the Japanese do the same sort of thing and perhaps some of us have misunderstood them. But it is difficult when the invitation comes in writing from an important priest to believe that he is merely being polite. Therefore we would suggest that you do not refuse such invitations but that you think very carefully twice before accepting them.

I wonder if it was necessary to put such a thing in the newsletter? I know *why* he put it in. Since Zenji Sama's death there have been many, many discussions in the Tokyo temple as to whether I was ever really invited to come to Japan. Some people, including Rev. Hajime, even discussed it whilst he lived, saying that Zenji Sama had told them that he had never issued the invitation. All this in spite of the fact that back in England I have several letters to prove that I was invited as also the special letter for my visa guaranteeing me to the Japanese government. In my own mind there is absolutely no doubt that I was invited; that other people think I was or wasn't doesn't really matter. But Harry is quite right, I suppose, to talk about this because several other people have had similar experiences—one of them went back to San Francisco last week almost crazed from what had happened.[136]

I shouldn't be talking like this in this diary. It is wrong. If he went crazy it was because there was something wrong with him. I must be very careful what I say. I must equally be very careful what Harry writes. We must not give wrong thoughts to people.[137]

The third warning Harry wrote said,

3. Be careful not to excite jealousy in the temple. The Japanese are no more jealous than any other nation but monasteries the world over are special and different from the ordinary world in that they are closed communities and, with everyone living in his next-door neighbor's pocket, as it were, character flaws show rapidly and molehills soon become mountains. Be specially careful of attracting the favor of the abbot or abbess of the temple concerned for their attendants and temple officials can be very jealous of their positions and jealousy sometimes drives them to create rumors and scandals of a most revolting nature. More important still, we know of two who were so insanely jealous of Jiyu Rōshi's success in Zen and her position in the temple that they thought nothing of trying to destroy her reputation in the eyes of the temple authorities and, for that matter, wherever else they went. There is much more I would like to tell you about this for Jiyu Rōshi has suffered bitterly owing to the late abbot's affection for her but she will not permit me to print it. She has never said anything and I would not have known if I had not accidentally found her diaries one night when I was acting as her night-nurse. She is not pleased that I read them.[138]

He's darned right I'm not pleased that he read them! He'd got no business fiddling about with this diary. Perhaps I ought to burn it—it might be the best thing—although the warning could be well taken. I know of somebody else up in Tokyo who had a really rough time. The female Rōshi at the temple she was in had an assistant who screamed and cried every time she had to do any work other than that of attending the Rōshi. Yes, maybe he's right in putting some of these things in. Maybe people should be warned of the dangers when they come here. I know that if I'd known a lot of things I certainly would have been far more careful.[138] I know something else too; under no circumstances would I ever have come without Zenji Sama's direct invitation. I'm not in the habit of going anywhere without invitations anyway. So whatever they say, whatever anyone believes, I *genuinely* believed myself to be invited and I *know* that Zenji Sama genuinely invited me.

3rd. March.

A letter came from my friend in Kyoto. I had written to her to ask if she could possibly come and help me since she had offered to—this was back in December when I first got here. I now have a reply—three months later. She talks at some length about how much she would love to come but can't do so because she mustn't stop her meditation and must be at Sesshin. She talks a tremendous lot about her 'shugyō' and her 'meditation' and how to sit and how she can't sit correctly in the half-lotus position any longer; and she *still* talks about how much she would love to be able to look after me. If she really wants to why doesn't she come and do it? This is what I was talking about only the other day—people who are always talking of how much they want to do things for others but never do them—the coldness of many who go into Zen for the sake of wisdom without first understanding the necessity of compassion and love. I might have died in these three months if it hadn't been for Harry. There have been times when I was close to it but Harry pulled me through. This letter talks of all the work she's had to do— she must clean the temple garden for the trainees there and she's got to help with the washing-up and help with the cooking— there are eight or ten other people there helping with her. Ah, forget it. If that's as far as her Zen has got, if that's all she understands after so many years in the East, she's best left alone where she is—and I'm best off with Harry.[139]

5th. March.

George arrived this morning. He was one of the original eight that Zenji Sama had early on for that first great Jūkai. He is going to be ordained as a priest. Zenji Sama had told me to ordain them all as they required it. This will be the first one. He'll be here for a short time getting together the necessary robes and other things before the ceremony takes place. I shall do the ceremony sometime in April then we can both go to Zenji Sama's funeral together.

10th. March.

I have been instructing Harry in various ceremonial duties so that he can assist me with the playing of the mokugyo and gong at the memorial ceremonies. We had four of them to-day. When they were over Harry went back to his previous conversations on the master-disciple relationship whilst I was lying down to rest. "Am I right in believing that you were learning from Rev. Hajime but were really Zenji Sama's disciple?" he asked.

"Yes," I said.

"So you were also Rev. Hajime's disciple."

"No, at no time was I ever legally Rev. Hajime's disciple. I did ask him once if I could become it and he pointed out to me the reasons why I couldn't."

"Why couldn't you?"

"Simply because I had been Transmitted by Zenji Sama. You cannot legally be Transmitted twice."

"I thought you could."

"I believe you still can be in Chinese Buddhism but I am not sure. If you think about it carefully you will know quite well why you can't. Transmission implies the seeing of Buddhahood within your own master. When you look at your master you see Shakyamuni Buddha in him just as he saw Shakyamuni Buddha in the master before him; and so did all the Patriarchs right back until the physical moment when Makakashyo beheld the historical Shakyamuni Buddha. If you go to a new master because you are not satisfied with the teaching of your present one you are virtually saying, 'This person is a master and that one is not completely so,' or 'This person is a master but that one is more of a master than this one is.' You remember I explained to you that enlightenment is not something you get piecemeal? Buddhahood is a whole thing—the whole of life *is* Buddhahood—every living thing, every animate, every inanimate thing is *the* whole of Buddhahood. That cup is the whole of Buddhahood; Zenji Sama is the whole of Buddhahood. Therefore, when you are Transmitted, your Transmission is whole. How *could* you change masters after Transmission?"

Harry was silent for some time then he said, "But there are people who do change masters."

"Yes," I said. "They are called 'zuishin' and they don't really *change* masters. The word 'zuishin' means a 'follower of another.' Usually a zuishin is somebody who, after Transmission, feels that there are still things he doesn't know and, his true master being dead, he goes off to continue learning from another master. But a zuishin is always looked down on by the entire Buddhist Church for he is dragging his true master's name in the mud, as it were, by implying that he didn't give him all of the teaching at his Transmission. I know of only one zuishin in this country. I very nearly became one once, when it was so difficult to get to Zenji Sama but, you know, after I thought about it deeply, I realised that another master had nothing to teach me that I hadn't already learned at my Transmission. And it was about then that I started seeing Rev. Hajime more clearly; then I *knew* I couldn't become his zuishin. After this I started understanding Buddhism a lot more clearly too. You either see your master as Shakyamuni Buddha or you don't. If you don't you are simply a person who has done a ceremony which is not a real Transmission. If you do see, as indeed I saw, there is no way in which you can really follow another even when you are hurt and angry as I was. You cannot tear up the Buddhahood of your own master.[140]

"Some people become zuishins, I'm told, simply because the new master they wish to follow is politically powerful and can give them a job in a really rich temple. I've heard of this happening. Fortunately I've never met such people. The Administration Department decries this practice horribly but there's not much it can do about it other than provide the stigma of being a zuishin. I think they are right in refusing to permit people to do Transmission twice."[141]

"Hmmm, I see. Tell me something else."

"Yes?" I said.

"Can you explain the cruelty of the Japanese to animals?"

"If we're going to have a long, long discussion on this sort of thing I suggest that we get some coffee first."

"All right," he said and went out to make it.

"Apropos of what we were saying earlier, before we get off on a new subject," I said, "I think you should perhaps know that there is, I have heard, the rather unfortunate custom of masters *selling* disciples in Japan."

"Selling them? What are you talking about?"

"Some priests can't get disciples at all, so they go to those who can get plenty and offer to pay cash to borrow one so that they can do Kessei. The disciple becomes the borrower's Chief Junior and goes back, after he's done his Chief Junior ceremony, to his original master. Then there are those who don't just want to borrow. These, it would seem, literally 'buy' a disciple for a large price. Since the disciple must obey his master he has no say in the matter. I got very worried when I discovered that Rev. Hajime had let one of his daughters go to a childless family. This wasn't, of course, so that she could become a priest; this was just because the other family hadn't got any children. The idea throughout Japan is that families shouldn't have more than two children. It's a good idea to prevent overpopulation but there's something in me that winces at the thought of a parent or master selling or giving away one of his kids."

"Yeah, I know what you mean but I'm not quite sure why it is so revolting."

"It is, isn't it?"

He nodded. "Tell me, do the people who get sold, the disciples, do they go willingly?"

"Not always. I believe Rev. Hajime told me of a couple who ran away after their masters had collected up the cash. Presumably there was a reason why the person they were sold to couldn't get a disciple in the beginning. Perhaps that was why they ran away."

Since the kettle had boiled and the coffee was already made we went to the living room.

"With regard to animals," I said, "you must understand that Buddhism has always taught very great compassion for *all* animal life. And you must also understand that the Japanese are not strictly Buddhists—they are Shintoists first and Buddhists, Christians or whatever else second. Their nationality, Japanese, and their national religion, Shintoism, come before everything. Shintoism deals with everything temporal—you get married in Shintoism and buried in Buddhism. Whereas Buddhism teaches compassion for all life, Shintoism teaches that the Emperor is God and you are his child from the moment you open your eyes because you are a Japanese. It seems that animals are for use and enjoyment. The feet of unwanted animals are tied and the poor creatures put underneath the temples. It's the Japanese compromise between the compassion of Buddhism and the omnipotence of Shintoism. You don't kill an animal because Buddhism says that killing is wrong; instead you put it underneath the temple. Thus it becomes the Buddha's problem since He refuses to allow you to kill."

Harry shuddered. "I don't *want* to know any more about it."

"If you do I suggest you get in touch with a friend of mine who works on one of the newspapers in Tokyo. He's been fighting this sort of thing for a very long time."

"I'm still worried about that article you wrote when you were in the Tokyo temple. You know the one? Why foreigners make a hash of Zen?"

"Yes, I now realise that it was a test—a test of my loyalty. Was I loyal to Japan or to the foreigners? Ever since the beginning there have been tests like this. Who was I in with—the Japanese or my own people? I sometimes wonder about the Buddhism of some in that Tokyo temple—there's still the 'them' and the 'us.' There are Japanese and there's the rest of the world. You remember when I first arrived how Rev. Ichirō told me about the terrible things that had happened to Japan as a result of the Hiroshima and Nagasaki bombings? I can remember how he reacted when he realised that I was going out on a limb for the sake of the Westerners who were killed in the war rather than the Japanese. If I'd been a bit more alert then I'd have recognised what was happening. All through my stay in the Tokyo temple I was constantly being asked, 'Are the foreigners who are coming here loyal to Japan or are they loyal to you? If they are loyal to you why are they studying Japanese Buddhism?' They weren't talking about me; I was merely the representative of the rest of the world. I can remember some really important people coming from one of the military bases. I was told that if they were loyal to Japan I should get them to arrange for the return of Okinawa. I remember Rev. Hajime telling me this and thinking how preposterous the idea was. Zenji Sama never mentioned anything of the sort and neither did the Director. As far as they were concerned Buddhism was one and undivided.[142]

"After Zenji Sama's death I was asked the same question again in a different form. 'Where *does* your loyalty lie?' I can guarantee you I would never have written that article if I hadn't been so ill."

He put a hand on my shoulder. "I can believe that; it's totally contrary to anything I've ever known you write."

"I'm awfully glad that the worst thing I said in it was why some foreigners make such a mess of Zen. What I wrote was true. But, if I'd not been so ill at the time, that article would never have been written at all."

I looked out of the window and saw the mayor coming up the path. "Quick," I said, "let's get rid of the coffee things. Here comes the mayor."

Harry went to the kitchen to get on with lunch and I sat back, hoping that the mayor brought good news about the mending of the temple roof.

12th. March.

I had a card from Rev. Hajime. The British friend who has been collecting my things from the Tokyo temple has told Rev. Hajime that he will pick up the rest within the next day or two and bring them down here to my temple sometime in April. It is good to know that the officials of the Tokyo temple are going to give my address to the foreigners who have been going there. It has been very worrying up to now for quite a number have been trying to get hold of me. It seems that some of the new staff members there have been unwilling to tell them where to find me. It was also good to know that the Cashier's Department will soon be sending the cash that has been promised to me if I run the Foreign Section from here.

One thing is somewhat disturbing, however. Rev. Hajime wrote that a bad rumour surrounding us is spreading and that we must fight for it for the sake of our honour. He will see me on the seventeenth. I wonder what bad rumour he's talking about now? I'm not there so it can't be about me. Maybe someone is trying to get rid of Rev. Hajime, and probably the Director.[143] I wonder what the rumour is about this time?

15th. March.

Harry has been doing much work on ceremonial and is now extremely valuable as an assistant—really valuable. Two of the local Japanese priests—one a man, the other a woman—are coming along regularly to help here also. The man especially has been doing a lot of work on getting the front of the temple rebuilt. He is the one I spoke of in my earlier reference (20th. February) who brings with him the expert carpenter. The temple looks so very different. It is so pleasant to have safe walls. I shall be glad when the mayor does something about the roof as he has promised.

16th. March.

Harry asked me to-day why it was that the Japanese have always referred to me as Jiyu San instead of Kennett San which is the polite form of address. I suppose one could say that it is because I am a woman and, as such, cannot be taken seriously. But that wouldn't be true since the other women I have met in monasteries are at least addressed correctly; they are not, as I was, spoken to in the familiar terminology reserved for children and servants. No-one is permitted to use another's first name without permission. Harry insisted on knowing about this but I didn't really want to discuss it. I don't see any point in discussing it. Whether they were rude or not, whether they couldn't be polite to a foreigner or whether they wanted to be deliberately rude to me as an individual is neither here nor there. I learned what I came here to learn. I met Zenji Sama; it is enough for me that I met Zenji Sama. I don't need to make idle speculations. I have too much to do.

In years to come maybe people will ask such questions; at the moment finding the answers is very difficult. I tried once to get the Japanese to change what they called me, to use my surname instead of my priest's given name, for I knew that what they were doing was, in their culture, very impolite, but they would not take the matter seriously.[144] What can one do under such circumstances? And why bother about it? It is a pity that people worry about unimportant things. I must really try to get Harry away from trying to discuss matters of this sort—they don't count. It matters so much more that one works upon oneself.

17th. March.

The 'phone was installed here to-day. I have been notifying all my friends of my 'phone number. A 'phone should make life a lot easier.

24th. March.

Harry went to Nagoya to-day and I went to Kyoto. Just as I was leaving the temple a small boy came up to me carrying a little kitten. It was black and white, very, very thin and looked very ill. He asked me if I would give it a home. I told him to keep it for a couple of days since I would not be back from Kyoto until the twenty-seventh when I would gladly accept it. He said he would look after it.

26th. March.

I got back from Kyoto earlier than I expected. I was somewhat appalled to hear dull cries coming from under the temple. When I looked I found the little kitten. It had been put under the temple, as is the custom with unwanted animals, so that 'Kami Sama' (the Shinto equivalent of God) could take care of it. This method of disposing of unwanted animals, which I find particularly irresponsible and cruel, I have been unfortunate enough to witness far too often. Hundreds of unwanted little creatures were disposed of in this way beneath the temple in Tokyo, sometimes stuffed into boxes and, according to friends of mine, sometimes with their feet tied. I was able to retrieve two little kittens once and looked after them until one was killed in a fight and the other left home. This little creature—the one that came to-day—is terribly thin; not a bone in its body that cannot be seen through the miserable fur and his little tail is broken. I find the breaking of cats' tails a revolting habit. The Japanese believe that there is a death-hair in a cat's tail. If the tail is waved over a person, and it has not been previously broken, then that person will die. This superstition is so powerful that people go around breaking cats' tails. I will keep this little fellow—I rather like him. I will call him Thomas.

28th. March.

Another letter from my friend in Kyoto. She's saying that she is sorry she wasn't able to come. I had hoped she might still have managed to since I felt that it would be better for me to have a woman in the house nursing me during my convalescence rather than a man. She said in her letter that she had hoped to be able to come but had waited for her Rōshi to come back to settle the programme for the next month or so. On his return he had arranged several Sesshins and she was going to have sanzen and numerous other things for a very long time to come so there was no way in which she could possibly come even for a short visit. Well, if that is the sort of teaching that her Rōshi is giving her, all I can say is that I was extraordinarily fortunate in whom I had to teach me.[145] There is so much more to Zen than just rushing off to Sesshin and going to sanzen. I can just picture what Zenji Sama would have said if someone had told him that they had a friend who'd been very ill and needed some help; not to have given it would have been an extraordinarily *good* way to get shied out of the Tokyo temple. She ended her letter with the suggestion that I get one of my "sporting priest-friends" to give me a "spin" in his car all the way to Kyoto. She informed me that, although her mornings and evenings were tight, she could generally muster a couple of hours during the day. She would find it awfully nice if I came down, and if I was driven in a car it might not be too much of a strain for me. As for her, should something unforeseen open, she would grab the 'phone and "rush it" with pleasure. Ah—the rest of that letter speaks for itself.[146]

31st. March.

A letter arrived from Rev. Hajime. It said that at the end of last month the office appointments meeting was held as usual and my name, 'Foreign Guest Master,' was crossed off the registration list by the opinions of many of the other officers. Zenji Sama,[147] he said, put his weight on their side. He writes that this is very sorry for me and the foreigners. At least from April I may get ten thousand yen for my work, not for study, as an outside officer of the temple. He said he was trying to tell this coolly, but there is some hope because the new Zenji Sama said that when the circumstances have changed (he thinks that means when some of the officers leave) he will do something for me and the foreigners. As of now, however, it is not worth trying to do anything there.

I am not at all surprised by this. They are at least paying me to look after the foreigners even if they don't want them in the temple itself. With regard to my own training I have no problems; I finished going up the seven ranks of the priesthood long before my Zenji Sama died. All I now have to do is settle in and look after the foreigners to the best of my ability. I rather like the idea.

I telephoned Rev. Hajime after receiving this letter and asked him if I had 'carte blanche' to go ahead and look after the foreigners here as I think best. He said that I had but that I should report what I am doing to the Tokyo temple once every month or so. I asked if I needed to check everything I did with them before doing it and he said he didn't think so. I expect *that* will come back to rebound on me at a later date; I shall do something and they'll say I hadn't the right to do it.[73] Well, that's fine by me—I'm not worried about it.

Harry came in from the kitchen wiping his hands. "Tell me," he said, "why did the Director embrace you and say 'magnificent' when there was no response from you?"

I sat back, stretched and smiled. "Oh, that's very comical," I said.

"What's funny about it?"

"You don't understand the Eastern mind. A man and woman able to touch each other without desire is regarded as something quite remarkable in the East. The East believes that no-one can touch a member of the opposite sex without going into transports of ecstasy therefore Orientals think all Westerners are extraordinarily lewd. One Chinese, who came to the Tokyo temple, shook hands with me at the Director's suggestion and trembled in terror afterwards. He said that he would never be able to again control his physical desires. As it seems to me Orientals just can't understand our being able to have physical contact with each other and yet not suffer from a desire to instantly jump into bed and rape one another."

"You mean to say the Director was testing you to see if you *did* have any physical desires when you touched another person?"

"Yes, and he found my lack of response absolutely magnificent. He told me once that it was one of the things that really made him respect foreigners—that they could touch each other and have no physical desire. He was always of the opinion, until the time he tried embracing me, that Westerners were extremely lewd. After that, after he found that there was no response from me, he said that his opinion of the West went up a hundred percent. I find the whole thing extraordinarily comical. Imagine what he would make of the 'kiss of peace' in the Catholic Church."

Harry gave me a queer look. "There are times when I'm awfully glad I'm Occidental!" I chuckled and he went back to the kitchen.

1st. April.

We started work on the newsletter for this month. Harry wrote much about the temple improvements, saying that the

Hondō should be completed sometime this month. He also talked
of the ordination that is going to take place soon; the ordination
of George who, by the way, is still here. He has been doing much
studying and getting his robes ready for the ceremony.

A couple of items of information that Harry put in the
newsletter I think should be mentioned here. One was concerning food and medicine. He wrote,

> For those intending to enter Japanese temples the big
> difficulty for most people in temples of our school is the
> lack of sweet foods in comparison to the large quantity of
> salty and sour ones. The priests compensate for this by eat-
> ing heartily, at the funerals and other outside ceremonies
> they attend, of the food offered to them by the parishioners
> but the average foreigner here in Japan cannot do this. Jiyu
> Rōshi was seldom allowed to go to outside ceremonies
> when in the Tokyo temple [not strictly true; I went to quite
> a few when I was with the Director but not a fraction as
> many as did other juniors;] and so she acquired the usual
> disease resulting from this deficiency of diet, i.e. inflam-
> mation of the salivary glands. This can be extremely
> painful and so we advise that you stock up on sweet things
> before you enter a temple and nibble at them occasionally.
> We also recommend that you bring a supply of your
> favorite antibiotic, laxative and any other medicine you
> may need. Remember that you will not be allowed outside
> the temple for some time after you enter it except with spe-
> cial permission and it is not wise to ask for this too often.
> So get visa papers and sightseeing done before you take up
> your residence in the temple buildings. Under no circum-
> stances get the desire to go on a shopping spree after enter-
> ing. If you get the wanderlust when you are inside you will
> only harm your own reputation and inadvertently the rep-
> utations of your fellow foreigners.

I'm glad he's talked about the problem of the sour and salty
foods. It's amazing what a strange deficiency that actually is,
the lack of sugar. The Japanese eat far too much of it in many
respects but, for some peculiar reason, it is not provided in the

temple diet and all the priests supplement that diet either by going out to funeral meals, as Harry says, or by buying huge boxes of bean jam cakes which are incredibly sweet and cloying. Without them they would be in great trouble. When I was in the Tokyo temple it was extremely difficult in the early days and so I had this problem with my salivary glands; getting antibiotics to treat it was well nigh impossible. I eventually succeeded, it is true, in curing it but it was very painful and I still have a lot of problems when eating sour foods. I'm glad Harry has put this into the newsletter.

He put in something else too. I must really watch that young man. His comments were concerning experience.

> I once asked Jiyu Rōshi what a Bodhisattva was and she replied, "You can see them everywhere all the time." Giving thought to this during the past few months I have come to think of anyone who does anything for others as a Bodhisattva. Applying my thought to the above comments on food I get the following:– Jiyu Rōshi bought her experience the hard way in the Tokyo temple and she is giving it gladly and freely for our benefit. If she had been willing to break the temple rules she could have saved herself the illness she had as a result of food deficiency but we would not have known of the problem nor would we have known how to deal with it and we would have suffered in consequence. We do not like having to tell you to bring food into the temple but we cannot honestly think of any other solution to the problem. This is another side of Bodhisattvahood; striving for perfection but accepting the inevitable when faced with a common sense problem. Next time someone does you a good turn gratis think about his or her Bodhisattva potential. Don't just say thank you and wonder what they're going to get out of it for doing it for you. And having thought, do something about discovering the joys of genuine gratitude.

I'm not quite sure what that young man's learning. He's certainly on the right lines although he hasn't got very far. But he worries me. He seems to be taking up cudgels in my defense like a white knight. I don't *need* one.[148] I'm quite complete without his assistance.[149]

I tried to tell this to Harry, as best I could without hurting his feelings, for I know that what he's doing he believes to be for my good and his reply was, "If you won't look after yourself then someone else must do it for you." Well, perhaps I'm *not* looking after myself. I feel very well. I'm doing plenty of work now; yesterday I started digging the pond in the garden. My body is beginning to get straighter. I hope that, by the time I do George's ordination, I shall be able to stand completely straight. No, I'm doing this all wrong. I must be very grateful to Harry. He's done a wonderful job looking after me. I know that he doesn't understand a lot of what went on in the Tokyo temple. I know that he's very angry with them about it. Until he can understand the mind of the master and disciple, until he can appreciate that which existed between Zenji Sama and I, he is going to feel anger at what went on and my duty now, my training, is to be patient with him and understand that what he is doing is for my good just as what was done in the temple in Tokyo was for my good. I will ask his forgiveness to-morrow for having had such wicked thoughts concerning him; for having even contemplated being angry with him over this.

2nd. April.

I explained to Harry what I wrote in my previous entry and asked his forgiveness for having misjudged him. I tried to explain to him that he and I, if we are to truly understand and practice Zen together, must try to practice it on the same level at the same time. I don't think he understood me so I told him to listen not to my words with his ears but with that part of him that meditated within his guts; then he would understand my meaning. He gave me a very strange look, made gasshō and went to meditate.

15th. April.

There are many, many ceremonies to-day. We have had so many funerals this year. There are so many memorials.

The author ordaining one of her disciples at Unpukuji.

16th. April.

George finished his robes and everything is ready for his ordination on the eighteenth.

18th. April.

I ordained George this morning; this is the first ordination done by my own wish. When I ordained Jim it was by order of Zenji Sama and so he was not really my disciple; he was his. The same is true of the Chinese girl but George is mine because I didn't *have* to do it. I didn't do it because there would be trouble if I refused; I did it because I wanted to. He is an extremely capable man but unfortunately has asthma which is not helped by the climate in this part of Japan. We had a big party afterwards. The priest from the local temple who has been helping me, as well as the woman priest from the other local temple, were also there.

The rebuilding of my temple is completed now, except for the roof, and it looks very beautiful. This ordination will be the first big ceremony we have had since the temple's completion.

I telegraphed Tokyo to tell them of George's ordination and several telegrams of congratulation arrived from the new Zenji Sama and the officers there. Since I am still officially working for them, although I am doing it down here, I felt that it was my duty to let them know. I telephoned Rev. Hajime and he said that I was quite right in sending the telegram. He told me that I should report everything of importance.

19th. April.

It was good having both Harry and George helping here with the many ceremonies that took place to-day. One of them played the mokugyo and the other the gongs; I was the celebrant. George has come to all the lectures and discussions that Harry and I have had in the past few weeks but he's extremely quiet and hardly ever offers an opinion except when alone with me.

23rd. April.

George went back to Tokyo this morning; I was sorry to see him go. It has been very enjoyable having him here.

26th. April.

I received a letter from Rev. Hajime congratulating me on George's ordination. He told me that I can have one new Chief Junior each year but not more and that I should find out from the priest who has been helping me how the necessary forms are filled in for this. He also told me that if I elevate the status of my temple, which would cost two-hundred thousand yen, I can have several Chief Juniors each year. I don't see the point of doing that. I can't see myself having more than one Chief Junior a year anyway. He says that if I do want more than one he, Rev. Hajime, will have to be the priest who does the ceremonies unless I pay the two-hundred thousand yen. He also said that George's ordination papers should be sent in by the priest who has been helping me; if I study them I will know how to write out future ones. If the priest cannot do them, or doesn't know how to, I should go to Rev. Hajime's temple on the first of May since he will be there on the thirtieth of this month. He then said something else. At the beginning of next month the governing body of our school of Zen will meet after which he thinks that many problems will be settled. I wonder exactly what problems he's talking about? I wonder if they have anything to do with the foreigners coming to the Tokyo temple?

27th. April.

I went to Tokyo to-day since Zenji Sama's state funeral will take place to-morrow. It is the first time I have made so long a journey since my illness. Tokyo looked very different from when I saw it last. I suppose I was still so ill I didn't really see it very clearly. I am staying in my old room; I never noticed how grubby and old it was before. It's really surprising. I had no idea it was in this state nor had I any idea that the authorities had never mended the mats on the floor. Odd how one doesn't notice such things when one is living in a place permanently. It is almost as though this is the only room they have never bothered to do anything about. There is also only one other room in the temple that has glass doors instead of paper ones. I asked Rev. Hajime about that once and he said that it was because this room and the one next door to it are not really in the temple. I asked him what he meant by that and he wouldn't answer me. It seems the Japanese make the distinction of using glass doors in houses for rooms that aren't really there. I asked another priest about this once and he said that such rooms were given to people who were unwelcome guests.

28th. April.

Zenji Sama's state funeral took place to-day; George came to the ceremony with me. I was told I must sit with Zenji Sama's disciples. Unfortunately the girl disciple who has always been very anti me objected to my sitting beside her and complained to the priest in charge of the seating arrangements. He told me to go and sit elsewhere. I did so and was grumbled at by the temple officers for not wishing to sit with my Zenji Sama's ashes. I went back to my rightful place behind the catafalque and the girl disciple complained again; so I took no notice whatsoever of either side and just sat there with Zenji Sama; it was the most sensible thing to do.

I have never been a demonstrative person but during the procession I was swept by such a flood of tears that I could not control them. Someone jumped up from the audience (it's a little difficult to call it a congregation for they were very noisy) and pushed a camera in my face to photograph me. I'm past caring with these people; in the old days, when I first came here, I would have been very angry. Now it doesn't matter at all. If they have no manners that is their problem.

When the ceremony was over there was a big feast and George and I, as members of (the dead) Zenji Sama's religious family, went to it. I was asked what we were doing there by one of the priests in charge. I was rather startled by this and said, "Why, I am Zenji Sama's foreign disciple." He huffed and went off to ask if this was true; presumably someone told him that it was. All the disciples, including George and I, were given copies of Zenji Sama's translation of the works of Keizan Zenji as well as a beautiful plate; Zenji Sama's calligraphy was painted on it.

When the meal was over and the gifts had been given out I went back to my room. Rev. Hajime came to see me. I told him what had happened at the ceremony and banquet and he became very angry.

"Who was it asked if you were Zenji Sama's disciple? Who was it said you couldn't sit there?"

"Forget about it, Rev. Hajime. It is over."

I thought of going to the bath house but decided against it. Why create problems? I can always go elsewhere. I walked along the corridors to take a look at the gardens and met one of my friends. He asked me if I was going to be at the Jōdō ceremony for the new Zenji Sama in the morning and I told him no.

"You're staying here the night though?" he said.

I stopped to think for a moment then I said, "No, I'm not. I'm going off now. This may be the last time you'll see me. I really don't know," and I held out my hand. He looked at it and then shook it.

"All right," he said with a grin, "foreign style."

We smiled and gasshōed. I went back to my room. The Director was there to see me, hovering by the door.

"Next time you come," he said, "if you do come again, will probably be the last time you will ever see me."

"Why, Reverend Director?"

"I will have to leave here very soon. I have told you that whilst I am here you will always be welcome but you would be well advised never to spend another night in this house."

"I will remember that, Reverend Director."

"You would be well advised also to remember that many overtures will be made to you; and there may be some threats. Politicians——. You must choose wisely. Will you promise me you will?"

"I'll try, Reverend Director."

"Come to my room for a cup of tea."

I went to his room and made the tea for him. We sat and looked at each other for a long time.

Then I said, "I'm going to stay with a Japanese friend of mine tonight just outside the city. I'm not going to stay here. I don't think it would be wise for I don't intend to come to the new Zenji Sama's Jōdō in the morning. He might be very unhappy to see foreigners there at the moment and, if he is friendly towards them, I don't want to cause him any problems with the officers that may antagonize him."

"You have to see him," he said.

"What about?"

"He's going to be giving out the gifts that Zenji Sama left for people and you are on the list. You will have to see him to-day."

"But it's already late, Reverend Director."

"It's only five in the evening. The gift-giving starts in about half an hour. Come, I will take you."

He took me to Zenji Sama's house, the house that had been specially built for him and in which all my brother and sister disciples were waiting for the new Zenji Sama. When my turn came I went up to him. He handed me a piece of paper informing me that a sum of money had been left to me by the will of the former

Chief Abbot. I thanked him. He was not very friendly nor were the officials around him. I bowed and left the room.

Outside the Director took both my hands in his and gasshōed them to his head. "Good-bye, Jiyu San," he said.

"Good-bye, Reverend Director." I turned and left Zenji Sama's house, collected up my small bag and went off to my friend's house.

29th. April.

My friend says that he is arranging for me to have another temple, much closer to Tokyo than my present one, so that I can look after the foreigners better. He is very angry over what has been happening at the big Tokyo temple. He feels that their attitude to foreigners is very wrong. It will be interesting to see what develops as a result of his work.

1st. May.

I returned to my own temple to-day and found Harry busily at work mending things. There have been quite a number of ceremonies and he has very competently handled them although he is a layman.

After I had rested he talked to me about what he wishes to do with this month's newsletter. It seems that fourteen people have written to complain that I ordained George but would not ordain them. It is true that quite a number of people have asked in the past but I refused to ordain them because I didn't think they understood the meaning of discipleship properly; I don't think that ordination should be entered into at all lightly or in a hurry. Bearing this in mind Harry has written quite a long piece about discipleship and the difficulties of being ordained in Japan. He also wrote a lot on the difficulties for women when living in Japanese monasteries; the innumerable privileges accorded men and the prejudices against women. Well, I suppose it is advisable for people to know these things and so enter monasteries with both eyes wide open. I suppose it is wise but it is indeed regrettable.

We now have a regular Zazenkai twice a month for the local villagers and anyone else who wants to come. It is proving very valuable. The village is much more behind us than it ever was before.

Unfortunately Harry will be leaving in July. He's always been one of those people that has itchy feet and he now wants to wander off again, this time to see what mainland China is like. I shall be very sorry to see him go. He has been one of the most helpful people, and one of the best friends, I have ever had; the sort of person whom you don't expect to do things but who always seems to come out of the woodwork when you're in need of help whilst those whom you always thought were your friends are busy trying not to be around.[150] Bearing in mind the fact that he is going to be going away, we put an advertisement in the newsletter for this month saying that I needed a permanent companion-assistant. Harry pointed out that financially it was a rotten job but a wonderful opportunity. Financially there's nothing attached to it at all. I very much doubt if he'll get any applicants but it was very kind of him to try.

6th. May.

George, who came down on the train with me from Tokyo to make sure I was safe, left to-day. It's amazing how much I am enjoying the company of my trainees. It is so very pleasant to have sincere people with whom to discuss religion. Every day I feel the wings beating softly. I wonder where they want to take me? I wonder if I'm imagining it?

15th. May.

A letter came from Rev. Hajime, a rather important letter. He sent the papers for the registration of George's ordination, telling me that I must send with them a copy of George's birth certificate and two photographs to prove that the ordination had taken place. Then he said something else. When I was in Tokyo for Zenji Sama's funeral I had again heard of the problems being caused by the very heavy hospital bill that I still have not been able to pay. Apparently the hospital sent it to the Tokyo temple authorities since I had said that I had no money, the hospital being of the opinion that they, being my employer, should pay it for me. Rev. Hajime told them that the temple would not touch the bill under any circumstances and telephoned the British Consul to tell him that paying it was the duty of the British authorities. The Consul was not pleased about this since he had told me that the only way he could pay the bill was if someone were to lodge a complaint against me and have me deported. Some time ago I asked the new Zenji Sama if he would be good enough to lend me the money on condition that I guaranteed to pay him back at a later date. According to Rev. Hajime's letter he is not willing to lend me anything at all and I know of no-one else with sufficient cash.

The letter ended very strangely, Rev. Hajime saying that he was coming down to his own temple. I have been asked to lecture at one of the temples of another school of Buddhism and I asked Rev. Hajime if this were permissible when I rang him this evening. He was quite cold about it and said that what I did was of no concern to anyone.

Whenever he ends a letter in the way he did the one that came this morning it means that he wants me to pay him a visit but, after what I heard him say, after hearing his tone of voice on the 'phone, I don't think I had better go. I must write to the hospital and explain to them that they should not, under any circumstances, write to the Tokyo temple about the money for the hospital bill. I don't know how I'm going to pay it—I honestly don't think I'll *ever* be able to pay it—and I know for certain that the Japanese never will. If Zenji Sama had lived there would have been no problem but it is different with the people who are in power now; such things are impossible.

We were having supper late this evening when a special delivery postcard arrived from Rev. Hajime to say that the temple in Tokyo, that has offered me work, wants me on the twenty-fourth of this month. I'm not at all sure how I'm supposed to get there unless they are paying my fare to do so. I cannot go back and forth to Tokyo any longer as I did in the old days; I just cannot afford it. I will ring the temple sometime to-morrow and find out what the arrangements are.

22nd. May.

I went to Tokyo to-day since the lecture that I am required for takes place on the twenty-fourth and I had promised some friends that I would stay with them whilst in the area. The temple I am lecturing at has paid my expenses and promises me a fee as well. My friends actually live beyond Tokyo in Saitama; they are the ones who are arranging a new temple for me in the Tokyo area. The husband, a very important Japanese and an extremely wealthy landowner, has quite a number of temples on his land; he is going to let me have one of the empty ones for the foreigners. He speaks excellent English and has been around the world several times. It was good seeing him this evening. We talked much about the new temple and to-morrow we shall go to see it. We shall also visit a priest who lives in another temple nearby under whose protection the empty temple has been for some time.

23rd. May.

I visited the priest I spoke of yesterday and he was overjoyed to see me. He is not of our school of Zen[151] but, as far as he is concerned, my being different does not matter; he just dislikes seeing empty temples. I did not realise that there were so many empty temples in the country. They are under the auspices of other priests, one priest having perhaps as many as six or ten. He lives in one and visits the others, as occasion requires, to do funerals. The particular temple they are thinking of for the foreigners is large but rather difficult to get to. In many respects I think it is more difficult to get to than is my own one in the west; there are far fewer buses. In addition to this the bus doesn't stop anywhere close but we will see how it is for people to get here, see which of the two is the most convenient and make our decision after a few months as to which we keep; the new one or the one in the west.

24th. May.

I went to the temple in Tokyo to-day and eventually lectured there. It was rather strange. I had understood I was *expected* to give a lecture. It had been arranged by a young priest and his wife, who know me very well, who speak excellent English. But the temple belongs to the young priest's father and mother and it seems that the younger pair had not fully checked out the willingness of their parents for me to give the lecture. This was very odd. I had been told they had agreed and were inviting me; now it seems they were unwilling for me to come although they sent the cash. I have a horrible feeling that their change of mind has something to do with the political machinations of the Tokyo temple or, worse still, stem directly from my 'phone call to Rev. Hajime. I have an equally horrible feeling that *he* is no *true* friend of mine but, if I do not trust *him*, *who* can I trust?

The mother, who is also a priest of their school of Buddhism, seemed particularly annoyed about my coming; I'm not quite sure what to make of her. She was obviously very worried about the political implications of having someone from an Imperial temple lecturing at her temple. I suppose it *is* all temple politics again. I really don't understand it and I don't very much care. I went along to lecture as required and that is what I've done. I shall be staying the night here.

There was a large banquet when the lecture was over during which the mother asked me many questions about the Tokyo temple. I felt that a lot of them were of a political nature and I sensed that it was very dangerous for me to answer them. It was very difficult to keep the conversation on something other than this. She seemed very anxious to know what the temple's attitude to foreigners was. I can see that I could be placed in some extremely difficult situations if I were to go to other temples regularly and yet I have to earn a living. The young couple definitely wanted me to come again but the parents obviously had second thoughts, all of them connected with the political dangers of having someone from the head temple. I sensed that if the Imperial Tokyo temple didn't want foreigners then no other temple should really consider them. I can see this attitude being a great danger to the foreigners here. I must think more and more about the possibilities of leaving Japan. England is definitely out; Malaysia is not a good idea for I can only stay there for a limited time. I can, of course, go to the temple in Tokyo, the new one, or I can stay at my one in the west, or I can go to one of the Commonwealth countries or to America. America would probably be the sanest place to go to since so many of the people I originally taught live there and would like to have me. But I just haven't the wherewithal on which to go and I see no means of getting it. So probably the best thing I can do is just sit still, either in the new temple or the one in the west, do what I can to obey Zenji Sama's orders to keep the foreigners together and see what happens. It is obvious that this is not the place to be; it is rampant with politics and I don't want to be played off against the Tokyo temple and this one by turns. That would be really terrible—and disastrous.

25th. May.

I went to the Tokyo temple this morning and visited Rev. Hajime. He was very unfriendly—very unfriendly indeed. It was as though we barely knew each other. I wonder what is wrong?

I told him of the possibility of the new temple and he said that he would go with me to see the officials to make sure that I would be all right there. Something in me feels worried about this; something about the way in which he said it. I find myself wondering, "Am I with a friend or an enemy?"[152] I wish I knew. There are no such things as enemies in *true* Buddhism but this temple has changed so much that I no longer really know it. The peace inside me is magnificent. The wings tell me, "Don't stay, don't stay, pass on by. These people are not Zenji Sama's any longer. You will always belong to him. Do not stay." But I *must* trust someone in a foreign country; if I don't trust Rev. Hajime who else *is* there to trust?

As I left Rev. Hajime's room I saw the Director waiting for me. He held my hands and said, "Whilst I am here you will *always* be welcome—understand? *Always.*" He then left me.

I have arranged to meet Rev. Hajime to-morrow outside one of the local train stations. We will meet the officials of the new temple together. I will spend the night with friends.

26th. May.

I met Rev. Hajime outside Shinjuku Station and the two of us went in a friend's car to the village where the new temple is situated. It is indeed a beautiful temple but it is far from anywhere and I find myself wondering if it will be possible for the foreigners to get here. I see no way unless they actually have cars of their own; it will be very difficult otherwise. The village council and the mayor talked with my friend and Rev. Hajime, discussing the possibility of my becoming the priest. It became obvious that Rev. Hajime was suggesting that I *didn't* become the actual priest of the temple, only its temporary caretaker. This rather surprised the council although some of them seemed to have been expecting it. It certainly surprised me. I cannot understand fully what is going on; I thought I was to become the priest. I know that my friend had told me that I would be caretaker temporarily, to see how the villagers and I liked each other, but it seems that Rev. Hajime is determined that that is all I ever shall be. He was constantly speaking about the priest who owns this temple as part of his string and saying that we had to consider how he would feel about a foreigner taking it. I was under the impression that this had already been arranged. I can see many sticky problems coming out of this. I must be very careful or there will be great difficulties.

After we had left Rev. Hajime at Shinjuku Station my friend told me that he felt that the villagers were not too happy at having Rev. Hajime there. Neither he nor they really trusted the officials of big and important temples. This had certainly come over very loudly during the interview. He asked me to return to his house and spend the night there. His wife was very kind and so were his family.

27th. May.

I went to the Tokyo temple to-day, out of politeness, to thank Rev. Hajime for having gone with me yesterday. He and I both went to see the Director. He told the Director that it was indeed a large and apparently very prosperous temple. He pointed out that the priest who owns it will be very upset at losing its revenues and that he was originally trained in the Tokyo temple. The Director was obviously unquiet about the whole matter and unhappy at what was being said. Rev. Hajime continued in this vein for some time saying how far off the temple was and how difficult it would be for the foreigners to get to; I almost felt as though I were stealing it from its rightful owner; his attitude was *so* negative.

After he had gone the Director took my hands in his again. "You are always welcome remember. But I think you should consider somewhere other than Japan. I shall not be here longer than next March at most. They may get rid of me sooner than that."

"Get rid of you, Reverend Director?"

"Yes, things like that happen in our school of Zen."

His comment reminded me of something I had been told a long time ago—something that I hadn't even noticed at the time as worthy of writing down—an instance that had happened when I had been here only a very short time. It was when people were arguing about my right to be in the Tokyo temple—whether or not Zenji Sama had really invited me. It was way back in my first year and I had deliberately hunted round to find the person who had been the interpreter for Zenji Sama when he was in London. He had been a teacher of English at one of the local universities and I had had great difficulty in finding him. Finally I managed to; he was working for an obscure company in Tokyo. He had been very anxious *not* to be found by me and, although I had set up the appointment, would only stay with me for a very few moments. I asked him why he was no longer teaching at the university and his answer had been, "When you know more about our school of Zen you will understand these things"—almost exactly the same words as those of the Director. Even at that early date he had been warning me of the political problems as had also the Director once so long ago—as Rev. Hajime had warned me of them and now as the Director was warning me of them again. I can remember asking this young interpreter about Zenji Sama's invitation—had he *really* invited me or not? and he had refused to give me a direct answer—yet he knew that Zenji Sama had; thus do politics change situations. I would be well advised to go somewhere else but I haven't the money. I will sit still, as I said yesterday, either in my own temple or in the new one, and see what happens.

I said good-bye to the Director. Each time we say good-bye he seems to look at me for a longer period as though he wants to take with him a lasting impression. I get so much of the feel of Zenji Sama from him; there is so much sadness in his heart and such complete acceptance of the situation.

I returned to my own temple. It was good to be home again.

28th. May.

Many ceremonies were waiting for me for several people who should have had memorials during the days I was away had held them over so that they could have them done when I got back. At about three in the afternoon we were finished and Harry wanted to talk about many things again. He wanted to understand clearly what it was that had happened when the British couple were here; he wanted to understand what it really meant to 'mirror' somebody as I had explained it to him.

"Why didn't it work?" he asked. "After all, Rev. Hajime is a very competent priest. Why couldn't they understand him?"

"Possibly because Rev. Hajime is no longer as excellent a priest as he once was."[153]

Harry stared at me. "What do you mean? He's an enlightened man."

"Enlightenment isn't something that stays with you just because you once had a kenshō; you have to work hard at your training to be really and truly enlightened. A master once said, 'Unless you keep up your meditation, unless you keep up your training, even the greatest kenshō will remain only a beautiful memory.'[154] You see, knowing that you have the potential of

Buddhahood is one thing; working on yourself at all times so that this potential will always show, so that you are always literally 'becoming Buddha,' as it says in the last part of the 'Hannyashingyō,' is quite another. Many people are satisfied with knowing of the possibility of Buddhahood within themselves without ever realising that the knowledge of the possibility entails doing something about it. There are those who think that because they have the Buddha potential they need to do nothing. I watched Rev. Hajime; I worshipped at his shrine; I thought him the most intelligent, most holy priest I had ever seen. I watched him as he taught when a simple lecturer in the Tokyo temple—a joy to behold, someone in whose Truth one could lie back and bask. Then I watched contrivance appear. I saw him behaving like a saint in others' presence but as a selfish man in mine. I was a nuisance. One time I saw him he told me I and other foreigners would be welcome as servants but nothing more. The next minute he was smirking and fawning over his foreign guests whilst hating them in his heart. Naturally they wouldn't believe me if I were to tell them such things. You know, in many respects the priests who marched up and down the Hondō with their pride showing were a lot better than was he when he walked in one morning, deliberately trying to look artless, deliberately humble—you knew he wasn't because you could feel something stirring within him—ambition. This was the day he said to me that he didn't want advancement in the temple simply because he was helping me. At the time I couldn't work out what it was that worried me about him; now I know. It was the recognition within himself that I could be very useful to him and the fact that he didn't like the knowledge. One of the troubles with a big place like that Tokyo temple is that to remain a saint within it may mean going completely against the will of the majority."

"Do you realise what you're saying?"

"Yes, that saints aren't to be found in great temples; they're where I found them—in back streets—or else trying to do a magnificent job against incredible odds as were Zenji Sama, the Director and some of the very old seniors."

"What went wrong with what was being done with that British couple?"

"Self was still in the way. Rev. Hajime was *trying* to teach them something. When a priest mirrors another person he doesn't deliberately *try* to reflect anything. He should have his own self so much out of the way that the other person reflects in him quite naturally. The moon and its reflection are one but Rev. Hajime and that couple were not. There was Rev. Hajime who was trying to teach and there was the couple that were to be taught; so he was using contrivance in the mirroring rather than just using that which came naturally, rather than being completely himself—with no *visible* self—and therefore a reflector for what was in front of him. Can you understand what I'm trying to say?"

"I think so," he replied, "but not completely."

"Do you remember that other couple that came up from Kyoto—that very strange pair who, after they came here—? Do you remember I told you that I felt that they were evil, really evil and I didn't know the reason why? They were interested in manipulating people, and they wanted to see what would happen to people in stress situations. They had caught me, as they thought—a tame Zen master living alone—and could put me into stressful situations and see what would happen. I can remember the husband telling me that I needed to be taught how to eat spaghetti and I told him I didn't need to learn. He then said, 'But if you want me to stay in your house you must allow me to teach you many things. After all, that is what I've come for.' I pointed out to him that I hadn't invited him to come to my house nor had I asked to become his student; he had asked me if he could learn Zen; either he came and learned or he could get out. After that they spent hours and hours trying to put me under stress. One of the things that kept me from being in difficulties was the fact that I was ringing the gong every hour on the hour and holding myself very still inside. It infuriated them because all I was doing was going on with my work without getting involved in their manipulations. I was not *trying* to create an artificial situation so there was no way they could get at me. They managed to get at some of the other temple priests in the places they visited.

"What I'm trying to say, in a very mixed-up way of course, is that this pair were trying to mirror others without ever having done anything about themselves; their mirroring was an attempt at controlling the minds of others; and Rev. Hajime was fast going along the same road. Someone who truly mirrors another knows that the moon and its reflection are one and that there is no difference whatsoever between them. This is real mirroring—the mirror image which is not separate from the real thing. All is one and all is different. You must understand the 'all is one' and the 'all is different.'"

"I've never heard you talk like this before."

"That's primarily because you've always discussed very earthy matters. It's worrying when you just discuss worldly things. I want you to go to much higher ones and stop worrying about silly people."

"But if I don't know the mistakes they made how am I going to know how not to make them myself?"

"Well, try to understand that any situation that is controlled or contrived is the result of the egocentric self's will; anything that arises naturally is not contrived by the egocentric self's will. Remember the difference between deliberate thought and natural thought during meditation? It is *deliberate* thought that you have to cut off; natural thought is right and unavoidable. You cannot avoid hearing a dog barking outside when you are meditating; it is not going to damage your meditation unless you deliberately think, 'What a nuisance—a dog is barking.' You should understand mirroring from that angle. If you meditate properly just there is a dog barking and you continue to sit; you have not thought about the thought; you have not taken it apart, analyzed whether it is annoying *you* or not—just you have continued to sit. Do you remember I told you of how I asked Rev. Hajime—I think it was Rev. Hajime, I can't remember now—about the problem of wandering thoughts during meditation and he said, 'This morning under my robe a flea was walking; just I noticed it had strong legs'? That's how you have to think of wandering thoughts—don't *deliberately* think; be natural. Mirroring is done in the same way. Natural mirroring is quite right for then one catches the Lord as He flashes by. But contrived mirroring is willful and ends in brainwashing—it's dangerous, wrong and evil for it is a *deliberate* attempt to control another being and to usurp the prerogative of the Lord of the House."

"This is the first time I've ever heard you say anything about Rev. Hajime."

"I know, and it's very wicked of me to have done so. But I've watched him change so much over the years. In the end I found myself putting on the brakes for fear of what I might learn from him. I can remember standing, as it were, on the edge of a precipice and realising that he was hurtling over it; and I put on my brakes to stop myself following him. After that the Director started teaching me. I think he knew that I needed to go on and that the person I was with had ceased his training in the real sense.

"There are pitfalls all the way, Harry, both for new trainees and for masters; you need to know and remember that. I've found them—so help me *have* I found them! If Zenji Sama were here I know he would agree with me on this."

"But don't some people, in the early stages, deliberately mirror others?"

"If you get someone in a temple in the very early days who absolutely will *not* understand what is going on deliberate mirroring is sometimes used. An American acquaintance of mine in another big temple was given a mirror trainee who went with her everywhere and was scolded, beaten and grumbled at all day long whilst, in fact, it was she that they wanted to scold and beat. She cottoned on to what was happening in the space of a few hours and wrote an article about it saying how, in the end, she screamed inside herself with the horror of what she was really like. Oh, yes, it is done occasionally but for it to work you've got to have somebody who's really very, very sincere and you only want to do it once; if it doesn't work that once you never want to try it again."

"Maybe Rev. Hajime thought that that British couple had got that far."

"He may have thought it as a result of what their letters said but when he met them he should have realised that their words didn't match their behaviour at all. He should never have attempted mirroring under the circumstances. So often people's words are excellent but their knowledge of Buddhism, as shown within their actions, is non-existent. A true Buddhist can show his understanding of the 'all is one' and 'all is different' at all times in every movement he makes. He shows the reflection of the moon to be the moon itself and the moon itself to be the reflection; and he can exhibit this in the way in which he lifts the needle or waves the hossu or eats his food. Harry, I'm awfully tired. Can we stop for now?"

"If you really want to but this is getting very interesting."

"I'll talk more about it to-morrow or the day after, depending on what we've got time to do. We've got to start the newsletter to-morrow."

We left the subject and I went into my room to rest. I still get these dizzy spells. I wonder what they are? There's a sort of dull headache at the back of my head. Well, I wasn't imagining the last thing so I suppose I'm not imagining these either. But I certainly haven't the cash to have them checked out. I doubt, as things are, if I ever shall.

2nd. June.

A card came from Rev. Hajime. He thanked me for my letter (I had written to him concerning the new temple, telling him that I felt that he was perhaps not a hundred percent behind my idea of going there). Regarding the many things that I told him, he wishes to talk when I see him next time. He writes that the new staff around the new Zenji Sama seems to be trying to get rid of us by making several rumours and that we are in the process of fighting with them. No letters have come from foreigners for Zenji Sama. All the letters that have come have been sent off to me. He says that I do not need to pay the postage.

I had also written to say that several of my friends felt that their letters weren't getting through to me since they had not had replies. I wonder what the rumours are that he is talking about?

I showed this card to Harry.

"Do you think the rumours he's talking about are concerning you and him?"

"I honestly don't know," I replied. "The card specifically says that the new staffs are trying to get rid of *us* by making rumours and that *we* are fighting with them. I'm not fighting with anybody; I'm not even there so I don't really see how it *can* be me. But, knowing Rev. Hajime's knowledge of English, it could *well* be me."

"What could they be making a rumour about now?"

"Don't ask me! When somebody wants to make a rumour it's very easy to do. You know that as well as I do. Let's get on with the newsletter—that's a lot more important."

"What shall we write about this month?" he asked.

"Well, we have an ordination. You remember that psychiatrist from one of the bases who wants to be ordained—one of the original eight who was with Zenji Sama for the first big Jūkai? He's coming down sometime to be ordained. We can certainly write about that."

"What's his name?" he asked.

"Fred," I answered.

"Ah, yes, I remember him. That's one article," he said. "Good. What else?"

"Well, there's the possibility of opening the Foreign Section in the Tokyo temple as well as that of opening it in the other one that my friend has found for me. I don't think we should put the last in just yet, however, just in case it falls through."

"What are the possibilities of our opening up again in the Tokyo temple, the royal one?"

"As far as I can understand the new Zenji Sama wants a study group rather than actual disciples. He's not too happy about the idea of having foreign disciples—thanks, I suspect, to the behaviour of certain people who were in the original group with Zenji

Sama. But there weren't all that number of problems—I know that and so do you. There were four-hundred people; out of them three or four caused difficulties. But it's always the three or four that cause difficulties that stick out like sore thumbs. They're the ones that everybody hears about; not the three-hundred and ninety-six. The three or four are the ones that the new Zenji Sama is talking about right now; he prefers a study group."

"Yes."

"So we'll put that in too."

"All right."

"We can put something in about the Zazenkai. We should also, I think, make sure that the people who pay subscriptions for the newsletter send them to the Tokyo temple rather than here; Tokyo is paying me to do this job."

"Do you think that's wise? If they are trying to get rid of you . . . ."

"Who ever said anything about that?"

"Well, I don't know; I wonder sometimes. If they are they would have all the cash and the addresses of the subscribers— and you'd be left in the lurch."

"I don't believe that of them; I *can't* believe it of them."

"O.K., if you want to act that innocent— —."

"Harry, there are times when you worry me very much."

"All right, have it your way."

"We should also put in something about the new main altar," I said quickly in order to change the subject. "It's completely finished but not yet paid for."

"All right, we'll do just that. Have you written a lecture yet?"

"No. I'll do one on books this afternoon."

5th. June.

A large number of people arrived to-day from one of the American universities. The class is, at the moment, travelling round the country to various seminars. They are going to be here for about a week. One of the professors who came with them seems to be very concerned that Zen is going to try and take over the world, everything he believes in and has ever believed in. One feels worried about such people. Zen doesn't do things like that; it's not out to control the world. It's funny what these psychologists think up.

9th. June.

Harry left this morning for a couple of days to attend to personal affairs. Also, this morning I ordained Fred. He arrived, together with his wife and two children, and we had a very pleasant ceremony. It was unfortunate that I had not been able to get all the forms sorted out before his arrival but I really didn't know that he was coming to-day; his letter has not reached me. There was nothing prepared in the way of paper work but that can be done later. I sent a telegram to the Tokyo temple explaining to them that I had just ordained the second one of the eight of Zenji Sama's original disciples.

Rev. Hajime who, it seems, is on a visit to his temple, rang me up to say that he was coming over to see Fred and was very upset that he had not been able to come to the ordination. Had I known that he'd been in his own temple I would have been glad to invite him.

10th. June.

Rev. Hajime arrived to-day instead of yesterday. Since Fred and his wife and family had stayed in my temple he was still able to see and talk with them. He brought Fred a present.

I asked him what exactly the rumours were that he had written about on his last card and he said, "Did I write about any? Oh . . . ." and that was all. One wonders about that man sometimes.

He talked to Fred for a long time and then I told him that we were planning to have another Kessei here in September so that George could become Chief Junior before I went to the new temple. He promised that he would come as the lecturer.

12th. June.

A number of people have arrived and, apart from our daily lectures, we are very busy perfecting the garden, putting in many beautiful trees. The pond is now finished and we are about to build a fountain; we'll then stock the pond with fish. The mayor has promised a load of gravel for the paths to complete the garden and it should look very beautiful when it is done.

We are also starting the Wesak dance classes for the local children. Admittedly Wesak will be about a month late this year but the children love the idea and we will celebrate it in the garden.

30th. June.

We had Wesak, the Buddha's birthday celebration, to-day. All the flowers and trees were in full bloom. The sun streamed down on the lovely garden and the statue of the Baby Buddha, underneath its flower-trimmed canopy, was on the steps outside the front door of the temple. The place was exquisite; the joy around wonderful. All the parents came to watch the children, wearing their best kimonos, dance. A friend of mine came from a nearby temple to lecture.

1st. July.

Harry and I started work to-day on the last newsletter he will do before he leaves. As this is our fifth anniversary he wants to do a special article on our history and how the Foreign Section started rather than have me write a lecture. I have agreed to this. We put something in about the book of my lectures that is being published in Singapore. We spoke of the Sesshin and the fact that George will be doing his Chief Junior during that time. We also said that I would be in Tokyo from the twelfth to the eighteenth of this month. I am going to see the new temple again although I don't know if I like the idea of having it; I have grown very happy here. But we will see.

Harry was very concerned about a Buddhist priest in England who, at the moment, is having a lot of difficulties. Someone, it seems, is trying to give him a very bad reputation. Harry wanted me to take up cudgels in his defense.

"No," I replied, "there is no point in it."

"But you can't just let them sacrifice him like this."

"If there are true Buddhists in England they will meditate and their hearts will tell them the truth of the situation. As for the rest, let them go their own way—leave them be; there is nothing we can do."

"But you can't just leave people like this."

"Yes, you can and sometimes you have to; sometimes there is no alternative. Get on with your meditation; leave them to get on with their meditation—and let those who want to make rumours and fight, the scandalmongers, get on with making rumours, scandalmongering and fighting. There is nothing else one *can* do. If he is a true priest he will sit still within his own heart as I did long ago; there will be no problem."

"Well, if you won't write something about it then I will!"

"That is up to you—you are a free agent, Harry."

"Can I quote what you said?"

"About what?"

"That if they are true, all they will do is meditate?"

"You may tell them from me to get on with their meditation and leave those who want to fight to fight. That is *all* you may tell them from me." I turned from him and went to my room.

12th. July.

I went to Tokyo to-day and visited the Tokyo temple to make arrangements for some of the foreigners who, it seems, are having difficulties in getting hold of me; I also took several articles to the newspaper for which I am now working since it was on my way. The atmosphere in the temple is very strange; it does not feel right. The Director seems to be going round in a little shell of his own, isolated in the midst of everything.

I asked Rev. Hajime about the rumour—I wanted to know what it was but again he wouldn't tell me. I feel sure that it has something to do with me but he will not speak. He was extremely unfriendly until the last moment of my visit, quite different from when he visited me in my temple. I stayed only a short while—just long enough to complete my business. I have far too many friends in the area to stay in a place where I feel so uncomfortable—and I have much too much work to do.

14th. July.

I spent yesterday with friends in Tokyo and to-day I am looking after the affairs of the new temple. I shall be moving in sometime in September and I have to make a lot of arrangements with regard to furnishings and various other things. I shall be staying there for a period of two weeks out of each month; this way it will be fair to both the temple in the west and to this one. I made an attempt to find the priest whom Rev. Hajime says owns it. I wanted to talk to him since I had heard so many rumours about his unwillingness for me to have it, but it seems extraordinarily difficult to find him.[155]

16th. July.

After much work with many friends here in Tokyo I am returning to my own temple to-day.

17th. July.

I received a letter from Kyoto. I am going to be lecturing there on the twenty-third of this month and the friend who had originally promised to look after me says that she will be glad and happy to see me on that date, or possibly the day before. She also wants to know if my 'phone has been connected yet. It's been in some time—I thought she knew. The rest of her letter was simply gossip about various Britons we know. She is glad that I have recovered.

22nd. July.

Went to Kyoto to-day and was able to meet my friend. She was unfortunately very busy at her own temple and so could only spare an hour for me which we spent in a coffee shop. I stayed at another friend's temple—not the one at which she was staying. It was obvious that she was not happy at the idea of my going there and I didn't press the point.

23rd. July.

The lecture, which was to an American university class studying here in Kyoto, went extremely well. Many of the students are coming to my own temple to continue their studies.

28th. July.

I've been making arrangements for George's Chief Junior which will coincide, of course, with my again doing Kessei. I have also been busy with raising the status of the temple; to-day the confirmation arrived. It is good to know that I and the temple now have the right to do many other ceremonies.

A letter came from Rev. Hajime enclosing the receipts for the cash I had sent to the Administration Section for Kessei and raising the temple's status. I had previously complained to him about one of the junior trainees sent to help me because of his incompetence. Now Rev. Hajime was considerably annoyed. Whether he is annoyed or not, I refuse to pay out money, hard-earned money from the American point of view, for people to help me here if they are incompetent at the job.

Harry left this morning; I was very sorry to see him go. The rebuilding of the temple is now complete except for the roof which the villagers themselves will be doing in a few weeks' time. I'm going to miss Harry but the wanderlust has caught him again; I hope he finds what he is looking for. I had to come all the way to Japan—I wonder where he has to go to, all the way from New Zealand?

31st. July.

A card came from Rev. Hajime apologising for complaining about my comments concerning the junior who didn't know how to recite the Scriptures. He has tested several others and discovered that two of them do not even know how to recite the "Hannyashingyō." It is very easy for this sort of thing to happen in a temple as big as the Tokyo one where people are constantly having to ask off from ceremonies and classes because of conflicting duties. And it's so easy not to notice who is and is not in a class when the class is of over two-hundred people.

Rev. Hajime says he cannot come down as early as he had hoped on the first; he will only be able to arrive here on the second because the new Zenji Sama and many of the officers of the Tokyo temple are temporarily away and will not be back until the first. He asks if I can rearrange some of the Kessei ceremonies so as to be certain that he can be here for all of them. He does say, however, that if it's not possible he won't mind. I really don't think that it is possible. I can't put off a whole lot of people just because he isn't here.

George arrived late this afternoon; he has got all the necessary things ready for his Chief Junior. A new young man, Robert, also arrived; he is going to act as cook for the Sesshin. I worry a bit about him. He seems to be very much involved in doing things at very high speed. If I were—well, no, I'm not a doctor; I can't make that sort of a decision—but he does remind me of someone I once met who suffered from manic-depression. I hope he's not ill. He says he had an extremely rough time with the trainees in the Tokyo temple, one of whom, when he stayed there the night, was particularly obnoxious.[156] I must try and find out more about that.

1st. August.

Sesshin started to-day and so did Kessei. George is doing a magnificent job as Chief Junior. Unfortunately a couple of the trainees who have come to help me from other temples, since there are over thirty people here, are causing considerable problems by spending money on food and various other things that the temple can ill afford. I hope that this does not continue. I have had to tell them very firmly to take the food back. This caused a lot of trouble but there was no alternative.

Robert is also causing quite a bit of trouble. He is convinced the world is against him.

The newsletter will be late this month owing to Sesshin—there is no alternative to that.

434 · THE WILD, WHITE GOOSE

2nd. August.

Rev. Hajime arrived early this morning and was overjoyed to see the temple so beautifully mended and the garden blooming. He was amazed at the new Meditation Hall. George did his Chief Junior well and all the ceremonies went well too. The manager of the local head office was duly impressed with what he saw. The Americans who are here (most of them young) are all extremely keen but the intense heat is not helping the Sesshin and we have had to put up five electric fans in the Meditation Hall. All the girls are sleeping in what was originally the club and which will, when finished, become a separate Meditation Hall. An elderly lady has very kindly consented to look after them. She fussed about them as though they were the royal princesses. Most of them understood it as kindness; only one or two found it annoying.

8th. August.

Sesshin ended to-day and we were able to start work on the newsletter. The news this month consists mainly of information with regard to the Sesshin and the fact that Segaki will be held on the twenty-fifth. I am concerned about Robert. He seems to be deteriorating fast. The only time he is really competent is when he is able to rush round and not think about anything, when he can work himself into a frenzy. If he has to sit still and think he becomes very strange and ill.

George and I have been working on getting the papers sorted out for the administration. He leaves for Tokyo to-morrow.

16th. August.

Robert has now become extremely ill. He spent all day yesterday being so terribly paranoid that I became quite frightened—not frightened in the sense that I was afraid of what would happen to me but of what was going to happen to him. I notified a doctor friend of mine on the base where he works of his condition. There is no doubt in my mind that this young man is very seriously ill. There are things I cannot even confide to this diary for they would be too dangerous; and I was so exhausted yesterday from trying to keep him on the right side of sanity that I couldn't write anything.

Last night Robert started screaming because his room was only separated from mine by paper walls and he said that he could not possibly sleep that near someone else because of the fear of them taking him over, of being possessed. I took a bed out into the garden. Sleeping there meant getting bitten by the mosquitoes but at least Robert felt safe.

17th. August.

This morning I took Robert to the train and said good-bye to him; I do hope he sees the doctor. Life really is sitting beneath the eternal Bo tree; every day the demons attack, every day comes the eternal kyosaku; every day one is enlightened by calling the earth to witness the effort of eternal training and meditation. Now I know why a master cannot handle delusion cases until many years after his own understanding.

I went to Rev. Hajime's temple in order to help there. His wife was extremely cold. The whole atmosphere of this temple has changed amazingly from when I was last here. Then I had actually begun to think that Rev. Hajime's wife was beginning to like me a little but now she is looking at me most peculiarly and making it quite obvious that she does not want me here. I asked Rev. Hajime if it were possible for me not to come to help in future, since I did not wish to so upset his wife, but he said that I was imagining things. He insists that I stay here the night.

18th. August.

I stayed the night very unwillingly and this morning the wife was ruder than ever before. Rev. Hajime's disciples are copying her and Rev. Hajime, although in English he is saying he is against what they are doing, is encouraging them to do it when he speaks Japanese. He forgets that I speak Japanese well enough to know what he is saying. In one breath he tells me not to worry about what is going on and in the next is aiding and abetting it. As soon as the ceremonies were over I got ready to leave but he refused to let me, insisting that I stay another night because the villagers would talk about him if I didn't. I still wanted to go and he threatened to give me no more help with the authorities unless I stayed. Knowing how dangerous this could be for both me and the other foreigners I agreed very unwillingly to stay.

19th. August.
I returned to my own temple this morning.

25th. August.
Another letter came from my friend in Kyoto. It contained much the same things that her letters have always contained—promises of meetings and nothing more—hopes that friends of mine will take me to Kyoto to see her. I'm getting rather tired of this sort of letter.

The British friend who has been kindly helping me with my moving, etc., arrived to-day with a relative of his plus several boxes of things that I had left in various places. He intends to take me to Kyoto for a day out. George also arrived.

George had problems registering his Chief Junior papers with the local Administration Section. They insisted that I, as a woman, cannot have a male Chief Junior since no man would study under a woman—ergo, George is not a man! We took George along to the local Administration Office. My British friend stayed outside whilst George and I went in; the local priest who has been such a good friend to me in the past also went. The official there refused to do anything with regard to the papers—I could not have a male Chief Junior and that was that. I pointed out to him that I had already got one, that the ceremony was already done; he said that George *must* be a woman. I explained that Rev. Hajime understood that George was a *man* and so did the Tokyo temple officials; George offered, if necessary, to prove that he was male. The official told him he could have the certificate but it would have to say that he was a woman. I said that Rev. Hajime was willing to be responsible for the situation. The official grudgingly put the seals on the papers and told me to take them to Tokyo. Rev. Hajime was senior to him so if he said it was all right then it was not his responsibility. I *must* find some priest to take Rev. Hajime's place. Having to stay in his temple is a high price to pay for such dubious advantages as using his name provides.

26th. August.

My British friend took us sightseeing to-day to several different places. It was very enjoyable for I have done almost no sightseeing in Japan and one of the things I am looking forward to is being able to go round and see something of the actual countryside.

27th. August.

I went to Tokyo to-day. One of my main purposes in doing so was, of course, to take the papers for Rev. Hajime's seals so that they can go to the Administrative Branch. There was absolutely no problem with the seals, however the Administration Section now says that I've put the papers in too late for this season so they are going to have to ante-date George's Chief Junior by three months. I agreed.[157] I really cannot be bothered with arguing about this sort of thing any longer.

I went to stay with the friend who has arranged the new temple; the last details were finalised for my moving in. However, I was still unable to get hold of the actual priest who owns this particular temple. Since I move in some time in September I feel I really must contact him.

28th. August.

I returned to the Tokyo temple. The atmosphere with regard to foreign guests was very, very strange so I did not stay there.

29th. August.

I returned to the Tokyo temple to-day and found an Australian woman and an American pianist there. It was odd that both were in the Vice-Abbot's guest department instead of being in either my, or Rev. Hajime's, rooms. The whole atmosphere was one of:– keep all foreigners as far out of here as possible.

Rev. Hajime and the others were still polite in a way but not *really* polite. I wanted to get away as soon as I could. I promised I would take the Australian to my own temple in the morning. Both are spending the night temporarily at a hotel in Tokyo.

I spent the evening with George, the two of us discussing many things with regard to Buddhism. Rev. Hajime is of the opinion that George is ready for Transmission. I am not sure about this; I personally do not think that he *is* ready for Transmission, but since it is Rev. Hajime's opinion, and so *may* have been Zenji Sama's, I'm going to go ahead with the Transmission ceremony. I shall write for the silks.

30th. August.
Returned to my own temple with the Australian.

5th. September.
A card came from Rev. Hajime to-day. I really think they must have their affairs in an awful muddle in that Administration Section. This card says that they have decided to make an exception in George's case and accept his papers for Chief Junior. Will I please send them back to them. As I understood it this had already been arranged and they'd already got them! At the same time Rev. Hajime says I should send in the Transmission papers so that the silks may arrive on time for George to do his Transmission. The card ended by saying that everything was going very well and that he wanted to write. How different he is on paper from what he is when I meet him. There is something very odd going on in his temple and in the one in Tokyo—and, above all, in him.

The Australian woman is creating a lot of problems with regard to training. She has great objections to what it is. She is like the Chinese girl who suffered from the idea that all you had to do in Zen was sit still and everything would be done for you.

I have been packing a few things ready for going to the new temple.

17th. September.

Another letter came from Rev. Hajime to-day. It said that the Administration Section has accepted George's Chief Junior and is now waiting for his seal so that they can send his Transmission papers. I had asked Rev. Hajime several things about the advisability of performing ceremonies in the new temple since I have not yet been able to meet the priest who owns it; Rev. Hajime's answer was rather strange. He said that the previous "housekeeper" was asked to start doing ceremonies gradually and that it will be the same with me. He says that it is best that way. I can't help feeling that I had better stay in my own temple, where I definitely *am* the priest, rather than try to move in such an uncertain situation but, if I do not take the temple, my friend will be very upset after all the work he has done. Rev. Hajime says I should ask the priest of the other local temple about the legal owner. He also says that the new Zenji Sama has shown no change from when I met his son during my last visit. He is still, I suppose, not interested in foreigners. I do not know what else he can be referring to. I don't remember meeting the son.

The last part of Rev. Hajime's letter was almost sinister. He said that he has been thinking about the quarrel between us when we went to the Administration Section and to my new temple and he has found that the fault was his. He then likened himself to someone who carries something and feels that it is becoming heavier but who cannot throw it away. He asked me what such a person feels about it and said that that was his feeling now and he did not know the reason.

I had not been conscious of the fact that we were quarelling. I knew that he was not at ease and I knew that he was very angry over the fact that I had a man for a Chief Junior and was thus causing problems with the Administration Section. Yet they themselves had said in the first place that it was all right and so had Zenji Sama. One minute they say I am to do these things and the next that I am not to. I remember asking them if they were also angry about his ordination and was he all right, was he really ordained? They had said yes, any woman could ordain anyone. I had then asked about Chief Juniors and they said, sometimes yes, sometimes no. It is not *customary* for a woman to have a male Chief Junior. I asked them why they had permitted me to go ahead if they were so uncertain and they had no answer.

I am sorry if I am becoming a burden to Rev. Hajime. I knew that something was wrong but this is the first sign he has made openly concerning it. I must make sure that he does not have to bear anything unnecessarily because of me. I really wonder about what is going on in that Tokyo temple; I know there is much more than I am hearing of.

18th. September.

A film company from Canada wants to make a film of village life in Japan. I have been making the necessary arrangements for them but there are considerable problems since they wish, of all things, to photograph a Japanese family bathing together. Quite reasonably the Japanese feel that this is not polite—I honestly don't blame them.

20th. September.

The Australian woman is refusing to do any training whatsoever and is pretending to be ill. I know there is nothing wrong with her but there is nothing I can do. The weather is very hot and she insists on having almost every piece of bedding in the temple around her in a temperature that is eighty-five in the shade. What is really wrong is she wants attention.

21st. September.

The Australian declared that she was better to-day and wanted me to take her sightseeing in Kyoto and Nara. She says that she will pay all expenses. I feel worried about going for I don't feel that she can be trusted. Anyway, I agreed to go with her. On arrival in Kyoto she made several very unfortunate scenes about the cost of the hotel. I foresee a very gruelling three days. I should have trusted my instincts.

24th. September.

I am extremely glad to be back from Kyoto. The whole visit was a fiasco. The Australian is again saying that she is ill and can do absolutely nothing. She spends all her time lying in bed.

26th. September.

George arrived and the Australian was immediately better. George is ready for his Transmission; the papers and silks arrived to-day. The Administration Section may or may not have objections to my doing things, I really don't know, but it works awfully hard to make sure that I get everything on time to do them with—even if it makes difficulties about their being registered. They sent a certificate giving me the right to do sanzen together with the silks; so I now have my teaching certificate ratifying Zenji Sama's True Transmission.

27th. September.

George started the written part of his Transmission to-day. He'll be doing the paper work first; this is fortunate since the Canadian film unit will be here to-morrow.

28th. September.

The Canadian film unit arrived as well as many of the priests whom I had arranged to come for the ceremonies they wished to film. The Australian got up, completely recovered as I suspected she would be when the filming started.

29th. September.

The Australian is trying to cause estrangement between George and I. It is extraordinarily unfortunate that she is here during his Transmission.

One of the people from the Canadian film unit telephoned me to complain about being charged a thousand yen each for the services of the priests who came yesterday. She seemed shocked at finding out that one does have to pay people who work in this country just as one has to pay them in others!

4th. October.

It is fortunate that George has so much to write otherwise this Australian would cause him unbelievable problems. I have suggested she leaves and have telephoned to my British friend, the one who took me to Kyoto, to say that, if he is in the area of my temple, could he possibly come by, collect her and take her back to Tokyo. She says she cannot possibly travel alone and George must look after her. George doesn't know quite what to do and I foresee problems if she is still here on the day when he does his Transmission ceremony; at the moment I see no way in which this can be avoided.

5th. October.

George's Transmission day to-day and the Australian is insisting that she comes to the ceremony. No Transmission has ever been witnessed by anyone other than the priest, the disciple and the priest's assistant who is usually in the same line as that of the priest or master doing the ceremony. I tried vainly to explain this to the Australian and got a girl in to keep her company during the ceremony itself but she spent most of the day crying and saying that I am casting her off and refusing to let her see things. This evening she went into a torrent of rage, screaming that I was doing secret witch ceremonies to harm others. Fortunately George was bathing and so out of ear-shot. She has so much the attitude of mind of a voyeur that just having her near me is sickening.[158] Whether George was ready for his Transmission or not I know one thing for certain—what has been going on has definitely concerned and upset him. I hope and pray that it may not harm his training.

6th. October.

We completed George's Transmission at midnight. The Australian woman created an atrociously bad atmosphere but the ceremony went, on the whole, well. I think, however, it would have gone a lot better if we had not had the Australian here.[159]

It is possible that he was not ready—very possible. But many such ceremonies have been done in the past on people

who were not completely ready and, at a later date, they understood fully what had happened; I do not feel that there is anything to worry about. It has always been George's way to
believe that he wasn't really sincere or wasn't really interested.
For a man who is not interested in Zen, or not really sincere
about it, I have never seen anybody work so hard. He does
excellent training every day of the week. This Transmission
will be all right but it may take a year or two to crystallise.

My British friend arrived with his car and has agreed to take
all of us back to Tokyo. I, in any case, have to move in to the
new temple and officially take it over so, since he has such a
large car, I have been able to pack all the stuff I need to take
with me. I am not taking more than I absolutely need—just the
bare essentials. Something tells me that this temple is not going
to work out—I don't know why. My friend is going to start late
this evening because he wants to drive throughout the night. He
has a strange liking for visiting shrines late in the evening and
he wants to visit the one in Ise before we go. That means that
we've got something like a twelve to fourteen hour journey
through the night.

7th. October.

We arrived in Tokyo this morning. The Australian complained most of the night about the lack of room in the car and
because I had taken little Tom in a basket at my feet. She is of
the opinion that the cat has been horribly spoiled ever since she
arrived. Considering the state the poor little creature was in
when I first saw him the least I can do is try and give him some
comfort now. We left the Australian at a hotel. She said good-
bye to George and my friend and gave me a triumphant sneer
over her shoulder as she swept through the hotel door; it was one
of the most expensive hotels in Tokyo. Both George and my
friend were obviously embarrassed. George went to his club.

We got to the new temple to discover that it was still locked
and that no arrangements whatsoever had been made for my
arrival. I got my friend, after leaving my things at one of the
houses in the village, to take me to the Tokyo temple whilst the

necessary arrangements were made. When I arrived there it was obvious that no foreigner whatsoever was welcome. I waited in Rev. Hajime's room for him to come, hoping he might explain what was going on. His assistant walked in with a broom and started sweeping—an extremely rude thing to do when someone is sitting in a Japanese room. He informed me that if I didn't get out he would sweep the dust over me. I went to the Director's room and found that he was just getting ready to go out.

"I'm going temporarily to my temple in the north," he said, "I told you that whilst I was here you would always be welcome but I am the last of Zenji Sama's people. Do *not* come back to this temple."

"I have nowhere to go to-night, Reverend Director."

He looked worried. "Be gone before the bell goes in the morning."

"Yes, Reverend Director, I understand you."

"And don't *ever* come back." He put his hands on my shoulders. "Promise me you won't *ever* come back."

"My Zenji Sama's grave is here."

"That's in the garden—that's all right. Guard yourself."

"I will, Reverend Director."

I went back to Rev. Hajime's room. He was there and looked up shocked at my entrance.

"Why have you come?" he asked.

"To collect up the few oddments I left here and just say hello to you. Is there anything wrong in that?"

He sighed, got up and lit a cigarette. "Whenever you come I smoke much more than I should," he said.

"Rev. Hajime, what on earth is wrong with you? If you don't want to have anything to do with me at all I'm quite happy about it. If I'm such a burden to you for heaven's sake say so—and let's be done with it."

"No, no." He turned back and his face had changed completely. "Let's have some tea together," he said.

We both had tea. Presently the door opened and in came the girl who had had the abortion.

"I brought your 'phone bill," she said.

"My 'phone bill?" I said. "What are you talking about?"

"You've been making 'phone calls while you were here, you were sending out for meals, you were . . . ."

"Look here," I said, "I haven't touched the 'phone in this temple since I left and the last 'phone call I made was temple business. Now let's stop assing about—I am paying no 'phone bill at all."

"It's two thousand yen," she said, "and I'm not leaving until I've got it."

I turned away from her and tried to continue my conversation with Rev. Hajime but he was looking worried.

"You must pay her," he said, "I know you've been calling out for food to be sent in. You always were."

"I shall *not* pay her," I replied. "I do not have a 'phone bill in this temple and I am not going to be forced into paying one. What do you think you're up to?"

The girl, instantly realising that he was on her side, came in quickly, "Yes, you've got to pay it."

"I shall not."

Rev. Hajime lost his temper and yelled, "I'll be damned if I'm going to put up with being in the middle of two women!"

"As you wish," I said. I held my mind very still, stared into the fire-pot, meditated and continued to drink my tea. The girl took the telephone slips, tore them up, threw them in my face, walked out of the room and slammed the sliding door.

"You mustn't worry me like this!" cried Rev. Hajime. "I can't have it; I can't put up with it. I can't stand it!"

"Rev. Hajime, what's been going on? I need to know and I'm *not* going to be put off. Your behaviour has become steadily more insulting."

"She says that you're in love with me; that you told her so when you were on the ship going to Malaysia; that you cried in her arms about it. My wife knows. Everyone here knows." He jumped up. "I *want* to insult you; I'm *going* to insult you."

"That's *really* funny!"

"What do you mean? It isn't funny at all."

"It *is* funny! Do you realise that my cabin was packed full with twenty or thirty people having a party, seeing me off; that we were drinking pink champagne? You were there."

"I don't remember much."

"No, I can believe that; you were too drunk. I doubt if you could remember anything of that night. But I *do* remember a lot about it because I was *not* drunk at all and a lot of other people remember too if they are honest. I'm not at all surprised at what she's saying concerning me."

"Why?" He stared at me in amazement.

"Well, if you knew a bit more about women you'd know. She wanted very much to have your body and you wouldn't give it to her; you told me so yourself. So she presumed I had got it."

"Yes, I know; I ought to have given it to her."

"You ought to have done no such thing! Because you didn't give it to her she felt that I was the one in the way. I feared she might be jealous a long time ago but I didn't let myself believe it. And now she's blaming me, in a weird way, for the fact that she never got you. She made up this tale—it sounds good. In her type of logic it even makes sense."

He looked at me in concern. "You really think so?"

"I don't think, I know. But stop worrying, Rev. Hajime. To-day will be the last time I shall ever be in this temple if I can avoid coming."

"Don't say that—it isn't true—you mustn't say things that aren't true!"

"It is true. Good-bye, Rev. Hajime."

"Please at least telephone me; please write to me."

"*No*, Rev. Hajime, I will *not*. If our relationship ever starts up again it will be by your doing; it will never be by mine."

I rose and left the room.

"I still have two or three of your things," he said.

"Be good enough to put them outside your room, or out-side my room, by to-morrow morning so that I may take them with me."

"All right," he said.

I went back to my room. It was the second time I had noticed how dark and dingy it was, and how uncared for by the Maintenance Department compared to the rest of the temple. The notice outside the door that said "Foreign Guest Department" had been painted once and never painted again; normally such notices are painted every three months. The mats on the floor were in an atrocious condition. Little Tom nestled up close to me (I had left him in the room whilst I was waiting to see Rev. Hajime). I had some fish for him and he ate them. I borrowed a bed from one of the cupboards in the Guest Department and slept very badly. At three in the morning I rose and, with little Tom in his basket, went to an all-night restaurant in the city.

7th. October.

This is really a continuation of yesterday's entry for I wrote most of that in the restaurant that I am in at the moment. I shall go to my new temple as soon as it gets light.

Later. I returned to the new temple and found one of the village elders waiting for me. I was able to put my things away and get somewhat settled in. Unfortunately two newspaper reporters were there also, summoned by the village elder. I foresee much trouble with this again.

8th. October.

Things are very quiet here and I'm able to do much meditation and work cleaning up the place; it is badly in need of being looked after. But I see no way in which the foreigners can possibly be induced to help pay for the mending of another temple. My British friend, as well as the British Consul's wife, have visited me here.

8th. November.

Another Japanese friend of mine to-day went with me to see the priest who really owns this place. He is not at all friendly and not pleased that I am here. He is more or less saying that everything was done without his knowledge and then publicised in the newspapers. My Japanese friend has advised me to leave the temple at once and return to my own one.

9th. November.

Returned to my own temple. There were a number of letters waiting for me, notably one from my friend in Kyoto wanting to know many things—how I was getting on—just news as usual but no sign of her coming here to help me. I still get very dizzy now and then but I have noticed that this is primarily when I eat certain types of food. It's very difficult to buy the other types on my salary, however, because they're so expensive.

The newspaper articles I am writing are being well received— that, at least, is something.

13th. November.

Another letter from Kyoto—just chatty news as usual.

14th. November.

The dizziness comes and goes every time I eat bread, sugar or rice. I wonder why?[120] It really is worrying—yet every day the wings beat more strongly—and the desire to go somewhere else (but where the heck to?) grows stronger, too.

A local priest visited me to-day. He told me that if I were to offer myself as a disciple to the new Zenji Sama he'd probably be glad and happy to reopen the Foreign Section in Tokyo. I wonder if that was a piece of official information or just a fishing expedition?[160]

1st. December.

I appeared on Japanese television to-day, discussing the work of the former Foreign Section of the Tokyo temple and the overseas branches that have come out of it—their development and plans for the future. On the program with me was a Western junior trainee from the Tendai school of Buddhism; a Japanese priest and scholar were also on the program. They were obviously not too happy about the success that the Foreign Section has had.[161]

5th. December.

A letter came to-day from Rev. Hajime. He has somehow found out that I am visiting the Administration Branch on the fifteenth of December and wants to go there with me; he wants me to change the date to the sixteenth since the fifteenth is a Sunday—that was an oversight on my part. He then went on to say that he feels that he will soon grow tired of playing religious politics, although he does not like it even now. He says he is thinking of removing "this stone" [i.e. this Stone Buddha—himself] from the Tokyo temple. The new staff apparently does not like my having a room in the temple there. They can have my dark, grubby little room, no problem. Rev. Hajime said he would see me on the sixteenth and suggested that we have supper together at that time. What on earth does he want to have supper with me for? I see no point in it.

9th. December.

Another letter from my friend in Kyoto who is all agog about the new temple. Not much else except news of what she is doing.

16th. December.

I went to Tokyo to-day. Rev. Hajime was at the Administration Office when I arrived there; I handed in the papers for George's Transmission. Rev. Hajime was very charming. He informed me that he had specially taken ten thousand yen out of the bank to pay for dinner for the two of us this evening. I could see no reason for such a spendthrift action; after all, that's more than I have to live on for a whole month!

He took me to a Chinese restaurant not far from the station outside which stands the Hachikō statue and ordered a huge feast but I was not hungry. He ate hurriedly, obviously enjoying it very much, and got very drunk. Then he started asking me questions. Perhaps it was the relaxed atmosphere, perhaps it was because we were away from the temple, socializing together for the first time in our lives, that caused me to relax sufficiently to tell him of my future plans for the Foreign

Section and my own temple even when all my instincts told me not to. It must have been the saké he had drunk, I don't know what else, but I saw something appear in his face that appalled me. Before this I do not think I have ever seen such greed, ambition or—I don't know what it was—it was horrifying. It happened when I mentioned the Japanese friend of mine who arranged the new temple for me. He said, "Such a person should belong to me in my temple, not to you, a foreigner." Seeing that look, everything that had happened since I met him somehow fell into place—every single thing. I couldn't explain why but it did. The look passed in a flash, gone, over—but I had seen it; and nothing could ever be the same again between us. What I had been seeing in Rev. Hajime was what I had wanted to see, not what was really there. I had seen a man one could respect, who was just training and training and training, doing a magnificent job on himself. Now it was as if a veil had been torn from my eyes. I saw an ambitious, greedy, selfish little creature, afraid for its own position in the Tokyo temple, not caring a damn who it hurt in consequence. No wonder *something* in my guts had always seemed uneasy when I was with him. What a fool I had been to always think I was imagining it.

We said good-bye to each other and I went back to the new temple. I decided I would try to give it a few more days and see if I could sort things out with the legal priest, apologising to him for having taken it over before asking his permission.

17th. December.

Two friends of mine came this morning and we all had lunch together. It was very enjoyable.

21st. December.

I had to go to the Tokyo temple, like it or lump it, to pick up two or three things I had left in the main Guest Department. The temple office had notified the temple down the road that the things were there and they would like me to collect them. I had no intention of visiting Rev. Hajime but unfortunately couldn't find the chief guest master and was told that he was in

Rev. Hajime's room. The priest who told me said, "Come on, let's go together." He knew me quite well and I could think of no good reason, that was explainable, as to why I couldn't go. So, very reluctantly, I went. The chief guest master was over-joyed to see me.

"Ah, you've come back to look after the foreigners who are coming to-day. I asked Rev. Hajime to tell you," he said. "There's quite a lot of them. We've got to have someone to take them round the temple. I was just asking where you were."

Rev. Hajime made a grimace. "Shhhh, don't say that to her!" he said.

I looked at him, I looked at the chief guest master—the latter was nonplussed. "Why, isn't that what she's come for?"

"Shhhh," was all Rev. Hajime would say.

The chief guest master went away looking worried and I was following him when Rev. Hajime stopped me. He called a young priest in the Guest Department. A very unfortunate scene ensued for it was obvious that he wanted to hurt me as much as he possibly could in front of this young man; he was very annoyed when he realised that he wasn't succeeding. I just sat still. The young priest told me that hundreds of foreigners had come to the temple and that he and Rev. Hajime were looking after them; that they would be looking after them in future; that I needed never to come again. I turned to Rev. Hajime.

"Is this true?" I asked.

"Oh, you need never come again," he said.

"That's *not* what I asked. I asked you if it was true that hundreds of foreigners were coming here."

He exchanged a knowing look with the young trainee and said, "Of course not. I've told you the truth."

"Yes, of course, Rev. Hajime. Forgive me." I rose. "I have to get back to my own temple. Good-bye."

I went along the corridor to find the chief guest master waiting for me near the door.

"I really thought you had come back to look after the foreigners," he said. "A lot of people are wondering why you are not here."

"Really? I was under the impression that I was not expected to be here."

The chief guest master shook his head. "I really don't know what's going on," he said.

"Reverend Guest Master, neither do I but it was good to see you again. Good-bye." I left him and returned to the new temple.[162]

23rd. December.

A letter came to-day asking me to go with the wife of a doctor friend of mine to see Rev. Hajime. The doctor wished to complain about the ill-treatment of foreigners. I did not want to go but felt that I had no alternative. I wanted to go back to my own temple to-day, there having been more problems with the rightful owner of the new one.

I was appalled at the way in which Rev. Hajime treated the doctor's wife, taking no notice whatsoever of her complaints. She was obviously feeling extremely uncomfortable. When she left she gave me a strange look and said, "Is this how Buddhists behave?"

I went back to my own temple immediately after this and found several letters there, one from a young man who, it seems, went to the Tokyo temple, applied to enter and was refused by Rev. Hajime. This letter has been waiting for me since the nineteenth. Rev. Hajime had certainly not told me about it yet he had either written to him or seen him in person.

24th. December.

It was very enjoyable to go to Nagoya to-day and buy something tasty for Christmas dinner, to be alone in my own house without others about.

Lately I have been feeling weak every time I get the dizziness. I really must be careful what I eat. I am listless and very thirsty.

25th. December.

Christmas was very solitary and *very* enjoyable. I don't think I can remember one which was more enjoyable. I ate my little Christmas dinner alone, I watched my little T.V. set alone and I meditated in my temple alone. I know that's awfully bad Buddhism but, by golly, I did enjoy it!

31st. December.

A card came from Rev. Hajime saying that he had translated the letter I had sent to the new Zenji Sama requesting that he be my guarantor if I stay in the country. I sent that letter ages ago. Why is it only now that he has translated it? I sent off another letter immediately saying that I had already arranged for my guarantor to be the head of the Administration Section since he is also someone in my Zenji Sama's line.

To-night it looks as though I shall spend the coming of the New Year completely alone. I shall ring my bell at midnight and on the altar will be the great mochi that one of the parishioners brought some time this afternoon; I shall have the celebration wine for those who wish to come and drink it. I'm really looking forward to this new year—a new year without ever having to go up to Tokyo, for I'm not going back to the new temple ever again any more than I am going back to the Tokyo one. The new one belongs to someone else; I should never have gone there. The last person I know who really matters to me, the Reverend Director, has either left the Tokyo temple permanently or will soon; I know Rev. Hajime for what he really is. From here on I do indeed walk alone—and I am looking forward to it. How strong the wings seem to have become in the last few hours. My fledgling days are past.

1st. January.

I spent a most enjoyable birthday. The big mochi, brought by the parishioners, was on the altar; the mayor came to see me and was annoyed because the mochi had been put on my altar instead of on that of one of the other temples in the village.

2nd. January.

I received a notification from a bank to-day telling me that Zenji Sama has left me two hundred thousand yen for whenever

I am in need. It is a wonderful present—I certainly never expected it. I knew that he had left me something—but I never really believed I would get anything.

3rd. January.

The young man, who has been waiting in Tokyo for my reply to his letter, is arriving sometime to-morrow night. His name is Peter.

4th. January.

Peter arrived late to-night and wants to study here for some time. He is tall with extraordinarily vacant blue eyes. It is as though he has lost his soul and is hungrily hunting for it.

5th. January.

A letter came from Charles in America telling me that he is sending five thousand dollars in American stock for me to sell so as to be able to go to the United States any time I want to—so that I can look round and possibly found the Foreign Section in America. I knew that if I sat still and waited Zenji Sama and the Buddhas and Patriarchs would show me the way. As a leaf I went where the wind blew me—to the new temple, to Tokyo, here to my own temple. It seems now that the wind could very well blow me to America. But I also know something else. It is my duty as a Buddhist priest to leave no stone unturned in my attempts to try at all times no matter what the odds. Therefore, before deciding to go to America or anywhere else, I will make one last great attempt to try and keep the Foreign Section here in Japan; not because it *must* stay here, but because it feels like unfinished business. I will make one last attempt with all of them in Tokyo—with Rev. Hajime, with all the new officials and with the new Zenji Sama. If it fails I will believe that the wind *is* blowing the leaf away from Japan and back to the West. During this one year I will wait and see if anyone in England writes. If they want me I will go; they know that I have lost Zenji Sama; I must always keep the door open for anyone and everyone. Just as at my Kessei I said that the temple gate would always stand open to every living thing whilst I am here, so will I keep open the gate of the Buddha Nature within me for the entire universe, for anyone and everything that wishes to enter. I will try once more—then make the decision to go or stay. The wings fan softly; I know they seem to be telling me to go now but my instinct is to try just once more and, with this young man here, maybe it will be easier. He wishes to live here permanently and I believe that he is sincere.

15th. January.

I have been teaching Peter many things. He needs to know so much. In many respects he has to start Buddhism almost from scratch. This is a blessing in disguise. If he wasn't starting from scratch I would probably have to get him to get rid of an awful lot of pre-conceived ideas. This young man speaks Korean haltingly. Such a talent will be useful later on.

A letter came from Rev. Hajime—an extremely sad letter. The day after Christmas I sent him a New Year card and a mochi[163] out of politeness, since he had taught me many things in the past, but had received no reply. Then this letter came. After wishing me a happy New Year and a happy birthday, he said that I should recheck the affair of the new temple since he felt sure that there had been misunderstandings there. He then went on to say that he was very sorry for me, regarding his wife. Apparently when I 'phoned last year to speak about what had happened with regard to the new temple she had looked very hurt. After that, for three days during his stay in the temple, she apparently spoke not a word to him. He did not understand the reason. Then, on the last day, she told him many things about me which she said had happened in his temple during the past several years, things which have hurt her very much. He suggested that perhaps the problems arose from the difference of customs between Westerners and Easterners. It seems his wife behaved to me as she had to a delinquent youth who had once been placed on probation with Rev. Hajime in his temple. She seemed to think of me in the same way as him in spite of everything Rev. Hajime did. So long as she knows that he is in contact with me, apparently she will continue to behave this way. He concludes that it is indeed a very piteous thing and hopes that I may come to work in a more broad-minded setting without having to think of shallow-minded people such as them. It seems that, although he thinks that I can do this, he himself cannot "abandon" them and so, after leaving the Tokyo temple, he will live his life as a poor priest of a temple in the country.

I find myself wondering very much what he is talking about. I know that last year, and in the years past, there have been differences of opinion between his wife and I, primarily due to misunderstandings of customs. But I had not thought that I had done anything to hurt this woman so deeply. After all, I barely know her and I have not visited the house much except for my stay during the first year. It seems very strange that she should be behaving like this after so many, many years. If Rev. Hajime does not even want a New Year greeting I am content; in any case I am not happy with his double dealing in the Tokyo temple. I told him last year that I did not wish to see him again. In his mind perhaps the differences between East and West are so great that there *is* no way in which the two can come to mutual understanding—absolutely no way in which they can ever really get together. If this is so I know that his thinking is wrong but I cannot give him my experience. He may *know* that all is one within himself but he does not know how to stay in unity with it in the all is different. United by the all is one he is yet separated by the all is different. How many centuries will it take for East and West to come together, and live together, completely in harmony, without worrying about the small things, the shallow things, that make them different?

16th. January.

Peter has been finding many of the old manuscripts that I translated with Rev. Hajime. He located quite a number of them whilst doing various jobs throughout the temple—not least of which was covering jam pots. Having in the old days got what information I felt was important from them, I had started to make use of the paper—paper being somewhat expensive and therefore scarce. Peter is very pleased with these manuscripts and is studying them avidly. Over the next few weeks I intend to teach him much. He has expressed an interest in becoming a member of the priesthood. I am thinking that it would be a good idea to allow him to become a junior trainee fairly soon. Unlike a Transmitted priest, a junior trainee can leave any time. I do not like hurried ordinations but if I ordain him quickly he will not be so easily made a pawn of by unscrupulous people. If he is my legal disciple he will at least have a modicum of protection whilst in Japan. The priest who has been helping me and the woman-priest next-door agree with me about this.

20th. January.

I went to a very famous temple not far from here, in the mountains of Ise, to interview the priest for an article for the newspaper.

31st. January.

To-day I ordained Peter as a junior trainee. It was a very simple and a very happy ceremony. The two priests—the one who has been helping us and the woman—both came as witnesses.

I have noticed, as I said, that every time I have a dizzy spell I seem to become weaker, but I seem to become weakest in the afternoons as well as being dizzy when I wake up in the morning. I cannot help thinking that it would perhaps *be* wiser to go back to the West so as to be able to get proper medical help—I see no way in which I can ever afford a doctor here. But it is wise that I do not speak of these things. I do not wish to worry this young man.

1st. February.

My friend in Tokyo who helped me get the new temple has sent me some translations of the works of Dōgen. I intend to correct the English for him to the best of my ability and send them back.

The two priests who were at Peter's ordination have many outside ceremonies and the woman-priest is shortly to do

Kessei—she wishes me to help her. These things keep me very busy. There were many ceremonies to-day.

2nd. February.

I received a card from Rev. Hajime. I had not expected to ever hear anything more from him. I had telephoned the Tokyo temple's Financial Department to say that it had not sent my monthly cash; Rev. Hajime's card said that the treasurer will be sending it shortly. He informed me that the head of the Administration Section wants to talk with him about becoming my sponsor although I have already arranged everything. He also told me that he did not wish to come to any more Kesseis in my temple. I was not expecting him to.

Peter has to go to Korea in order to renew his visa since the Japanese authorites will never permit anyone to change their visa status within the country. Since Peter is now going to have a totally different type of visa, thanks to the head of the Administration Section in Tokyo who has agreed to become his sponsor as well as mine, it is necessary for him to go to Korea to get the status changed. I shall go to Kōbe on the twenty-eighth to see him off on the ship.

28th. February.

We went to Kōbe to-day and stayed with the treasurer of the Tokyo temple who is the priest of a very large temple in the Kōbe area. He had come home specially after hearing from his wife that I had telephoned. He was extremely rude, wanting to know why we wished to stay in his temple and why I had telephoned his wife to ask if we could. I pointed out that one of my disciples, Peter, was going to Korea to get a new visa and that all we needed was a night's lodging; if it was inconvenient we would gladly go to a hotel; I had only asked to stay there since priests were supposed to stay in temples.[164] He grudgingly allowed us to stay.

1st. March.

We spent a rather uncomfortable night in the treasurer's temple. This morning the wife, who has always been an extremely good friend of mine, apologised for the behaviour of her husband, begged me to forget all about it and also begged me to visit her regularly. I said that I would certainly think about it.

I saw Peter off on the ship to Korea and then I returned to my own temple.

2nd. March.

I started work on the March newsletter. It will be a joint effort for March and April. The newsletter has suffered sadly since Harry went away. I have been asked to do a lecture tour in the United States for a couple of months and have agreed to do it. I spoke of this in the newsletter as well as Peter's ordination.

3rd. March.

I was invited to assist at a very important ceremony in a large temple in the neighbouring city. There was a large meal after the ceremony and then one of the priests approached me with the suggestion that, since it was obvious that I could get many foreigners for disciples, especially young ones, he and several others would be glad and happy to pay a sum of money to me if I would acquire disciples for them. I couldn't believe what I was hearing—I didn't *want* to believe what I was hearing. I had heard of such things being done; I told Harry about them but I didn't really believe it—not until now. After all, where I come from we don't sell our children. I tried to explain this to him but he said that it was quite usual in Japan for a priest who had a large number of disciples to send some of them to other people; thus all priests could have a disciple and be able to do Kessei. If a priest couldn't do Kessei then he couldn't make money at ceremonies for he was not regarded as being high enough up to demand good fees. I was too disgusted with this to say what I wanted to say about it. The priests were very upset when I would not agree to help them; they said I was in

Japan and should follow Japanese ways.[165] I suppose this will be another nail in my coffin as far as they are concerned.

7th. March.

I had a letter to-day from Rev. Hajime—just a short note saying that he had translated a lecture I had left behind in the Tokyo temple and which I had originally intended to give at a temple near here. It is good to have the translation—two years late!

I went to another temple to-day for an interview so as to write another article for the newspaper. The finances here are so far working out fairly well—so long as I can continue to write articles and the Tokyo temple continues to send my monthly cash. Peter has a very limited amount of money. The time will soon come when I shall probably have to finance him.

I had a letter from England to-day; from a young man who is interested in my going to England to lecture if I am actually going to be in the United States. It is the first letter of this sort I have had from anyone in England. If my fare can be raised I will definitely go. I have written to tell him this.

8th. March.

The villagers have been collecting the money for the new roof and I have been going round with the town council to help with the collection. It was unfortunate that the roof didn't get put up last year but I suppose it was only to be expected. After all, we had done a lot of mending.

9th. March.

There was a big funeral in the city west of here to-day to which I was invited. I couldn't understand the reason why for I knew none of the priests at the temple and it is very strange to receive an invitation from so far away for something like a funeral. But, since they were going to pay and I needed the money, I went.

During the meal, when the funeral was over, the priest of the temple took me aside to ask if I was going to America with Rev. Hajime. I was startled for I had no idea that Rev. Hajime was going to America. The priest laughed and looked knowing when I said that I didn't know, making it quite clear that he knew that I knew and understood why I wasn't telling. The knowing smiles going round were quite revolting. As soon as possible I returned home and wrote a letter to Rev. Hajime demanding information as to what he had been saying concerning me.

10th. March.

The Kessei of the woman in the temple next to mine took place to-day. It was obvious that people were not too happy about my being there.

21st. March.

I received a reply from Rev. Hajime to my somewhat terse card concerning the incident in the distant temple. He said he had been invited to lecture in a certain city in America at the beginning of July, that the schedule was up to the person who had invited him and that my going to America had nothing whatsoever to do with him. He continued that he was surprised to know that I was seeing only the bad side of him, that in my eyes he had no good point whatsoever.

I don't know who to believe and I was stupid to write him the letter in the first place. He is quite right to grumble—I should not have allowed myself to be pulled off centre by a bunch of idiots[166] at a funeral.

1st. April.

Peter returned to-day. The mayor of the town here is not too happy about my having another foreigner living here perma-nently. I find this strange because originally he was extremely pleased with the idea of a large number of foreigners here and had even given us the parish hall to turn into a Zendō. I suspect that the parish hall has always belonged to us but was sequestered by the town when the temple became derelict. However, the mayor is not happy that a large number of for-eigners may be here and says that I must not ordain any more without his express permission.

A Japanese lady arrived this afternoon bringing with her two young American girls who are on an exchange program and wish to study Zen. I have been teaching them together with Peter.

The mayor gets ruder every time he comes. There is something going on of which I have no knowledge but, as I said earlier, the leaf will obey the wind. If the wind is blowing it away from Japan then it will leave; if the wind does not blow then it will stay.

5th. May.

We started rehearsing the village children for the dances for the Buddha's birthday celebration which will take place in about two week's time. Peter was extremely good at helping with this.

I heard on my grape-vine that the Director of the Tokyo temple officially left, after almost forty years there, on the 31st. of March. He went, as he had come, carrying his trainee's box and wearing a black robe, down the temple path to the station on foot.

15th. May.

We celebrated the Buddha's birthday to-day. The children came in beautiful kimonos for the dancing and their parents were overjoyed with the celebration. As of old, a friend of mine came to give the lecture. Peter took a number of slide photographs. Some day perhaps they will remind us of much that has happened here.

15th. June.

About thirty people from one of the university classes in Kyoto arrived to do Sesshin here. Another professor was again somewhat worried about the spread of Zen in America since he felt that it was going to try and take over the world. He was especially frightened by the two of us. I wonder what he thinks one middle-aged female and one young man barely in his twenties can do to take over the world?

18th. June.

Went to Kyoto with the university class and took them on a tour of Mount Hyei as well as giving a couple of lectures at the Kyoto International House. It was a very enjoyable day. I stayed in an inexpensive hotel rather than bother anybody in a temple.[167]

I have received no money whatsoever from the Tokyo temple since the first of March and our financial situation is now very serious. At the beginning of May I wrote to the wife of the treasurer in Kōbe to ask her if she knew what had happened to my monthly cash and begged her to use her influence with her husband to get him to send it. By way of reply she telephoned to say that if I'd go to Kōbe once a week to teach English to her daughter she would arrange that I got ten thousand yen a month, the equivalent of what I was getting from Tokyo. It seemed a peculiar way of solving the problem but I agreed.

I have been going to Kōbe every Saturday, in consequence of this, since about the middle of May. It has caused a lot of problems with the village for they feel that *I* should be there to deal with *their* ceremonies; they're not happy with a mere junior, Peter, doing them for them. But I have to earn sufficient money to run the temple and I see no other means than this teaching. Now, from to-day, Peter has no more cash and I must support him too.

I telephoned the Tokyo temple to ask the treasurer what had happened but there was no reply from the Treasury Office. I thought of telephoning Rev. Hajime but decided against it.

3rd. July.

To-day a young priestess came from a temple in the north of Japan. She wants us to go to her temple for a big festival and appear on television there. She originally came solely for me but, when she discovered that I had Peter with me, she wanted him to come as well.

10th. July.

We went to the young priestess's temple to-day. We were wined, dined and fêted; then we appeared on television. It was

obvious that the young priestess's family, however, was not terribly pleased to see us.[161]

12th. July.

We returned to my own temple this morning. The young
priestess has asked Peter to marry her! My mind boggles.

13th. July.

I have to make arrangements for my trip to America.
George has been helping me through a friend of his to whom I
wrote. To-morrow I must go to the American Consulate and see
about the necessary visas for myself.

14th. July.

I went to the American Consulate. It seems there are going
to be some problems with regard to my going to America for
this lecture-tour. Unless I misunderstood what I heard, I must
get a letter of sponsorship from every university that is inviting
me. I'll write to a friend in Tokyo about it; I felt that the
Japanese clerk didn't fully understand me.

My weakness is increasing as is the dizziness. I wish I could
afford better food.

10th. August.

Many villagers arrived to-day to mend the temple roof.
They say it will take two to three days. Peter is unhappy since
they will not let him help them mix the mud. They say that a
foreigner does not know how to.

11th. August.

To-day there was a typhoon which caused great havoc at the
back of the temple, almost ruining the new mats that we have
just put down. The roof had been stripped off and it had not
occurred to the villagers to put tarpaulin over the huge hole.
Unfortunately it was my bedroom that suffered.

12th. August.

The villagers finished mending the roof to-day. It looks extremely good from the front but the mayor put all the new tiles on the front for cosmetic effect and all the bad ones on the back— which means that the living quarters still leak badly. He also insisted on taking the new tiles off the gate roof (Peter had done a good job tiling this) and put old ones there instead. He says he is not willing to mend the living quarters, only the Hondō.

13th. August.

I was too weak to take the long walk from three this morning until noon to open the houses for OBon so Peter did it for me. The mayor was extremely angry over this saying that I had not obtained his express permission to do it. It is no use pointing out to him that he has no jurisdiction over the town temples; it is equally no use pointing out to him that I am not well.

To-morrow Peter will do his Chief Junior ceremony. He has done extraordinarily well up to now. To-morrow will be the first time that Rev. Hajime has not come to the ceremonies. I have invited someone as lecturer. I hope all will go well.

14th. August.

We did Kessei to-day so that Peter could become Chief Junior. It was very different from the first one. Only five people were present—the necessary number of witnesses, as well as an American friend of Peter's and several other people who came for the Hossen ceremony only. But it was very enjoyable. Unfortunately the lecturer was useless since he couldn't believe that foreigners could understand what he was talking about. He was amazed when he discovered that I could translate what he was saying. The Japanese never cease to be amazed at a foreigner who can speak their language.

There is still no money whatsoever from the Tokyo temple. This going to Kōbe every week is taking its toll of my strength. Peter went with me once in order to help me but I can't allow that to happen often; I cannot allow myself to become completely useless.

28th. August.

To-day was the great Segaki for OBon. The temple was packed and it was good to have at least two assistants for Peter's friend has stayed on. When it was over we all spent a very happy evening together.

29th. August.

I took some of the money Zenji Sama left me and we all went to Kyoto to-day to shop for temple equipment of our own to take with us as and when we leave Japan. I think somehow all of us know that we are going to leave fairly soon although nothing has actually been said. It was also the first day of real sightseeing I've ever had here—sightseeing that was worth doing, that is. We visited several temples that I'd always wanted to see including Nanzenji where Dōgen Zenji himself was once abbot—the temple he walked out of when he felt he wasn't yet ready to teach. How well I understand that feeling.

We spent the night in an inexpensive ryokan[167] and Peter and his friend played chess.

30th. August.

We returned to my own temple, after seeing Peter's friend off on the train, to find that a letter from Rev. Tarō had arrived. He wants me to go to his home temple in Hyogo where his master, who is now an official of the Tokyo temple, wishes to meet me. He says there will be a big feast in my honour as well as a lecture for me to give to his parishioners. I was overjoyed at receiving the letter and telephoned Rev. Tarō at once to say that I would be delighted to come.

1st. September.

I went to Rev. Tarō's temple. He was very, very pleased to see me and we spent a happy day together talking over old times in the Tokyo temple. His master arrived late in the evening and I was truly fêted with very great honour, being served from the red-stemmed tea bowls and cake stands used only for very great priests. But there was something about the whole thing that didn't feel right. I knew, from the moment his master entered the room, that Rev. Tarō was worried about something. He couldn't look me in the eye. He obviously didn't want to be there.

His master continued to wine and dine me into the night; he talked more and more about the Foreign Section, about affairs in the Tokyo temple, about the new Zenji Sama, what his new staff wanted done. And he made it very clear that I would be welcome in the Tokyo temple if I became the zuishin of the new Zenji Sama. He explained patiently that I could not officially become the new Zenji Sama's disciple because no-one who has become a full priest can ever again become a true disciple of another, only a zuishin. He continued to talk soothingly, waiting for my answer. I evaded giving one. I needed to think clearly without wine in my head. I could be misunderstanding what he was saying. But I couldn't help knowing that I had been invited to this temple, and fêted in this way, to show me that if I were willing to desert Zenji Sama, if I were willing to become the follower of another, there would be no difficulty with regard to my staying in the Tokyo temple and reopening the Foreign Section there.

2nd. September.

To-day there were several important ceremonies for OHigan after which I lectured. Rev. Tarō's master then went back to Tokyo and Rev. Tarō and I were left alone. He still could not meet my eyes and I knew that he was not happy about what he had heard.

3rd. September.

Rev. Tarō saw me off on the train this morning. We took a long look at each other on the platform. I think both of us knew that we might never see the other again. As I got into the train I said, "It won't happen."

He nodded. "I know." The train pulled out of the station.

When I got back to my own temple I was surprised to hear loud laughter and the television set going full-blast in the living room. I entered to find the priest from the big temple in the nearby city sitting at the table with his son, together with Peter, smoking and drinking. I asked what they were doing there and learned that they had come to invite my disciple, but not me, to an outside ceremony. I refused to let him go.

When the priest and his son had gone I suggested that Peter went to meditate; I went to my room. After Peter had gone to bed I went to the Hondō and sat in front of the statue of Kanzeon. I knew I was looking down a deep abyss; I knew that I was saying, "Why not? Why not chuck it all? Why not go over to this new Zenji Sama? Peace and quiet from want will be yours. They are promising you everything—security, a good job, cash, food, medical benefits, maybe even honour—you name it, they're offering it. You can have the lot; you don't ever have to worry again; you don't have to go off into a strange, cold world to a foreign country." I also knew that I could just give up utterly. I *need* not keep trying to do this—to *hell* with the other foreigners, let them find someone else to fight for them, to teach them, to help them out of their troubles. I can sit here in my little temple until I starve—just like the priestess who had this temple before me. What is the point of trying? I found what I came for and I can die without regrets, even alone and in poverty. It was as if Kanzeon pointed to the two roads— both completely open, both completely mine. Everything in the temple was still. I could go whichever way I wanted, any time I wanted. I looked at the two roads, one leading to glory, comfort and ease, the other into despair. Between them rose a mountain range,[168] faced by a sheer cliff, with no visible way up. Beyond that mountain range I knew lay a new life, a distant land, unknown challenges, and unforeseen hardships. I felt the wings fanning softly, strong and vibrant, and I felt something else. I felt Zenji Sama there saying, "You are free. Go whatever way you wish." And I knew completely and utterly that I *was* free and that I *could* choose whatever way I wanted. Again I looked at the two roads and the sheer cliff. I was not conscious of making a decision, only that I did not go down either of the two roads; I was only conscious of leaving the Hondō, going to my room and there writing a letter to Rev. Tarō's master. I told him that I was Zenji Sama's disciple, that I always had been and always would be; there was no way in which I could possibly become the zuishin of another. The offer from the new Zenji Sama was a great honour. Perhaps in years to come I may be able to reconsider but I could see no possibility of it whatsoever now. No other priest n the Tokyo temple was required to give up his master in order to work there. If I were to become the zuishin of another I would be denying, in my own mind and indeed in the eyes of the Buddhist world, the complete enlightenment, the complete Buddhahood of Zenji Sama; this I could under no circumstances do. I said that I would gladly and happily serve the Foreign Section and make all the foreigners loyal to the new Zenji Sama but I belonged to my Zenji Sama and always would. I folded the letter and went straight out to post it although it was midnight.

The dizziness I have been experiencing has been joined by a dull headache whenever I eat certain foods, always starchy items. I will get this checked out when I get to London.

9th. September.

To-day I had what I *know* will be the last letter I shall ever receive from Rev. Hajime. It said that he had talked about my coming to the Tokyo temple again with the officers and that they do not agree to my coming here. According to Rev. Hajime, the new Zenji Sama has the same opinion. So now there is no hope for me in the Tokyo temple. He says the cash due to me since April will be given when I leave Japan (about sixty thousand yen).

He also spoke of a young Japanese who very much wants to be ordained by me. He says that his father is completely against it; I suspect that that is at Rev. Hajime's instigation.[169]

10th. September.

We went to the American Consulate. Since I have, in any case, to go on to England, there seems to be no problem whatsoever in my getting a short-term visit visa for the purpose of doing the lectures although I have indicated that I would like to immigrate; it will be the business type. I shall go on to England when the tour is over and decide where I will eventually settle after seeing my own country again. I am still in six minds as to whether to take everything with me now or leave some of it here just in case I ever come back, but a large part of me says I should take everything and find a place to store it until I decide whether I am going to immigrate to America or live in England.

27th. October.

We have been packing steadily and making arrangements to leave. The dull headache and the weakness is with me permanently now; I feel that I must get to a doctor soon or it may be too late. I have told the mayor that I may return and he is happy. He is willing to look after the temple until that time. The priest who has been so kind in helping us mend things is going to take quite a lot of our furniture, either to store or to keep if we do not return. To-morrow, after everything has been moved, I shall leave this temple and go to stay with him whilst we make the final arrangements.

28th. October.

To-day we left my own temple. After going through the gate I turned to have one more look at it, to fix it in my mind. I had seen my possessions taken away in two lorries, one to be stored or kept by the priest who has helped us, the other to a ship in Nagoya harbour which will take it to a friend of mine, there to wait the final decision of where I shall settle.

We stayed with the priest who is my friend. We shall be with him for three days whilst arranging the shipping and customs release of our things.[170]

29th. October.

The ship carrying our effects sailed to-day.

30th. October.

My priest friend took us for a farewell dinner; oddly enough in Rev. Hajime's home town. It was very enjoyable.

31st. October.

We left on the bullet train for Tokyo and went to stay with the British friend who has helped us so much in the past with mending the temple and lending us his car on so many different occasions. I took little Thomas with us in his basket.

1st. November.

Peter wanted to meet Rev. Hajime to arrange the registration of some of his papers. We went to the Tokyo temple garden to see Zenji Sama's tomb and he had his photograph taken beside it; he then insisted on paying Rev. Hajime the visit. I said he could and went to wait for him in a small restaurant in the town where I had coffee. When he returned he was obviously not willing to talk about anything that had happened and it was with great difficulty that I finally pried out of him the information that Rev. Hajime had a young American with him—a girl living in the room next-door to his. This didn't surprise me in the least; he had no need to worry about hurting me with the information; I had long ago suspected as much. When I refused to become the new Zenji Sama's zuishin I knew that I had signed my own death warrant in the Tokyo temple. Rev. Hajime had told them that I could not be there any longer since I had fallen in love with him and his wife had found out. It is amazing how wishful thinking can produce a certainty.[171]

This evening we had dinner with George at a Tokyo hotel. Rev. Hajime turned up for just a few minutes, together with the treasurer. Apparently he had asked Peter where he could see me, since he must discuss the registration with me, and he had told him of the hotel to which we were going for dinner. Rev. Hajime told me that he had brought the treasurer with him as a chaperon. Apparently the girl who had the abortion told his wife I was in love with him and he is now terrified she may write to her again. He had a drink with us, asked me about Peter, asked what his name was (which seemed strange since he'd met him only that afternoon) and then left; thereafter the dinner became enjoyable.[172]

2nd. November.

We left my British friend to-day and went to stay for the last night with the American friend who looked after me during the three days of my illness in Tokyo. I was not at all happy about the way in which I had behaved to Rev. Hajime the previous evening; perhaps it had been because the treasurer was there. I felt that, since I was leaving Japan, perhaps for ever, I should make one last attempt to make our parting a pleasant one.

Peter was out shopping so I telephoned the Tokyo temple and got straight through to Rev. Hajime. The first thing he said was that he would not be able to see us off on the 'plane in the morning although I had not asked him to; that he had to go to the new Zenji Sama's Kessei. He was obviously trying to be friendly, telling me how much he was interested in what we were doing, but I felt that his heart was not in his words. We talked of mundane things for a few moments then I heard my American friend coming in at the front door and said good-bye. I have made my last attempt; I have done everything within my power; there *is* an end.[173]

3rd. November.

> *And each man kills the thing he loves,*
> *Let this by all be heard;*
> *A coward does it with a kiss,*
> *The brave man with a sword.* *

This poem has been going through and through my mind ever since I got up this morning; and it was with me during most of the night. Rev. Hajime's friendship; how easily it could be shattered as soon as it was not politically advisable for him to retain it. 'The coward does it with a kiss'—the betrayal of all his old friends in the Foreign Section. What was the cause? Political manoeuvring? A new Zenji Sama? Or his own personal ambition so that he, Rev. Hajime, could take over the Foreign Section, could go to America?[174] Oh, who the heck cares?

---

*From *The Ballad of Reading Gaol*, by Oscar Wilde, Unicorn Press, London, 1948.

We arrived at Tokyo airport. I wrote the above poem on a sheet of airport stationery and posted it to Rev. Hajime; it was the only way I could stop it running through my head.[175]

George, several Japanese friends of mine and the gentleman who had helped me get the new temple were all there to say good-bye to us. The last had got over his bad temper as a result of my leaving the new temple. Our things were safely on the 'plane; all we had to carry on was our hand luggage and Thomas. It was good that he was able to travel with us in the cabin.

I said good-bye to everyone and we made our way to the immigration desk. I turned to wave to them and then went through the barrier. We waited in the lounge for a few minutes and then they called us to the 'plane. As I went up the ramp I knew that my eyes were filling with tears; I felt a grief that I have never before known at any time; I was extremely glad that Peter was in front of me. As I stepped off the ramp onto the 'plane itself there, in the doorway just above me, was the vision of the old priest, this time wearing brown robes, whom I had seen once before so very long ago wearing black in the Tokyo temple. But the tatte-mōsu no longer hid the face; and it was the face of Zenji Sama. He sat completely still, utterly at peace, filling me with himself. My eyes streamed with tears and the vision was gone but within my heart I heard, loud and clear, the words "Lo, I am with you always, even unto the ends of the world." The wings surged with life and I felt my spirit soar into the sky. The eaglet had left the nest; no longer an eaglet but an eagle. The stewardess closed the doors of the 'plane and I looked out of the window. I saw the little Japanese boy who had so badly wanted to become one of my disciples dashing the tears from his eyes as he waved from the parapet. Tom sat on my lap; the stewardess had been very kind—she had said he did not have to stay in his basket. The 'plane was already airborne, high above the clouds. For a moment they parted and I had my last glimpse of that great, sprawling city which is Tokyo; the clouds closed over it as we continued to climb. And then we were indeed in the blue sky which stretched to eternity.

Gyate, gyate, haragyate, harasōgyate, Bodhi, sowaka.
Going, going, going on, always going on, always *becoming* Buddha.

Annotations.

1. My reactions here were very mixed. I half wanted to be ordained in Malaysia instead of in Japan; letters between Rev. Jones and I reflected this. The only one *still* in my possession makes it clear that *I* wished the ordination to take place in Japan and that he agreed. At this distance in time this whole situation is a mess but it is possible that there had been later letters agreeing with his wishes. One thing *is* certain however—I did *not* agree to having reporters or publicity of any sort and they were *never* mentioned in our correspondence. That they were there shattered the beauty and purity of what was about to happen and impugned my motives.

2. I had told my mother in England what I *proposed* to do but, because of her fear of *all* religion in spite of her professing otherwise, had not perhaps explained the matter as fully as I should to satisfy the Chinese. I *know* I told her I was thinking of being ordained, if not in Malaysia then in Japan. I *remember* there being another of our frequent and distressing quarrels, my assuring her that I was going to teach at Tsurumi University, in Yokohama, and her saying good-bye to me on the ship in Southampton.

3. If I had been a true Buddhist at this time I would not have done this for I would have had my emotions under better control.

4. This is non-Buddhist thinking.

5. Un-Buddhist behavior and speech.

6. I was actually getting desperate to meditate.

7. This can only be *fully* comprehended at the time of kenshō when it becomes a flowing reality.

8. It is contrary to the Precepts to say or think ill of others.

9. It was wrong of me to write such things of Rev. Ichirō, even if true. I repeat them here that the reader may understand how far I was from being a true Buddhist at this time and thus learn not to copy my mistakes in his own training.

10. See also *How to Grow a Lotus Blossom*, Plate XI:– The Voice of the Eternal Lord.*

11. See *How to Grow a Lotus Blossom*, Plate LXII:– Heaven and Earth Are One.*

12. This was the reliving of a past life. See *How to Grow a Lotus Blossom*, Plates XIII through XVIII:– Vast Emptiness.*

13. See *How to Grow a Lotus Blossom,* Plates L through LII:– The True Being.*

---

*If I had understood more of Zen at this time I would have known that all of the experiences mentioned in 10–13 were the beginning of the kenshō that took place on 5th. October of that year. However, it is customary in Zen monasteries to keep very silent about such things where new trainees are concerned and only explain them when the first kenshō is completed and training is *obviously* continuing as it should. In addition to this it is not usual, although it does *occasionally* happen, for so many of them in a first *kenshō* (see *How to Grow a Lotus Blossom*, Foreward).

14. This is probably the most important sentence in the book from the point of view of someone who wishes to learn Zen. The two sentences which follow it are almost equally important.

15. The ability and *willingness* to 'catch the Lord' are vital to a peaceful death as well as having a kenshō in life (see *How to Grow a Lotus Blossom*, Plate XI:– The Voice of the Eternal Lord). What is happening here is no idle parlour game for the purpose of sharpening my wits. The master stands in place of the Lord in relation to the disciple and, if he knows his job, will behave as such whilst knowing that he is *not*—a concept very difficult for Western people to comprehend. It is for the above reason, and no other, that the disciple serves his master in many ways such as cooking and cleaning.

16. This was the start of an unfortunate trend in my thinking which was to colour, and even sour to a certain extent, the rest of my years in the temple. It is very important *not* to allow oneself to be influenced by the prejudices and opinions of others that are of a dualistic nature; when a teacher makes such statements it is important to remember that he is showing the disciple how *not* to think and behave. If this point is not taken to heart the disciple may get caught in the trap of non-Buddhist dualism, as I did, from which it is difficult to escape. That the master *believes* in his prejudices or not is none of the disciple's business; the disciple's job *solely* is to train himself to the best of his ability and not make other people's problems his own.

17. I did not know it at the time but this was very important. Until one can actually *see* the Buddha in one's fellow beings one cannot find It within oneself.

18. Such feeling is un-Buddhist.

19. The answer to this question is yes. This was also seeing the Buddha in these three seniors in varying degrees and ways.

20. When a person is doing true training there is an atmosphere of light about them to such an extent that, if one keeps up one's own meditation, one seems to see it. The three mentioned in Note No. 19. and Zenji Sama were thus as well as those in other parts of this book where this note number is appended.

21. Meditation heightens one's ability to hear the Voice of the Eternal Lord; Note No. 10. applies here also.

22. Pitying others is the breakage of the Precept against pride. I was very wrong here in the ideal sense of the word; however, it is important to make allowances for human nature whilst not condoning it.

23. It is important to get to this state without giving in to one's feelings; by so doing I made the kenshō possible. If I had allowed myself to lose my grip on my temper, I would have put it off indefinitely. Herein lies one of the greatest uses of meditation.

24. When the world around one seems crazy it is time to meditate deepest; one can then jump beyond both craziness and sanity. What happened in this incident caused me to make the leap I otherwise may not have taken (see entry for 5th. October). Constant beatings with the kyosaku in the meditation hall can do the same thing, if one is truly training, simply because they become meaningless and have to be transcended. Any impossible situation will cause a trainee to leap beyond the opposites if he is really meditating.

25. What follows is seeing one's past in this life-time as in a mirror; seeing the *immediate* causes of one's character traits enables one to know what to look for in one's former lives and thus remove the potential those traits hold for the future.

26. Both children and adults often hear the Lord's Voice and follow its advice without knowing why or even that it *is* His Voice; such people enter religion.

27. My reactions to the incidents and comments of my mother and others in this entry were un-Buddhist at the time they occurred thus they rose as shadows during the kenshō to show me how and where I had caused my body and mind to become unharmonised.

28. Elements of this, much expanded, are to be found in *How to Grow a Lotus Blossom*; this entry, and those numbered as Notes 10–13 and 20, should be studied in conjunction therewith.

29. Kenshō enables one to see the True Self of others clearly. Rev. Tarō was doing good training so seeing him was easy but kenshō heightens one's ability to such an extent that radiance can be seen around those who are not training so well also. Thus one can *know* for certain that *all* have the Buddha Nature or Light of the Lord.

30. The passage quoted is found in the Old Testament in Chapter 2 of the "Song of Songs," also known as the "Canticle of Canticles" or the "Song of Solomon."

31. See *How to Grow a Lotus Blossom*, Plates XIX and XX:– The Army of Mara, and the Foreward.

32. This indeed happened at my Transmission and again last year (see *How to Grow a Lotus Blossom*, Plates XXX through XXXIII:– Struck by the Sword of Buddha's Wisdom, which explains the 'flooding' of the Spirit). It happens totally differently from the way in which I described it to Rev. Hajime and he was right to be annoyed—however, perhaps the person I first heard about it from experienced the real thing but was at a loss to describe it; after all, I did get the story third hand.

33. If a layman has a kenshō it will *not* be *confirmed* by a priest for the reason that he may cease training himself and just live off the kenshō. This would lead to stagnation and, eventually, a return to evil ways which would now be far more dangerous

than before—in other words he would become a Buddhist sorcerer. The keeping of the Precepts is imperative—without certain knowledge of a trainee's doing this any confirmation of a kenshō is highly dangerous.

34. Refer to pages 515–516 of "Questions and Answers" at the end of this book.

35. Dangerous thinking. To even allow the *possibility* of doubt, wrong thoughts or duality to arise is dangerous. From such small beginnings karma is born—even after kenshō. The solving of the kōan is an on-going process.

36. About a dollar.

37. This is part of the On-Going Fugen Kenshō (see *How to Grow a Lotus Blossom*, Foreward).

38. This is by no means a general opinion; there are some Zenists who make out a doctrinal case for the hells.

39. If meditation is done properly it is possible to be still when everything around one is in turmoil. Thus one frequently sees pictures of monks sitting still on rocks whilst demons attack them from all sides but can do nothing to harm them. As with demons, so with situations like this; the secret of dealing with such events is *not* to allow oneself to be pulled out of meditation.

40. Only one priest, either male or female, is necessary to legally ordain priests in Japanese Sōtō Zen.

41. Since the master stands in place of the Lord of the House, his will is sacred to a true disciple.

42. After one has once had a kenshō one is *always* saved from despair and turning from the Lord *provided* one does not *will* oneself away from Him; *willfulness* in turning from the Lord is

the *one* and *only* thing that can separate a person from the Lord, *never* external pressures.

43. This was a prophecy that unfortunately came true.

44. Master Dōgen said:– "You should remember Nansen's anecdote of cutting a cat in half. Once his students, divided into two factions, were quarreling over a cat. Nansen suddenly took hold of it and said, 'Boil down your contention to one word. If you can do so I will not cut this cat in half but, if you cannot, I will.' None of them could answer so he cut it in two with one stroke."

"Later Nansen told Chao-Chou of this and the latter took off his straw sandals and went out with them on his head. What this behaviour of Chao-Chou's means is the main point of Nansen's cutting the cat in two. This is a far more splendid measure, suited to the occasion."

The Master went on:–

"If I had been Nansen I should have said, 'Even if you can answer in one word I will kill the cat and, if you cannot I will still kill it. Who on earth was quarreling over the cat? Who can help it out of the difficulty?' And I should have said, in place of the students, 'It is because we all have realised the Way that we all keep silence. Now, Master, kill the cat please.' And I should have continued, 'The Rev. Nansen knows how to cut in two but he does not know how to cut in one.'"

I, Ejō, asked:–

"What do you mean by cutting in one?"

Master Dōgen answered:–

"If the students say nothing and keep silence for a while Nansen may say, 'When you keep silence the whole Way reveals itself and you express It' and let the cat loose. (The cat runs away. This is how to cut it in one.) There is an old saying that one should not be scrupulous about trifles in performing a great function. (He should not have cut the cat in two; he should have cut it in one.)"

The Master continued:–

"This deed of Nansen's cutting the cat is a great operation of the Way, and the phrase 'cutting the cat' is what carries momentum to a new turn to enlightenment. Without this phrase you cannot penetrate the mental attitude of enlightenment in which all the earth, mountains and rivers are the crystallization of the pure and mysterious Mind of Buddha; and this Mind cannot be the Buddha. On hearing the phrase you must promptly understand that this cat is not a mere cat; it is the Buddha's Body. Then the students will directly open their eyes to the reality of things."

The Master said again:–

"This deed of cutting the cat is the deed of a Buddha."

"What do you call this deed?"

"You may call it cutting the cat."

I asked again:–

"Is it a sinful act?"

The Master answered:–

"Yes, it is."

"How can we be delivered from the sin?"

"To awake the students to the reality of things by the act of a Buddha is one thing; that it is a sinful act is another. It partakes of both a Buddha act and a sinful act."

"Pratimoksa applies to this case, does it not?"

The Master answered:–

"So it does."

And he continued:–

"However, the idea of awakening the students to the reality of things may be right, but you are best advised to do without such an idea."

– *Shōbōgenzō Zuimonki*, by Koun Ejō, translated by Rev. Genkai Shoyu with assistance of Rev. Jiyu-Kennett, mimeo, 1965.

45. This certificate came directly from the administration not from the temple.

46. Unless one keeps up one's training, even *after* kenshō, its beauty will fade and more karma will be accrued as a direct

result of one's lack of awareness. It was for this reason that Shakyamuni Buddha *always* carried His begging bowl and wore His robes after His Enlightenment.

47. There were very few bamboo and paper dividers and what there were had only rags of paper upon them.

48. A first class Kyoshi is possible after two years of training in a head temple but takes three years in any other training temple. It is roughly equivalent to a master's degree.

49. When making such observations it is imperative to keep an open mind—I could be mistaken. Judging others is a very dangerous occupation.

50. I personally do not consider this to be a sound idea.

51. Fortunately the front of the temple had glass doors rather than paper ones and I had put up the wooden shutters on all the paper doors. If it had not been thus I am not at all sure what would have been the outcome of this incident.

52. My fellow foreigners thought that I was rich; this was my fault owing to the fact that I did not dare let them or the Japanese know otherwise. It was a lie I abhorred having to live but, since the Japanese are terribly paranoid about poor foreigners in their country, I had no alternative. My studies in Japan were financed primarily by the Chinese abbot who had ordained me. This was extraordinarily kind of him but he was able to give me only enough for the bare necessities.

53. At this time a pound was worth three dollars.

54. This has a spiritual as well as a practical meaning, the physical body being the House of the Lord which is cleansed and purified through Zen training.

55. Photographs of this procession and all the ceremonies are in the possession of Shasta Abbey.

56. The priest's body is also the 'Temple of the Lord.' 'The opening of the gate' signifies the priest's willingness to 'be open' to giving help to all who come.

57. The word 'master' here has the double meaning of both Zenji Sama and the Cosmic Buddha.

58. Substitute 'He' for 'master' in Note No. 57.

59. Substitute 'Zenji Sama' for 'master' in Note No. 57.

60. Criticising others is un-Buddhist of me.

61. A true Buddhist would find no difference.

62. In actual fact, the Sōtō Sect registers their rōshis with the Head Office and the Rinzai Sect publishes the names of theirs in a book. It is also the normal thing in Zen for people to write and publish their kenshō experiences. Many are also found in manuscript form in the libraries of various great temples.

63. It was actually Andy who suggested the wording of the note to Rev. Hajime, who then told it to Zenji Sama, who then dictated it as his. Andy, at this time, became very difficult, saying that *I* had caused the trouble in England by asking others to write letters about it! This was the beginning, for me, of a wonder as to whom I could trust, since even my closest friends seemed untrustworthy; it was the beginning of a feeling that haunted me much afterwards; a feeling of standing in quicksand whenever anyone tried to get close to me. This was eventually to make me strong enough to rise above what happened at this time and lead me to greater depths of spirituality.

64. The political manoeuvrings of some of the descendants of the various Ancestral lines is the main reason why *true* Zen masters are more often found in small temples than large ones; the ambitious usually get the latter. However occasionally, there is an excellent Zen master appointed to a large temple, as in the case of Zenji Sama. Such people have a very difficult time, as he did, as a result of the political machinations by which they are surrounded.

65. It was a grave fault in me to be so unalert.

66. The officers of a large temple, all being abbots in their own right, albeit of smaller temples, are placed on a duty roster as celebrant for the day's ceremonies. It is because all are of the same rank that Zenji Sama was called the *"Chief* Abbot."

67. I was wrong to make this comment. No true Buddhist passes judgement on, or moralises over, the acts of others.

68. It is un-Buddhist to get angry for any reason whatsoever.

69. World War II.

70. Such despairing statements are anti-Buddhist since they call up despairing thoughts and recollections in both oneself and others. In true religion to despair oneself, and to cause others to suffer, is *the* "unforgiveable sin" if such it may be called.

71. This is a wrong assumption since it could lead to my closing my mind to him. "The gate must always stand open to those in need"—"the gate" being my mind in this case.

72. This actually happened in 1976—interestingly enough as a result of my third kenshō described in *How to Grow a Lotus Blossom.* I can only conclude that Britain's age-old distrust of authority in any religion, and her desire for a protestant type of lay ministry as opposed to a priesthood, is the root cause of the

problem. Every time there has been the chance of a genuine Sangha there some lay Buddhist has attempted to destroy it either by rumour or innuendo with very fair success. My personal life being unassailable, the attempt on me could only be launched, as in the case of the man who wrote the letters, against the validity and truth of my teaching and experience— to my knowledge a first in the line of attacks on the Sangha in England. *Editor's Note:* There is now a well-established Sangha in England. See "About the Order of Buddhist Contemplatives" and "About the Monasteries of the Order: Throssel Hole Buddhist Abbey" at the end of this book.

73. It is wrong to think thus of others.

74. In the East this is *not* true.

75. In the ultimate sense there is no such thing as an enemy; all is one.

76. Note No. 67 does not mean, however, that one should not take precautions; this instance certainly required them.

77. I should not have made this comment; a true Buddhist should take notice of such incidents but neither praise nor blame their originator.

78. Such thoughts are sometimes unavoidable but they should never be voiced.

79. It is wrong to describe others thus.

80. Throughout all this time my meditation was deepening greatly. One of the great advantages that came out of all the problems mentioned in books three and four of this diary was the way that they caused both my faith and my meditation to deepen in order to be able both to handle, and rise above, them.

81. Bad language is *always* wrong.

82. This is explained in the text of the next entry.

83. To refuse to recognise the Buddha Nature in another by refusing respect is a very dangerous thing. The secret papers tell us that Buddhism will only last as long as bowing lasts. I was very wrong to act thus.

84. I had no right to say this; it is anti-Buddhist and I had no proof of it.

85. A form of address used for small boys in Japan.

86. This is wrong thinking. I should not have such thoughts.

87. It is wrong to allow such thoughts as these.

88. I had asked if my rank could be raised some time earlier so that I could qualify for an office and get help from the juniors with the foreigners as well as, perhaps, acceptance from the seniors.

89. All of this interview with Rev. Hajime was wrong behaviour on my part.

90. The shock of what I had overheard had made me forget my promise to Zenji Sama.

91. *Editor's Comment:* There is a belief in some Western circles that once a person has experienced a kenshō and been named a rōshi his or her every act must necessarily be the embodiment of enlightenment or else he or she is not a real rōshi. This is not true. Even the most excellent and experienced rōshi, whether of the Sōtō, Rinzai, or Ōbaku Sect, is human and not a god; he or she can and will make mistakes as long as he lives. What an enlightenment experience does is to show one without doubt

the truth of the way of continuous religious training. He or she who continues to follow this way fearlessly, who learns from his mistakes, and who is not afraid of letting other people see them is fit to teach others and be called a rōshi. D.M.

92. This interview exhibits wrong behaviour on my part. These things should not have affected me emotionally in the way they did.

93. I have no personal proof of this matter concerning the Koreans but have heard that it is so from several people. I would be glad to hear from any source whatsoever that I am misinformed on this matter since I have no desire whatsoever to leave the reader with a wrong impression concerning the Japanese.

94. This comment proved to be very prophetic when I returned to England and continues to be so to this day, (16th. January, 1978).

95. From here on my part of this interview no longer exhibits wrong thought.

96. The word used here would be better translated as 'visions' rather than 'dreams.'

97. Even with an unassailable character this was not to be (see also Note No. 72).

98. The fact that I am a rōshi was ratified again in the Journal of Eiheiji, *Sanshō*, last November, (1977,) in an article in Japanese concerning this and other Buddhist centres in America.

99. 'Quarrel' is the wrong word, 'mistrust' would be better. The situation described should not be contrived artificially, because of the Director's words, as some people have *tried* to contrive it here in Shasta simply because it happened to *me* and, ipso

facto, should happen to them since they are my disciples! The master-disciple relationship is based on absolute trust; I should have had greater faith in Zenji Sama than I did.

100. Wrong thinking.

101. The temple had a number of lay employees; this was one of them.

102. I should have added that life is sacred.

103. Wrong thinking even if true.

104. I must apologise to any Buddhist writer from whom I *may* have borrowed ideas or turns of phrase in these answers. I do not recall deliberately *quoting* from anyone but this does not preclude the possibility of my having done so. Should this indeed be the case, and I find the sources in the future, I will gladly acknowledge them in future editions but, at the time of going to print, I can recollect none. Incidentally, I would no longer answer these questions quite as I did here.

105. There are two occasions when transmission can take place, a.)when a person begins to truly train and, b.)after a first kenshō (see article in *Journal of Shasta Abbey,* "A Note on Transmission and Priestly Rank," by Daizui MacPhillamy, August-September, 1977).

106. The same principle applies here as in Note No. 99. It was this incident which caused me to leave Zenji Sama, in spite of my promise, prior to his death; a fact which, although I returned and apologised quickly, I have regretted ever since.

107. I had moved into a much larger room some time before the previous Jūkai.

108. It is *always* wrong to go against the master's wishes. I knew it and I still went; I have regretted it ever since.

109. At this time there was a great push on the part of the Malaysian government to force everyone to become Mohammedan and to have no language other than Malayan in a multi-racial, multi-cultural and multi-religious country.

110. The constant vacillations of opinions for and against foreigners was one of the most difficult things for me to cope with whilst I was in Japan—and one of the most difficult to keep up with!

111. The mistrust and despair that was bred in many of the foreigners by the situation in Note No. 110 was one of the saddest things I was forced to witness during my stay in Japan. If I had not had my first kenshō *I* would have been inundated by them also; as it was, it was many years after I left Japan, and two further kenshōs, before I could again trust anyone absolutely. At every turn it was faith and meditation that helped, and ultimately saved, me from spiritual destruction.

112. Those who cannot understand this should read my article on discipleship in the Twenty-fifth Anniversary Issue of *The Journal of the Order of Buddhist Contemplatives*, Volume 10, nos. 3 & 4 (Autumn–Winter 1995), pp. 21–24. This article was first published in *Gesar* magazine, Fall 1977.

113. Whatever went wrong at the sub-temple he was staying at I never found out; it is still a mystery. It kept him free for a number of months so his behaviour would seem to have been very ungrateful.

114. This woman was one of the truest friends I had during my entire stay in Japan.

115. A reference to the Lord of the House (see *Denkōroku*, by Keizan Zenji, in *Zen is Eternal Life*, and *How to Grow a Lotus Blossom*).

116. I should have bowed to both of them in spite of what was happening.

117. I had said to him that it was a pity someone else did not talk to the authorities and was glad when he went to do so and worried at the same time for I knew it was unwise.

118. All of this later proved to be political manoeuvring for the purpose of upsetting Zenji Sama's relationship with me on the part of persons unknown, *none* of whom were in power in the head office. Both then, and to this day, both I and the Foreign Section (now the Shasta Abbey community) have maintained good relations with the Sōtō Zen authorities; the article concerning us in the prestigious Sōtō Zen journal, *Sanshō*, (November 1977) and the visit of Matsunaga Rōshi and Harada Rōshi in 1978 attest to this.

119. I was right about Zenji Sama's real reactions as I later found out. He was very upset by what he had been told, blew up, cooled and changed his mind. In the meantime the letter had been sent.

120. I was later to find out that this was a warning sign of the onset of diabetes that had been brought on by malnutrition and worry. The immense weight that I put on was also later diagnosed as having been caused by malnutrition. My diet during most of the time I was in Japan consisted of rice gruel for breakfast, rice and miso soup for lunch (the latter containing tofu, or bean curd, and vegetables) and noodles and soup for supper, the soup being made from water and soya sauce. If I had been allowed to go to as many outside ceremonies as were the other trainees during the first four years this illness would not have happened; it was only when I started going to outside ceremonies (approximately twice a week

or less) that I was able to supplement my diet with the meals offered by the congregation. A "feast" was held in the temple once a month consisting of an extra dish of vegetables and friends helped after the first three years also; unfortunately, by that time, the damage was already done.

121. This effect of the malnutrition has still not been reversed.

122. It was these higher teachings that, through being discovered too soon, caused another person to return to England recently and cause a recurrence of the problems upon which Note No. 94 comments. The higher teachings of Zen are not for cowards.

123. This was not true.

124. Nevertheless sitting meditation in the Zazen position can *never*, and must *never*, be dispensed with; nor must it be *clung* to as Dōgen Zenji points out in the "Zazen Rules."

125. It proved to be the latter; the latest of the political moves.

126. Although they had X-rayed me many times in this area when I had visited doctors in the past I had always been told they could see nothing on the plates. The unbelievable truth was that the growth was so large that the doctors thought the plates were defective (presumably every time!) since no *Japanese* could have a tumour that big. It had not occurred to them it seems that they were X-raying a foreigner who was much larger than the average Japanese. It was a Western doctor that made the final diagnosis and ordered the surgery. I remember very little of what happened during the time between being at my friend's house and the incidents mentioned here.

127. It appears that those in charge of the hospital were divided in their opinion as to whether or not my treatment should have been rendered without charge, as apparently was customary for Christian clerics and their relatives. I was repeatedly assured

that the matter had been settled and I left Japan believing it to be so. Many years later my doctor had need to request my records from this hospital during my recent illness and he was informed that they would not be released until I paid the hospital some one thousand dollars in past-due charges. Some of my disciples and friends kindly raised the money to pay the hospital and the records were eventually released.

128. Wrong speech.

129. *Very* wrong speech; it breaks the Precepts concerning speaking against others and judging others. I was very *wrong* to write this.

130. The exact date of this event is not known. 17th. December is a close approximation. The entries from here to 12th. February were all written down at a much later date.

131. In the ultimate sense, other people's behaviour can never be a difficulty to a trainee; in the worldly sense, however, this statement was an accurate description.

132. As a result of meditation I have been able to discover that this and some other facts of my childhood were incorrect, and the obtention of my early hospital records through a doctor friend has proved the truth of what my meditations revealed concerning myself. If it had not been for the exaggeration of minor ailments before my fifth year into major illnesses, of which I was later told, I would have had a totally different childhood and youth and my kōan would have developed differently. Thanks to meditation I have been able to clear up many cloudy areas of my early life.

133. Even where such comments concerning others as the above are true, it is still wrong for a true student of Zen to make them since they involve the breaking of the Precept against speaking or thinking ill of others. I include this paragraph here as a warning to both the reader and myself. It is important to remember

that one does not lead others into making mistakes similar to one's own.

134. This was a personal view. I have no proof of this and therefore such a comment should not have been made.

135. The following comments only apply to married couples wishing to enter *Japanese* temples; they do *not* apply to married couples wishing to enter *American* ones. I wrote these comments for the Japan of 1968.

136. This person did not go to a Zen temple but to one of a different sect; he is now well again.

137. This paragraph is very important. It is *always* wrong to break the Precepts and yet one seems sometimes to *have* to speak out. If I had been a better monk at the time of writing this I would have handled the situations differently; I pray that the reader does not copy my bad example as a result of this entry. I also am not sure that my motives were entirely good in writing the passage.

138. Read the previous footnote, excluding the first sentence.

139. The whole of this entry shows self-pity and temper and is, therefore, bad teaching. It is included here to show how humanly frail a Zen teacher can be.

140. One could, hypothetically, be Transmitted by a thousand different masters and, in one sense, is so Transmitted once the 'all is one' is completely understood; but Harry was not, at this time, ready for such teaching, being still in the stage of comparing masters rather than recognising their intrinsic oneness.

141. I agree because of the implication that the first master is not truly Buddha and because of the tendency for people to otherwise gather up a number of "Transmissions" for their own

political or financial advantage, since being Transmitted by a monk gives them the right to possibly become abbot or abbess of that monk's temple. Some monks actually have collected the revenues of several temples in the past prior to this rule being made.

142. This information should not have been given to Harry since it partakes of gossip and thus breaks the Precepts. It is repeated here as a warning to the reader to learn from my mistakes and guard his speech. My motives may not have been pure when writing this.

143. Such speculation is idle and not conducive to true training.

144. Maybe they thought they were emulating my culture. If so, then my comments here are very wicked for their sole purpose was kindness.

145. It is wrong of me to criticise in this way without certain knowledge. There is no way in which a rōshi of any school of Zen, whether Sōtō, Rinzai or Ōbaku, would ever agree with the kind of thinking found in her letter; I can only conclude that she never told him. True Zen training is synonymous with service to one's fellow men. I say this in no way to criticise her either but, in accordance with the purpose of this book, to point out my own mistakes in training.

146. This is a wrong attitude of mind; other people's karma and training is not my business; each person makes his or her own karma.

147. The abbot who took over after my Zenji Sama's death.

148. Ingratitude and embarrassment for *anything* and negative criticism of others is always wrong however, as will be seen by what follows, I was, at this time, beginning to be more alert

concerning such things. It is important to remain still and be pulled off centre by neither praise nor blame at such times.

149. I should not be thinking thus.

150. Wrong thought; such thinking can lead to the despising of others and is thus a breakage of the Precepts.

151. He is Rinzai.

152. In the *real* sense of religion there are no such things as friends and enemies whilst, in the worldly sense, they exist. So, whilst *knowing* that one is invulnerable, one must still take precautions. "Trust in God and tie your camel" is as applicable in Zen as it is in Mohammedanism with the proviso that one must be on the alert for any sign of paranoia.

153. Although it is wrong to break the Precepts one nevertheless is occasionally forced by circumstances and moral obligation into doing so; the keeping of the Precepts does not permit of moral cowardice. However, when one does do such a thing one must fully accept the karmic consequence of having done it without complaint. One may not blame the relinquishing of *personal* responsibility on the teachings of the Buddhas and Ancestors or the results of having taken it. In the above instance to speak of Rev. Hajime as I did was to break the Precepts; not to speak would have been morally irresponsible—and I must still keep my mind open to the fact that I could be wrong.

154. Dōgen Zenji once said, "It is hard to keep the initial humility to the end but it is *absolutely* imperative." Seeing the Cosmic Buddha is one thing, being worthy of it is quite another. Unfortunately, in the West, the *"moment"* of kenshō is frequently regarded as the *whole* of training rather than its commencement and therefore we often find so-called "enlightened" Westerners who are very unsatisfactory people. This is solely

because they experienced a first kenshō (see Foreward in *How to Grow a Lotus Blossom*) and decided that their training was over.

155. The friend who arranged this temple for me is a sort of "feudal Lord" of which there are many in Japan. Since the temple was on his land he could, by ancient right, give it to whomsoever he wished irrespective of its legal owner's wishes!

156. He stayed there whilst I was in hospital.

157. Compromise such as this is always wrong.

158. This is wrong thinking—the temple gate must stand open to all.

159. Her presence actually did do damage; normally priests guard both the Transmission room and the master and disciple at the time of Transmission because of the danger of disturbance. At this time such guards were not available but the whole incident served to teach me their importance.

160. It is wrong to become suspicious.

161. A foreigner who successfully competes with a Japanese is in a very dangerous position with regard to creating jealousy. To a very large extent this was my problem in the Tokyo temple also. Jealousy is, unfortunately, a Japanese national trait.

162. *Editor's Comment:* In the years which have passed since Rōshi Jiyu-Kennett's arrival in America, some of the events recorded in these diaries have taken on a new perspective. It now appears that almost all of the difficulties which she encountered in the Tokyo monastery were caused by the political machinations of only two of the officers who, it would seem, provided her and others with misleading information on a number of occasions. These two used every letter which came from England and every mistake made by people who came to

the Foreign Guest Department to further their anti-foreign cause. Rōshi Jiyu-Kennett did not know this at the time of writing the diary and of leaving Japan. Their actions should not give the reader the impression that the majority of the Japanese priesthood is anti-foreign nor anti-Rōshi Jiyu-Kennett herself, as later events both in Japan and America have proved. The Sōtō Sect authorities provided her with all necessary certification before she came to America and she has remained in good standing up to the time of her death in 1996. D.M.

163. One always sends a mochi to someone who has taught you anything in Zen at the New Year whether you are still friends or not.

164. I was following the correct custom in doing this.

165. It is quite customary for the parents of large Japanese families to give, or sell, a child to a childless family. If I had been a Japanese I would not have been appalled by this.

166. Calling someone an idiot is not good Buddhism.

167. I should have stayed in a temple; this is a sign that I was allowing myself to be influenced by circumstances and external things.

168. What is being described here is one of the "little moments" of the On-Going Fūgen kenshō (see *How to Grow a Lotus Blossom,* Foreward). I was at this place again at the beginning of my last kenshō. One is in the same place every time a kenshō, however deep, takes place.

169. Such presumption is wrong.

170. During this time I received a certificate asking me to become the official pioneer missionary of the Sōtō Sect in America and a contract for four years to do this from the Head

Office. So, in spite of appearances, I became their official representative when going to America and England.

171. This is wrong thinking on my part; I have no proof of this.

172. This was wrong of me; his going or coming should have made no difference.

173. There is *never* an end.

174. Such speculation is a waste of time; staying still in meditation is the only thing that matters. One must not be pulled off centre by such considerations, whether they represent that which is real or imagined. The danger of allowing sadness to enter one's heart is that such speculation can arise.

175. A human, rather than a Buddhist, act.

Glossary.

The following abbreviations are used:
Liturgy—*The Liturgy of the Order of Buddhist
Contemplatives for the Laity*, second edition
Liturgy, Priests' edition—*The Liturgy of the Order of
Buddhist Contemplatives*
ZEL—*Zen is Eternal Life*, fourth edition
C—Chinese
J—Japanese
P—Pali
S—Sanskrit

ANANDA (S). The Buddha's personal jiisha. See *Denkōroku*,
chap. 3, in ZEL, p. 231.
ANCESTOR. Refers to any teacher, male or female, who has
fully understood Buddhism and who is in the line of succes-
sion. See Ancestral line, Liturgy, pp. 66–69 and *Denkōroku*,
ZEL, pp. 217–296.
ANICCA (P), anitya (S), impermanence. Transience. See
Gakudō-yōjinshū, ZEL, p. 162ff, and "Uji," ZEL, p. 198ff.
ASURA (S), those who do not shine, i.e. Titan.
AVATAMSAKA SUTRA (S), Hua-yen Ching (C), Kegonkyō
(J), Garland Scripture. The teaching of Shakyamuni Buddha
during the three weeks immediately after His enlightenment
while He was still in a deep state of meditation. The

Gandavyuha and *Dasabhumika Scripture* are sections of this Scripture.

BETSUIN (J), a sub-temple. In other words, I could call my temple a temple that was representing the Tokyo temple.

BODHIDHARMA (S), c. 530, Bodaidaruma or Daruma (J). The Indian Ancestor who brought Zen teaching to China; known to the Chinese as the First Ancestor.

BODHISATTVA (S), bosatsu (J), pu-sa (C), enlightened being. See ZEL, pp. 36–65.

BODHISATTVA VOW, see FOUR VOWS.

BUDDHA (S), Butsu (J). Enlightened One, Awakened One. (1) A person with direct understanding of the Truth. A completely awakened person. (2) The historical Shakyamuni Buddha.

BUDDHA MIND. The mind without attachment and discrimination which is the real mind of all beings, although they themselves may not recognise it: another name for the Buddha Nature.

BUDDHA'S NOBLE TRUTHS, see FOUR NOBLE TRUTHS.

CHIEF JUNIOR, Shusōshō (J). A trainee selected by the Abbot for a training term of one hundred days to lead all trainees in the monastery. See "The Ceremonies Necessary for the Training Term," Liturgy, Priests' edition, pp. 530–586; see also ZEL, Book 1, chap. 9, pp. 73–87.

CHIGO-SAN (J). The name given to the princes and princesses who came to greet the Buddha after his enlightenment. Nowadays it is traditional for the children of the parishioners to relive this incident when a new priest is installed in a temple.

CHIKORYŌ (J), the cashier's office.

COSMIC BUDDHA. THAT which appears in every place and time and in all beings; also called by various other names such as Vairocana Buddha, Amitabha Buddha, Dharmakaya, Buddha Nature and Lord of the House. IT can be revealed through genuine training but cannot be explained as existing or not existing being beyond dualism.

DAI KAIDŌ (J), literally 'great hall of shadows;' the home of Buddha Nature within a being, where it remains hidden unless revealed by training. Although it is not spatial, it can manifest itself in the hara.

DEVA (S), ten (J). (1) Gods; heavenly beings; beings in possession of supernatural powers. (2) A great person who, having understood the Truth, leads others to it.

DHARMA (S), hō (J), fa (C). (1) Law, Truth, the Teachings of the Buddhas and Ancestors. (2) The second of the Three Treasures and Refuges:– "I take refuge in the Dharma." The Dharma is the medicine for all suffering as it teaches the way to transcend greed, hate and delusion.

DIAMOND SCRIPTURE, Vajracchedika Prajnaparamita Sutra (S), Kongō-kyō (J). One of the Great Wisdom Scriptures which succinctly deals with the training of the Bodhisattva especially relating to the awakening of True Wisdom and to the practice of the Six Paramitas. The *Diamond Scripture* is widely used in all Mahayana traditions and it was this Scripture which Daikan Enō used to teach his disciples.

DŌGEN ZENJI (J), 1200–1253. Founder of the Sōtō Zen Church in Japan. He was of noble birth and was orphaned as a child. He entered the priesthood at the age of twelve, studied Tendai on Mt. Hiei and then went on to study under Myoan Eisai at Kenninji Temple. In 1223 he journeyed to China with Eisai's disciple, Myozen, in order to study Zen, eventually entering Tendōzan Keitokuji where he became the disciple of Tendō Nyojō Zenji, one of the great Sōtō Zen teachers then alive: he became Nyojō Zenji's Dharma Heir receiving the Transmission from him. He returned to Japan in 1227; he was at first Abbot of Kenninji, then Abbot of Kōshōji and later founded Eiheiji in 1244. His chief disciple was Koun Ejō. His major works are the *Shōbōgenzō*, the *Eihei-kōroku*, the *Eihei-shingi* and the *Kyōjukaimon*. He was given the posthumous title of Kōsō Jōyō Daishi. He is widely acknowledged to be Japan's greatest religious thinker. In ZEL, pp. 89–214.

EIGHTFOLD PATH. The way to transcend suffering as taught
by Shakyamuni Buddha in the fourth Noble Truth. The
eight stages are right understanding, right thought, right
speech, right action, right livelihood, right effort, right
mindfulness and right concentration. See also FOUR
NOBLE TRUTHS.

EKŌ (J), offertory giving merit of ceremony or scripture reci-
tation to someone else. See Offertories in Liturgy and
Liturgy, Priests' edition.

ENLIGHTENMENT, Nirvana (S), Bodhi (S). Religious reali-
zation or understanding.

ENLIGHTENMENT BY OTHERS, Sravaka-bodhi (S), becoming enlightened as a result of hearing the teaching and putting it into practice to realise no-self but not the emptiness
of all things, without undertaking the Bodhisattva practice.
The first level in Hinayana, the other being single enlightenment. Both of these levels retain the idea of training for oneself, which is abandoned in the Mahayana practice of the
Bodhisattva path.

FIVE LAWS OF THE UNIVERSE. The five laws by which the
universe operates are:– (1) the laws of the physical world—
the world is not answerable to one's personal will; (2) the
laws of the organic world—all things flow; (3) the laws of
morality—karma is inexorable; (4) the laws of the Dharma
—evil is vanquished and good prevails; (5) the laws of
mind—the will to enlightenment: the intuitive knowledge
of the Buddha Nature occurs to all men.

FOUR NOBLE TRUTHS. These are:– (1) suffering exists; (2)
suffering's cause; (3) suffering's end; (4) the Eightfold Path.
See the EIGHTFOLD PATH.

FOUR VOWS. The four Bodhisattva vows. (1) However innumerable beings are, I vow to save them; (2) However inex-
haustible the passions are, I vow to transform them; (3)
However limitless the Dharma is, I vow to understand it
completely; (4) However infinite the Buddha's Truth is, I vow
to attain it. See ZEL, pp. 36–65, see Liturgy, pp. 48–52, 93.

FUGEN (J), Samantabhadra (S), Full of Virtue. See "Activity in the Heart of Samantabhadra," ZEL, pp. 46–53.

FUTONS, large rectangular cushions used as mattresses.

FULL-LOTUS. The form of cross-legged sitting in which each foot is placed over the opposite thigh. See *Serene Reflection Meditation*, 6th edition, 1996, p. 26.

GASSHŌ (J). The Buddhist mudra which expresses gratitude and humility.

GOI THEORY (J). Tōzan's Five Ranks.

HACHIKŌ (J). The famous "faithful dog of Japan" who, after his master's death, continued to come every day to meet his train.

HAISEKI (J), Bowing seat.

HALF-LOTUS. A form of cross-legged sitting in which one foot is placed on the opposite thigh whilst the other rests on the sitting place See *Serene Reflection Meditation*, 6th edition, 1996, p. 26.

HANAMATSURI (J), 'flower festival,' The Buddha's birthday, May 8. See Liturgy, Priests' edition, pp. 277–282.

HARA (J). The triangular region of the front of the body formed from the base of the sternum and reaching down the sides of the rib cage to just below the navel.

HŌKYŌZAMMAI (J), Pao-ching San-wei (C), The Most Excellent Mirror-Samādhi. Scripture written by Tōzan Ryokai, one of the founders of the Sōtō Zen Church. Liturgy, pp. 61–65.

HONDŌ (J). Hall of a temple where ceremonies are held and lectures given.

HOSSU (J). A sceptre carried by a celebrant during ceremonies. Symbol of the priest's compassion.

HUNGRY GHOST, gaki (J), preta (S). An occupant of one of the Six Worlds depicted with a tiny throat and bloated stomach. See "The Ceremony for Feeding the Hungry Ghosts," Liturgy, pp. 158–175.

IMPREGNATIONS, vasana (S), remnants of karma from the past which must still be dealt with after the roots of greed, hate and delusion have been cut. Even though no new karma is created, the effects of past karma remain.

IRON MAN, tetsugen (J), Vajrasattva (S). The immovable, imperturbable and indestructible Buddha Nature within one. See *Denkōroku*, chap. 1, ZEL, pp. 224–227.

JŌDŌ (J). (1) The festival of the attainment of Buddhahood held on December 8th. (2) A Zen ceremony in which the Abbot ascends the high altar to be tested in mondo (question and answer) on his realisation of the Truth. One of the Kessei ceremonies. See Liturgy, Priests' edition, "The Abbot's Dharma Ceremony," pp. 566–573.

KAIDŌ (J), see DAI KAIDŌ.

KAISHAKU (J), wooden clappers used as signals during Zen ceremonies.

KANZEON BOSATSU (J), Avalokitesvara Bodhisattva (S), Kuan-shi-yin, Kuan Yin (C), also Kannon (J). He who hears the cries of the world. Kanzeon is the Bodhisattva who exhibits Great Compassion and Mercy.

KARMA (S), kamma (P). Action, resulting from cause, and its effect. The Law of Cause and Effect; the third of the Five Laws of the Universe.

KENSHŌ (J), to see into one's own nature. The experience of enlightenment, satori (J).

KESA (J), kasaya (S). The Buddhist priest's robe. See also RAKUSU.

KŌAN (J), kung-an (C), public case. A statement or story, used usually by a Rinzai Zen Master, as a teaching device.

KOTATSU (J). Traditionally, a table beneath which there is a sunken well containing charcoal sticks embedded in sand, nowadays sometimes heated by an electric heater or charcoal briquettes affixed to the bottom of the table.

KYŌJUKAIMON (J). Dōgen's explanation of the Buddhist Precepts. In ZEL, pp. 211–214.

KYOKUROKU (J), celebrant's chair.

KYOSAKU (J), awakening stick.

LAW, see DHARMA.

LORD OF THE HOUSE. Buddha in each being, Buddha Nature, Cosmic Buddha; That which is not explicable in terms of existence and non-existence or self and other. Another term for Buddha Mind, Iron Man, True Heart.

LOTUS SCRIPTURE, Hokke-kyō or Myō-hō-renge-kyō (J), Saddharma Pundarika (S). *The Lotus of the Good Law Scripture.* A Mahayana Buddhist Scripture which teaches that all living things have the Buddha Nature and can attain Buddhahood.

MAKAKASHYŌ (J), Mahakasyapa (S), also called Kasyapa, Kashō. One of the ten great disciples of Shakyamuni Buddha. Born into a Brahmin family, he became a disciple of the Buddha and reached Understanding in only eight days. See *Denkōroku*, ZEL, pp. 227–236.

MAKYŌ (J). Hallucinations, which must be distinguished from genuine religious visions, which may arise during meditation; usually due to incorrect breathing, posture or physical or mental stress.

MANDALA (S), mandara (J). A diagram which expresses a religious view of the universe by means of symbols or portraits of Buddhas and Bodhisattvas.

MANJUSRI BODHISATTVA (S), Monju Bosatsu (J). Manjusri personifies great wisdom (prajna).

MARA (S). The personification of all temptations to evil and distractions from training.

MOCHI (J), solid beaten rice cakes.

MOKUGYO (J), carved wooden drum in the shape of a fish holding a ball in its mouth.

NENGE (J), a procession which expresses a Buddhist doctrine.

NENJU (J), Meditation Hall Closing Ceremony. Liturgy, pp. 112–113.

NYOI (J). A sceptre carried by a celebrant during ceremonies.

OBON (J). The time of Segaki in Japan, usually July 15, called the Festival of Lanterns.

OHIGAN (J), crossing over. The Japanese festival held at the equinox.

OX-HERDING PICTURES. A series of ten pictures depicting Zen training. These drawings are attributed to Kaku-an Shi-en, a Chinese Zen priest of the twelfth century.

PATRIARCH, see ANCESTOR.

PRECEPTS, kai (J), sila (S). The ways of living that are in accordance with the Dharma.

QUIETISM. A spiritual disease caused by a grave misunderstanding of karma.

RAKUSU (J). A small kesa (priest's robe) worn around the neck.

RŌSHI (J), reverend master.

RYOKAN (J), a Japanese-style family inn, as opposed to a Western-style hotel.

SAMSARA (S), shōji (J), this world of life and death.

SANDŌKAI (J), Ts'an-t'ung-chi (C), the harmonising of the all is one and the all is different. A Zen Scripture written by Sekitō Kisen. In Liturgy, pp. 59–61.

SANGE (J), contrition, confession, repentance. The sincere recognition of all that is wrong within one and the acceptance of one's past karma. Sange is the true source of religious humility and a principal gateway to enlightenment.

SANGHA (S), sō (J). The community of those who follow the Buddha's Teaching: male priests, female priests, laymen, laywomen.

SANZEN (J). Spiritual direction under a Zen Master.

SCRIPTURE OF GREAT WISDOM; Hannya-Shingyō; full name:– Makahannya haramita shingyō (J); Mahaprajna Paramita Hrdaya Sutra (S). Sometimes called the *Heart Scripture* since it is considered to be the essence, or heart, of the Great Wisdom Scripture.

SEGAKI (J), feeding the hungry spirits. A ceremony performed annually for all those who have died the previous year without having become enlightened, or on special occasions as needed. Held at Shasta Abbey on October 31. In Liturgy, pp. 158–175.

SESSHIN (J), searching the heart.

SHAKYAMUNI BUDDHA (J), sage of the Shakyas. Refers to the historical Buddha after His enlightenment. See ZEL, pp. 3–7, 224–231.

SHŌNAWASHYU (J), Sanavasa (S). The third Ancestor in India, successor to Ananda. See ZEL, pp. 237–245.

SHŌSAN (J). Ceremony similar to Jōdō held every two weeks in Zen monasteries, in which all trainees bring their kōans to the Abbot.

SHUGYŌ (J), hard training.

SINGLE ENLIGHTENMENT, pratyeka-bodhi (S). Enlightenment reached by oneself alone and not passed on to others. The second level of Hinayana.

SKANDHAS (S), heaps, aggregates. The psycho/physical existence of a human being is categorised into five aggregates. They are:– (1) form or matter; (2) sensations or feelings; (3) thoughts and perceptions; (4) mental activity or impulses; (5) consciousness. When the skandhas are viewed through ignorance, a false notion of a self is created.

SURANGAMA SUTRA (S), Ryōgonkyō (J). A Mahayana Buddhist Scripture which discusses many of the obstacles that arise in training as well as the various states into which one can fall as a result of confusion and attachment. Excerpted in ZEL, pp. 55–56.

SUTRA (S), kyō (J), sutta (P). A Buddhist Scripture. The first division of the *Tripitaka*.

TAIKAI (J), "Great Meeting."

TAOISM, the teachings of Lao-tzu, Chuang-tzu and their successors.

TATHAGATA (S), Nyorai (J), Thus come One, Thus gone One. A title for a Buddha.

TATTE-MŌSU (J). High hat worn by an abbot during ceremonies.

TEN BUDDHAS. The names of the Ten Buddhas are recited in many Zen ceremonies. Note that the Ten Buddhas include Scriptures, Bodhisattvas and Ancestors, indicating every form of Buddha.

THREE TREASURES, Sambō (J). The Buddha, the Dharma
and the Sangha; they are also referred to as the Three
Jewels.

TITAN ASURAS, see ASURA.

TOKO-NO-MA (J). The most important place in the chief guest
room of a Japanese house, where flowers, a scroll and incense burner may be found.

TRANSMISSION, Dembō (J). In the Zen tradition, the Truth is
passed down heart to heart and this has been called the
Transmission of Mind or Dharma. This Transmission is
beyond all words and concepts and only takes place when
the Master and disciple are One in the Buddha Mind. The
first example of the Transmission is the story in the
Denkōroku of Makakashyō, the First Ancestor.

UNSUI (J), cloud and water. A priest trainee, male or female.

VASANA (S), see IMPREGNATIONS.

ZAZEN (J), sitting meditation. Zen meditation done in the formal seated position. See *Rules for Meditation* in Liturgy,
pp. 97–100.

ZENJI (J), ch'an-shih (C), Zen Master.

Questions and Answers.

The following questions and answers were recorded during discussions of both monks and lay Buddhists with Rōshi Jiyu-Kennett on the subject of this book. They have been edited, paraphrased, and printed here in hopes that they may clarify some of the questions which readers may have.

QUESTION: The pettiness and political manoeuvring of some of the monks shocked me; are all monasteries like this?

Rōshi Jiyu-Kennett: Yes, to a certain degree. People suffer from the idea that monasteries are a collection of saints; they don't realise that people who go to monasteries are human. The ones who appeared petty or dishonest when I was there were trying to do what was right as best they knew how at the time. One of the most important lessons to learn if you would profit from monastic training is not to be disappointed by your fellow trainees; learn from them but do not judge them. When you do see someone who sets an incredible example for you, as did Zenji Sama, the old Cook, the Chief Lecturer, the Director and the old Disciplinarian for me, then count yourself very fortunate and follow their teaching.

Monk: And it is important to realise that this has nothing to do with the East or the West. There are plenty of examples of this sort of behaviour in Western monasteries. For example there is the story of St. John of the Cross being flogged

511

every night at supper time for six months because he refused to wear shoes! That is at least as peculiar as anything described in this book.

QUESTION: I noticed that your kenshō occurred after you had been driven to the point of illness and exhaustion and that people were beaten to bring them to a state of desperation. Is this the only way to find the Truth? Is it the best way?

Rōshi Jiyu-Kennett: No; beating people is not the ancient way. Of course you can put a person in the right situation, beat him, deprive him and, if he takes it positively, you can drive him into a kenshō in a few months; but consider the damage that was done to me physically by that system. Sometimes the beating produced a kenshō but far more often people simply left in a rage, resigned themselves to it stoically or fled into flower arrangement, calligraphy and the like, none of which did them much good spiritually. Beating is a form of manipulation. In America we do not have to do it that way so I see no reason to copy Japan in that respect. Yes, you have to be desperate enough to be willing to give up everything if you would know the Lord of the House, but people do that naturally if they meditate and really look at the hell that they are in. You do not need to manufacture artificial desperation.

QUESTION: What advice would you give to someone who is thinking of going to Japan to study Zen?

Rōshi Jiyu-Kennett: First, understand that the Japanese are human. Too many people who go to Japan, especially young Americans, have the idea that every Japanese is wise, polite and, in all ways wonderful; such people, if they stay in the country longer than a month or two, are usually very disappointed and disillusioned. I did not have that problem perhaps because I went there relatively soon after the Second World War. I remember several friends begging me not to go—showing me the scars from the tortures the Japanese had inflicted on them in prisoner-of-war camps—

telling me that they were monsters. In fact, the Japanese, like everyone else, are neither a nation of saints nor a nation of fiends; they are human.

Next, it is extremely important to know the language well, especially be able to read and write it before you go. Third, do not expect anything; conditions change rapidly and things could be very much the same as they were for me or they could be very different. Do not go unless you have a written invitation from the Abbot of the temple where you wish to study or from the head office of the sect to which the temple belongs; keep the invitation with you and do not give it to anyone lest it disappear and you be thrown out. Specify everything in advance: cash, visa guarantee, whether or not you are willing to grant interviews to the media. You must even specify which media you will and will not appear in—you will have to list them—otherwise they may say that you have refused to see the newspaper reporters so they have brought in a magazine writer or a T.V. crew. Above all do not spend time in a small country temple with just one or two priests; go to one of the big training temples—Eiheiji, Myoshinji or Sōjiji for instance. If you go to a small temple to train you are almost certain to be turned into a temple pet and given no real teaching. There are, of course, rare exceptions, but be very wary of the small temples.

Layman: You have talked about going to a temple in Japan. What about advice for someone who is serious about undertaking Zen training in a temple in the United States?

Rōshi Jiyu-Kennett: There are three things you need to know. Visit the place and first have a good look at the other students, especially the ones who have been there a while. Are they as you would like to become? Can they think and act for themselves or are they automatons: gutless and brainwashed? Next, observe and speak with the teacher. Does he say that his students are free to go and learn from whomsoever they wish or does he claim to own them forever once they have accepted his teaching? Third, are the students

permitted to visit their family on occasion if they wish?
Most good temples will say that you should not leave the
temple at all for the first three months except for a real
emergency and they will discourage going home in the middle of term just because you feel like it. However, any religious community which flatly prohibits visiting your family
or permits you to see them only in the temple or in the company of other students or staff is probably trying to brain-
wash you and is a very dangerous place. If you find a
problem in any of these three areas, you would do well to
go elsewhere. If these problems are not found, and if the
place feels like "home" to you spiritually, it is probably the
right place for you. There are a number of such good temples and monasteries in America.

QUESTION: What about the Oriental monks who have come
to the West?

Rōshi Jiyu-Kennett: We tend to get coming to the West people
who are ambitious or who do not fit in well with the average Oriental temple; occasionally they are extraordinarily
good and their standards are so high that they are somewhat
unpopular; frequently they are the rejects with whom no
one wants to study in the East. The West rarely gets an average monk. This means, of course, that it is not necessary to
go to the Orient to find a top-quality teacher of Buddhism:
it also means that the student should be careful not to
assume that all Oriental teachers in the West are excellent.
Further, it means that what we get over here is not a fair
sample of what is over there. Orientals are just as much
human beings as are Westerners. Frankly, I think people are
better off studying with Americans.

QUESTION: One of the things which impressed me most in
your book was that it made it clear that it is the *person* who
does the training, not the situation.

Rōshi Jiyu-Kennett: Yes, I remember sitting there and saying, "I *must* take everything that has happened to me for my good; however badly they may seem to behave, it is for my good." That was what really drove me into that kenshō so quickly.

Monk: Then this book is really about how to train in Zen, isn't it?

Rōshi Jiyu-Kennett: Yes. It is about how you do it. Stop complaining in your own head about your circumstances, your past, how other people are not training and the like, and get on with doing something about *you.* Then everything that happens is an opportunity to train—to practice the Buddha's Way—and everything can be accepted positively and every situation met with positive action. You must develop faith or you will get nowhere.

Monk: You also must make a commitment. Nothing can be held back whatsoever. Nothing can be more important to you than finding the Truth.

QUESTION: Isn't your training a special case; I mean most people simply wouldn't have been willing to do what you did; was there something special in your background?

Rōshi Jiyu-Kennett: No. I just got on with my training.

Layman: You once mentioned having been educated in a British private or public school; did that have something to do with it?

Rōshi Jiyu-Kennett: Anyone who has been to such a school, as the private school I went to, or who has been in the armed forces, knows something about how to keep going and not get discouraged when things get tough but that is hardly something special. You do not need to be in a situation like the one I described in this book in order to find the Truth. What you need, wherever you are, is faith, commitment and a determination to go on, regardless of all obstacles, born of a desperation not to get stuck the way you are.

QUESTION: You discussed at some length the giving up of morality in order to abide by a morality beyond the normal moral codes. Could you say something more about the criteria for action if you have gone beyond the usual ones?

Rōshi Jiyu-Kennett: First of all I do *not* mean that you abandon morality and become immoral; that would be a complete perversion of Zen teachings. If you once really understand the basic spirit behind the usual moral code it will lead you to the Three Pure Precepts: Cease from Evil (or Cease from Harm), Do only Good and Do Good for Others, then there are times when the old morality rules apply and there are times when they don't; and, when they don't, you must accept the karma for breaking them. In the end, you have to go even further than that and just take refuge in the Buddha, Dharma and Sangha and do the very best you can. This happens when you are so at one with the Buddha's Way that the more specific sets of Precepts are your very blood and bones—when you *naturally* follow them so closely that it does not even occur to you to do otherwise as there is simply no point in so doing.

Monk: This is the danger of misunderstanding the freedom of Zen. If you go beyond the external set of moral standards, without having understood their spirit and made it a living part of you, you are in big trouble.

Rōshi Jiyu-Kennett: Yes. That is why, if people are not going to commit themselves to religion completely and take it the whole way, I would rather they be Christians or Jews than Buddhists. At its best Buddhism is magnificent, it transcends all other religions but, if you take it at its lowest common denominator, it is abominable. This is also why when you find a real Zen Master in Japan he is so magnificent and when you meet a mediocre priest he is often quite unpleasant to be with. The opposite of morality beyond morality is deceit in the name of Truth and this is what I mean by the lowest common denominator of Buddhism. Once you step outside normal morality this has to be guarded against, with great care, through the trebling of one's efforts to train.

About the Author.

Born in England in 1924, Reverend Master P.T.N.H. Jiyu-Kennett became a Buddhist at an early age, studying Theravada Buddhism. She was later introduced to Rinzai Zen Buddhism by D.T. Suzuki in London, where she held membership in, and lectured at, the London Buddhist Society. She studied at Trinity College of Music, London, and Durham University, and pursued a career as a professional musician before meeting her future master, the Very Reverend Keidō Chisan Kohō Zenji.

Rev. Master Jiyu-Kennett began her priest training in 1962, with her ordination into the Chinese Buddhist Sangha in Malaysia by the Very Reverend Seck Kim Seng, Archbishop of Malacca. She then continued her training in Japan under Kohō Zenji, who was then Chief Abbot of Dai Hon Zan Sōjiji, one of the two head temples of Sōtō Zen Buddhism in Japan. In 1963 she received Dharma Transmission from him and was later certified by him as a Rōshi (Zen Master). She held several positions during her years in Japan including that of Foreign Guestmaster of Dai Hon Zan Sōjiji and Abbess of her own temple in Mie Prefecture.

It had always been Kohō Zenji's sincere wish that Sōtō Zen Buddhism be successfully transmitted to the West by a Westerner. He worked very hard to make it possible for Rev. Master Jiyu-Kennett to train in Japan and, after his death, she left Japan in order to carry out this task. In November 1969, Rev. Master Jiyu-Kennett came to San Francisco on a lecture

517

tour, and as her following of disciples grew rapidly, the Zen Mission Society was founded and moved to Mount Shasta, where Shasta Abbey was founded in November 1970. The Zen Mission Society was reorganized as The Order of Buddhist Contemplatives in 1978.

Rev. Master Jiyu-Kennett served twenty-six years as Abbess and spiritual director of Shasta Abbey, ordaining and teaching monks and laypeople. She founded Throssel Hole Buddhist Abbey in England in 1972 and was Head of the Order of Buddhist Contemplatives. Her written legacy as a Zen Master includes the books *Zen is Eternal Life; How to Grow a Lotus Blossom; The Wild, White Goose; The Book of Life* and *The Liturgy of the Order of Buddhist Contemplatives for the Laity. The Roar of the Tigress*, a collection of her edited lectures, was published after her death. She died on November 6, 1996.

About the Order of
Buddhist Contemplatives.

The Order of Buddhist Contemplatives is a religious order practicing Serene Reflection Meditation (J. Sōtō Zen) as transmitted from The Very Reverend Keidō Chisan Kohō Zenji, Abbot of Dai Hon Zan Sōjiji in Yokohama, Japan, to Reverend Master P.T.N.H. Jiyu-Kennett. Rev. Master Jiyu-Kennett returned to the West in 1969, establishing Shasta Abbey in 1970 and Throssel Hole Buddhist Abbey in northern England in 1972. She founded the Order of Buddhist Contemplatives in 1978, serving as Head of the Order until her death in 1996. There are currently temples and meditation groups of the Order located in various places throughout Europe and North America. The daily practice of Buddhism which occurs at these temples and meditation groups uses Western forms and languages. The Order has male and female monks and lay ministers; women and men have equal status and train together. In our Order, the monastics are referred to as both monks and priests, and they follow the traditional Mahayana Buddhist monastic precepts, including being celibate and vegetarian. Lay ministers are householders who have long experience and deep commitment to the practice of this religious tradition, who serve in a wide variety of roles. The Head of the Order is Rev. Master Daizui MacPhillamy. The Order publishes *The Journal of the Order of Buddhist Contemplatives* quarterly.

For more information about the Order, and the location of its temples and meditation groups, please visit our website: www.obcon.org.

About the
Monasteries of the Order.

Shasta Abbey.

Shasta Abbey, located on sixteen forested acres near the city of Mount Shasta in northern California, is a seminary for the Buddhist priesthood and training monastery for both lay and monastic Buddhists and visitors. It was established in 1970 by Rev. Master P.T.N.H. Jiyu-Kennett, who was Abbess and spiritual director until her death in 1996. Buddhist training at Shasta Abbey is based on the practice of Serene Reflection Meditation and the keeping of the Buddhist Precepts. The monastery is home to twenty-five to thirty ordained male and female monks and its Abbot is Rev. Master Ekō Little, a senior disciple of Rev. Master Jiyu-Kennett.

Guests and visitors follow a schedule that is similar to that of the monastic community, providing a balance of sitting meditation, work, ceremonial, and instruction in Buddhism. The schedule allows the mind of meditation to be cultivated and maintained throughout all aspects of daily life. Retreat guests stay at the Abbey's guest house, which accommodates about forty people. All meals are vegetarian and are prepared in the Abbey kitchen. A stay at Shasta Abbey allows visitors to set aside their usual daily concerns so that they may participate wholeheartedly in the spiritual life of the monastery.

In addition to its monastic and lay training programs, Shasta Abbey publishes books through Shasta Abbey Press. For more information, call or write Shasta Abbey, 3724 Summit Drive,

Mt. Shasta, California, 96067-9102; phone: (530) 926-4208; fax: (530) 926-0428; website: www.shastaabbey.org; email: shastaabbey@shastaabbey.org.

Throssel Hole Buddhist Abbey.

Throssel Hole Buddhist Abbey is situated in a quiet valley in the north of England. It was founded in 1972 by Rev. Master P.T.N.H. Jiyu-Kennett as Throssel Hole Priory, and over the years has become a monastery and seminary for training priests of the Order, as well as a retreat and training center for a large European congregation. Its Abbot is Rev. Master Daishin Morgan, a senior disciple of Rev. Master Jiyu-Kennett.

The Abbey offers for lay guests a full and varied program to which all are warmly invited. Experienced senior priests teach both meditation and how to use the Buddhist Precepts in establishing a daily practice. Through these means one can find the Truth, or Buddha Nature, at the heart of oneself and all beings. Training shows how to let go of the clinging that causes suffering, thus allowing this inner compassion and wisdom to enrich our lives. Guests meditate in the bright and spacious ceremony hall, and sleep there at night, dormitory-style, with complete privacy between men and women maintained. A large dining hall includes a small library and common room area for guests. By following the monastery's daily schedule, guests experience how it is that all activities of life—working, relaxing, reading, eating, and sleeping—have true spiritual depth and value. For more information, call or write Throssel Hole Buddhist Abbey, Carrshield, Hexham, Northumberland NE47 8AL, United Kingdom; phone: +44 (0) 1434 345204; fax: +44 (0) 1434 345216; website: www.throssel.org.uk.